An Introduction
to Celtic Christianity

An Introduction
to Celtic Christianity

Edited by
James P. Mackey

T&T CLARK
EDINBURGH

T&T CLARK LTD
59 GEORGE STREET
EDINBURGH EH2 2LQ
SCOTLAND

First published 1989

ISBN 0 567 09507 X   HB
ISBN 0 567 29507 9   PB

British Library Cataloguing in Publication Data
An Introduction to Celtic Christianity.
1. Celtic church. History
I. Mackey, James P. (James Patrick), *1934 –*
274.1

Typeset by Bookworm Typesetting Ltd, Edinburgh
Printed and bound in Great Britain by Billing & Sons Ltd., Worcester

Contents

Introduction:
Is There a Celtic Christianity?

James P. Mackey

The aim of this volume is quite simple, and its ambition is not great. It aims to provide an introductory map for beginners. There seems to be a burgeoning interest these days in things Celtic, fuelled by varieties of motivation, and equally evident on both sides of the Atlantic. The publishing fraternity has responded with everything from weighty tomes on Celtic consciousness to some poor attempts at retelling ancient Celtic myths and legends. Of the people newly attracted to such literature many could not even begin to find their way around a Celtic culture still surviving, and in a few places still thriving, and some who might be quite familiar with one particular survival or revival might as yet be like people who had never left their own village and were consequently quite uncertain about extent of territory, the location of other villages, their direction and distance.

The map now offered is a map of Celtic Christianity, not of Celtic culture in general. It is further restricted to the two large islands off the north-west coast of Europe, with the most incidental of grid references to Brittany and the Isle of Man. Continental Celtic survivals and revivals would need another volume, and another language. There is, of course, the chapter on Irish monks wandering through the Continent, but the focus of that chapter is still Irish Celtic Christianity. Indeed, the complaint could well be made that the map has most detail on Ireland; the charge of chauvinism might even be raised against the editor: for the collection begins with St Patrick, even though Christianity had first been brought to the British (an original name for Celts) by Roman merchants; so many papers are devoted to Irish Christianity; Joyce is chosen instead of, say, McDiarmid, Ó Ríordáin instead of Jones. The charge, I am sure, can be sustained. The pleas I could enter, concerning my lack of control over the selection of authors which finally responded to the original batch of invitations, and other accidents along the way, would not quite win a reprieve. But if this collection provokes other editors, or more widely travelled Celts, to provide more balanced maps with greater coverage of ancient Celtic territories, then the chauvinism of its editor will have proved a happy fault. This map, in the meantime, can at least introduce beginners to some of the salient places, events and characters, all major landmarks in the long development of Celtic Christianity on the British (i.e. Celtic) Isles. Then the traveller in ancient lands and ancient ways may feel the pang of desire for riches yet to be seen, the anticipated thrill of the adventure as, with the quiet confidence which only a landmark can give, the byways are explored, and the hidden places that have kept some part of the secret of existence safe from the pathetic frenzy of modern life.

The concentration on the Christianity of the Celts, however, should scarcely be counted as a further restriction upon the aims and achievements of this volume. The fact of the matter is that the Celts seem to have taken quite quickly and early to Christianity. Correspondingly Christian scribes, annalists and historians enable us to see much more of Celtic pre-Christian culture than is the case with many another primal culture later christianized. Indeed, apart from archeological finds which of their very nature and in the absence of contemporary literature, reveal little of the cultural dimension of a people's existence, the originally oral tradition of the non-literate[1] Celts has been preserved in great abundance by Christian scribes and scholars and bards, though this was done more in Ireland than in any other traditionally Celtic territory.[2]

The christianizing of the Celt and the *quid pro quo* of the Christian preservation of pre-Christian Celtic culture justifies an introduction to Celtic Christianity, but it need not, and indeed it must not, involve us in the pretence that the conversion was smooth and its results final. Far from it. At least as long as the bardic institution survived in any substantial and truly continuous form, as it did in Ireland down to the seventeenth century, and in Scotland well into the eighteenth century, the residual resistance of the old paganism to the 'new' Christianity was sharply and deliberately maintained against all Christian complacency and occasional triumphalism. A poem of the *Fiannaiacht* from as late as the sixteenth century still cocks a snook at the *parvenu*:

> While Fionn was living and the Fianna,
> Dearer to them was the mountain than the church:
> Sweet they thought the song of blackbirds,
> Tinklings of bells they did not think sweet.

A new religion can never succeed except to the extent that it succeeds in embodying at least the best of the culture

---

[1]   People who prefer the adjective 'illiterate' here often betray by that very choice the fact that they have no inkling of the existence of extensive grounds for a positive preference for memory-retention and oral-transmission. One of the few things that Caesar got right about the Celts was the presence of a preference here, rather than some inability to write: 'we have it on Caesar's authority that the druids of Gaul considered it improper to commit their learning to writing, and on this point he is substantially borne out by the Irish evidence.' (P. MacCana, *Celtic Mythology*, London: Hamlyn, 1970, p.16) This is not the place to digress at length about the grounds for such a preference. They have much to do with the nature of spiritual rather than material retention/possession, and with the close relationship between imagination and memory. They have to do with the nature of ultimate wisdom, which a person really could not 'forget'; and there must surely be interesting contrasts with a computer age and in particular with a combination of electronic memory banks and the self-fulfilling prophecy of the obsolescene of the very idea of a uniquely human mind.
[2]   N. Chadwick, *The Celts*, Pelican Books, 1970, especially the section on Celtic literature.

to which it comes. Christianity recorded its greatest initial success in the Roman Empire by assimilating to itself so much of the Graeco-Roman culture, and that includes the predominantly Platonised religious culture of what are now counted as the first and most formative Christian centuries. Correspondingly, the great and sophisticated Platonic religious tradition which lasted for nigh on a thousand years from the time of Plato until a Christian emperor closed down the Academy at Athens in the sixth century (a genuine act of vandalism), survived to this day in so many of its salient features within the Christian cultural corpus. The trouble was that the recipe for this earliest and most elaborate success for Christianity was soon forgotten and the resulting form of Graeco-Roman Christianity, essentially invented by and for the western Mediterranean territories, was soon taken to be the one true form of the religion now attributed to a Jew called Jesus or Joshua, or Jehoshua of Nazareth. So the complaint is now constantly raised against the missionary expounders of Christianity in the modern period that, instead of resorting to the original recipe and assimilating the primal cultures of Africa and Asia and the Americas, they overlay these cultures with the values and structures of Graeco-Roman, European Christianity. Contemporary missionaries are urged to undo as much as possible of the damage then done, primal religions are back in vogue with Christian theologians, and Christian theology of missions is full of respect for languages as the repositories of the cultures of all kinds of peoples.

Much of Celtic Christianity too, of course, was Graeco-Romanized in the course of the centuries; some of it quite early in the ancient territory of Gaul; some quite late with the late decline of native institutions in Ireland. But there are probably some survivals of genuinely Celtic rather than (or more than) Graeco-Roman Christianity, at least on the very fringes of ancient Celtic territory, in places like Wales, Scotland and Ireland where the Romans never held much sway, if any at all, and where other Graeco-Roman churches never quite eradicated the alternative form. It may be that such survival of genuinely Celtic Christianity is now merely literary, that such monuments to a Christian consciousness as the collections of Carmichael and Hyde are all we have left. I doubt that. The characteristic mind and spirit of a people does not so easily or so quickly die. Anyway, however bad our case, part of the purpose of literature is to keep alive, so that we still have the opportunity to see and experience the christianizing of the Celt, the celticizing of Christianity. The presence of unreconciled Celtic pagan culture within the Christian literature of these Celtic territories allows us to do many things, all of which we are recommended to do nowadays by one set of gurus or another:

1.   To recover and refresh as much as we can the Celtic roots of our distinctive ethnic consciousness and this, of course, means a welcome to those pagan Celtic voices that have been allowed to speak to us, or have spoken up anyway in the literature that is still extant.
2.   To attempt to reconcile the still unreconciled elements of Celtic culture and Christianity in these territories – this may mean a critical stance towards some elements of the Graeco-Roman form of Christianity, including its Reformed and Evangelical versions, which has come to dominate these islands; but it should also mean a substantial contribution to the rich variety of Christian forms in the world as more ethnic groups are encouraged to preserve and develop their own distinctive mentalities and patterns of behaviour.

It is not, of course, suggested that this volume should attempt much, if any, of this. Only that all or most of this would be possible for those who could be successfully introduced to Celtic Christianity, and that all or most of this would be a very good thing indeed. However, it is all very well to be told that as human beings we badly need that revival of ethnic cultures which alone could stem the deadly monochrome superficiality of an increasingly international consumerist anti-culture; it is all very well to be told that as Christians we need to graft our Christianity onto the living trunk of our ancient and sacred tree, for fear that our Christianity too might prove in the end just as flashy and as transient as the lights we hang on Christmas trees or, to put the matter more positively, so that Christian grace might truly rejuvenate nature. But what if the word 'Celtic' can no longer be given any distinctive content? What if we have to admit that, due to a variety of reasons – amongst them perhaps the acts of cultural vandalism inevitably perpetrated by all empire builders, and amongst these the acts of killing off the tutelary languages except on the very periphery of ancient Celtic territory – nothing still living or revivable is distinctively Celtic? If there ever was a culture common at some level to all Celtic peoples who wandered between Asia Minor and the last islands on the north-west of the known world, what if nothing now remains of it except fragmentary and very local memories, the odd quaint customs in remote parts, a few provincial idiosyncrasies, and in the ivory towers of academia a literature that is no longer alive?

Neither can this little volume take on the mighty task of meeting such dark, deep suspicions; and I did not, in agreeing their topics with each of the contributors, attempt to place upon each the duty of revealing what in that topic was distinctly Celtic, though I did express the hope that something distinctly Celtic might appear between them all, and might show signs of life. Indeed, one or two who found in the end that they could not contribute, explicitly questioned the aptitude of the adjective 'Celtic' to the topic proposed to them: one said she would prefer to speak of 'insular art' instead of 'Celtic art'; others, for reasons which my ecclesiastical experience would lead me to suspect were present though not stated, insisted that there was nothing specifically Celtic about the theology of one of the very few Celts ever to make a name for themselves as theologians, Pelagius. Once again, the reader of this volume need expect no *fait accompli*; only the promise held out, for what it is worth to any reader, that use of this map may lead to further explorations and eventually to discernment of a distinctively Celtic mentality still living perhaps in the depths of consciousness, a Celtic culture still flowering in hidden places, still waiting to be fully christianized and to shape again a distinctive Christianity to all that is best in itself.

Two things may be said in introductory fashion, however, the second at greater length than the first.

First, it may be said that if some proponents of Celtic culture prove diffident at times about identifying it with any great clarity, its detractors in ancient and modern times show no such hesitation. Already at the beginning of the seventeenth century Geoffrey Keating felt it necessary to begin his *Foras Feasa ar Eirinn* (History of Ireland) by soundly berating a number of named writers who had set out, in his view, to defame the Irish in particular. These writers were, he said, like beetles who, when they took flight at the onset of summer, somehow managed to overshoot the beauty of flowers and to land in every available patch of cow-dung. Keating is anxious to categorize all of these beetles as *Nua-Gaill*, more recent foreigners, for his very name betrays the fact that he himself stems from the *Sean-Gaill*, the old foreigners, the Normans who became, in a hallowed phrase of Irish mythology, 'more Irish than the Irish themselves', and who, of course, could never be guilty of such crass misrepresentations of their own people.

Behind this mild conceit lies a general truth. Invaders who come to any shore or border with imperial intent inevitably engage in cultural vandalism. They destroy so much that is human in that rich array of individuality and uniqueness which is somewhere close to the very essence of being human. For they come not to enrich or receive, but to control and to despoil. It is necessary for them therefore to make the pathetic attempt to conceal their own inhumanity by attributing less than human status to those they would oppress. This is all the more necessary in that the majority of invading forces is made up of those who could not succeed at home. The need of such people to attempt to justify their new colonial privileges, riches and status out of all proportion to what their deserts would gain for them at home, requires a persistent effort to vilify and degrade people who are on any truly human scale their betters. Exactly the same syndrome can be seen in the post-colonial era in attitudes adopted to strangers in many lands who come to work and be exploited by the economic system of the so-called host country: the same attempt to portray as sub-human, or lower-human, an attempt which itself, with powerful poetic justice, reveals the inhumanity of the exploiter, his ignorance of the richness of human cultures and his moral bankruptcy. The Celts, who were never themselves imperialist, have suffered their share from such ignorance and moral degeneracy, and it is this that Keating felt he had to expose before beginning his history.

Ignorance aligned with prejudice did not cease with the *Nua Gaill* of Keating's time. Stewart Piggott's book *The Druids*[3] gives ample evidence of both; their presence all the better exposed by the many pompous pages on the method of the true scientist with which this otherwise able archeologist begins his book. With 'little corroborative material from literate sources' (and indeed he shows no evidence in the book of any competence in the original Celtic languages), he can yet paint us 'a picture of a society barbarous and uncivilised in its essentials'. Prejudice reveals itself in the passing word as much as ignorance does in the substance of the sentences. Consider, for example, the words 'gross' and 'decent' in the following phrases, and even the word 'swallowing': 'a world of gross meat-eaters', 'swallowing their imported wine neat, rather than diluted as a decent Greek or Roman would prefer' (p46). So dietary differences are forced to support allegations of inferiority, and later the fine and intricate social structures which characterised the Celtic tribal system is simply declared by our archeologist (who incidentally gives no evidence of having any substantial knowledge of it) 'in itself . . . incompatible with civilised government' (p.50).

A certain amount of this by now rather puerile prejudice is simply a repetition of prejudices which the Romans, the first extensive conquerors of the Celts, penned for the kind of questionable political purposes already explained: and classical literature seems to be the only early literature to which people like Piggott have any personal access. Indeed, a sample of the prejudices of Roman colonizers appears in the pages of this volume, when Hanson in explaining what the Britons (i.e. Celts) 'were for the Romans', describes their

---

[3]   London, Thames and Hudson, 1968.

art as favouring the 'grotesque'.[4] A very different judgment, this, from the kind of judgment passed on Celtic art in the chapter devoted to that subject in this collection. Little wonder that professional reviewers of scholarly work on early Celtic culture should now regard independence of inevitably prejudiced Roman viewpoints as a first and rather elementary criterion for critical acceptance in a new era of Celtic studies.[5]

There are then, and there have been for quite a long time, people who have pretended to know what was specifically Celtic, and the fact that their writing reveals a great deal more about their own ignorance and prejudice than it reveals about the Celts should nevertheless leave us with some hope that the task of discovering the distinctive characteristics of Celtic culture was never terribly difficult, and may still be quite manageable today.

Indeed it might not be too paradoxical to suggest that it is precisely when the Celts seem to have most clearly capitulated to Rome that the prospect of identifying their distinctive spirit can appear most substantial to those who are adequately informed about the range of their literary activities. For the Celts, particularly Irish Celts, almost as

---

[4] I presume that Hanson is still reflecting Roman prejudice when he later says of the Britons that they 'could not ever attain to the art of coining money'. Such supremely artistic metal-workers certainly *could* attain to such a relatively simple art, but as in the matter of writing, they may have had good reason to prefer other means of exchange. I am a little more suspicious of Hanson's judgment that the Irish had 'no system of education comparable to that of Britain'. This may represent another Roman view of the matter; even then much would depend on the qualitative-judgmental load the word comparable was meant to bear.

[5] Barry Cunliffe's review of H.D. Rankin's *Celts and the Classical world* in the *Times Higher Educational Supplement*, (4.3.88), under the heading 'Barbarian bogeys', must suffice here as one example of the new scholarly critical requirement that Celts must be understood from a better knowledge of their own most civilized values and structures, and not from those of the Romans, which were in many cases morally inferior, or at least more crassly pragmatic and materialist. Rankin meets the requirement to some extent. Simon Hornblower, in his review of the book (*Times Literary Supplement*, 26.2.88, p.227), points out that Rankin does at least suggest in his last chapter that we might 'speculate about the possible development of Celtic society had it not been enmeshed in the greedy, socially inflexible and militaristic reticulations of Roman overlordship'.

soon as they were converted to Christianity, began to master Latin, the language of Rome, and then to compose in that language in a great variety of *genres*. Thomas Finan's appreciative survey of their creative contribution, their Latin literature of confessions and lives, of voyage and vision, and of course, as always, their poetry, allows the reader to come to a personal conclusion on the prospects of encountering in the language of an alien empire the distinctive temper of a Celtic spirit.

Second, I think that little harm can be done if I myself attempt to say what I thought to be distinctive and striking, and possibly properly Celtic features, of the topics discussed in this volume. I use no other criterion than that of reverberation – whatever seems to reverberate within some depths of my own Celtic consciousness, as that too has been formed by my learning and use from my earliest childhood of the Irish language – that repository of a total and ancient culture – and my return to it in later life, when years of feeding upon largely teutonic philosophy and theology began at last to fail to refresh my spirit and was beginning to fail my Christian faith. Here too my selection and comments may do no more than tempt the reader to continue the quest for something specifically Celtic. At worst it need do no more than point the reader forward to some of the significant riches to be found in this collection, and that at least is a legitimate aim in any introduction.

In his piece on St Patrick's Breastplate O'Donoghue insists that no one who does not come to grips with the nearness of the spirit world will ever understand Celtic Christianity. Perhaps I can begin with that feature since it is a very general one and it draws the eye down to so many more particular aspects of the Celtic outlook. Its most obvious pre-Christian illustration took the form of the fairy-folk of popular imagination – themselves ancient gods and their retinues who lived on into Christian ages in reduced circumstances – who, as O'Donoghue reminds us, were only normally invisible. The nearness, the ubiquitous *presence* of the spiritual in all things and at all times, though needing its special times and places too as a picture needs a frame in order to focus its universality, is indeed a powerful, permanent, and characteristic Celtic conviction. And I mention it at the beginning because in the end it may prove to be the most important contribution which the Celtic mind can still offer to the modern world. I listened last night to some serious scientists anxious to communicate to a wide television audience the most recent discoveries about the human brain. One was at great pains to assure me that all of his advanced science would deal in fact with the brain, that I should not really worry about the word 'mind' (though he, for some reason which he failed to reveal to me, had to keep on using it). Mind was, he said and repeated several times, *nothing* other than a sequence of thoughts, feelings etc., set off by the brain in its interaction with our physical world. The chief presenter of the series said the brain produced or created what we called mind, but he too seemed anxious to prevent me from suspecting some further mysterious entity, something other than the physical grey, convoluted substance from which his science had already wrested so much information and on which it could provide so much more. It was all so innocently typical of that dogmatic materialism which constitutes the unscientific dogma of the scientific age; the orthodox, now as always in the past, anxious that we should shut our ears and eyes, and our *nothing* minds, to the very words of the few remaining heretics. It had not so much as occurred to those earnest communicators, those apostles of the latest metaphysic of all physics, to probe further the commonest of daily experiences; to ask, for example: if a thought is merely an epiphenomenon of the physical brain, how could it be termed true or false? and if it could be termed neither, why I should bother to accord to his thoughts on the subject any more credence than I give to the nearest pseudo-Romany mind-reader? Or how I was to account for the most persistent and formative of my conscious states – the consciousness of my-self, *something* certainly other than any and all of the sequences through which it continues to live? It almost seemed as if in some irrational, certainly unscientific way, these poor men had decided their science had taken them so far, they had to foreclose upon too much more probing in case they should lose some of what they had already gained. They seemed to lack a wider and more generous vision where spirit and matter did not pose as rivals but everywhere interpenetrated and enriched each other, as would also then the disciplines which in their methodical way divided the indivisible between them.

This pervasive sense of spiritual presence is brought to the reader's notice many times and in many different contexts in this collection. The presence is always ultimately the presence of the divine. But we should not let residual memories of arid theological disputes as to whether, for instance, 'spirit' in some religious literature is a person or an 'impersonal power', tempt us to try to divide and so constrict the richness of the material we are about to meet. When the spiritual powers present are depicted as persons, they are meant to be thought of as persons, not as ciphers for God's presence. They have their own efficacy, though they have it only by God's will and grace to them. Hence O'Donoghue remarks, the choirs of angels are as real as the sun and moon, and their power is invoked directly: they are not invoked as mere transmitters of prayers to God. So much is crystal clear from the prayers in Diarmuid O Laoghaire's article, prayers to Michael and the angels, prayers that go back to a tradition common to Ireland and Scotland and do so much to fill in the picture of pre-Reformation Christianity in both countries. In that tradition, the Celtic Christian at prayer was consciously a member of a great company that stretched from the persons of the Trinity through the powerful angelic throngs to the least of the spiritual persons, the risen saints.

The natural world too was absolutely real for the Celtic mentality, a well as being altogether good and salvific, as the locus, this natural world also with all its parts and elements, of the gracious power of God. It might seem strange to stress the reality of the natural world. I do so not only because men as far apart as Karl Barth and Seamus Heaney have given expression to the potentially devastating suspicion of its unreality and have linked this to an absence of a form of religious faith,[6] but also because the scientists of a few pages

---

[6] Seamus Heaney, *In Illo Tempore, Station Island*, London, Faber and Faber, 1984, p.118; Karl Barth, *Dogmatics in Outline*, London, SCM Press, 1949, pp.52-3.

back may well have imbibed from a less wholesome religious tradition such a sense of opposition between spiritual and material world as to make any suggestion of the efficacy, or even the existence, of the former, a threat to the latter. The full and uninhibited acceptance of the natural world, in full continuity with the spiritual, both indeed utterly interpenetrable, removes such rivalries and suspicions and relieves people of the need to protect their partial knowledge by self-imprisonment and by the bold gesture of throwing away the keys with which they had locked themselves in a world too small for the very minds they continue to talk about.

In Celtic Christianity God's gracious power, God's spirit, one might say God's grace, is everywhere in the natural world and in all our dealings in it, as much as it is in all those spiritual persons who are on God's side or have gone to God's side at last. For as there is no real dichotomy between spirits and material things, so there is no real distinction between modes of God's presence in the one and the other to the Celtic Christian who invokes them to protect or to praise. It is not that God's grace is an 'impersonal' created power whereas God's angels or the risen saints are personal powers, albeit always empowered by God. The great tragedy of the western theology of grace, for which even the great 'Doctor of grace', Augustine, must take his share of the blame, lies in the gradual overshadowing of uncreated grace (God's own personal presence or spirit), by concepts of created grace (effects or states produced within God's creatures). For grace in essence is a way of talking about God's creative, life-giving, beneficent presence to and within all, both personal and impersonal entities, spiritual and material. And that is the comprehensive impression conveyed by Celtic Christianity at its best and most characteristic.

When Tudur Jones asks what is characteristically Celtic about Welsh Evangelical Christianity he lists first the confidence that this is God's world and that nature and grace belong together, and after he has listed the need for a redeemer (and we shall come to that in a moment), he returns immediately to the powerful sense of the closeness of eternity to everyday things. But again it is the Breastplate and the prayers and hymns in the chapters already mentioned that put flesh on this abstract thesis, because of the concrete way in which they request and reveal this powerful love of God and of neighbour in every ordinary act and interaction, in sleeping and waking and eating, in journeying and sowing and harvesting; and not least because of the manner in which so many of the most traditional prayers are clearly derived from the Latin liturgy and the Latin Scriptures. The import of that last point is this: religion in practice, the encounter with the spiritual, is frequently thought to consist of special acts at special times and places and the reading and assimilating of special sacred texts; in short, it is thought to consist of the non-worldly. To paraphrase liturgy and Scripture for the purpose of everyday dealing with nature and society, is to make liturgy and Scripture the privileged focus of an experience of God that is everywhere available, rather than special substitutes for an otherwise godless life and world. And here it might not be out of order to add a few words in defence of the oft maligned Rosary. To meditate daily on the 'mysteries' of Jesus' life, death and destiny, while repeating in rhythmic fashion some scriptural phrases from the event that began it all, the Annunciation, and asking Mary repeatedly to 'pray for us now and at the hour of our death', is hardly a highly questionable way of keeping the great Christian drama at the very heart of daily life.

There are two chapters in this collection on Celtic monks, Peter O'Dwyer on Celtic monks and the Culdee Reform, and Cardinal O'Fee on Irish monks on the Continent; and the reader who has been following with some reluctance the line of argument so far might now wish to interject a mild objection: surely Celtic monasteries were a rejection of the world rather than a celebration of ubiquitous divine immanence? How does the fierce asceticism of the hermit, the harsh penances of the other monks, fit the picture painted so far? Undoubtedly the penances do seem harsh to a softer civilization: the vigils and fasting, the prostrations and the beatings. And a complete answer to this objection is not furnished by pointing to the rehabilitatory function of most of these penances, the motives, superior to much earlier official ecclesiastical penance, of restoring the lapsed as quickly and efficiently as possible to full membership of an élite and privileged community; so the glutton was made to fast, the sleepy-head to stay awake, the occasional deserter to suffer a term of exclusion. The full answer can come to one who stands, like I did, near the round tower at Ardmore and looks out across the breathtaking beauty of the bay; or to one who scales Skellig rock, miles out in the Atlantic from the westernmost point of Europe, and is overwhelmed by the vast expanse of naked, restless sea and in awe before its might; or to one who follows the steps of Irish monks on the Continent and comes to beautiful Annegray in the Vosges, where Columbanus restored a ruined temple to Diana to be his monastery church (an answer to the Romans more than once delivered). The motive of these emigrant monks also was ascetic, a detachment from home and family, and it led them as surely to nature and beauty. Heaney's poem 'The Hermit'[7] reveals well the release of a greater, more comprehensive force, for this was their aim in life; an encounter with a power and a grace beyond the experience of the gourmet and the drinker, the anxious entrepreneur and the ever-manoeuvring politician. It is little wonder that these monks carried into their Christian existence, almost without break, some of the finest of the nature poetry of their pagan Celtic predecessors; little wonder that the most abstract and the most naturalist is so intricately woven in their art, as Hilary Richardson notes. In these carefully chosen natural settings, in their own liturgical rhyming of the seasons, in prayer and work and study, and in their high creative art, they encountered the gracious power which their practical charity, the key to their whole existence, then pressed them to release to their secular counterparts in the clergy and to the laity.

---

[7]   Seamus Heaney, 'the Hermit', *Station Island*, p.109
    As he prowled the rim of his clearing
    where the blade of choice had not spared
    one stump of affection
    he was like a ploughshare
    interred to sustain the whole field
    of force.

Where then was original sin and the alleged corruption of nature? Where the need for a redeemer? Our long theological tutelage to that dark North African, Augustine, must no longer tempt us to overlook the correct Celtic answer to these questions. This natural world, this human nature, is good through and through as the Genesis refrain insists; and God saw that it as good, and God saw that it was good, and God saw that it was very good. The newborn child is innocent. That is the truth of the matter, and no amount of solemn dogma in the shadow of Augustine will ever alter it. In fact a God who punishes for eternity, however mildly, a newborn babe who dies before baptism, is an Augustinian monster (it is to such an image, rather than to anything found in Celtic art, that the adjective 'grotesque' properly applies). But this good world is in bondage, in the manner of a good land under occupation by malevolent forces. However much contemporary minds may feel like resisting the traditional Celtic personification of such forces, there can be no doubt that malevolent forces operate in our world and through our own spirits, and that we need saving from them. But the Christ of traditional Celtic imagery, as O'Donoghue points out, comes not to confront the corruption of nature, but to release a beautiful and holy world from its bondage; not to replace the revelatory light of nature with a new and different light, but to scatter the dark forces so that the original light (the light which the prologue to the Fourth Gospel says enlightens everyone who comes into the world) could shine for us again, and guide our footsteps home. Which brings us, inevitably, to Pelagius and to Monique Nicholson's article.

Celtic names do not occur very often in the history of theology. Like the earliest Greek philosophers they felt that poetry, preferably sung or at least intoned, was the only adequate medium for the highest of human spiritual possessions, the wisdom that told of the ways of God with the world. Theology, on the other hand, has tended towards the conceptual-analytic and the correspondingly prosaic. So Celtic Christians who in this respect also carried forward their pagan past, seldom wrote 'straight' theology. In this also they may have much to offer to a contemporary theological scene which is slowly rediscovering the primacy of the religious imagination; although we are still a long way from witnessing in this scene as privileged and influential a social place given to poet and artist as ancient pagan Celtic society gave them.

There are some great Celtic theologians. John Scotus Eriugena, a member of that band of Irish scholars which wielded such an influence on the developing civilization of Europe in the Middle Ages, would certainly merit a place in the shortest history of theology. But a combination of accident and personal design made me choose Pelagius as our sample Celtic theologian. I always suspected that there was not much that was Celtic about the substance of Eriugena's work; yet the more reluctance I found amongst potential contributors to regard Pelagius as a Celtic thinker, the more I increased my old suspicion that the very key to his theology is its Celtic character. There is something about the manner in which people dealing with the Celtic tradition try to dismiss Pelagius – Glanmor Williams attributes 'devastating success' to St Germanus of Auxerre in combating his followers in Wales in the fifth century, but he does not wonder why men of the stature of Germanus had to be sent for this purpose. There is something about the way in which admissions of Pelagius' continuing influence are followed immediately by the most stringent qualifications – Martin McNamara talks of Pelagius on Paul being used in the Irish Church down to 1079, but hastens to assure us that this does not mean the Irish Church was Pelagian. There is something reminiscent about all of this, of the family that wants anxiously to disown a son who has been condemned as a reprobate by a powerful establishment and subsequently by the world at large. Although, as far as implicit condemnation goes, the precise terms of an alleged Papal condemnation are curiously missing from our records; whereas the terms of the Emperor's condemnation of Pelagius are remarkably similar to the terms of an imperial condemnation of the Celtic druids! One does not need a very keen nose to get a strong whiff of cultural bias.

What is at issue in the chapter on Pelagius is not just the rehabilitation of a 'heretic' – a theological game in vogu over the last few decades – but the very real possibility that there is a characteristically Celtic theology of nature, sin and redemption which could be quite orthodox, or at least avoid the clear excesses and failures of its Augustinian counterpart. It is my personal conviction – and one which I should be prepared to argue at any theological length in the proper forum – that Pelagius' own thought, from what we know of it, is perfectly capable of giving an adequate and orthodox account of God's prevenient grace in all of our world and all our existence – thus avoiding the 'salvation by one's bootstraps' image which is the popular theological impression of 'Pelagianism' – while also dealing realistically with the power of sin and its universal sway. But the article on Pelagius is included in this collection more for the fascinating prospect it offers of a continuity of a certain Celtic vision of the ubiquity of God's gracious power in all our world, of the belonging together of nature and grace, of the total interpenetration of the spiritual and material worlds.

There is another very general feature of Celtic life which is mentioned by a number of our authors, by Hanson in writing of Patrick's surviving influence, by O'Fee as a further example of grace building on nature when the Irish monks now do this for Christ, and by Tudur Jones in a similar context. It is the Celtic penchant for wandering abroad. Other peoples, of course, had wandered, but with imperial intent, and the will to dominate other peoples is to this day the most destructive force in the long and dismal history of the race. Contemporary empire-builders, the Russians and the Americans, may use more sophisticated economic weapons to disguise a raw military force more obvious in times past, but their destruction of other cultures is no less devastating for that. Of course the Celts could be as greedy and destructive as their neighbours; they sacked Rome in 390 BC and Delphi in 279 BC. But there were features of their wanderings which are of value today, and therefore worth highlighting. Negatively, they did not attempt to create an empire. Some may see this, cynically, as an attempt to make a virtue of necessity: they simply lacked the organizational ability required for empire-building. I think this is an unnecessarily cynical view of the matter, and in line with other familiar and crude attempts to criticise the Celts. Rather was their social organisation extremely complex and inevitably varied; and thus more sensitive to the complexities of human relationships. One can think of the superior place of women in early Celtic society; and when early Celtic prayers address Christ as King they have a far greater sense of his intimacy with his people than a Roman could ever suggest by use of the same, or a similar, title. Imperial organisation is by contrast essentially destructive of cultural variety, for it positively institutionalizes domination and greed.[8]

Put more positively, we know from their earliest art that the wandering Celts had an inherent ability to assimilate and to enrich whatever the peoples they encountered had to offer, while leaving all essential differences intact. They could make quite distinctively their own forms borrowed from others, and contribute to the richness of the cultures of others without attempting to suppress these. It may well be that this ability has not been lost, or that it could be revived, for it is essential if the modern world is not to descend into a monochrome, materialist cultural limbo in which human life will not be worth living.

One can detect this ability in its religious version in many pages of this collection. Those who wandered for Christ left homeland and tribe permanently behind, like Abraham; they were not intent on expanding territorial or tribal boundaries. Meeting other forms of the Christian faith-in-practice they were often reduced to pleading for *lebensraum* for their ways, for cohabitation and mutual existence, in place of displacement of one Christian way by another. Roman authorities, then as now, seemed to have difficulty in accepting such a plea. The imperial temptation survives, often for centuries, the possession of the only force that can ensure its satisfaction, physical force and fear.

Not the least of the examples of the Celts' ability to adapt are those furnished by our two Welsh authors, Glanmor Williams and Tudur Jones, and by Terence McCaughey. Celts in the remaining Celtic lands of Scotland and Wales were well capable of assimilating to their Christianity all that seemed

---

[8] An Australian Prime Minister recently referred to this ability, in praise of the Irish in his country: the ability to contribute some things and assimilate others, rather than attempt to suppress or replace in imperial fashion.

best to them in the Protestant Reformation of the sixteenth century, and of doing this at every level of society, from the traditional Celtic warrior aristocracy of the Highlands to the poor and unlettered in the Welsh valleys. In fact, it seems to me to be clearly implied in McCaughey's chapter and to be almost explicit in Williams', that it is only when extraneous political motives and forces enter the equation that divisiveness and hostility begin to mar a process of assimilation and adaptation more natural to the spirit of Celtic Christianity. When in Scotland overt political allegiances began to effect the livings of clergymen, and in Wales a rewritten 'history' aligned Papacy with English rule and Protestantism with Tudor (i.e. British or Celtic) rule, although the 'history' could just as easily have been written the other way round if a Papist had taken the English throne, it becomes obvious that it is politics from extraneous sources which causes unnecessary divisions. All of which adds poignancy to Hanson's observation that one of the features of Patrician Christianity was its ability to unite parts of the British (i.e. Celtic) Isles now tragically at political loggerheads; and to McCaughey's plea for a return to the Gaelic as a repository of the pluralist experience of people who have lived over so many centuries in these islands. When one hears a Northern Irish Protestant talk dangerously these days about fighting for his faith, and one realises that he means to fight Irish nationalists who are generally regarded as being Roman Catholics, one feels an almost physical need for a return to common Christian roots, if these are any longer accessible through the tangled undergrowth of twisted imperial deadwood and political intrigue.

Is Celtic Christianity still accessible as a vital force? Robert Welsh's chapter on Seán Ó Ríordáin witnesses to its survival in all its characteristic features: the language, the poetry as privileged vehicle, the sense of tradition, the saints' places on remote islands, the prayer/joy-thrust in bird-song, the impatience with narrowness of imposed definitions. It is in the subversion of definitions, of course, and of identities imprisoned in iron conventions, that one meets James Joyce, whose 'weapons of resistance', as O'Leary points out, were 'language and religion (but a religion of art or one of absolute non-conformity)'. 'As for Irish Catholicism', he writes, 'if it

could swallow Joyce whole, while not abandoning the necessary critical discrimination, perhaps it would find at last the
contemporary adult application of its precious heritage of
faith'.

So there is hope; but much remains to be done, and not
least at the scholarly level. O'Fee talks about the need for
a *vue d'ensemble*; McNamara's article is, and could be, little
more than a survey of all the rich material now becoming available to scholars from the distinctive Irish tradition
of Scripture translations, glosses, homilies and apocrypha.
And so many intriguing questions remain to be answered,
and none, it would seem, without contemporary relevance.
O'Fee mentions the place of women in religious life, and the
wanderer's way with language; I would like to add again the
Celtic way of adapting the natural religious (or so-called
pagan) heritage and the prospect of yet completing that
task. If this collection motivates its readers to follow some of
these lines of questioning for themselves, it will have served
its purpose more than adequately; and the question of the
survival of Celtic Christianity will find that small part of its
answer that academia can offer.

I must end with a particular word of acknowledgement to
one of the contributors, Noel-Dermot O'Donoghue. It was
he in fact who first conceived of this enterprise, sought a
publisher, and began to look for contributors. I hope that
the end result has not fallen too far short of his original
goal, and that he can see the appearance of the work in
print as a fitting way to mark his retirement from Edinburgh
University, to the curriculum of which he added the study
of Celtic Christianity. I should also record, but this time with
sadness, the death of Richard Hanson since he contributed to
this collection. As an islandman like myself he will not mind,
I am sure, if I pray for him and for all of us in the language
and imagery of our common Celtic culture: *go mbuailfeadsa,
agus gach aon a léighfidh an leabhar so, leis i nOileán Parrthais.*

The Mission of Saint Patrick

R.P.C. Hanson

An enterprising young scholar could write an original and interesting doctoral thesis on the history of Patrician scholarship.[1] The study of Saint Patrick has undergone the usual course of discovery and change and controversy which studies of other people from Christian antiquity have undergone, ever since his story emerged from the Middle Ages adorned or smothered by a gaudy clothing of legend and invention. In Patrick's case, however, the efforts of slowly intensifying scholarship, gradually finding its most effective tools, in its efforts to pierce the mists of later tradition and trace the lineaments of the historical Patrick, have been for much of the time bedevilled, obstructed and distorted by the tendency to use him for the murky ends of denominational rivalry, a tendency which has now disappeared almost entirely among serious scholars, but which still survives in less informed circles. In the course of this history of

---

[1] The quotations from Patrick's works in this chapter are taken from their translation in my *The Life and Writings of the Historical Saint Patrick* (New York 1983) which is in its turn a rendering of the Latin text printed in *Saint Patrick: Confession et Lettre à Coroticus* (Sources Chrétiennes No. 249, Paris 1978).

scholarship almost every conceivable form of theory about
Patrick has been put forward, from the attempt to fit into a
single account every single detail related of Patrick, early
or late, legendary or historical (Healy), to the denial of any
historical existence to him altogether (Ledwich, Zimmer and
Weijenborg). His career has caught the attention of many
scholars, not only Irish, but also American, German, and
Italian (though surprisingly few English). Add to this the
growth of a large jungle of popular nonsense associated
with his name, exemplified by the practice of dyeing the
beer drunk on March 17th in New York the colour of green,
and the reader will appreciate that the subject of Patrick is a
complicated and delicate one.

This essay consequently, if it is not to exceed grossly in
length and bore its readers intolerably, will make the following assumptions, which are not arbitrary but are based on
many years spent in studying the subject and on a fairly large
consensus of reputable scholarship:

1.   The primary sources for reconstructing Patrick's life
must be the two pieces of writing which are indubitably
his, i.e. the *Letter to Coroticus* and the *Confession*, and whatever
can be gleaned about the history of the extreme north-west of
Europe during the fifth century.

2.   Later *Lives* of Patrick, even the earliest, those of Muirchú
and of Tirechán, can give us only the faintest gleams of light
about the historical Patrick and must be rigorously controlled
by what the earlier and more reliable sources tell us.

3.   The surviving Irish *Annals*, useful though they are for the
history of medieval Ireland, were written too late (at the earliest towards the middle of the eighth century) to throw any
light on Patrick's life.

4.   The only works which we can with confidence attribute
to Patrick are those listed under (1) above.

The result of this critical operation is to remove most of
the conventional appearance and activity associated with

St Patrick. He did not banish snakes from Ireland. He did not illustrate the doctrine of the Trinity by the example of the shamrock; he did not climb Croagh Patrick nor institute his Purgatory in Lough Derg in Donegal. He did not spend any time with a chieftain called Dichu on Mt Slemish in Co. Antrim. He did not meet any High-King, whether called Laoghaire or not, on the hill of Tara in Co. Meath. We cannot even with confidence associate him with the foundation of the see of Armagh, for archeological investigation has shown that the ancient Navan fort just outside the modern town was long sacked and deserted by the time Patrick reached Ireland.

That Patrick's origins and background were British is absolutely clear. He came from Britain, but not from the kind of country which the word 'British' suggests to us today. His Britain was a country almost wholly uninfluenced by any English or Anglo-Saxon culture or race whatever, a Britain which had been conquered by the Romans and occupied by them for two and a half centuries. And in his case the word 'British' had its original, now half-forgotten, meaning. It meant 'Celtic'. The Britons were for the Romans a congeries of tribes displaying all the usual characteristics of Celtic culture and tradition: they were fierce, though erratic, fighters; they liked to wear brightly-coloured garments and gold ornaments and jewels; they were great breeders of horses and cattle; they spoke a language which had never been written down, widely different from Latin; they liked to hear poetry and sagas recited; they were mostly tall and fair-haired; they worshipped a multitude of gods and goddesses, locally rather than nationally recognized; their society was tribal, much stratified into different classes, controlled by oral traditional law, and ruled at the top by kings some of whom were greater and more powerful than the others; their art was peculiar to themselves, intricate, delicate, shunning a straight line, favouring the grotesque, almost esoteric. These people and this culture had been for two centuries exposed to a process of Romanisation, strong and influential among the upper classes, less so among the peasants.

Among the influences emanating from Roman culture had come Christianity, anonymously, obscurely but steadily.

Long before St Columba inaugurated his monastic type of Christianity in Iona, long before St Augustine landed at Thanet bearing with him the Continental Christianity of the late sixth century, Christianity had reached Britain. This fact has only recently been recognized universally and consciously by scholars, but now literary and archeological research has put it beyond doubt. By the year 400 the Christian Church had been firmly established in Britain. There were bishops, presbyters and deacons, and quite possibly monks and nuns also. This was the religious background from which Patrick sprang, and for which he is one of our most informative sources, though this truth is still far from widely recognised. We know the sites of a few church buildings (Silchester, Caerwent, perhaps Canterbury) and can guess at others. We can name a very short list of sees – Eboracum (York), London, probably Lincoln – but by now there were far more than those few in Britain, perhaps as many as thirty in all. The British church had produced a few martyrs – Aaron, Julius and Alban, the last of whom had a shrine at Verulamium (St Alban's) which the faithful were wont to visit. We can even by Patrick's aid reconstruct the Rule of Faith of the British church as it stood in the first half of the fifth century (*Confession* 4). It bears the marks of the Trinitarian controversy of the fourth century, but not of the Christological disputes of the fifth. Clerical marriage was allowed: Patrick was the son of a deacon and grandson of a priest. The British church must by the year 400 have been transforming itself from being an urban church, as it surely was at first, into a church covering rural areas also: Patrick's father was a deacon attached to a village (*vicus*) not a town, and he had an estate upon which Patrick lived. Two pavements with Christian symbols have been discovered in villas, and at Lullingstone near Otford in Kent a Christian chapel designed to serve an estate, with fine wall-paintings. British Christians cannot all have been poor and of the lower classes. Some of the communion silver in the Water Newton Find which probably came from a church in Durobrivae (Ancaster in Northamptonshire) was expensive and of good craftsmanship.

But the British church was not a strong, thriving institution like the Gallic and Spanish churches. It was remote from centres of power and culture. We know the names of six or seven British Christians born in the fourth century, apart from Patrick, and the only eminent one was Pelagius, whose eminence largely came from the fact that in the fifth century he clashed with Augustine. As the Roman pagan poets and orators regularly cited the Britons as examples of the distant outreach of Roman power, so the theologians of the third and fourth centuries will sometimes cite Britain as a sign of the vast extent of territory where Christians now live, but that is all. We must imagine Patrick as one who has been much influenced by Roman civilization: he knows some Latin, he respects Roman law and Roman institutions; he has also, when our account of him begins, been baptized as a child and is a nominal Christian. But still underneath all this we must postulate the power of a basically Celtic culture. His native language is British, not Latin. If, as seems probable, he was born in the last decade of the fourth century, then he grew up in a Britain which in the year 410 or 411 threw off Roman government. The administrators and the mobile units of the Roman army withdrew, the country relapsed into sections of tribal territory ruled by kings or by warlords (*tyranni*) who must have retained some imitation of Roman administration, for they tended to adopt the titles of Roman officials, but who could not even attain to the art of coining money. A reversion to Celtic traditions and Celtic ways, as well as to the Celtic practice of inter-tribal fighting, must have washed over the Britons, Christians and others, like a wave.

It is easy to reconstruct the main outlines of Patrick's life from the information which he gives us in his *Confession*. He was the son of a well-off Briton who owned a *villa* (Patrick in fact calls it a *villula* (*Confession* 1) but he means a Roman-style estate) where there were many servants and employees. He had begun to learn Latin; he had been brought up as a Christian, though his religion meant little to him. His father, Calpornius, as well as owning an estate, was a deacon attached to a village whose name Patrick gives us but which no one has ever been able to identify. When he was almost sixteen, he was captured by Irish pirates and carried off to a remote part of Ireland, probably on the west coast, where he spent six years as a slave, tending cattle. Wrenched suddenly and ruthlessly away from everything familiar and dear to him and set down helpless among strangers, he turned to God, to whom, in spite of his father being a deacon, he had hitherto paid little attention. He became a devoutly religious youth.

After six years in captivity he was able to escape, to make his way to the east coast of Ireland, and to find a boat that would take him to Britain. Here he rejoined his family and spent an indefinite number of years with them. A significant dream suggested to him that he should go as a missionary to Ireland (*Conf.* 23), though he did not act on it immediately. Then or at some other time he was ordained deacon, and no doubt priest also later. At some point, when he was absent from Britain, almost certainly paying a visit to Gaul, his name was canvassed for the task of being sent as a bishop to Ireland, and after some debate caused by doubt as to whether his education, interrupted by his kidnapping and never completed, was sufficient for the assignment, he was chosen, consecrated bishop and sent to Ireland. We know nothing at all about his movements in Ireland thereafter, and not very much about what he did there. He certainly succeeded in converting thousands of Irish people to Christianity and ordaining many clergy. One incident is brightly illuminated for us. A British ruler or warlord called Coroticus, who, with his people, was a nominal Christian, organised a raid on Ireland as a result of which many Christians whom Patrick had very recently baptized, confirmed and admitted to communion were massacred, others held in captivity, and others sold as slaves to the Picts. This outrage evoked from Patrick a letter of angry protest, which survives as the *Letter to Coroticus*. Patrick remained in Ireland for the rest of his life once he went there as a bishop. We do not know where he is buried. He was probably not martyred but died as an old man, which is how he describes himself in his *Confession* (10), written at the end of his life.

The dates of his career are extraordinarily difficult to determine. He cannot have lived earlier than the mid-fourth century, because he mentions the *solidus* (*Letter* 14), a coin first minted by Constantine the Great, and his Rule of Faith shows signs of being marked by the Arian Controversy. It is wholly unlikely that he lived very far into the second half of the fifth century, because he gives no sign at all of encountering difficulty in communicating with the British church while he is in Ireland, and he not only has probably visited Gaul once already (*Conf.* 32) but contemplates the possibility of visiting Gaul again (*Conf.* 43); and though he dismisses this possibility it is not because he regards Gaul as inaccessible. Yet, if we are to put any confidence in the scanty historical sources available to us, Britain in the second half of the fifth century was a scene of civil war, and foreign invasion, many of its cities sacked and untenanted, many of its people living as refugees in the hills. And contact between Britain and Gaul is largely lost in the second half of that century. Patrick's *Letter to Coroticus* implies not only that this warlord (*tyrannus* is what Patrick virtually calls him, *Letter* 6) is nominally Christian, along with his people, but that he is undisputed ruler in his own territory, unhindered by any possibility of Roman power controlling or punishing him. Yet Patrick respects Roman civilisation and almost identifies being a Christian with absorbing Roman ways (*Letter* 14). He always calls Britain 'the Britains', i.e. the British provinces (as established by Rome) not the British Isles. These pieces of evidence all point to Patrick's career being placed at a time when Roman government no longer prevailed in Britain but had only recently departed. We know that in the year 431 Pope Celestine sent a missionary bishop to Ireland called Palladius, though it is wholly uncertain what happened to him. The Irish *Annals* with suspicious unanimity place Patrick's arrival in Ireland as a bishop in the year after the advent of Palladius, 432. It may be possible to detect an indirect reference to the mission of Palladius in Patrick's *Confession* ('that I should imitate those who the Lord had long ago foretold would declare his gospel . . . so you can see we are witnesses that the gospel has been preached as far as the point where there is no one beyond'). It is therefore reasonable to conclude that Patrick was born about the year 390, came to Ireland some time not long after 431, and died between 450 and 460. This at least seems the most tenable theory until further evidence can be produced.

But when we speak of the 'Mission of St Patrick' we must ask ourselves the further questions: who supplied him, who authorized him, to whom did he regard himself as responsible? And we must also seek to determine the motives both of those who sent him and of Patrick himself. Many theories have been held as to the sources of Patrick's mission. The *Annals* say that he was sent, or at least patronised, by the Pope (probably Leo the Great, who was Pope from 440 to 461). The later *Lives* connect him with a variety of eminent persons on the Continent, with Germanus of Auxerre and his predecessor Amator, with Martin of Tours and with the monastery of Lerins, off the southern coast of France near Nice. Conjectures have been made that he was despatched by the church of Gaul, or, quite differently, that he was a lone evangelist, self- empowered, self-supplied and even self-ordained. But if we confine ourselves, as we have at the outset undertaken to do, to the only reliable evidence, the words of Patrick himself, we can come to only one conclusion: Patrick was sent and supplied by the British church, and during the whole of his career held himself responsible to that church.

He certainly regarded Britain as his native land: 'And again a few years later I was in Britain with my family, who received me as their son', he says (*Conf.* 23). He refers five times to his native country (*Conf.* 17, 36, 43, *Letter* 1, 11), and in three of these occurrences he links with his country his family, his extended family in the Celtic fashion, using alliteration 'country and kin' (*patriam et parentes*). He counts the loss of direct contact with his kin among the trials which God has called him to accept in remaining as a bishop in Ireland for the rest of his life. When he was chosen to be a bishop in Ireland he himself was not then in Britain, but it is certain that the people who canvassed for him and who finally sent him there were in Britain. He speaks of his close friend (who was later to betray him) in these terms (*Conf.* 32):

> I even had entrusted my soul to him! And I learned from some of the brothers that before that occasion for defending myself (at a time when I was not present nor was I even in Britain nor was the matter initiated by me) he, even he, was canvassing for me. He even had said to me with his own mouth, "Listen!

You are to be promoted to the rank of bishop", though I was not worthy.

The British church was Patrick's church. It was that church which ordained him deacon and presbyter, which consecrated him bishop and which sent him to Ireland, and it was to the leaders of that church that he addressed his *Confession* at the end of his life. This remarkable document, a classic of its kind, in some respects unique, and not enough known to students of ancient Christian literature, was at once a paean of thanksgiving to God, a statement of Patrick's personal inadequacy, especially on the side of education, and a vindication of his conduct as a bishop aimed at those in the British church who were inclined to criticize him, as well as at his supporters there. Among other points, he is anxious to vindicate his integrity in handling finance and support, which he must have been receiving from the British church (*Conf.* 49-54). Even if we did not possess this strong evidence of Britain being the base of his mission, the inadequacy of his grasp of the Latin language would argue strongly in favour of a British provenance for Patrick. Had he been a protégé of the Gallic church, which is the only serious alternative to consider, he must have spent a considerable time (not a mere visit, which he probably did make (*Conf.* 32, 43, *Letter* 14)) in that country speaking and writing nothing but Latin; he must have acquired a certain fluency in the language. But that is just what Patrick's Latin lacks, on his own admission (*Conf.* 4-11). Latin learned for almost wholly ecclesiastical purposes, especially for reading the Bible, in Britain, a mixture of vulgar Latin, Biblical Latin and ecclesiastical Latin, which are the ingredients of Patrick's Latin, is just the kind of Latin which we might expect to find imparted and used, perhaps painfully used, in the backward and unsophisticated British church, where not Latin but British would be Patrick's native language.

The motives of British churchmen in sending Patrick as a bishop to Ireland can be conjectured without much difficulty. Ninian had earlier been sent to Whithorn. The territory today called Strathclyde had been evangelised by Patrick's day, or so we must assume if we identify Patrick's

Coroticus with a warlord of that name and approximately that date whose headquarters were Dumbarton on the Firth of Clyde. By the first half of the fifth century the British church, harassed occasionally by Irish and Saxon raids but immune from the wholesale invasion and occupation which was the fate of the rest of Western Europe during that period, was enjoying a time of relative prosperity and expansion. It would have seemed right and logical to extend its evangelizing activity to Ireland.

During that period British Christians begin to appear more frequently on the stage of history. Pelagius rises to prominence as a preacher, reformer, and opponent of Augustine. Faustus first resides as a monk in Lerins and then, becoming bishop of Riez, makes a name in the literary world. Eminent people visit the British church, Victoricus of Rouen early in the century, Germanus of Auxerre in the 'thirties and 'forties. And, as we have seen, in 431 Pope Celestine I (423-432) sent a bishop, Palladius, 'to the Irish who believed in Christ', as the chronicler Prosper says. There must have been many Christians in Ireland by 431. In the ancient world no bishop was ever sent to a place totally devoid of Christians. Later accounts of what happened to Palladius differ from each other and none is reliable, but we can be fairly sure that nothing much came of his mission. He may have been martyred soon, but if so no Martyrology records him. He may have quickly succumbed to illness. But it is likely that the Pope's action, done as far as we know without consulting the British church, gave that church a shock and jogged it into an awareness of its responsibility towards its sister-island. Patrick was sent as a sign of the British church's obligation to evangelise. The highlands of Scotland, a remote and almost inaccessible region inhabited at least partly by warlike Picts (to whom Patrick incidentally shows a violent hostility (*Letter* 2, 12, 15)), were not an attractive field for evangelising. Ireland, easily accessible from the west coast of Britain, offered fairer opportunities. Patrick had spent six years of his life there. He knew the language. He was a devout and single-minded priest. The chief argument against his being sent was his lack of education, of which he is keenly, obsessively conscious. His Latin was inadequate, his reading minimal. He knew his Latin Bible very well indeed, but that was all. But he had influential friends and he was finally convinced that God was calling him to Ireland (*Conf.* 23, 28, 32, 46, *Letter* 1). So to Ireland he went.

Patrick's religion was unselfconscious, deep and convincing. At the most terrible moment of his life he had turned to God and found Him, and he never let go of Him (*Conf.* 2):

> And it was there that the Lord opened the understanding of my unbelieving heart, so that I should relate my sins even though it was late and I should turn with all my heart to the Lord my God, and he took notice of my humble state and pitied my youth and my ignorance and protected me before I knew him and before I had sense or could distinguish between good and bad and strengthened me and comforted me as a father does his son.

He was always conscious of God's presence and providence exercised towards him. When, with the band of raiders with whom he had found the means of returning to Britain after his escape from captivity the whole party, lost and hungry, encountered a herd of wild pigs, this was God's guidance (*Conf.* 19). When, much later, as a bishop in Ireland, he was imprisoned (*Conf.* 21), he was confident that God would cause him to be delivered, and delivered he was. When, in circumstances which are very obscure to us, an attempt was made to discredit his character and his whole career by his close friend bringing up against him some sin which Patrick had committed before his conversion, and which he had later confessed to this friend, God once again protected him and vindicated him (*Conf.* 26-32). Indeed, the *Confession* is, in one aspect, simply a lyrical expression of praise and gratitude to God by Patrick for His gracious dealing with His unworthy servant. But Patrick is not unreasonably confident of protection and success. He knows that he is likely to be martyred; he positively expects death for the sake of the Gospel, and would welcome it (*Conf.* 59). And the horrible incident of the massacre of his converts by Coroticus' soldiers must have taught him, if nothing else did, that trust in God does not imply automatic immunity from disaster.

An outstanding feature of Patrick's religion is his interest in dreams. All ancient Christians, like many modern African Christians, were interested in dreams. But we may perhaps see a touch of Celtic temperament here. Patrick recounts for us no less than eight visions which he saw in dreams, and he regarded them all as messages from God (*Conf.* 17 (two), 20, 21, 23, 24, 25, 29). The most elaborate is that which presented to him a man with letters from the people of the place in Ireland where had spent his captivity, saying 'Holy boy, we are asking you to come and walk among us again' (23). But even this dream is not worked up and rationalised as most dreams recounted for edification by medieval writers are. Patrick's dreams are convincing because they have the inconsequence, the surrealist atmosphere, of dreams. Here is another (*Conf.* 20):

> But that same night I was sleeping and Satan tempted me strongly, which I shall remember as long as I shall be in this body, and there fell on me something like a huge stone, and none of my limbs capable of moving. But how was it that it occurred to me, ignorant in spirit that I was, to call on Elijah? And while this was taking place I saw the sun rising in the sky and while I was crying out, "Elijah! Elijah!" with all my strength, the next thing that happened was that the radiance of the sun fell on me and at once dispersed from me all paralysis, and I believe that I was succoured by Christ my Lord and his Spirit was at that moment crying out on my behalf, and I hope that so it shall be in the day of my tribulation.

This remarkable sense of authenticity which we derive from reading his accounts of his own religious experience attaches in fact to all Patrick's religion.

His motive for accepting the call to a mission in Ireland was of course the conviction that God was calling him, though he hints that he only woke up to this call at the last minute (*Conf.* 23, 46). There was, however, another powerful motive which operated in Patrick bringing him to accept the call. He believed that he was living in the last times and, in accordance with the perennial call of Christ to evangelize (*Conf.* 40), he must preach the Gospel among the last people. It is not surprising that Patrick thought that the world was ending, for certainly the world as it had been created by the Western Roman Empire was ending. The great system of Roman government which had begun a thousand years before and had for four hundred years at least dominated the life of all the countries bordering on the Mediterranean Sea, and every country in Western Europe except Ireland, was, in its Western territories at least, collapsing round him. Under stress of barbarian raids, insecurity and exploitation by pretenders to the imperial throne, Britain had cast off Roman rule; Spain and the Gauls and Germany were overrun by invaders who showed no sign of retreating across the frontier. North Africa either was falling or had fallen to the Vandals. The Belgian and German provinces were controlled by barbarians. Across the Channel the Franks were every year advancing further. The central Roman government was reduced to ruling Italy and a strip of Southern Gaul under an increasingly powerless Emperor manipulated by barbarian warlords. The Balkan provinces were in a state of confusion under the impact of invaders from beyond the Danube. Rome, the eternal city – *Capitoli immobile saxum*, the citadel which Virgil had declared would last forever – had now been taken and sacked once by the Goths and again by the Vandals.

The world which the Britons had known for hundreds of years was coming to an end. The last age of this small world of antiquity had arrived. And consistently with this the Irish were the last people in this antique world to be evangelized. They inhabited an island situated on the edge of the vast Atlantic Ocean which no one had ever crossed, beyond which was nothing but a waste of water extending to the edge of the world. Patrick thought of himself as living under the imminence of the end of history, of the winding-up of all things by God. When the last people had been evangelised in the last age, then the world would end. He speaks of his converts as 'the people of the Lord which in the last times he had well and carefully planted' (*Letter* 5) and of himself as having 'a part among those whom [God] called and predestined to preach the Gospel . . . even to the end of the earth' (*Letter* 6), and as 'one of the hunters or fishers whom God long ago predicted beforehand [as appearing] in the last days' (*Letter* 11); most explicitly in *Confession* 34:

[God] has taken notice of me so that in spite of my ignorance and [of our being] in the last days I should venture to undertake this task, good and wonderful as it is, in such a way that I should imitate those who the Lord had long ago foretold would declare his gospel as a testimony to all nations before the end of the world, and we see as a consequence that it has been fulfilled just so: you can see that we are witnesses that the gospel has been preached as far as the point where there is no one beyond.

It is remarkable that one who thought that there would be almost no future for the world should in fact have laboured with such success that he laid the foundations of Irish Christianity for the next thousand years. We observe the same phenomenon in Gregory the Great at the end of the sixth century.

What, then, did Patrick accomplish in his mission? The country to which he was sent was not at first sight a promising one for a man of Patrick's background. It had never been conquered by the Romans, and in consequence had no writing, no coinage, no Roman roads, no market towns, no uniform system of law nor administration, and no system of education comparable to that of Britain. Time was to prove, though after Patrick's day, that the hitherto almost universal unit of administration of the Christian church, the diocese governed by a bishop with presbyters and deacons under him, could not apply and could not be worked in Irish conditions. The Irish (or, as Patrick usually called them, the Scots, *Scotti*) represented the Celtic way of life, or polity, in its purest, least contaminated form. There was no such thing as the High-King with whom later legend credited the Ireland of Patrick's day. There was no single state, centralized or federal or other. It was the tribal form which still dominated Irish society, as it had dominated British and Gallic society before the arrival of the Romans. Irish society consisted of a congeries of tribes, each of which could be thought of as a greatly extended family, some larger, some smaller, and each headed by a king; among the smaller tribes he would be called a 'sub-king' (*regulus* is Patrick's word for this office, as *rex* for full king (*Conf.* 41, *Letter* 12, *Conf.* 52)). The lesser tribes with their sub-kings would owe some allegiance to the more powerful tribes with their kings, probably in the form of tribute paid in cattle and slaves. Sometimes a large tribe or group of tribes connected ultimately by blood would dominate a large area of the country, as the Ui Neill did in Ulster (from whom was later to spring St Columba).

Society within each tribe was stratified into various classes: royal kin, nobles, craftsmen, bards and brehons (keepers of the traditional law), herdsmen, retainers, slaves and so on. There was no written law, but the oral law, which must have differed in some ways from tribe to tribe, was sedulously handed down from father to son by hereditary officials, and 'law' here means a vast amalgam of custom and rite and saga as well as law proper. The formation of blood feuds and vendettas was obviated by a wise system of fixing a 'price' as the penalty of killing or injuring or devaluing the honour of everyone, price varying according to status, the unit the price of a slave or of a beast. Patrick alludes to this practice in *Confession* 53, 'I reckon that I spent among them not less than the price of fifteen men'. Another Celtic custom, found outside Ireland as well as within, was that of 'fosterage' whereby a king's or noble's son or sons would be 'fostered', i.e. spend some of the years of their childhood with some other king or noble, thereby creating a bond of friendship and obligation between the two. It is possible that some Irish kings used to give their sons to Patrick to 'foster' in this way: 'During this period', he says, 'I used to give presents to kings in addition to what I used to give as a salary to their sons who used to travel around with me' (*Conf.* 52). But, at any rate in his early years as a bishop, Patrick and his clergy would be formally outside Irish law, classifiable into no stratum of society, and therefore liable to attack or injury without any safeguard or compensation. The earliest canons of Irish synods and the earliest Irish Penitentials give us a fragmentary picture of the clergy of the Christian church gradually being absorbed into the structure of Irish society. But, judging by Patrick's asseveration that he is liable to martyrdom at any time, this assimilation did not happen in Patrick's day.

He had no particular love for the Irish. At one point, indeed, he appears to number himself among the Irish, 'They think it derogatory that we are Irish' (*Letter* 16). But more

often he speaks contemptuously of them; as he denounces
the soldiers of Coroticus, he says (*Letter* 2):

> I do not say, to my fellow-citizens, nor to the citizens of the
> Christian- Romans, but to the fellow-citizens of devils . . . They
> live in an atmosphere of enmity, associates of the Irish and the
> Picts and of outlaws.

He speaks of the delivery of Christians into the hands of
Irish and Picts as a crime (*Letter* 12). And his own people at
home when his mission to Ireland was being contemplated
described the Irish as 'enemies who do not know God' (*Conf.*
46). It is highly likely, indeed, that Patrick regarded himself
as, among other things, carrying out a civilising mission
to the Irish. He was to be followed in this conviction by
many visitors from the larger island to the smaller during
the next fifteen centuries. He certainly had no respect whatever for the religion of the Irish. It is in fact very difficult
to reconstruct what their religion was. We can list the
names of several Celtic gods worshipped by the Irish –
Dagda and Maeve and Lug and Brigid – but they were not
gods associated with particular activities like the gods of
the Greek Olympic pantheon, and it is virtually impossible
to reconstruct the ideas behind pagan Irish religion. There
was a cult of the dead and a belief in an underworld. There
were fertility cults. Geraldus Cambrensis as late as the twelfth
century says that when an important king was initiated into
his kingdom he had in the past been obliged to copulate at one
point with a mare. Patrick himself witnesses to the existence
in Ireland of a cult of the sun in some form (*Conf.* 60). All this
was anathema to Patrick. Unconverted Irish are worshippers
of fake idols (*Conf.* 38); he has rescued his converts from
worshipping 'idols and filthy things' (*Conf.* 41). All who worship the sun 'will come to a bad end in wretched punishment'
(*Conf.* 60). He knew the Irish language. He knew something of
Irish society, for he had lived as a slave in Ireland for six years,
and he displays an uncharacteristic pride when he records
that he had converted (*Conf.* 42) a very beautiful Irishwoman
of the noble class. But he had no sympathy with Irish culture
as such.

We must constantly remind ourselves that Patrick was a bishop of the Christian church of the fifth century, and we must resist the temptation to seem him as a prototype of any Christian minister of the church of our day, much more than a thousand years later. He was not like a modern Roman Catholic bishop, very much conditioned by an elaborate ecclesiastical law and constantly keeping in mind the existence of the autocrat of his centralised church. He was not like a modern Anglican bishop, existing in a much looser framework of ecclesiastical law, much concerned to reconcile different traditions within his diocese, conscious of exercising leadership within a national church. He was not like a Methodist or Presbyterian minister; far less did he resemble a lone evangelist on the model of the Plymouth Brethren. He certainly regarded the bishop of Rome as the leading bishop of the Western church and as on occasion entitled to exercise authority, not very carefully defined, over that church. But the bishop of Rome was remote and difficult to communicate with. For Patrick the most important church was the British church, his native church which had authorized his mission and was financing it. He regards himself as in some sense responsible to it. It seems likely that the accusation which he was obliged to endure when he was a bishop came from high authority in that church, quite possibly from a synod, and that it was a synod which finally cleared him. 'And when I was attacked by some of my seniors who came and [brought up] my sins against my onerous work as bishop . . .', he says (*Conf.* 26), and 'They found a charge against me after thirty years . . .' (*Conf.* 27), and 'Therefore on that day in which I was rejected by the people already mentioned above . . .' (*Conf.* 29), and calls it 'that occasion for defending myself' (*defensionem, Conf.* 32). But God supported him in the crisis and 'my faith was approved in the sight of God and men' (*Conf.* 30).

Patrick is, from our point of view, teasingly unexplicit in his references here. Perhaps it was his outspoken attack on Coroticus, a powerful British Christian, which ultimately caused this attack on his good name. He knows already when he writes the *Letter to Coroticus* that there are people who despise him and dislike him (*Conf.* 1, 6, 11, 12, 16). But this does not prevent him exercising the full spiritual power open to a fifth-century bishop. He directly and explicitly excommunicates Coroticus and his supporters (*Letter* 5, 7, 21). He claims to be one of God's priests (i.e. bishops, *sacerdotes*) 'whom he chose and granted to them supreme, divine, lofty power, that those whom they bound on earth are bound in heaven also' (*Letter* 6). The fact that this *Letter* was preserved and copied and has survived (its earliest manuscript is of the tenth century) shows that it must have had some effect.

In other respects Patrick acts as a normal fifth-century bishop might be expected to act. He converts and baptises a vast number of people ('thousands', he says, *Confession* 14, 50). This baptism included both confirmation and admission to Holy Communion. He ordains clergy, some of whom serve on his staff. He must have led a largely peripatetic life and there is little evidence that towards the end of his life, when he wrote the *Confession*, he was rather more stationary. He also encourages his converts to embrace the religious life as monks and nuns, or even as people simply vowed to continence (*Conf.* 42). He may even have lived such a life himself before he was made bishop. But it seems entirely likely (*Conf.* 42) that these religious did not form separate communities, enclosed and living on their own, but led their ascetic lives in their own households. Patrick imported the spirit and in a modest way the practice of monasticism to Ireland, but cannot be credited with the wholly monastic structure which the ministry of the Irish church later assumed; this was a development deriving from different impulses some time after his death. He never mentions other bishops as residing in Ireland nor any arrangements to be taken to appoint his successor. He certainly built some churches, no doubt of wood, because he refers to pious women throwing gifts on the altar (*Conf.* 49).

He taught, no doubt, the doctrine which he had learnt from his native church. He writes out for us early in the *Confession* (4) a doctrinal statement, which he later calls a 'rule of faith of the Trinity' (*mensura fidei trinitatis*, 14). It is a most interesting document, of which surprisingly little notice has been taken by the world of scholarship. It most resembles a

similar formula given us by Victorinus of Pettau (who also
calls his a 'rule of faith'), who was a bishop of a Balkan town
about the year 300 and was martyred in the persecution of
Diocletian. But Patrick's rule of faith is not a mere copy of
that of Victorinus. It shows signs of having been influenced
by the controversies about the divinity of Jesus Christ which
convulsed the fourth-century church after Victorinus' day;
it may even quote the Nicene Creed, and if this conjecture
is true it is one of the earliest documents, Latin or Greek, to
do so. The Latin of this rule of faith is not Patrick's, but it is
not redolent of Ciceronian eloquence. It is the homely Latin
of a homely church which admired a martyr and adopted his
language for its doctrine.

Patrick's doctrine as we can recover it from his two
works is what one might expect from one who was not
highly educated and could not appreciate theological subtleties. But it is neither naïve nor perfunctory. It springs from
his heart and he has firmly grasped the very marrow of
Christianity. Our redemption through Christ, the dwelling
of the Holy Spirit in our hearts, our duty of continual praise
to God's, God's love and providence, the necessity of faith,
the hope of and in the case of those murdered by the agency
of Coroticus, the certainty of heaven, the call to imitate
Christ (*Conf.* 42, 47, 50), the judgment to come. These are
his themes, set out with a refreshing and convincing lack
of rhetoric or artificiality of any kind. It was not in Patrick's
nature to be artificial, and anyway his command of Latin
was too weak for him to write rhetorically (as he admits
Conf. 9-13). It is one of his charms. He has no acquaintance with any book, so far as we can ascertain, except the
Latin (pre-Vulgate) Bible. But that book he knows very well
and uses constantly, even when biblical quotations are not
called for. Indeed, against Coroticus he almost uses it as
if it was ammunition (*Letter* 20). We look in vain for signs
in Patrick of what might be regarded as popular medieval
religion. He is interested in visions, but not in miracles. He
does not invoke saints (unless we are to count his calling on
Elijah in a dream *Conf.* 20). He just may make one reference
to Purgatory in *Letter* 17, but it is not likely. He was not,
of course, a Protestant before his time, but a fifth-century

bishop who had grasped clearly and firmly the essentials of the Christian message.

We can know nothing about how he went about his work of evangelising nor where his evangelising activities led him, though later legend gaudily filled this void. He probably penetrated as far as the west coast of Ireland, for the 'Cry of the Irish' from 'the voice of those who were by the Wood of Voclut which is near the Western Sea' (*Conf.* 23) which he heard in his dream must have come from the district which is round the town now known as Killala in Co. Mayo, near the border with Co. Sligo. It is wholly likely that Patrick went there, especially as he says that he had penetrated to parts where nobody (i.e. no Christian, or no evangelist) had been before (*Conf.* 34, 51).

His was certainly a peripatetic ministry. He used to travel round accompanied by the sons of kings whom he was educating or 'fostering' (*Conf.* 52). He distributed gifts among their fathers. The sons and daughters of the Irish and of their sub-kings (*reguli*) were persuaded to become monks and nuns (*Conf.* 41). He received the news of the massacre of his converts at a place which was at some distance from where they had been baptized; he had apparently moved on after the ceremony (*Letter* 3). He had endured temporary captivity many times (*Conf.* 21, 37, 52). He is quite confident that he has securely established the Christian faith in Ireland; he speaks (*Letter* 5) of:

> the people of the Lord . . . which in the last times [Christ] had well and carefully planted, and it was established by the favour of God.

His desire that he should be martyred was not granted. We do not know where he died and was buried. We can be certain that we do do not know, for the monastery of Armagh, when in the seventh and eighth centuries it was propagating the cult of Patrick in every possible way, admitted that nobody knew where he was buried; had the monks of Armagh known, they would certainly have exploited the fact. Neither Downpatrick nor Saul can make good any claim to possess Patrick's body. This anonymity about his burial-place would probably have pleased Patrick.

He had established in Ireland a diocesan organization such as prevailed throughout the church at the time. We cannot envisage him dividing the country into dioceses. To Coroticus he says 'I Patrick . . . in Ireland declare myself to be a bishop'; the sentence could be translated 'declare myself to be a bishop (or even 'the bishop') in Ireland' (*Letter* 1). This almost excludes the possibility of other bishops co-existing with him. It would be anachronistic to picture Patrick forming parishes, because the parochial system was at that time only at a rudimentary stage even in those parts of the church which were most developed. We need not doubt that the British church sent somebody else to succeed Patrick as bishop in Ireland, but we do not know his name. The later *Lives* give us plentiful but quite unreliable information on the subject.

The fact that the first source to name Patrick after his death can be dated no earlier than the year 632 should not cause us much surprise because the later fifth and sixth centuries are the darkest period of dark ages when our information on almost any subject is scanty. By the time we hear of him again the Irish church has undergone a great transformation, and has adopted that wholly monastic structure which distinguished it, and to a lesser degree all the churches of the Celtic area, from the other churches. Neither Adamnan's *Life of St. Columba* (688-92) nor Bede's *Ecclesiastical History of the English People* (731), which shows considerable interest in and respect for Irish Christianity, mentions him. But he was not forgotten. His *Confession* and *Letter to Coroticus* continued to be read and probably to be copied. The earliest *Lives*, those of Muirchú and of Tirechán, show knowledge of these works. By the seventh century Patrick had become a fruitful subject for legend and embroidery, as useful for ecclesiastical politics as for popular religion.

The legacy of Patrick is hard to estimate. Of course he has the credit, if not of bringing Christianity to Ireland, at least of establishing it there. He deserves the title 'Apostle of the Irish People'. We can perhaps credit him also with that missionary impulse which was so strong a trait in early Irish Christianity. The world did not end, as he expected, but the horizon became darker and darker as far as the survival of

Roman culture and education went during the two or three centuries after Patrick's death. It was to be lightened by the arrival of Irish monks during the seventh and eighth centuries, who upheld a higher level of learning and zeal than their contemporaries on the Continent. Learning Patrick could never have bequeathed to them, but missionary zeal was certainly close to his heart. Perhaps this tradition owed its genesis to him; certainly anybody who read his *Confession* might be infected by it.

Another legacy of Patrick may have been the friendship which existed between British and Irish Christians, even after the arrival of the Anglo-Saxons, and even after the Synod of Whitby in 664 had committed the Anglo-Saxon church to a definitely Continental and not Celtic form of ecclesiastical polity. The Iris and the British, as the Irish and the Anglo-Saxon churches, were not enemies, but regarded each other with a respect and an admiration which Bede in his history cannot conceal, for all his adherence to the Continental model; together they contributed a great deal to what is called the Carolingian Renaissance. Patrick came from Britain and was entirely loyal to its church. We can justly ascribe some share of glory in the cultural achievement of the British Isles to one who founded their religious concord.

Finally, we can perhaps see in the peculiar self-abandonment of the Irish monks of the sixth and seventh centuries something of Patrick's spirit. Patrick was not somebody to do things by halves, and neither were they. He would not accept the gifts given him by pious women (*Conf.* 49); he determined, once having set foot on Irish soil as a bishop, never to leave the island nor to visit his 'native country and kin'; he hoped ardently for martyrdom. 'Today', he says, 'I can offer to [God] confidently my life as a living victim to Christ my God' (*Conf.* 34), and these were no empty words. The Irish monks left their native country to live the perfect life (an expression of Patrick's) abroad, with no intention of ever returning. They penetrated to the furthest parts of Western Europe. Their ascetic rules and practices were severer than any others. Columbanus at the end of the sixth century calls upon his monks directly and drastically to renounce all worldly hope and comfort, and persuades the sons and relations of ferocious and unscrupulous Merovingian kings and nobles to follow his regime. There is no remote, stormswept island off the west coasts of Ireland, Brittany and Scotland which has not the remains of a Celtic monastery on it. Here Patrick's example and spirit were bearing their finest fruit.

St Patrick's Breastplate

N. D. O'Donoghue

Introduction

The ancient hymn known as the *Lorica Sancti Patritii*, the Deer's Cry (*Faeth Fiada*), and *St Patrick's Breastplate* is one of the most remarkable single expressions of Christian piety and practice. The Patrick, son of Calpornius, who wrote the *Confession* and *Letter to Coroticus*, belongs to the fifth century, and as the Breastplate in its extant form cannot be traced further back than the eighth century, the connection with the man whose name it bears is no longer defended by scholars of the period. Logically, all this means is that in its extant form it belongs linguistically to a time later than that of St Patrick; it leaves wide open the question as to whether the hymn, as we have it, may have come from an earlier form dating back to the fifth century or even to pre-Patrician times. One thing is certain: the *Breastplate*, as it has come down to us, is a messenger from a world at once familiar and strange, a messenger that is put in question by our contemporary sense or senses of the meaning of Christianity, but also a messenger that puts our contemporary understanding of Christianity in question, and may well have much to say to us that can illuminate our journey into the future.

The original *Lorica* is in Old Irish with a Latin ending. There are many English translations available, the best-known of which is that of a certain Mrs Alexander, and I have used these freely in working out the translation that follows, literal basically, yet aiming at echoing, however faintly, the sound and flow of the original, something that has not as a general characteristic entirely vanished from modern and contemporary Gaelic speech, nor from the Anglo-Irish speech that was born of it and is still with us.[1]

The Hymn

I

For my shield this day I call:
A mighty power:
The Holy Trinity!
Affirming threeness,
Confessing oneness,
In the making of all
Through love . . .

---

[1] The Old Irish text is to be found in *The Irish Liber Hymnorum* edited by J.H. Bernard and R. Atkinson as volume XIII of the publication of the Henry Bradshaw Society, London 1897, Vol I p.133. It is also to be found, with full critical apparatus, in *Thesaurus Palaeohibernicus* edited W. Stokes and J. Strachan, Cambridge University Press, 1903. The most accessible source for the Old Irish text is *A Golden Treasury of Irish Poetry* by D. Greene and F. O'Connor, Macmillan 1967. Unfortunately this book is now out of print, but is widely available in libraries. All these editions provide a literal English translation, as does also *St Patrick: His Life and Writings* by N.D.J. White, SPCK 1920. There are many popular and poetic translations of which those of George Sigerson and James Clarence Mangan are outstanding as literary works. The best-known of the popular translations is that (noted already) of Mrs Alexander. Well-known also is that of R.A.S. McAlister. Both are reasonably accurate, and both manage to convey the force and spirit of the original.

II

For my shield this day I call:
    Christ's power in his coming
    and in his baptising,
    Christ's power in his dying
    On the cross, his arising
    from the tomb, his ascending;
    Christ's power in his coming
    for judgment and ending.

III

For my shield this day I call:
    strong power of the seraphim,
    with angels obeying,
    and archangels attending,
    in the glorious company
    of the holy and risen ones,
    in the prayers of the fathers,
    in visions prophetic
    and commands apostolic,
    in the annals of witness,
    in virginal innocence,
    in the deeds of steadfast men.

IV

For my shield this day I call:
    Heaven's might,
    Sun's brightness,
    Moon's whiteness,
    Fire's glory,
    Lightning's swiftness,
    Wind's wildness,
    Ocean's depth,
    Earth's solidity,
    Rock's immobility.

V

This day I call to me:
    God's strength to direct me,
    God's power to sustain me,
    God's wisdom to guide me,
    God's vision to light me,
    God's ear to my hearing,
    God's word to my speaking,
    God's hand to uphold me,
    God's pathway before me,
    God's shield to protect me,
    God's legions to save me:

from snares of the demons,
from evil enticements,
from failings of nature,
from one man or many
that seek to destroy me,
anear or afar.

VI

Around me I gather
these forces to save
my soul and my body
from dark powers that assail me:
against false prophesyings,
against pagan devisings,
against heretical lying
and false gods all around me.
Against spells cast by women
by blacksmiths, by Druids,
against knowledge unlawful
that injures the body,
that injures the spirit.

VII

Be Christ this day my strong protector;
against poison and burning,
against drowning and wounding,
through reward wide and plenty . . .
Christ beside me, Christ before me;
Christ behind me, Christ within me;
Christ beneath me, Christ above me;
Christ to right of me, Christ to left of me;
Christ in my lying, my sitting, my rising;
Christ in heart of all who know me,
Christ on tongue of all who meet me,
Christ in eye of all who see me,
Christ in ear of all who hear me.

VIII

For my shield this day I call
a mighty power:
the Holy Trinity!
affirming threeness,
confessing oneness
in the making of all –
through love . . .

IX

For to the Lord belongs salvation,
and to the Lord belongs salvation
and to Christ belongs salvation.

May your salvation, Lord, be
with us always.
(Domini est salus, Domini est salus,
Christi est salus;
Salus tua, Domine, sit semper nobiscum).

Structure and Themes: The Deity

The Latin stanza that concludes the hymn is a kind of seal
or closure, almost an official stamp in the common language
of Christendom, in what was to *remain* the common language
of Christendom in its western and missionary form until
the middle of the twentieth century. Reading these fluent
and well-known phrases at the end of one of the earliest
vernacular hymns of the West we realise with sharp regret
that irrecoverable loss which Christendom, and Western culture, has sustained by the sudden departure of that common
companion of all the world's languages that shared the one
Gospel and the one form of worship. At any rate, here they
stand, these clear and haunting Latin phrases, witness to that
marriage of Gaelic and Latin which lies at the foundation of
Western religion and culture.

This seal is a trinitarian seal as befits the hymn itself, for this
is bracketed by a trinitarian invocation which, identically
repeated, encloses the hymn and gives it its horizon. The
language of this trinitarian invocation is simple and strong, as
if carved on stone; the phrases come to us across the years in
easily recognisable Gaelic: *niurt triun*, (*neart trean*), two sharp
heavy words, almost forming a palindrome as they strengthen
each other in expressing the unbreakable power of the triune
protection.

In this first stanza, already and fully, the central theme
and direction of the hymn is clearly stated. The *Lorica* is a
protection prayer, a deeply Christian protection prayer that
yet carries along with it some of the flavour of pre-Christian

invocations that were no less sincerely spoken and sung for the same purpose of protection. The sense of need and the sense of earnest entreaty and confidence have not changed, only the final direction and focus has changed. And yet within this horizon, or focal point, some of the more ancient way of invocation remains, as we shall see.

It is noteworthy that the Trinity, or rather the Deity, at once three and one, is invoked in its creative power and presence: the 'strong power' is not simply a massive overshadowing presence but a vibrant all-sustaining, all-permeating energy. Following Professor P.L. Henry I have translated *dail* in the original as 'through love'.[2] The word strikes, as clear as a bell, the note of tenderness and closeness that runs through the whole composition and is one of the constants of Celtic piety: the Triune God with his heavenly Host and his marvellous creation of earth and sky and ocean is a living intimate presence, the 'divine milieu' of Teilhard de Chardin, the 'breathing together of all things' of which the first philosophers of the West spoke so feelingly.

In the second stanza, the power of Christ is invoked in all its main manifestations: his birth, his baptism, his death and burial, his resurrection, his coming in judgment. Again, it is protection that is the main theme and the 'mighty acts' of Christ are invoked to serve this purpose. Neither here, nor elsewhere in the *Lorica*, are we in the world of face-to-face encounter with the Deity, or with Christ, or with heavenly beings. We are in a different prayer-world from that of the directness of the Lord's Prayer and of thousands of Christian prayers in the same direct vocative mood. Neither are we in the world of the Psalms, or of the Old Testament prophets who contended with the Lord face to face. Yet the more indirect invocational mode of prayer shows through, especially in Job and the Wisdom Books, and in the fact that both Moses and Elias, and indeed Abraham, are distinguished by their relationship with a deity not to be approached directly except in answer to a special call. And it may be true, as some

---

[2]   P.L. Henry, *Saoithiulacht na Sean-Ghaeilge*. Dublin: Government Publications, 1978, p.136.

scholars hold, that the step into full Father-and-Son intimacy with God had to wait for Jesus Christ as his special sign and signature.[3]

The Heavenly Host

The third stanza of our hymn descends from the sphere of deity and 'the Word made flesh' to the world of the first creation by which, in the Old Testament, the Most High God is the Lord God *of Hosts*. These heavenly beings are not seen as material in the sense of corruptible and visible to common sight. They are spirits, and to their sphere of being belong the spirits of the saints, those human beings who have died – 'they seem to the eyes of the foolish to have died, but in truth they live in the world of peace' – and are still part of the Church and alive in the service of the faithful. All this is the world of the *invisibilia* named clearly, and in contrast to the visible world, in the Nicene Creed. In our day, and ever since, in the sixteenth century, René Descartes made a clear and unbridgeable dichotomy between matter and spirit, we assume that an invisible world is quite alien to our senses and thus *absolutely* invisible and closed off from our field of perception. But for the people of the *Lorica* the angelic world was no more than *normally* invisible and inapprehensible. Not only was this world very close in a spiritual way, but it could shine through or otherwise impress itself on human perception. If one does not understand the nearness and apprehensibility of this 'other world' of the angels and saints, there is no hope at all of understanding Celtic Christianity either in its marvellous flowering in the 'Dark Ages' or in its pathetic and tenacious survival in what is left of that ancient faith and culture.

So it is that the invocation of the angels and saints is deeply meant and intimately felt. There is question of presences no less real than the Deity in its trinitarian and incarnational

---

[3]   See: J. Jeremias, *The Prayer of Jesus* (London 1976); C. Geffre, 'Father' as the Proper Name of God, *Concilium* (Edinburgh) March 1981.

manifestation, no less immediate and proximate than the world of nature that is invoked in the following stanza.

The link here with pre-Christian animism and the fairy-world of Celtic folk imagination is clear, and only those who wish to break all continuity between 'paganism' and Christianity would wish to deny it.

But let us look a little more closely at the invocation of the heavenly Host and of 'the holy and risen ones'. Traditionally, there are nine choirs or hierarchies of the heavenly host, ranging from the Cherubim and Seraphim at the top to the Archangels and Angels at the lowest level, reaching in a kind of continuity to man as 'a little less than the angels'. All these may find their way into the early Christian liturgies; indeed, they, rather incongruously, survive in the somewhat demythologized formularies of the present Catholic mass: they have vanished from the Confession formula but still find a place in the *trisagion* at the end of the preface. It must be said that, on the whole, the shapers of today's liturgies seem to have found the angelic hierarchies an embarrassment.

Not so the shapers of the *Lorica*. Three of the traditional nine 'choirs' appear, and one has the feeling that the others are not far away. What is significant, nevertheless, is that the 'choirs' that are immediately invoked are each given a specific function or role that bears directly on their presence as protectors. The Cherubim are strong in their radiant love; the Angels are obedient, ready to be God's messengers; the Archangels, who have a rank just above the Angels and far beneath the Cherubim and Seraphim, are God's ministers, a heavenly priesthood, as it were. There is no question of a merely imaginary or ornamental region of beings: they are as real as the sun and moon, the wind and the sea that are invoked in the succeeding stanza; in a sense they are more real, for they are eternal and indestructible, and their constant presence in human life touches the immortal part of us. Their presence, creaturely and deathless, is a kind of token of eternal life. To invoke these beings is to look beyond our mortal state.

The invocation of the angels moves naturally into the invocation of the saints: men and women like ourselves who now dwell in the world of Christian Resurrection which is identifiably or continuously the world of the angels. The reference to resurrection is plain and clear in itself, and it uses the word still in use in Gaelic prayers and liturgies today: *esseirgi* or *aiseiri*. But it is not at all clear whether the resurrection refers to the saints who are about to be invoked, or to the hope of resurrection on the part of the suppliant who is seeking protection. Most translators take it in this latter sense, and the text certainly leans in that direction. This breaks the flow of the prayer rather harshly, and I prefer to see the reference as bearing ultimately on the risen presence of the saints. There is a formidable ambiguity in Christian theology as to the status of 'the Just' in the time between their death and the general resurrection, but the invocation of the saints, here and elsewhere, makes it clear that the 'good dead' are living presences and, in some sense, already risen. Yet something of the ambiguity remains, and it may be that this is reflected in the ambiguity of our present text.

It is noteworthy that the saints, as also the angels, are called on directly to provide protection. Generally, Christian invocation of the heavenly host, angelic and human, has been intermediary or intercessory: they are asked to place the requests of the faithful before God. So, too, Mary is an interecessory figure never correctly the object of prayer. Indeed, Christ himself, though he can be the direct object of prayer, is far more usually an intercessor: *through Jesus Christ Our Lord* etc. We are in a world of hierarchies, celestial and terrestrial. It seems to me that in the Celtic tradition as represented by the *Lorica* and, later, by the *Carmina Gadelica* this hierarchical vision is dim and intermittent. Rather, there is a kind of domestication of the heavenly world all the way from the Trinity (and including it) to the least of the people of heaven whereby they all 'stand around', as it were, and may be honoured or invoked as need arises: indeed, the *Carmina* prayers and hymns give a distinct impression that the sweep of the invocations gives space to all of them. In the present instance the angelic list is sketchy, but the list of saints is fairly complete, including prophets, apostles, confessors, virgins and all great servants of God: an open-ended list but complete enough to let the whole of heaven in.

The Invocation of Nature

The sweep of the *Lorica* dips down, as it were, from the heavenly host to the visible cosmos in its spheres and elements: sun, moon and firmament, and the four elements: fire, air, water and earth. All this we tend to see as inanimate nature, but our hymn clearly sees it as somehow capable of responding to the human voice of invocation. The closest parallel to this kind of attitude to nature, outside the Celtic tradition, is the *Benedicite* or 'Song of the Three Children' from the third chapter of the Book of Daniel. This formed part of the Christian liturgy from early times and presumably would have been known to the composer(s) of the *Lorica*. In the *Benedicite* also, the spheres and the elements, as well as all living beings upon the earth, are called on to give glory to God; yet it is clear that here the physical world is seen rather as a 'theatre of God's glory' within which the voices of Daniel and his companions find space and resonance rather than as active partners in praise. In the *Lorica*, on the other hand, the world of nature is really invoked, called on for help, seen as in this regard no less responsive than the angels and saints. Sun and moon, fire and lightning, as well as the unchanging rocks and the ever-changing sea, are all seen as living and powerful friends and companions. And, conversely, man is seen as friend and companion to the world in which he lives.

Contemporary Christians sometimes find this fourth stanza of the *Lorica* disconcerting, and it is sometimes omitted either from the hymn book or from the performance of the hymn. It can, of course, be treated as metaphorical or ornamental: one does not *really* invoke the elements or really expect them to give us protection. Yet the words of this stanza tend to break through such distancing enterprises and to bring with them a kind of animism that seems pagan rather than Christian. So it is that P.L. Henry remarks that whereas the first three stanzas of the *Lorica* are 'very Christian, very orthodox', stanza IV 'has the savour of pre-Christian Religion'.[4] There would seem to be a case, then, for 'purifying' the *Lorica* from its residual paganism, a case very much strengthened by the

---

[4] *Saoithiulacht na Sean-Ghaeilge*, p.137

reference in the sixth stanzas to 'women, blacksmiths and druids' as among the evil powers against whom protection is invoked.

Yet any such 'purification' would turn a living organism into a corpse or mummy, something retaining enough 'form' to be capable of serving as a model or inspiration for a contemporary hymn but from which its own principle of life has departed. For it is precisely the invocation of the elements that gives the *Lorica* its immediacy and vibrancy both in what is invoked and what is feared. It is the prayer of a man or woman, a wayfarer, setting forth across a landscape that is overlighted by the Lord God of Hosts and overshadowed by dark spirits. The wayfarer is continually accompanied by elemental spirits that, as good and supportive, are natural and at home in the physical creation itself and, as evil, have invaded this world and are on the way to invading men and women. Indeed, these evil spirits have succeeded in, as it were, staking a claim in certain holy places of the earth: the womb (women), the sanctuary (druids) and the place where the elements meet most dramatically, the fiery forge and its human artisan (blacksmiths).

The belief that the world of elemental nature is a place of spirits has persisted through all the vicissitudes of the history of Gaelic Ireland, a history which, it must be remembered, was largely unaffected by either the Renaissance, the Reformation, the Enlightenment or the Scientific Revolution, and has been without a modern-style university or educational system until this century. This spirit-consciousness can be, and has been, put down to a kind of naïveté and credulity in part, at least, explicable by lack of education, or, more positively, as typical of folk-consciousness. However, it can survive the most complete system of education, and in Ireland it has survived the radical linguistic break of the nineteenth century, so much so that the English language when imposed on the Irish took on the colours of the Irish imagination and flowered in great literature. It has survived but, all the same, it has largely faded. All that can be said is that enough of it is left to provide a habitat for the kind of rediscovery of the spirit-world that is being made today in various ways and measures, wisely or wildly, all over the world. All the more reason for identifying and retaining this spirit-life in an ancient hymn.

Perhaps, however, it is not entirely accurate to see the physical world as it is invoked in the *Lorica* as merely the *place* of spirits. This indeed would have been accepted in the tradition to which the hymn belongs; yet the hymn does not invoke the spirits of earth or water or whatever, but rather these elements in themselves as benign and powerful presences. This does not mean that the elements are personalised in any general sense: only their protective power is invoked as if they carried the divine creative energy within them. In fact it is becoming clear at this point that the theme of creation briefly announced in the opening stanza is central to the whole composition.

The Invocation of the Godhead

In the fifth stanza we are back at the source of creation, a natural progression from the invocation of created nature in the fourth stanza. Already, in the opening stanza, the affirmation of the Trinity is followed immediately by the affirmation of the unity of the One, and it seems to me that it is the One rather than the Three that is seen as the Creator of all. Theologically the *Lorica* swings on two hinges: the Godhead is source and creator, Christ is God-with-us as a human presence, very dear and very near. The Holy Spirit has no direct presence in the hymn except as locked into the Trinity or Triunity. Neither is there any direct reference to Mary, already named Mother of God at the Council of Ephesus (431), though the invocation of 'the innocence of virgins' (stanza 3) carries an implicit reference to the Gospel accounts of the virgin birth of the Son of God and the central place of 'the Virgin' in these accounts.

At any rate, this fifth stanza of our hymn invokes the Godhead in several of Its attributes: strength, wisdom, vision etc.; and from this it goes on to face the enemy for the first time, the being or beings against whose presence and destructive power the *Lorica* is seen as a protection. Indeed the *Lorica*, as its title indicates, is first and last and all the way a protective formula, and what calls forth this protection is essential to the significance of the hymn. So it is that at this point the hymn goes on to name this enemy and these enemies.[5]

The Demonic Powers

Since the *Lorica* is a protection prayer it can be called functional inasmuch as its main purpose is to deal with the enemies that menace the wayfarer. Stanzas Vb, VI and VIIa are devoted to an enumeration of these enemies, an enumeration that usually involves some vivid descriptive epithet relating the enemy closely to the various circumstances of life.

Some of the enemies against which protection is sought are the evil chances of life: death by fire, by poison, by wounding, by drowning. Some take the form of human foes that attack the body and, more dangerously, the soul: the suppliant seems to gather around him a tight cloak of orthodoxy as he faces 'false prophesyings, pagan devisings and heretical lying'. This is the sharp and divisive voice of theological intolerance that has arguably been the Christian's worst enemy from the beginning, an enemy within that sows seeds of bitterness and pharisaism. It is less constantly and stridently present in Celtic Christianity than in either Catholic or Reformed Christianity, but is there all the same, and in passages such as the present it blows across the page like an east wind; and one feels the chill.

But clearly the great enemy is the demon, who comes first in the list and is present as felt and feared in all the other snares and dangers that menace the wayfarer. For the people of the *Lorica* the demon is a very concrete and personal reality, powerful, subtle, cruel, unrelenting. Above all the demon

---

[5] Greene and O'Connor (*op.cit*) see the *Lorica* as providing protection for a particular journey. This is true, but it cannot be said that this is the only or even the main purpose of the prayer. It seems to me that it is the journey of life for wayfaring men and women that is primarily in question, and that the hymn could be used as a kind of morning prayer, or generally, by individuals or communities.

is a deceiver, 'a liar and the father of lies' (*Jn* 8.44) from the beginning and capable of taking on the appearance of 'an angel of light' (2 *Cor* 11.14). So it is that protection is sought primarily not against the power of the demon, but against 'the snares of the demon'. The Christian wayfarer has to be sceptical of fair appearances and must walk warily. This is not a pessimistic theology of the radical evil of a fallen world. The world is good; nature is good; men and women are good. We are in a world of shadows, but the shadows do not emanate from the world. So it is that nature can be called in to protect us. Even though all creation groans and waits (*Romans* 8.19), yet creation still bears the imprint of the creator and carries within it, held captive as it were, an original purity and power that can answer to the right kind of invocation.

The Power of Spells

Before going on to consider the right kind of invocation it is necessary to look at those curious denunciations that close the sixth stanza. Protection is sought against spells cast by women and blacksmiths and druids. One can understand the reference to druids, only noting that the druids are still a power to be feared in the eighth century, assuming that the *Lorica* is as late as that. The reference to blacksmiths (or 'smiths', as most translations have it) is a little more difficult, though the idea of the forge as a place of power has lingered on, and appears now and then in the sagas and folk-tales. But women? Why should women cast spells any more effectively than men? It is not, be it noted, a question of women being dangerous but of *women who cast spells* being dangerous.

Of course there is a certain connection here between the feminine and a certain power to bind men or other women, but especially men, by words. The word is woman's weapon, as many a man has known to his cost, and this fact of life became ritualised in the Gaelic tradition. It is a recurrent theme in the heroic cycles that a woman could place a man under *geasa* or 'bonds' to protect her or even to take her as lover and wife at the utmost risk to himself; so Gràinne put Diarmid under *geasa*, and Deirdre the son of Uisneach. *Geasa* is plural, and it implies a kind of binding and weaving of spells. Obviously it was something the Christian wayfarer could do without.

At a less heroic level there was 'the widow's curse', the widow being the woman who did not have a man to defend her but was not left defenceless. She had the power of the word, and she could use it without fault wherever person or rights were invaded. This tradition still remains on in parts of Ireland, and there are women who still use it. Some time ago the case was reported in the Irish papers of two young men who overcame an old woman and took all her savings. Whereupon she cursed them roundly and eloquently, so much so that they felt they had to return; they did so, and found the police waiting for them! It is a short step from this well-earned cursing to the kind of curse that might come from less worthy motives and which our wayfarer wants to guard against.

But of course the word of power is not spoken only by woman; it can also be spoken by druids, as our hymn testifies, and by blacksmiths as well. By poets, too, as we know from other sources. These men are all professionals, trained to shape and sharpen, to hammer out and weld together the words of power. The woman has this power by nature; man has it by a skill passed down across the generations and often guarded as a secret. Much of this was taken over by the Celtic understanding of the Christian priesthood, and some of it remains to this day.[6]

The Invocation of Christ

Stanza 2 and stanza 7 go together, and they form the beginning and culmination of the main body of the *Lorica*, which is bracketed by the trinitarian invocation. Stanza 2 is a

---

[6] There is also the curious reference to 'knowledge unlawful that injures the spirit', *fri cach fiss ara-chuil, corp ocus animain duini*. Most scholars translate *fiss* as 'knowledge' (modern Irish *fios*) but Greene-O'Connor translates it as 'skill'. Probably the reference is to secret magical knowledge (which makes 'skills' a reasonable interpretation), but it is also possible that certain kinds of knowledge of high mysteries is dangerous and hence forbidden in accordance with St Paul's statement in 2 *Cor* 12.4 that he had heard things in his vision that it was not permitted to speak of.

Christology, a brief but comprehensive statement of the central mysteries of Christianity: incarnation, baptism, death, resurrection, ascension, second coming, last judgment. As we have seen, this summary of 'the mighty acts of God in Christ' fits in with the general theme of the prayer; the wayfarer invokes all these mysteries to provide protection. Yet it is worth noting that this powerful and comprehensive Christological invocation does not rule out the need or rightness of invoking the heavenly host and the physical universe. The light of Christ does not dim or outshine or extinguish all other lights; rather does it seem to affirm or disclose their original glory.

We are here at a central insight of Celtic theology, if that name may be taken to stand for the doctrinal world and Christian life-style from which the *Lorica* comes. It is the insight that Christ comes not to show up or illuminate the deformity of a fallen world but rather to release a beautiful and holy world from bondage; most of all, to release the human person, body and soul, from bondage, and to dissipate the shadows that lie across all creation through the presence of the enemy and his dark angels. The new light of Christ is an enabling light, allowing the original glory of creation to glow and radiate, not a new light to take the place of that original light, of man and created nature, become darkness. So it is that the asceticism, sometimes extreme, that goes with this tradition, is not the expression of a human righteousness confronting the divine righteousness of Christ, but rather an affirmation, difficult but possible, of an original righteousness which is the created image of the eternal Father and the all-holy Trinity. This affirmation is made in and through and with Christ and, indeed, involves a Christ-mysticism beautifully and comprehensively expressed in the seventh stanza of our hymn.

Le Christique

I take the heading of this section from Pierre Teilhard de Chardin, firstly because there is no word or phrase in English (or in Gaelic either) to name the spiritual atmosphere of the

Christ-prayer in which the *Lorica* culminates, and secondly because I think the cosmic vision of Teilhard may be seen as a contemporary statement or restatement of the vision that shines through the interstices of this ancient Irish hymn.[7]

The Christ-prayer is frequently separated from the main text of the *Lorica* and used as a prayer with a thematic and structural unity of its own. This is understandable and, in a sense, legitimate, inasmuch as a new style of invocation comes in at this point: the protection theme is deepened by the theme of union and transformation. It as as if the image of the shield (*Lorica*) gives way to the image of a cloak or even a shirt drawn closely about the wayfarer, so closely, indeed, that it becomes a kind of second skin or body. But I think the most helpful image is that of anointing. Christ is the anointed one, the man totally, in his whole being, anointed by that Spirit-flowing which is at once corporeal and spiritual. Let us notice how the words create their own space, which is neither physical nor yet spiritual, but includes both, and affirms another dimension.

> Christ beside me, Christ before me;
> Christ behind me, Christ within me;
> Christ beneath me, Christ above me.

'Christ within me' might be taken to say it all, as a terminus or point of arrival echoing St Paul's 'I live now not I but Christ lives in me' (*Gal* 2.20), but, as in St Paul, this way of absorption is balanced by the otherness of 'Christ beneath me, Christ above me'. The wayfarer is not dissolved into divinity or divine humanity, but remains entirely himself:

---

[7] I am thinking especially of *Le Milieu Divin* (1957, English translation, with French title, London 1960) and of the theme of the cosmic nature of Christ which occurs in various places in his writings and has been brilliantly explored in *The Cosmic Christ in Origen and Teilhard de Chardin* by J.A. Lyons (Oxford University Press, 1982). As far as I know, *Le Christique* has not been translated into English; it is included in Vol 13 of *Oeuvres de Pierre Teilhard de Chardin* (Paris: Éditions du Seuil, 1955-1976). One of Teilhard's most fruitful principles is 'union differentiates', i.e. the more completely any two things form a unity, the more each becomes its own differentiated self within the union: it is the key to human marriage and all creative unity. I use this principle below as bearing on the union of the wayfarer with Christ.

there is question of the kind of union that differentiates and that affirms difference-in-unity.

To speak of anointing is to name the work as special to the Holy Spirit; at the level of the human-receptive it is to affirm that at this point the *Lorica* opens up to the dimension of Christian mysticism. The mystical is the first commandment of Judaism and Christianity as fully experienced in its givenness; likewise it is the Lord's Prayer as the divine response and divine gift, as St Teresa of Avila explains so eloquently in her *Way of Perfection*, at once a volcanic eruption from the depths of the human spirit or psyche and the equally divine presence descending in abundance of joy and peace, a joy and peace that gradually percolates into the quiet depths of the spirit and never disappears.

For the Christian, this experience of God is mediated by the divine humanity of Christ opening towards the Trinity of Persons and the unity of the divine essence.

The Christ-presence – *Le Christique* – is total, all-encompassing, intimate and ecstatic. Ecstatic, that is, in the original sense of going outside oneself – and in this self-transcendence the mystical wayfarer meets one and the same Christ in others.

> Christ in heart of all who know me,
> Christ on tongue of all who meet me,
> Christ in eye of all who see me,
> Christ in ear of all who hear me.

There is no 'privatism' here – there never is in the true mystic – but rather radiance and connectedness and a deep holy respect for all human relationships. In this vision of Christ in everybody the whole of creation becomes luminous, and the shadows of Satan are pierced if not dissipated. This is 'the right invocation of nature' of which I have spoken at the end of the seventh section, an invocation that calls on the primordial goodness of all that is made. This is not a covering-up of the human and the natural world but a recovery of that essential goodness which has never lost the image of the creator. In its realism and optimism it stands as a clear alternative to that Augustinian pessimism that has entered so deeply into our main theological traditions. The man or woman who has entered fully into the spirituality of the *Lorica* walks freely through a world where innocence and goodness are at home and where evil is an alien power from which there is nothing to fear.

Conclusion

And so we return at the end to the trinitarian invocation with which the hymn began, followed here at the end by the triple Latin affirmation of salvation by God and His anointed one. It is only here, at the very end, that invocation gives way to a direct vocative: *O Lord, may your salvation be with us always.* The wayfarer at journey's end looks up to the face of the Lord, the Lord who is at once Christ and the Father. These Latin phrases at the end are well-worn liturgical clichés, open to either a perfunctory or truly significant enunciation. All that has gone before in this marvellously fresh and power-ful hymn, in which nature and grace speak harmoniously together, inclines us strongly to accord to these oft-used Latin phrases their original freshness and resonance. Yes and Yes and Yes; 'To the Lord truly belongs salvation'; and this is indeed fully and freely given.

Hiberno-Latin Christian Literature

Thomas Finan

Context and Beginnings

The written literature of Ireland actually begins in Latin. Despite a rich oral literary tradition, later to be written down under the influence of Latin and Christianity, there was no commodious system of writing in Ireland until in the fifth century the language of the Christianity and Empire of Rome came with St Patrick. His Latin *Confession* and *Letter to Coroticus* constitute the earliest works of Irish literature. It is not colonial to claim them as Irish, though written by a man in exile from another country. Patrick himself, from Romano-Celtic Britain, was probably of Celtic blood. He was certainly a Celt in character, fiery, religious, visionary, mystical. And like many a later Briton he became Irish of the Irish among his adopted people. His writings are steeped in that sentiment. In one pithy sentence he positively asserts it by implication. A sentence addressed to his opponents in Britain. A sentence that also utters for the first time in literature another sentiment that has often since been thought but rarely so well expressed.

'To them it is annoying and unbecoming that we should be the Irishry!'[1]

Before sampling that beginning of Irish literature it will be helpful if we sketch the historical background to it, in Celtic Ireland, Romano-Celtic Britain and imperial Roman Europe. Two dramatic moments in history frame the picture for us.

The first is a moment in the definitive Roman conquest of Britain, in a series of campaigns by the Roman commander Agricola from 77 to 84 AD. By the fifth year of campaigning in 81 or 82, Agricola had advanced probably to the coast of Cumberland. From there he looked westwards across the narrow sea. We can leave the vivid view to the Roman historian Tacitus.[2]

> The whole side of Britain that faces Ireland was lined with his forces. But his motive was rather hope than fear. Ireland, lying between Britain and Spain, and easily accessible also from the Gallic sea, might, to great general advantage, bind in close union that powerful section of the empire. Ireland is small in extent as compared to Britain, but larger than the islands of the Mediterranean. In soil, in climate and in the character and civilization of its inhabitants it is much like Britain. Its approaches and harbours are tolerably well known from merchants who trade there. Agricola had given a welcome to an Irish prince, who had been driven from home by a rebellion; nominally a friend, he might be used as a pawn in the game. I have often heard Agricola say that Ireland could be reduced and held by a single legion and a few auxiliaries, and that the conquest would also pay from the point of view of Britain, if Roman arms were in evidence on every side and liberty vanished off the map.

It was not to be. As some commentator has remarked, Agricola was the first of many optimists about Ireland. The Roman legions never came across the sea to Ireland. But then neither did the language and literature of Rome, the material civilization and organization of Rome, nor the intellectual discipline of Greco-Roman Europe. Ireland remained the

---

[1] *Letter to Coroticus*, 16.
[2] *Agricola*, 24 (Penguin Classics).

only surviving nation of that Celtic race and culture that was once nearly co-extensive with Western Europe – until the Romans came and overlaid it all.

That is why 'until the coming of Patrick speech was not suffered to be given in Ireland but to three: to a historian for narration and the relating of tales; to a poet for eulogy and satire; to a brehon lawyer for giving judgement according to the old tradition and precedent. But after the coming of Patrick every speech of these men is under the yoke of the white [blessed] language, that is, the Scriptures,'[3] – i.e. Latin, and written.

The second of the two dramatic moments of our historical backdrop belongs to the times of Patrick's coming. For our present purposes let us accept the traditional dates of his mission in Ireland, 432-461. In 432 he would be in his late forties, born therefore about 385. His lifespan then coincides with the last stages of the fall of the Roman Empire in the West – from internal maladies and the external blows of invaders in flood-tide across the frontiers. The last western Emperor was deposed fifteen years after Patrick's death. Patrick was a young man of twenty-five in 410 when the unbelievable happened. Rome, the city they already called eternal, was put to fire and sword by Alaric and his Goths.

That was also the year in which Rome decided she could no longer defend Britain – and told them so – from invading Picts, Scots [Irish], Angles and Saxons. Bede provides a convenient and vivid picture of the consequences.[4]

On the departure of the Romans, the Picts and Scots, learning that they would not return, were quick to attack, and becoming bolder than ever, occupied all the northern and outer part of the island up to the wall. Here a dispirited British garrison stationed on the fortifications pined in terror night and day, while from beyond the wall the enemy constantly harassed them with hooked weapons, dragging the cowardly defenders down from their wall, and dashing them to the ground.

[3] Quoted from old Irish by Robin Flower, *The Irish Tradition*, Oxford, 1947, p.4.
[4] *A History of the English Church and People*, 1.12 (Penguin Classics).

At length the Britons abandoned their cities and wall and fled in disorder. Pursued by their foes, the slaughter was more ghastly than ever before, and the wretched citizens were torn in pieces by their enemies, as lambs are torn by wild beasts. They were driven from their homes, and sought to save themselves from starvation by robbery and violence against one another, their own internal anarchy adding to the miseries caused by others, until there was no food left in the whole land except whatever could be obtained by hunting.

There we get a glimpse of the times and conditions in which the sixteen-year-old Patrick was first taken to Ireland as a slave, of the conditions in which on escaping back to Britain after six years he could walk twenty-eight days through deserted country,[5] of the conditions which, many decades later, drew from the missionary Bishop the burning *Letter to Coroticus*, chieftain of the raiding Picts and Scots who slaughtered Patrick's freshly anointed Irish Christians or sold them into slavery.

Out of such dark times did Patrick write. In a world breaking down, where an ancient civilization in decline was being given the *coup de grâce* by barbarians on the march, where an already ancient Christianity was being overrun by the resurgent heathen. A world in which language itself was breaking down, the universal language of Western Europe, Latin the once stiff-jointed medium of the Seven Hills, enriched and refined into subtlety over a thousand years and forged into the *Romani sermonis maiestas*.

This matter of language is relevant to the understanding of Patrick. His often seemingly dim wrestlings with Latin are mostly not due at all to his own much-professed rusticity. His Latin is 'bad' only by the standards of a too academic classicism. His Latin is the Latin of his day, 'as she was spoke', – and often written. Broken down, of course, but clear enough once its idiom is understood. What opacity remains we may ascribe to the conditions of the text, to the quest for brevity that becomes obscure, and to that running

---

[5] *Confession*, 19.

Pauline intensity that sets thought and feeling out of synchro-mesh with syntax.

Genres of the Literature

Although the vernacular took over in Ireland as the literary medium earlier than elsewhere Irish Christianity did leave a considerable body of writing in Latin,[6] and of a great variety. But like much of Irish civilization it has not all survived, or only in fragmentary form, much of it scattered through the ancient libraries of Europe, in the places to which it wandered with the Irish monks and scholars, or in which they actually wrote it. It is beyond our present scope to survey all of that.[7] Our business is with religion. We shall confine ourselves to that, and within that to important mainline works.

Chronologically those works will take us from the beginnings of Christianity and Latin literature in Ireland down to the twelfth century – the moment of one of the reforms in Irish Christianity. About works extending over such an extended period one thing should be noted at once, as we shall not be constantly referring to it. Our concern here is with the nature and flavour of those works as representative of *Celtic Christianity*, of 'the Celtic *fringe*' as the phrase has it. This does not mean that they are *only* 'insular'. They are European-influenced – as had to be the case, given the sources of Irish Christianity. Patrick himself was certainly trained in France. In turn they influenced Europe,[8] sometimes profoundly, as we shall note. As again had to be the case, given the *leitmotiv* of Irish Christianity and its learning for centuries – to voyage for Christ, *peregrinari pro Christo*.

In kind those works cover most of the important genres of Christian literature. And that is the organization I propose to follow, keeping also to a chronological sequence.

---

[6] For major texts, many in the course of editing and publication, with translation, by the Dublin Institute for Advanced Studies, see the series *Scriptores Latini Hiberniae* (S.L.H.).

[7] See chapters VI and VII of Kenney, *Sources for the Early History of Ireland*, Vol.I.

[8] See e.g. Ludwig Bieler, *Ireland, Harbinger of the Middle Ages*, OUP, 1963.

In St Patrick's *Confession* we have one of the two most famous examples of a genre which owes its impulse and origins to Judeo-Christianity, rooted as it is deep down into the Old Testament sense of man before God, and deep down into the enhanced sense of man's inner life that emerged with Christianity, the sense of the abyss of the human soul, the *abyssus humanae conscientiae*, as St Augustine sounded and phrased it. And *qua* 'confession' as I have briefly explained the genre, Patrick's does bear comparison with the *Confessions* of Augustine. And indeed, quite apart from hints in the text, it is hardly conceivable that without the example of Augustine he should have so explicitly written in the genre. 'Behold, again and again I would set down the words of my confession . . . This is my confession before I die.'⁹

We have lives of the Irish saints, including two of St Patrick.¹⁰ Hagiography of course is a genre not of the most inspiring as learned from Europe. But even that genre occasionally took on a particular coloration in Ireland. And one particular example is positively beautiful, the most beautiful, I should think, in the genre anywhere. And, as a bonus, it must even be largely true – as true as the traditions about St Francis, however strange, that produced the *Fioretti*. No such portrait of a man could emerge, and in a very Celtic tone, except from the living form. I refer to Adamnan's Life of Columba

---

⁹ *Confession*, 61-62.
¹⁰ By Muirchú and Tírechán, both seventh-century. Both in Ludwig Bieler, *The Patrician Texts in the Book of Armagh* (S.L.H. Vol.X). Muirchú informs us that his only predecessor in the genre in Ireland was Cogitosus, who wrote a Life of St Brigid of Kildare.

In both Muirchú and Tírechán we have some striking illustrations of one aspect of Irish hagiography, the coloration of Lives of the Saints by the indigenous sagas. Tírechán is deeply imbued with another Irish characteristic, the cultivation of the traditional lore of famous sites and ancient places. His work is not so much a Life of St Patrick as a gathering of all the traditions of places associated with him. It is the adaptation to hagiographical purposes of the indigenous genre of the *dindshenchas*. Tírechán had good reason to be interested. He came from the region around the most famous place of all, the Wood of Foclut, 'by the western sea', where Patrick must have served his six years of captivity, and whence he heard the call in a vision to come again to Ireland (*Confession*, 23).

of Iona. [11] Columba from 'Derry all full of white angels', who in 565, the year Justinian died in Constantinople, founded the famous community from which half of Britain was re-Christianized. And so much in Celtic colours that the somewhat self-satisfied Anglo-Saxon Bede, while not as radical as Coroticus, certainly has a superiority complex towards the Celts and their Christianity.

If we could limit ourselves to Adamnan's Life of Columba that alone would give us an object lesson in all that is best and beautiful and 'Celtic' in Celtic Christianity. As also an illustration of the reasons why its spirit is so often compared to the Franciscan. I have mentioned the *Fioretti*.

The spirit of St Columba is a spirit which, like that of St Francis, combines, and ranges between, the two poles of earth and Heaven, between what we might call for want of better terms, a mystique and a mysticism. A mystique of the natural world and a mysticism towards its Creator.

Like the typical Irish saint he sought the exile and silence of the hermitage, the 'desert', the 'desert of God' as they called it, the *díseart Dé*. But never to the deadening of their Celtic sense of the beauty of nature, so prominent in indigenous Irish literature, and which produced such gems of nature poetry in Old Irish. 'Let us adore the Lord, /maker of wondrous works, /great bright heaven with its angels, /the white-waved sea on the earth'. [12] The aura that surrounds Columba is one of a love and tenderness and *sympathie* towards all creatures great and small, the weary stormbird or the elements of earth and sea and sky. Famous is the episode in his approaching death, (an account of a Saint's death in itself unsurpassed in hagiography), when the old white horse that used to carry the milk-pail came up and wept into his lap. Beautiful too his gesture when he told his monks of his approaching death – his blessing of the whole island. ' "My sons, I know that from

---

[11] Text and translation by A.O. and M.O. Anderson, *Adomnan's Life of Columba*, London and New York, 1961. Adamnan was a kinsman of Columba. Died in 704 as Abbot of Iona. Author also of a contemporary description of a visit to the Holy Land, as recounted to him by a French Bishop (*De Locis Sanctis*, ed. Denis Meehan in S.L.H. Vol.III).
[12] From the ninth-century Irish.

this day forward you will never more be able to see my face within this little plain." When he saw that they were greatly saddened by hearing this, he tried to comfort them as far as might be, and raising both his holy hands he blessed all this island of ours . . .'[13]

In a word, outside the *Odyssey*, I know of no piece of literature where one so inhales the tang of the earth and the wind and the sea and the islands as around Columba's isle of Iona in Adamnan's *Life*.

This mystique of the earth not just because nature is 'natural', but because it is open and translucent to the *super*natural. A trait of even the pre-Christian Celtic, as we shall explain later.

And hence the other pole of the spirit of Columba, the mystical, as I have called it, loosely but also in its strictly valid sense. He was a man of higher spiritual experiences, a man of prayer, and, as the Irish used to say, a man who had 'power'. The three Books of the Life are divided into prophecies, miracles, and phenomena of light and angelic visitations.

Now this of course is 'hagiography' . . . But it is also a spiritual climate. A climate where we see striking parallels to the phenomena attaching to the tradition of St Francis and his early followers. And critical history has no more right to reject *all* the phenomena in the one case than it has in the other. And in any case, even if the world were not like that, even the world of the saints, would we not *like* it to be so in our dreaming?! Certainly the Celts did, and the followers of St Columba and St Francis.

There is one mystical experience recounted of Columba – authentic or borrowed?! – that bridges the two poles of his spirituality. It also makes him one of the company of a few saints of whom the same experience is told – St Benedict, the Franciscan Brother John, Julian of Norwich, and others I am sure I do not know of.

Is prophecy of the future possible? And perception of things absent? Yes, according to Adamnan, if we believe

---

[13] *Life*, 2.28, ed.cit.

the words of St Paul, that 'he who clings to the Lord is one spirit.' 'So too, as this holy man of the Lord, Columba, himself admitted to a few brothers who once questioned him closely about this very thing, in some speculations made with divine favour the scope of his mind was miraculously enlarged and he saw plainly, and contemplated, even the whole world as it were caught up in one ray of the sun.'[14]

We have also the genre of the Sermon or Instruction. The most notable example is the series of Sermons or Instructions by Columbanus, who voyaged from Bangor to France, Germany, Switzerland and Italy, to found and end his days in the monastery at Bobbio. In them we find that blend of the Celtic and the European that I referred to earlier.

The Celtic in him is both general and particular. That is to say, it pertains both to the background and to the special temper of the man. Columbanus was not only a Celtic Christian but a 'twice-born' one as well. He underwent some profound 'conversion' experience in his youth. We can imagine what metal this produced when fused with his own intense, fiery and fearless temperament. No Irish saint was ever more consumed by 'zeal for thy house', more restlessly driven by the Celtic longing *peregrinari pro Christo*.[15]

With all that he was a man of imagination and sentiment. The imagination comes out in his image-strewn language, in his ability to paint a scene or make the abstract concretely vivid. The sentiment is seen in his affection for people and places, in the sadness of disappointments and partings.

But the imagination and the sentiment go much deeper than the surface of things. If it be true of the Celts that 'all their songs are sad', none ever felt a sadder interior melody than Columbanus. He has a Pascalian sense of the *misère* of the human condition, a Celtic as well as a metaphysical sense

[14]   Ibid., 1.1.
[15]   There is a vivid Life of him by Jonas, a seventh-century monk of Bobbio (ed. by Krusch in *Monumenta Germaniae Historica*). See also Tomás Ó Fiaich, *Columbanus in his own Words*, Dublin, 1974. Text and translation of his writings by G.S.M. Walker, *Sancti Columbani Opera* (S.L.H. Vol.II), from which I take the quotations.

of the transience and relativity and ultimate unreality of the visible world.[16] 'O human life, feeble and mortal, how many have you deceived, beguiled and blinded! While you fly you are nothing, while you are seen you are like a shadow, while you arise you are but smoke . . .' (*Serm.* 5.1). 'What, I ask, is the difference between what I saw yesterday and dreamt this night? Do they not seem to you today to be equally unreal?' (*Serm.* 6.1)

It is not surprising that reality for him is elsewhere. 'I shall hasten towards death that there I may see sure things and true, and all things together in one, which is impossible for me here.' (*Serm.* 6.1) So the complement to his sense of *misère* is his *Sehnsucht* for God and Heaven – as the heroes of both pre-Christian and Christianized Irish tales voyaged in search of the Island of Delights or the Land of Promise of the Saints. 'Wretched man that I am, if there I shall not see life, which I never see [here] in its truth; for it must be true there, where eternity dwells.' (*Serm.* 6.2)

Truth and reality are 'over there' . . . But over there too the ultimate *unreality*, the fulfilling of the unreality here in the ultimate negativity of Hell. This is the other pole of Columbanus's sense of the human condition. Both poles, as we shall see, are prominent in the Irish tradition – from the old vision literature to James Joyce's retreat, with its famous sermon on Hell (answering, it should be noted, to his own private sense of it!) and its subsequent brief season in Heaven.[17]

Add to all this that Columbanus is an artist and a poet – in temper and performance. His poetry shows it, but also his prose. Not even Augustine in his *Confessions* rises to higher levels of sustained stylistic eloquence than does Columbanus at high points in his *Sermons*.

I said that this Celt was European too. I am not referring to his work and influence in Europe.[18] Rather to that organizing and controlling intellect the lack of which has often left the products of Celtic imagination unstructured. In his Sermons

---

[16] One of his poems is *On the World's Impermanence*.
[17] In *Portrait of the Artist as a Young Man*.
[18] See e.g. M.M. Dubois, *St Columban. A Pioneer of Western Civilization*, Dublin, 1961.

Columbanus shows his intellect not only in the ordering of his theme within each instruction but also in the sequence of themes from Sermon to Sermon. His favourite metaphor is the Christian life as a road and a journey. In the order of his tracing of the journey our end is in our beginning. '. . . Our doctrine should commence from that point whence all that is arises . . . ,' that is from God, 'wholly invisible, inconceivable, ineffable, whose property it is ever to exist . . .' (*Serm.* 1.1) The final Sermon ends with a lyrically intense and longing invocation of God that constitutes one of the great mystical passages in any literature.

Hiberno-Latin has made a distinguished contribution to the great corpus of another specifically Christian literary genre, religious poetry born of the Christian vision of reality, and the hymnody directly related to the Christian liturgy.[19] A specifically Christian genre because we can trace its historical emergence in Greek and Latin Christianity. In the West the genre first found fitting form and style in the hymns by Ambrose of Milan. There is a precious passage in St Augustine's *Confessions*[20] describing the occasion on which Ambrose, 'after the manner of the Eastern churches', introduced 'this kind of consolation and exultation', the singing of hymns and psalms in Church. 'The custom has been retained from that day to this, and has been imitated by many. Indeed in almost all congregations throughout the world.' We can also trace how the style and forms of Christian poetry and hymnody were determined by its various functions. The Sequence is the most remarkably beautiful and original example of this. And there is good reason to believe that this form first attained its marvellous verbal music and its symmetries of feeling, thought and structure under Irish influence. That is, as we see it in the Sequences of Notker of St Gall, an Irish

---

[19]   Two important sources survive. The seventh-century *Antiphonary of Bangor* (ed. Warren in the Henry Bradshaw Society series). And the eleventh-century Irish *Liber Hymnorum* (ed. Bernard and Atkinson in the same series). See also Michael Curran, *The Antiphonary of Bangor and the Early Irish Monastic Liturgy*, Irish Academic Press, 1984.
[20]   9.7.

foundation by the companion of Columbanus after whom it is named, where Notker had an Irish teacher.

For the unique formal quality of Hiberno-Latin hymns at their best is in their verbal music. The genre of course the Irish learned from Europe. Metres also, and to some extent the impulse to rhyme – which in the Latin language first emerges in Christian poetry. Of continental Christian Latin poetry it has been said that until the Christian poets introduced rhyme and new accentual rhythms nobody could have imagined, on the basis of classical pagan poetry, what enchanting music lay unsounded in the language. It sounded now because its strings vibrated to a new melody, the'interior melody' of those new depths of interior life mentioned earlier. But nothing had been heard yet, so to speak, until the Irish plucked the strings of their acquired instrument. Even the best rhyming Christian Latin poetry on the Continent is a taste mechanical beside the subtleties of sound woven by the Irish in filigree patterns of alliteration, assonance and rhyme – end-rhyme and internal rhyme.

Whence did they get the impulse and the skills? We can see from very early in the Irish tradition the magic they felt in music and their magical genius for it. It is one of the few qualities of any kind, not to mention genius, for which the Irish are given credit by Gerald of Wales,[21] that outstanding medieval Anglo-Norman qualifier for the sardonic sentence quoted earlier from Patrick's *Letter to Coroticus*. And to this day a gust for the music of language is thought to be very Celtic in general and Irish in particular. What is certainly true is that the forms and music of Hiberno-Latin poetry are closely parallel to those of poetry in the early Irish vernacular.

Further there are certain qualities of that vernacular itself, at least as the poets use it, which have clearly come across into the way the religious poets use the Latin language. It gives a uniquely Irish quality to the best of their compositions. Early Irish could be very strict and concise in structure,

---

[21]   In his *Topographia Hibernica* (*History and Topography of Ireland*, Penguin Classics, chap.94).

asyntactical, exclamatory. With that quality of the language went a parallel quality in the Celtic way of seeing and stating, an economy of details, a concentration on the simple, the essential and the vivid, a tendency to state core facts and pass on rather than elaborate and develop into drawn-out chains of argument or doctrine. Both these qualities, in the language and the users of it, are surprising given the conventional Celtic reputation for rhetoric. But they are none the less true. And the result, both in Irish and in Latin, is poetry of a very special beauty in both content and form, a poetry that outdoes the Roman in the well-known genius of Latin for conciseness and lapidarity. The result is a restrained pointillism, a grave and strong simplicity, ballasted but limpid.

Here is an example translated from the old Irish.[22]

> My tidings for you: the stag bells,
> Winter snows, summer is gone.
>
> Wind high and cold, low the sun,
> Short his course, sea running high.
>
> Deep-red the bracken, its shape all gone -
> The wild-goose has raised his wonted cry.
>
> Cold has caught the wings of birds;
> Season of ice – these are my tidings

And even this is wordy by comparison with the linguistic economy of the original – and lacks its subtle rhyme and alliteration.

And here is a stanza to God from a Hiberno-Latin hymn in the Antiphonary of Bangor.

> Universorum
> Fontis jubar luminum
> Aethereorum
> Et orbi lucentium.

---

[22] Quoted from Kuno Meyer, *Selections from Ancient Irish Poetry*, London, 1959.

Brightness of the fount of every light
shining from heaven on the world.

For tone, mood and spirituality the Celtic background
also provided a mould and world-view into which Christian
Latin poetry could easily fit. The native Irish temperament
had a profoundly religious view of the universe. Earlier I
connected the otherworldly *Sehnsucht* of St Columbanus
to something already native to the Celtic temper, a kind
of natural Platonism in its sense of a world 'beyond' the
present, 'behind' appearances. But unlike Plato that 'other'
world is felt to be near at hand. A trembling of the veil and
it can appear, or the one around us disappear. Native Irish
literature is often characteristically unquiet with a sense
of the relativity of time and space and appearances.[23] The
seeming solid world is unstable. One set of appearances can
metamorphose into another – as in the magical verses from
The Voyage of Bran that I refer to later. Yeats is still a master in
catching the mood. In an early poem, *The Song of Wandering
Aengus*, 'a little silver trout' is caught from the stream.

> When I had laid it on the floor
> I went to blow the fire aflame,
> And something rustled on the floor,
> And someone called me by my name:
> It had become a glimmering girl
> With apple blossom in her hair
> Who called me by my name and ran
> And faded through the brightening air.

At the religious level, this cast of feeling generates a sense
of sacrality in which 'all things are filled with God', or
gods – in a pagan pantheism or a Christian panentheism of
omnipresence. Here is a medieval example from Irish:[24]

---

[23] Much in James Joyce still gives this impression. See also his theory of
'epiphany' in *Stephen Hero*. Compare too the nature of Celtic art – non-
representational, non-classical and – dare we say it! – romantic. Still so in
the painting of Jack B. Yeats.
[24] Quoted from Patrick Murray (ed.), *The Deer's Cry. A Treasury of Irish Religious Verse*, Dublin, 1986.

I am the wind which breathes upon the sea,
I am the wave of the ocean,
I am the murmur of the billows . . .
I am a beam of the sun . . .
I am a salmon in the water,
I am a lake in the plain,
I am a word of knowledge . . .
I am the God who created the fire in the head . . .

And here is a stanza from the Latin of St Columba's *Altus Prosator*,[25] a long poem on creation.

From the divine powers of the great God is suspended
the globe of the earth, and thereto is appended
the circle of the great deep,
sustained by the strong hand of almighty God;
promontories and rocks upholding that deep,
with columns like bars on solid foundations
immovable . . .

It is a way of seeing the world which makes nature poetry in the Irish language the earliest and the freshest in any vernacular, fresher than anything in classical Greek or Latin lyric for that matter. Firstly because nature itself is seen with the natural eye in the concrete detail that was also a Celtic characteristic, despite the modern Celtic reputation for the mistily mystical and the vaguely twilit. Secondly because nature is also soon *through*, in its transparence to the Divine. As only St Francis elsewhere saw it. And with the same faculty of perception, a *spiritual* eye washed clean and clear to clarity of seeing by concentration and contemplation.[26]

But it is not only in poetry that we see this spiritualized vision of reality. I have already suggested that it irradiates the spiritual aura that envelops St Columba of Iona, Franciscan *avant la lettre*. It is also the background to a moment in the most beautiful and artistically elaborated

---

[25] In the *Liber Hymnorum*.

[26] Compare still in modern times Joseph Mary Plunkett:
I see His blood in the rose
    And in the stars the glory of His eyes.
His body gleams amid eternal snows,
    His tears fall from the skies.

episode in Tírechán's Life of St Patrick. 'God above heaven and in heaven and under heaven; he has his dwelling in heaven and earth and sea and in everything that is in them; he breathes in all things and makes all things live, surpasses all things, sustains all things; he illumines the light of the sun, he consolidates the light of the night and the stars . . .' (chap. 26).

We have reached a cosmic range in those last remarks. We noted it earlier in Columbanus, in the 'totalizing' framework of his religious instruction, a journey from the Beginning back to the Beginning, from God the source and ground of existence back to God the end and fulfilment of existence. It is an appropriate moment to introduce John Scotus Eriugena, the ninth-century Irish philosopher theologian who taught and wrote in post-Carolingian France. We shall not have the space to say much about him – he is too big for our scope. But it would be inappropriate not to mention him at all. We are surveying genres, and philosophical theology is an important one, even if it goes beyond the literary. And in the matter of 'totalizing' range of reflection his range is the most elaborate and totalizing that early Christian Ireland produced. Or early Christian Europe for that matter. A barbarian from the ends of the earth was how a continental contemporary described him. But his major work has been described as the most impressive piece of philosophical writing between the ages of Augustine and Thomas Aquinas.

The major work in question is entitled *On the Division of Nature (De Divisione Naturae)*.[27] The 'nature' in question is the whole of reality, from the Creator down to the lowest limits of the created. And the 'division' refers to the classifications and grades of reality within those 'totalizing' cadres.

'Gyring in a gyre the Spirit goes forth and [then] comes back to its own place.' We might think it is Yeats, but Eriugena is quoting Ecclesiastes 1.6.[28] It is a good motif to indicate theme and range. For the theme is all existence as

---

[27] In course of publication in S.L.H., the first volumes being by I.P. Sheldon-Williams.
[28] Page 166 of S.L.H., Vol. XI.

seen in relation to God, the Beginning, the Middle and the End of all that exists. A way of putting it which of course he owes to Platonism as well as to Scripture. 'He is the causal Beginning of all those things, and the essential Middle which fulfils them, and the End in which they are consummated and which brings all movement to rest . . .'[29]

This of course is Neoplatonism. It echoes a pattern of movement, from source unto source, which is one of the great patterns of speculation we owe to Platonism in thought's struggle to net and order the universe. A triple movement: outgoing from Source, turning or 'conversion', return to Source.

It is, however, Christian Platonism. Eriugena learned it through reading and translating the great Greek Christian Platonist Fathers of the Eastern Church. And one of the mysteries about the achievement of Eriugena is where he learned his own Greek, almost the only man in Latin Europe at the time to have achieved such mastery of that language – in Ireland or on the Continent? The effect the Christian Platonist Greek Fathers had upon him can perhaps be explained by that kind of natural Platonism of the Celtic world-view that I mentioned earlier. Sheldon-Williams writes somewhere that 'the effect of their influence upon him was to bring him as wholly into the Greek tradition as if he had been a Byzantine writing in Greek, and to make of him the agent through whom the Western world came into this valuable inheritance.' (And in passing we might remark that as far as Christianity is concerned it has not yet come into that inheritance.)

To explain the way his own genius caught fire from the Greek Christian contact perhaps we can point to something more precise than that natural Celtic Platonism. It has been observed that one strand in early Irish Christian writing is a fondness precisely for cosmological speculation. One of the earliest Hiberno-Latin poems is the *Altus Prosator* of Columba, quoted already. It is in fact a kind of little cosmological epic of the origin, history and destiny of creation. From its issuing from the hands of the High Creator, the *Altus Prosator*, to its

29   Ibid., p.32.

consummation in destruction or transformation at the end of time, when for mankind there will remain but the two ultimates, Hell and heavenly glory. It runs the whole gamut of the cosmic epic, the creation and fall of choirs of angels, the creation of the rich harmony of the complex universe (*mundi machinam . . . et harmoniam*), the heavens and the earth, the stars and the great luminaries of the sky – at the making of which the faithful angels sang to the glory of the Creator for the marvellous making of the whole immensity (*factura pro mirabili/immensae molis*). And so on down to the end of time, at which point the concluding stanzas give us one of the great treatments of the perennial Judeo-Christian theme of the Last Judgement. And interestingly the author of all this seems also to have caught fire from a contact with the East – the Jewish-Hellenistic farrago of the apocryphal Book of Enoch.

One notices this 'totalizing' tendency in other ways too in Hiberno-Latin poems. For instance hymns to or poems about Christ tend to tell the *whole* story, to set him in the context of the complete cosmic epic of creation, Fall, Incarnation, redemption and consummation.

Relevant also in the Celtic background is the Irish contribution to the literature of visions, transcendent cosmic visions that is, the journey through Hell, Purgatory and Heaven that was to culminate in the cosmic epic of Dante. In Eriugena's own treatment of the 'beyond' – naturally very 'demythologizing' – there are some indications that he was familiar with this kind of material. But to it we come later.

Relevant too is that Celtic intensity of religious longing, that *desiderium* that we have noted many times already. I have referred to Eriugena as a 'philosopher theologian'. This because there is no speculative theology without philosophy, and in those days there was no compartmentalized philosophy outside a theological setting. In fact Eriugena sets the whole work in the traditional frame for 'totalizing' questions, a commentary on the creation narrative in the Book of Genesis.

But in none of these roles is Eriugena merely 'academic'. He is fired by his own drive, religious as well as metaphysical. He is one of those types called pilgrims of the absolute.

And the arrow he shoots is tipped with the mystical. After St John's own Prologue to his Gospel it is hard to find anything more inspired, more full of fire and light, than Eriugena's Homily on that Prologue.

One magnificent excursus into prayer towards the end of *The Division of Nature* makes explicit the goal of it all.[30]

'Lord Jesus, I ask no other reward of you, no other beatitude, no other joy, except clear, pure understanding . . . of your words, words inspired by your Holy Spirit. For this is the sum of my happiness, this is the goal of perfect contemplation. Since no rational soul, even the purest, will find anything beyond that. For beyond that there is nothing . . . For it is there you dwell, and thither you lead those who seek you and love you. There for your elect you prepare the spiritual banquet of true knowing, there you pass and minister to them. And what, O Lord, is that passing of yours, if not the ascent through the infinite levels of your contemplation? For ever and always you pass in the understandings of those who seek you and find you. By them you are ever sought and ever found . . . You are found in your theophanies, in which in multiple modes, as in a certain kind of mirror, you come to meet the minds of those who understand you. In that mode and measure in which you allow understanding of you, understanding not of *what* you are but of what you are *not*, and of the fact *that* you are. But you are not found in your superessential essence, in which you pass beyond and above any intellect desiring and climbing to grasp you. That is why to your friends you grant your presence by appearing to them in some way that cannot be expressed. But you pass away beyond them in the ungraspable sublimity and infinity of your essential nature.'

We now come to two genres, distinct but related, about which I have suggested above that they are not unrelated to the matter and range of Eriugena. They are related at least by the fact that the voyage or journey ends in or includes a vision, and that conversely the vision is itself a journey to

---

30 Migne, *P.L..*, 122.1010.

and through the regions of the Otherworld. Indeed Dante fused the two modes in the epic poem that is a *summa* of the Christian Middle Ages. I refer to the literature of voyages or journeys and that of visions, comprehensive visions of the Otherworld – on all three storeys, Hell, Purgatory and Heaven. Both pre-Christian and Christian Irish literature is rich in these two genres, and in both languages, Irish and Latin.[31] And in them we can see a particularly obvious influence of the Celtic on the Christian. And the converse too, since the indigenous stories were to some extent Christianized when they came to be written down in Christian times. At this point too we can mention the fact that some of the Hiberno-Latin examples came to be widely known on the Continent. Deservedly so. Because there is no doubt but that the Irish imposed on those age-old genres (not unique to Ireland) a degree of shape and structure which they did not have before. In this way, and because some of them were well known in Europe, they represent important stages in the progress of the genre that culminated in the *Divine Comedy*. And it has been suggested, with some plausibility, that Dante may in fact have known certain of them.

The connection that I have suggested between the impulse that produced those two genres, especially the vision literature, and the impulse behind the work of Eriugena, may not at first sight be very obvious. They are in two very different modes. One might explain the connection somewhat as follows.

The anthropologists tell us of two stages in the development of man's thinking about the world, the pre-logical or mythic, and the abstract philosophical. We might easily suppose that it is only in the second stage, with the crossing of the threshold into strict philosophical thinking, that the great ultimate boundary-questions should come into consciousness. The questions about the nature of all that exists, and why, in the famous phrase, anything at all should exist and

---

[31] See e.g. St John D. Seymour, *Irish Visions of the Other World*, London, 1930; C.S. Boswell, *An Irish Precursor of Dante*, London, 1908; A. D'Ancona, *Scritti Danteschi* (Florence, 1912), on *I Precursori di Dante*.

not just nothing. It is not so, however. Cosmogonies and cosmologies are as old as our written records of humanity – and indeed obviously older. As someone has put it, man had scarcely opened his eyes on the universe than he began the effort to understand it and reconstruct it in thought. So all civilizations, even the most ancient, have their cosmogonies. The 'thought' at work of course is not logical, abstract, philosophical. It is imaginative, pictured, visionary, mythic. But, as Aristotle observed, even the myth-makers are doing philosophy. And Lucretius, in his philosophical epic *On the Nature of the Universe* (*De Rerum Natura*) is in a tradition that begins with the myths in Hesiod's *Theogony* (which is in fact a *cosmogony* too).

Now even the at first sight endless variety in mythic attempts to see into the nature of things tends to follow certain archetypal and recurring patterns of organization – which in turn have led to certain archetypal and recurring structures of plot in literature. The voyage or journey is one such. The *apocalypsis* or vision is another. *Odyssey* and *Aeneid* have become common nouns. And 'apocalyptic' literature is a genre more extensive than just the last book of the Bible.

The earliest journey in literature is as old again as Homer is older than us. It is the Sumerian *Epic of Gilgamesh* from the third millennium BC. It is still the most concentrated and powerful example of the metaphysical significance that I am suggesting even a mythic story can have. It turns on man's existential awakening to the reality, finality and anguish of mortality. *Timor mortis conturbat me*, as the refrain of a medieval poem puts it. ' . . . Man perishes with despair in his heart. I have looked over the wall and I see the bodies floating on the river, and that will be my lot also.'[32] There are two journeys in the poem. The first is a forest journey – itself archetypal. Its purpose is to assuage mortal anguish by winning the immortality of heroic fame at least, mainly by slaying the giant Humbaba, who represents some principle of evil in the world. When that goes wrong, and the hero's own

[32] Quoted from N.K. Sandars, *The Epic of Gilgamesh* (Penguin Classics, 1977), p.72.

companion dies, Gilgamesh sets out on a second journey, with the purpose of wresting immortal life from the jealous gods. 'Because I am afraid of death I will go as best I can to find Utnapishtim, whom they call the Faraway, for he has entered the assembly of the gods.'[33]

The journey ends in definitive and tragic failure. But the fact that he does reach that faraway region illustrates the fact that the journey can include the vision. In the great epic journeys it nearly always does. The *Odyssey* and the *Aeneid* have their descents into the *Under*world. They are really passages to the *Other*world, motivated by the quest for a larger enlightenment, and haunted particularly by the *lacrimae rerum* of mortality. 'I had not thought death had undone so many . . . ' A sentiment which, by the way, in its Dantean original (*Inf.* 3.56f) is remarkably parallel to a sentence in the twelfth-century Hiberno-Latin *Vision of Tundal*. At the pit of Hell Satan is surrounded by 'a multitude of souls and demons so great that no one could believe the world would bring forth so many souls from its beginning.'[34]

The apocalyptic or revelational otherworldly vision on its own is equally archetypal, and often entails a journey as well. The Vision of Er at the end of Plato's *Republic* is well known. It is perhaps the first example in literature of something beginning to be *à la mode* at the moment, the so- called 'near death experience'. It is in fact a constant throughout the history of this kind of thing. And the Hiberno-Latin *Vision of Tundal* is the highest point of its development before Dante. Er dies, or appears to die, is taken on a journey in which he is shown not only the ancient equivalent of Hell, Purgatory and Heaven, but also the whole system and governance of the universe. After which his soul returns to his body, so that he can tell the whole story of the ultimate nature of the world and of human destiny.

Long before Plato Hesiod attributes the 'wisdom' of his *Theogony* to a vision of the Muses. Either he or they were already cannier than some. 'We know how to speak many

---

[33]   Sandars, p.97.
[34]   Page 36 of Wagner, ed. given *infra* n.53.

false things as though they were true; but we also know, when we will, how to utter true things.'[35]

Mention of the Muses reminds us of the archetypal role of woman as the mediatrix of the vision and the knowledge – from the Lady Philosophy in Boethius' work of theodicy, *The Consolation of Philosophy*, down to Beatrice in the *Divine Comedy*. It is a constant in Ireland. The most magical instance in any literature is in the eighth-century Irish-language *Voyage of Bran* – a voyage which begins in vision and consists in a further quest for it. The motif continues through the Irish-language literature of the late Middle Ages, and is still alive in Yeats's *Wanderings of Oisín*, enchanted away to Tír na nÓg and back by the visionary visitant Niamh –

> A pearl-pale, high-born lady who rode
> On a horse with bridle of findrinny,
> And like a sunset were her lips;
> A stormy sunset on doomed ships . . .

The tone of that may be out of fashion in these days of grit and cinders. But the genres of voyages and visions which we have been illustrating as archetypal and universal were particularly fruitful in Celtic Ireland. And they took on a uniquely Celtic coloration. It is necessary to appreciate both points of background to those genres in Hiberno-Latin. Now for obvious reasons due to the limitations of translation it is not easy to reproduce the qualities of the original Irish-language examples, especially the poetic parts of them. But Yeats's poem is an original composition. And he does capture that Celtic coloration of the old tales – even if perhaps he does gild the lily a bit. For these reasons an extended quotation will replace a lot of explanation.

> O Oisín, mount by me and ride
> To shores by the wash of the tremulous tide,
> Where men have heaped no burial-mounds,
> And the days pass by like a wayward tune,
> Where broken faith has never been known
> And the blushes of first love never have flown . . .

---

[35] *Theogony*, 27f.

We galloped over the glossy sea;
I know not if days passed or hours.
We galloped; now a hornless deer
Passed by us, chased by a phantom hound
All pearly white, save one red ear;
And now a lady rode like the wind
With an apple of gold in her tossing hand;
And a beautiful young man followed behind
With quenchless gaze and fluttering hair.
'Were these two born in the Danaan land,
Or have they breathed the mortal air?' . . .

Thus Gilgamesh's Garden of the gods, Homer's island of Calypso, his Isles of the Blessed, Virgil's Elysian Fields – all these archetypal and universal goals of the human quest for higher enlightenment, for liberation from mortality and the human lot, took on in Ireland the Celtic colours of The Land of Youth, Tír na nÓg, Islands of Delights, Lands of Promise beyond the sea, or just behind the veil of the unsteady appearances of the only relatively normal. They gave not only the impulse but often their coloration to the Hiberno-Latin Christian examples of the genres. The indigenous lands of promise or islands of delights became the lands of promise of the *saints*, or the lost Earthly Paradise, where, in this particular tradition, even the Blessed (unlike Dante's) remained until they were admitted to the Heavenly Paradise, only after the final universal judgement. (Incidentally the Earthly Paradise provides a good example of the frequently multiple sources of a highly developed theme in Christian literature. The first and most beautiful literary elaboration of it is in another 'myth' or 'story' of Plato's, in the *Phaedo*, 108ff).

Of course the indigenous were not the only sources of impulse and influence. The genres existed on the Continent too. And there they came not only from the Greco-Roman tradition but from Christianity's own tradition of apocryphal works like the *Book of Enoch* or the *Apocalypse of Paul*. (The Apocrypha in general seem to have been well known in Ireland.) But this is to say no more than what we underlined from the beginning, that Celtic Irish Latin writing underwent European influence too. But also the converse. And there is no better example of the converse than the genres of voyage and vision. I have already referred to the fact that the

Hiberno-Latin examples – and indeed one in medieval Irish – prepared the way to Dante by giving order and architecture to a domain of the Judeo-Christian quest and imagination which in the tradition was a farrago.

We have devoted some considerable time to explaining the nature, genesis and rationale of those two genres. It has been necessary, especially as it is not easy even for the native unskilled in the field to find his way through that element in the Irish tradition. For the same reason it is time to come to some specifics about the principal works in the genres.

To take the voyage first, we are lucky to have many indigenous examples in Irish. I shall mention two – pre-Christian though somewhat 'contaminated'. And also, it must be said, somewhat incomplete and disorganized by the time they came to be written down. They are *The Voyage of Bran* (*Immram Brain*), probably written down in the eighth century, and *The Voyage of Máel Dúin* (*Immram Máele Dúin*) from the same period.[36]

Of the two much the more sequential, elaborated and poetic is the Voyage of Bran. It shows all the motifs of the genre. The mysterious call to the hero heard in magical music, and in the magical poetry in which a mysterious woman visitant from 'The Land of Wonders' describes the Otherworld. Then the voyage over the sea – in which the Celtic theme of relativity marvellously emerges. For Bran and his shipboard companions meet one Manannán mac Lir driving over the sea in a chariot. What for Bran is the open clear bright ocean is for Manannán a flowery plain of dry land! And that is not all. In strict fact, as Manannán tells him, Bran is really rowing over a rich and blossoming forest! The inhabitants of the land below are described – without age or decay of freshness since the beginning of creation, because they have never sinned. Thus Christian elements are introduced – the Fall, and a prophecy of the coming of Christ. Bran reaches an 'Island of Joy', and eventually

---

[36] Editions, with translation, in Séamas Mac Mathúna, *Immram Brain*, Tübingen, 1985; and H.P.A. Oskamp, *The Voyage of Máel Dúin*, Groningen, 1970.

an 'Island of Women'. His companions go ashore, but not Bran . . . Many years they stay there, though it seemed only one. But as always there is one who is overcome by nostalgia for home, by longing from the midst of Circe's delights for plainer Penelope and Rocky Ithaca! The returned sentimental jumps ashore in Ireland – and becomes a heap of ashes. Bran writes down his adventure, says farewell – and is never heard of again.

I quoted Yeats earlier to give the tone of such Celtic tales. Precisely because here we must make do with translation. But some of it should be quoted. In the prose introduction, 'one day Bran went about alone in the neighbourhood of his fort. He heard music behind him. When he would look back it was still behind him the music was. Finally he fell sleep on account of the sweetness of the music . . . '

When he wakes up his mysterious visitant is there. And this (as they say) was the song she sang.[37]

> There is an island far away
> around which sea-horses glisten;
> a fair course against the little white-sided wave,
> four legs hold it up . . .
>
> Legs of white silver are under it;
> it shines through ages of beauty;
> a fair country throughout the world's age
> on which the many blossoms drop.
>
> There is an ancient tree in blossom there
> on which the birds call to the Hours . . .

Islands of Birds are one of the motifs in the indigenous genre. But the reference to the Hours is clearly a christian modification. And in fact an Island of Birds, with their calls to the chanting of the Hours of the monastic Office, is one of the principal and most beautiful motifs in the Hiberno-Latin *Voyage of St Brendan*.[38]

---

[37] Quoted from Mac Mathúna.
[38] Edition and translation by Carl Selmer, *Navigatio Sancti Brendani Abbatis*, University of Notre Dame, 1959.

The Voyage of Brendan is probably from the ninth century. Later than *Bran*, but clearly influenced by it and its kind. It is more than just influenced. It is clearly parallel, only adapting the idea and its motifs to the new Christian context. In addition to the rationale of the whole genre as suggested earlier, the adaptation suggested itself all the more easily to the island Irish, given the characteristic urge of its monks to 'voyage for Christ', *peregrinari pro Christo*. Whether to carry the Gospel or to find their own personal island of retreat and contemplation wheresoever they might find, in the Spirit, if not in the world, that Land of Wonders, that Land of Promise, which their own spirit longed for and their imagination bodied forth.

In *The Voyage of St Brendan* those lands fuse with the Judeo-Christian myth of the Earthly Paradise and become the Land of Promise of *the Saints*, that abode of lower-lighted bliss where, as already indicated, the blessed await the Paradise of Heaven after the General Judgement. 'From the very beginning of the world it has remained exactly as you see it now. Do you need any food, drink or clothing? You have been here a whole year already without tasting food or drink. You have never felt the need for sleep, for it has been daylight all the time. Here there is no obscuring darkness but only perpetual day, the Lord Jesus Christ being Himself our light.'[39]

Brendan's search for it takes seven years. In the course of which many other strange islands are visited, some of them as strange and primordial as episodes in Homer's *Odyssey* or in Apuleius' tale of *Cupid and Psyche*. But the atmosphere of the whole is bathed in a gentle religious light and in the pervasive Celtic world of wonders. 'The Lord Jesus Christ did not allow you to find it immediately because first He wished to show you the richness of His wonders in the deep.'[40] The years are cycles marked by the Christian seasons and the great feasts of the liturgical year, for which the voyagers always return to the same islands. And ever investing everything, even at sea, the aura of the monastic ritual of the daily Hours, linking hours, days, seasons and years in a rosary of prayer.

[39] Chap.1, quoted in the translation of F.J. Webb, *The Age of Bede* (Penguin Classics).
[40] Chap.28, quoted from Webb.

In the details there are many parallels with the *Voyages* of Bran and Máel Dúin. I have already referred to the Island of Birds. Suffice it to mention further the beginning and the end of the Brendan *Voyage*. The mysterious enchanting visitant who occasions the voyage of Bran becomes in *The Voyage of Brendan* the monk Barinthus, who visits Brendan at his monastery. He is sad and weeping, because he has a story both of joy and sorrow to tell. He has been there and back – to the island Land of Promise of the Saints. Brendan is at once consumed with a desire to seek it out. 'I have resolved, if it be God's will, to seek out that Land of Promise of the Saints which our father Barinthus described.' When he does reach it after seven years it is also to be told that here below death is the end of all voyaging – as it was for Odysseus as well as for Bran and his companion. 'The day of your final journey is at hand: you shall soon be laid to rest with your fathers.'[41]

On returning to his monastery Brendan told the whole story to his enraptured community. But he also told them of the prophecy. 'Events proved him right; he put all his affairs in order, and very shortly afterwards, fortified with the Sacraments of the Church, lay back in the arms of his disciples and gave up his illustrious spirit to the Lord . . .'[42]

In telling his tale the author of *Brendan* sometimes gives us the feeling that he goes round in cycles in more ways than the liturgical. But he did have the sense of an ending.

We come to apocalyptic, the visionary genre in the fully developed sense of the vision of, or more fully still, the journey through, the three realms of the Otherworld, Hell, Purgatory and Heaven. Four realms in fact when we bear in mind the function of the Earthly Paradise in that tradition. A function present as far back as the Book of Enoch and the Apocalypse of Paul, but particularly elaborated in Ireland – due no doubt to the influence of the indigenous motif of the Land of Wonders, the Land of Promise and so on, that we have seen in the voyage literature.

[41] Ibid.
[42] Ibid.

The earliest Hiberno-Latin vision literature seems to have been in a work no longer extant in its original state. It was in a Life of the seventh-century Irishman Fursey. Bede cites it as his source for his own account of Fursey.[43] (He also tells us that he himself knew an old brother in Bede's own monastery who testified to the historical truth of Fursey's experience, on the evidence of an older man who professed to have been told of it by Fursey himself . . .) This Fursey, in the tradition of Irish pilgrims for Christ, founded a monastery in East Anglia in the mid-seventh century, and later another at Lagny on the Marne in France.

The Life of him referred to by Bede must be the basis of the later medieval Life[44] which gives a good deal of space to the experiences summarized by Bede.

Fursey's vision occurs in the context of the 'near death experience', in which the soul leaves the body, to all appearances dead, and later returns to it, often unwillingly in the light of what it has seen. To the stupefaction of the temporarily bereaved, but also to their edification, since the experience is for reporting to them. Very 'modern', as I have said. But it is as old as Plato, and is the setting for most of the Irish apocalyptic literature.

Fursey's description of the Otherworld is not elaborate. But it has the beginnings of that new precision which, as I have said, the Irish gave it. It also has the beginnings of something else that the Irish gave it more and more. About the nature of the Heavenly Paradise it has that sense of the final ineffability of it which was to reach supreme expression in Dante – 'to the high imagination here power failed'. Like Dante, after their best efforts – and they are very good – the Irish reiterate that sentiment. Doubtless both the degree of success and the admission of the impossible are related to their native imagination and its literary preoccupation with Lands of Wonders and the Otherworld.

The elements of the medium in which they paint it are often Celtic, with its marvellous sense of colour, of the ornamental,

[43]   *History* . . . ,3.19.
[44]   In W.W. Heist, *Vitae Sanctorum Hiberniae*, Brussels, 1965.

the precious, the golden. But like Dante they typically culminate in the two media par excellence of the ineffable, light and
music – the latter also characteristic of the Celtic genius, as
we saw earlier.

Thus Fursey. 'He saw a great brightness . . . and hosts of
angels in four choirs singing and repeating: Holy, holy, holy,
Lord God of hosts.' Fursey's soul is 'filled with the sweetness
of supernal song and the sound of ineffable joy'. He knows
that it must come from an even loftier heaven than the one he
is in. 'Then the holy Angel said to him: "Do you know where
such gladness and joy is lived?" When he answered that he
knew not the holy Angel replied: "Among the supernal company, in the region from which we also are come." '[45]

The earliest completely apocalyptic work we have is not in
Latin but in medieval Irish. It is the eleventh-century *Vision
of* (pseudo-)*Adamnan* (*Fís Adamnáin*).[46] All the features I mentioned à propos of Fursey are so wonderfully developed in it
that it has been described as the best example of the genre
before Dante. I would reserve that accolade for the twelfth-
century *Vision of Tundal*. The vision of Adamnan, 'the High
Scholar of the Western World', is set in the great tradition of
Christian apocalyptic seers, since St Paul (2 Cor. 12.2-4) and
the apocryphal tradition that on the day of Mary's dormition
'all the apostles were brought to look upon the pains and
miserable punishments of the unblest.' Yet much of that
tradition is transposed into Celtic colours.

Here we have again the clear distinction of Hell, Purgatory
and Heaven – and of course the Earthly Paradise, that temporary Land of the Saints. But we have the beginnings of something else, namely that gradation within each realm which
Tundal develops further and which was given definitive form
by Dante.

Here there is a more elaborate attempt to rise to the evocation of the Heavenly Paradise – and a realization of its final
impossibility. 'Great and vast as are the splendour and the
radiance in the Land of Saints . . . , more vast, a thousand

---

[45] *Vita*, 1.14 (Heist, p.43).
[46] Translation in Boswell, *op.cit.*, from which quotations are taken.

times, the splendour in the region of the Heavenly Host, around the Lord's own throne.' But in the end 'to describe the mighty Lord that is upon that throne is not for any, unless Himself should do so, or should so direct the heavenly dignitaries.'[47]

Yet the attempt is made – in the Celtic colours we have seen before. 'This throne is fashioned like unto a canopied chair, and beneath it are four columns of precious stone. Though one should have no minstrelsy at all, save the harmonious music of these four columns, yet would he have his fill of melody and delight. Three stately birds are perched upon that chair, in front of the King, their minds intent upon the Creator throughout all ages, for that is their vocation. They celebrate the Hours, praising and adoring the Lord, and the Archangels accompany them. For the birds and the Archangels lead the music and then the Heavenly Host with the Saints and Virgins make response.'[48]

We are reminded of a much later Celtic singer and seer, dreaming of his state 'once out of nature'.

> Once out of nature I shall never take
> My bodily form from any natural thing,
> But such a form as Grecian goldsmiths make
> Of hammered gold and gold enamelling
> To keep a drowsy Emperor awake;
> Or set upon a golden bough to sing
> To lords and ladies of Byzantium
> Of what is past, or passing, or to come.[49]

In Hiberno-Latin there are three main successors to *The Vision of Adamnan*. Certain writings of Bishop Patrick of Dublin (1084), the *Vision of Tundal* (1149), and *St Patrick's Purgatory* (about 1180) – the last the best known, no doubt, but in fact inferior to all the others.

Bishop Patrick[50] is particularly interesting, as both a contrast and a complement to *Adamnan*. He is so close to

---

[47] Chap.7.
[48] Ibid.
[49] Yeats, *Sailing to Byzantium*.
[50] Text and translation in Aubrey Gwynn, *The Writings of Bishop Patrick* (S.L.H. Vol.I), from which quotations are taken.

Adamnan in time, possibly a generation later. Yet he is steeped in the European scholastic intellect, particularly in Augustinianism, which he acquired apparently as a Benedictine at Worcester in England. Yet for all that he is also steeped in the Irish tradition. There is no better proof of this than one of his long poems, *On the Wonders of Ireland* (*De Mirabilibus Hiberniae*). We know how Celtic that theme is. But it seems to be an early effusion of Patrick's, and not one of his best. Some of the 'wonders' have the unfortunate effect of weakening our resolve against Gerald of Wales a century later. But then the family's private right to private yarns at its own expense does not confer the right on intruders.

Bishop Patrick reminds us in many ways of Columbanus as we have described him. Intense, evangelical, pessimistic about the human lot, spiritual, mystical even, and, for our particular purposes here, preoccupied with the last things, Heaven and/or Hell. As we saw, one of Columbanus' poems is *On the World's Impermanence* (*De Mundi Transitu*). One of Bishop Patrick's is *On the Frailty of Life* (*De Caduca Vita*). And so to the same intense conclusion of mystical *desiderium*.

> So may I seek Thee Christ: so yearn for Thee in the depth of my heart
> As he who thirsts for water, as the beggar for wealth.
> So may my mind, so also may my body cleave to Thee
> As light to the sun in heaven, as stars to the sky.[51]

It is an easy step to the personal genesis of the inherited theme of the 'last things'.

He treats that theme in two of his writings. One is a long allegorical poem, *Versus Allegorici*. The other a prose tractate, *On the three Dwelling Places of the Soul* (*De Tribus Habitaculis Animae*). Those three places do not include Purgatory. They refer to the world and the Church here below, and Heaven and Hell beyond. The two pieces are complementary. The poem deals with the first, the prose with the other two. But the title of the prose is accurate. For the world is here again the third dwelling-place, seen with characteristic pessimism as a permanently unsatisfying composite of that good and

---

[51]   Lines 69ff.

evil which attain their separate and absolute condition only hereafter, in Heaven and Hell.

Now apart from their theme the Celtic relevance of these two pieces lies in their mode of presentation. In their matter and argument they are doctrinal, rigorously and scholastically logical. But stylistically eloquent too. At times more linkedly logical and eloquent even than the Augustine in the background. Yet the substance is presented through the make-believe form of vision, especially in the *Allegorical Verses*.

Of course the allegory owes much to Europe. But it is also clearly a forerunner of a later prolific convention in Irish poetry, the *aisling* or vision poem. The core of all the elements can be illustrated in lines towards the end of the poem which summarize what has gone before and anticipate the theme of the prose.[52]

> . . . I have sung the midmost, and pass by unsung the lowest
> and the highest.
> Who, who could sing them? who could mark their numbers?
>
> * * *
>
> Who could sing the silent speech of people who see men's
> hearts?
> Who the endless abiding joy of the mind?
> Who the united choirs singing hymns and praises,
> And the love that burns in the hearts of each and all?
> Who the lyres and every apt form of melody?
> Psalter and strange harps or threefold organs?
> The golden temples, the market-place, the throne, the seated
> King?
> Who could tell how great, how wondrous the good? Who the
> hidden time
> Of the star-bearing blessed summit where all these are to be
> found;
> That like a citadel stands forth far above the aforesaid city?
>   . . .
> As its members to the head, as the slight shadow is less
> Than that which casts the shadow, as dreams are less than
> real   things,
> So the former city is less than this in beauty and all splendour
>   . . .

---

[52] Lines 192ff.

With *The Vision of Tundal*[53] we advance nearly a century. But we revert from exposition, literal or thinly veiled, to the more traditional vision, from the systematic and doctrinal to the vividly imagined. Yet one of the principal points to note will be how profound the doctrine that underlies the imagined – or seen! – at its best. Thus we shall see, looking back, how far the genre has come since *Adamnan*. And, looking forward, how close the development has come to Dante. So close in some details that, unless there is another source, one is led to think that Dante must have known *The Vision of Tundal*. As he could have, since it was written on the Continent and was widely known there.

The vision is explicitly dated to 1149. The dating is further defined by reference to some contemporary events and persons in Irish ecclesiastical history, such as Malachy of Down and the account of him written by Bernard of Clairvaux. The vision purports to be written by a certain Marcus for the benefit of an unidentified Mother Abbess in Ratisbon, where there was, a traditional Irish presence. The vision is presented as the narrative of Tundal himself to whom it happened. He was a noble knight of Cashel, but unruly and irreligious. Hence the elaborate lesson he was given when, after apparently dying, suddenly of a Wednesday, his soul was given a guided tour by his guardian angel. Down to Hell, up through Purgatory, into the Earthly Paradise, and beyond it through the spheres of the Heavenly Paradise to the Dantean summit where vision of the Creator of all is given. And with the vision knowledge and understanding of all. 'Not only vision . . . but unparalleled knowledge, so that he no longer had any need to enquire about anything, but everything he desired to know he now knew clearly and totally.'[54] 'Within its depths I saw ingathered, bound by love in one volume, the scattered leaves of all the universe.'[55]

[53] Edition in Albrecht Wagner, *Visio Tnugdali*, Erlangen, 1882.
[54] Wagner, p.53.
[55] Dante, *Paradiso*, 33.85-87. Bishop Patrick is splendid on this supreme knowledge – what Dante calls (*Par.* 33.91) 'the universal form of this complex', *la forma universal di questo nodo*. Patrick owes it to two sources – the Columbanian intensity of his own longing for the light, and the Augustinian epistemology and metaphysics of that light, subsistent *Veritas*, Truth in the absolute.

Four days it took. On the Saturday his soul returned to its body, and to the amazement of clergy and people who were gathered for his funeral.

'A long road lies before us' says the Angel at the start. 'The way is long and the road hard' says Virgil to Dante.[56] And so for us. We cannot walk it in detail here.

In the architecture of the whole to be noted is the great advance in the clear demarcation of the realms of the Otherworld, Hell, Purgatory, Earthly Paradise and Heaven. And an even more remarkable advance towards Dante is the grading within each realm, into circles and spheres according to the degrees of guilt or bliss. And in the guilt and the bliss, as in Dante, a high degree of the fitting of the punishment and the reward to the sin and the virtue. And in the degrees of bliss, as in Dante, the harmonious contentment of each with his own.[57] And, as in both Dante and the developing Irish tradition, a sense, at the appropriate points, of the unsounded depths and the unscalable heights. With the concomitant sense of the need to rise to the height of the great argument, and finally to yield before the inexpressible.

We see this sense intensifying as Tundal descends through the circles of Hell. There, as in Dante, the tormented souls 'longed for death and could not find it'.[58] 'These have no hope of death . . . '[59] The way grows narrower as Tundal and his guide descend to the ultimate pit, past a Dantean frozen lake, through regions where 'all the foundations of the world seemed to shake', down to the Dantean well or cistern, at the bottom of which reigns the very principle of evil and negativity in the world, the Prince of Darkness in person. Here 'none who once enters will ever exit.'[60] 'Abandon all hope, you who enter.'[61]

---

[56] *Inferno*, 34.95.
[57] *Paradiso*, 3.52-54. A sentiment made explicit in *St Patrick's Purgatory*: 'Each individual rejoiced in his own felicity, but they all exulted at the joy of each of the others . . . ' (Quoted from J.-M. Picard and Y. de Pontfarcy, *St Patrick's Purgatory* (Blackrock, 1985), p.67). Cf. Bishop Patrick, *On the Three Dwelling Places . . .*, lines 116ff.
[58] Wagner, p.31.
[59] *Inferno*, 3.46.
[60] Wagner, p.38.
[61] *Inferno*, 3.1ff.

The emergence from Hell into Purgatory is the emergence from darkness into light. A fresh dawn light like that in Dante at the same point.[62] There is suffering but there is hope, and even a kind of joy, and even a kind of rest. *Requies* is a thematic word here.

With the transition to the Earthly Paradise and the ascending spheres of Heaven the thematic word is glory, *gloria*. *Ascendamus!* Let us climb. And as they climb – often not knowing how, as in Dante – an ever-growing sense of the dazzle of the glory and the impossibility of expressing it. Here especially we observe Celtic details in the description. Light is everywhere, as in Dante. But above all music, as in the Irish tradition, and of course again in Dante. 'And they sang Alleluia to the lord, with a new song and such sweet melody that for the soul who once heard it all memory of the past would sink into oblivion.'[63] *Un punto solo* . . . 'A single moment brings me deeper lethargy than five-and-twenty centuries . . .'[64]

The summit of the vision has already been quoted. Let us end therefore with one moment of particular glory shortly before the summit is reached. It is a glimpse into one of the highest spheres, the one where the monks and the nuns abide, those 'monks and virgins for Christ', as St Patrick loved to call them.[65] There all is a radiance of light and a vibrant symphony of musical sound. The glory of that light and sound 'surpassed all the glory seen before'. The instruments played without touch. The lips of the singers sang without movement.

But more splendid still is the 'firmament' above their heads. From it 'hung chains of the purest gold, intermingled with rods of silver . . . from which in turn perfumed censers were suspended, cymbals and bells, lilies and little golden spheres. And all through them a great host of angels floated, flying on golden wings, in between the golden chains, with wafting

---

[62] *Purgatorio*, 1.13ff.
[63] Wagner, p.48.
[64] *Paradiso*, 33.94f.
[65] *Confession*, 41; *Letter to Coroticus*, 12.

wings emitting to the hearer sounds the most pleasing and the sweetest ever.'[66]

Most of the elements in that high point of description, and certainly their combination, could come from nowhere but a Celtic climate. I wonder could Dante have known the passage? For just so, at a comparable point near the summit, just so do the flying angels minister between God above and the ranks of the Blessed ranged in the petals of the White Rose below.

> As bees ply back and forth, now in the flowers
> Busying themselves, and now intent to wend
> Where all their toil is turned to sweetest stores,
>
> So did the host of Angels now descend
> Amid the Flower of the countless leaves,
> Now rise to where their love dwells without end.
>
> Their glowing faces were as fire that gives
> Forth flame, golden their wings; the purest snow
> The whiteness of their raiment ne'er achieves.
>
> Down floating to the Flower, from row to row,
> Each ministered the peace and burning love
> They gathered in their waftings to and fro.
>
> Between the Flower and that which blazed above
> The volant concourse interposed no screen
> To dim the splendour and the sight thereof;
>
> For God's rays penetrate with shafts so keen
> Through all the universe, in due degree,
> There's naught can parry them or intervene.[67]

[66] Wagner, p.50.
[67] *Paradiso*, 31.7ff, in the version by Dorothy Sayers and Barbara Reynolds (Penguin Classics).

Irish Monks on the Continent

Tomás Ó Fiaich

Introduction

One of the most important religious and cultural phenomena on the European mainland during the early middle ages was the ceaseless activity there of monks from Ireland. From the departure of St Columban shortly before the year 600 they poured into modern France in ever-increasing numbers and gradually fanned out to include Belgium, Switzerland, Austria, Southern Germany and Northern Italy within their spheres of influence. An occasional foray was made further afield, into the modern Poland, Hungary, Jugo-Slavia and the USSR, but these were without long-term significance. For a period of about a century and a half, i.e. from the beginning of the seventh century until the middle of the eighth century, the Irish monks constituted, first on their own and later together with Anglo-Saxon missionaries, the most important religious and cultural influence which was at work within the future Carolingian Empire. After the setting-up of that empire in 800 the Irish influence was less marked in the religious than in the cultural field. When Charlemagne's Empire was transformed into the Holy Roman Empire of the

German nation in the tenth century, the Irish monks followed the centre of civil government across the Rhine, but never regained the pre-eminent position in religion and learning which earlier generations of Irish monks had occupied.

In this essay we shall examine the religious and cultural contribution of the 'Irish Mission' to Continental Europe. It is necessary to explain at the outset that the Irish are usually known as the *Scotti* in early medieval sources. In Roman times, however, the term *Hibernia* was also applied to Ireland and *Hibernici* to its inhabitants. When colonists from Ireland began to settle in Western Scotland from the fourth century on, they brought the Gaelic language along 'with them, and ultimately the term *Scotti* was applied to the inhabitants of northern Britain, giving the modern Scotland its name.

There can be no doubt that when someone on the Continent is named *Scottus* in early medieval times, i.e. from the first exodus of Irish monks until the twelfth century, approximately, he is an Irishman. A change takes place from the twelfth century on, after the invasion of Ireland by the Anglo-Normans. Henceforth the word *Scottus* comes to be retained more and more for a native of Scotland, while the word *Hibernicus* is the term normally used in Latin documents for an Irishman. Thus the ninth-century Johannes Scottus was Irish-born, as were Sedulius Scottus, Martinus Hibernensis and so on. But the thirteenth-century Duns Scottus was born in Scotland, despite the efforts made by Irish scholars of a later age to claim him as one of their own.

The movement of Irish monks into France towards the end of the sixth century was not, of course, the first monastic outreach of the Irish church. It was preceded by the departure of Colmcille to Iona in 563 and the considerable amount of evangelizing work carried out among the Picts and Scots by the saint and his followers. From Iona Aidan led a band of Irish missionaries to Lindisfarne for the conversion of Northumbria in the next generation, and Irish influence gradually spread over much of Eastern Britain and the Midlands. Irish hermits, too, seeking to abandon the world, found remote homes in many of the islands to the west and north of Scotland and ultimately reached Iceland.

This monastic movement to Great Britain and the islands does not form part of our story here. It was different in many respects from the movement to the Continent. The erection of island monasteries was already in full swing around the Irish coast. In a sense Colmcille in going to Iona did the same as Enda in going to Aran but went a longer journey. He settled in Gaelic-speaking territory and the links of the Scottish and Northumbrian missions with Ireland remained strong and unbroken. Iona continued culturally as part of Ireland. It was different with the Continental mission in its early stages. When the monks left Ireland, say, for France, they were facing a *terra ignota*, whose inhabitants were different in race, language and customs. They had little hope of ever seeing their native land and their family relations again, and this was the sacrifice which they embraced eagerly for the love of God.

The Birth of a Tradition

The exodus of the Irish monks and scholars had little of the modern foreign missionary movement about it. For one thing, the primary motive was ascetical rather than evangelical. The same ideal which led to repeated acts of mortification and self-denial as a significant feature of the religious life of early Ireland brought great numbers to leave home and seek more penitential surroundings on the rocky islands off the west coast from Skellig to Aran, in the remote islands to the west and north of Scotland as far as Iceland, and ultimately in many countries of Western Europe.

Peregrinatio is the word often used by contemporary writers to describe the movement abroad of these Irish religious. It did not normally mean 'pilgrimage' in the modern meaning of that word. The Irish *peregrinus* throughout the middle ages was not an Irishman who visited a shrine abroad and then returned home, but rather the man who for his soul's welfare abandoned his homeland for good or at least for many years. Gougaud has pointed out that the command to Abraham: 'Egredere de terra tua et de cognatione tua' always seems to have had a special appeal to the Irish people as a call from God to sacrifice what was most dear to them.

A secondary motive which soon came to the fore among the *peregrini* was the desire to spread Christ's kingdom. In France and Belgium and Germany and further east the Irish monks and hermits began to preach the gospel to their pagan neighbours and to Christians who had fallen into laxity and immorality. Even if this had not been the dominant motive for their departure from Ireland, it spurred them on to greater activity abroad. In this they were encouraged also by local rulers and churchmen on the Continent. The hermit's cell gradually grew into a monastery, the centre for the diffusion of Irish Christianity in the surrounding area. In this way, as Kenney says, 'Irish monastic discipline, Irish ecclesiastical law, Irish penitential rules and customs, Irish biblical texts, even a certain amount of Irish learning passed into the life of Europe'. To their new mission-field they brought some of the characteristics of the Irish church – emphasis on self-sacrifice, the independence of the monastery vis-à-vis the diocese, the duty of hospitality, the superior jurisdiction of the abbot to the bishop, the linking of the monastery with pastoral work, the repeated study of Scripture and especially of the psalms. They also brought some penitential and liturgical practices of the Irish church which took root in Europe and one day became part of the Church Universal – personal confession of sins, use of penitential books with prescribed penances, the lighting of the Easter Fire.

Historians seem to agree about the outstanding contribution of these Irish exiles to the christianization of Europe, but no such agreement exists among them regarding the significance of the Irish contribution in the fields of learning and culture. Perhaps both sides were guilty of exaggeration in the past. Scholars like Zimmer and Meyer claim that it was Ireland that saved the classical tradition after the fall of the Roman Empire in the fifth century and rebuilt it in Europe through the work of Irish scholars. This naturally provoked a reaction during the past few decades. Esposito tried to show that there was little knowledge of Greek in the Irish monastic schools and that Irish scholars of Greek gained their knowledge on the Continent. Cappuyns left little place for Eriugena's Irish background in his study of the philosopher's mental development. Masai sought to prove that the greatest influence in the development of manuscript painting came not from Ireland but from the East. Smit dismissed the writings of St Columban as providing no evidence for a knowledge of the Latin classics in sixth-century Ireland. Perhaps we can rejoice that both *Iromania* and *Irophobia*, as Duft called them, have now run their course.

The early Irish monks and scholars abroad were just as prone to argument as at home. Just as Colmcille's dispute with Finnian was said to have led to a civil war and his exile to Scotland, those who went to the Continent engaged in some mighty disputes – Columban against the kings and bishops of Gaul, Kilian against Geilana, Virgil against Boniface. It remained a characteristic of Irish clerics on the Continent till the bitter end – as late as the eighteenth century a French writer said the Irish priests in Paris 'lived on Masses and arguments'.

For some reason Irish art took no root on the Continent under the influence of the *peregrini*. Apart from a few stray examples like the *Schottenportal* in Regensburg, there is nothing in the architecture, sculpture or mural painting of Europe between 600 and 1200 which would indicate that an Irishman ever stood on the Continent. Yet it was the era of the Ardagh Chalice and Muiredach's Cross at home. Only in the illumination of manuscripts did the *peregrini* have a strong impact through the fine examples which they brought from Ireland. Fortunately a great number of the latter have survived. It is remarkable that while only ten manuscripts written before 1000 have survived on Irish soil, more than fifty such manuscripts from Ireland remain in Continental libraries. There is no better illustration of the history of the Irish monks than the style and content of their manuscripts. No wonder that Johann Kaspar Zeuss and his followers had to base their reconstruction of Early Irish on manuscripts in Würzburg, St Gallen and Milan. If the early Irish *peregrini* had left their books at home in Ireland, our knowledge of the Irish language would be very limited today.

The typical group of Irish *peregrini* travelled on foot overland. They would have left some of the larger monasteries like Bangor or Clonmacnois in groups of twelve and a leader, in memory of Christ and the apostles. Each wears a white tunic covered by a cowl and is tonsured from ear to ear. Many carry the pilgrim's staff, a leather water-bottle hanging from a belt and perhaps a gospel-book in its leather case slung across the shoulder. Most of these groups first cross to Britain and proceed to one of the ports on the Kentish coast, perhaps Richborough which was already in use in Roman times. They come ashore at Quentovic or Boulogne or Wissant. Perhaps for the overland journey they join forces with a group of traders on the way to the fair of Aachen or Lagny or Limoges. They will endure plenty of hunger and fatigue before they find a kindly prince or a generous bishop to act as their patron. One of their number spoke for all the rest when he wrote:

Nocte dieque gemo quia sum peregrinus et egens.

It would be difficult to say who was the first Irish *peregrinus* to reach the Continent. Brittany, for instance, has a host of Irish saints – Briac, Fiac, Maudez, Ninnoc, Ronán and many others – some of whom are pushed back to St Patrick's era. But their *Vitae* are late and unreliable. Similarly the legends of the sixth-century Irish saints in Italy – Frediano in Lucca, Ursus in Aosta, even Cataldo in Taranto in the seventh century – must be approached with a lot of scepticism. Their alleged Irish origin will probably never be either proved or disproved. But there is no scientific reason why they must all be rejected.

It is unlikely, therefore, that Columban was the first Irish monk to visit Continental Europe. But he was certainly the pioneer who inspired the mass exodus later. We are fortunate to have a biography of him written by the monk Jonas, who entered the monastery of Bobbio only three years after Columban's death. Like most hagiographers of that era Jonas emphasized the miraculous powers of his hero and played down or even omitted his failings. But he provides us with a lively, consecutive narrative, something which is missing for most of those who followed Columban to the Continent in subsequent centuries.

It has been conjectured that Columban was born in 543 on the borders of the modern counties of Wexford and Carlow. Jonas records his mother's dream that out of her body came a resplendent sun which illuminated the whole earth. Jonas is also responsible for the story by which Columban is most vividly remembered in Ireland, explaining how as a teenager he was warned by a local anchoress to fly from the girls who would try to ensnare him and how, when his mother sought to prevent his departure from home, he stepped over her prostrate body. It was in tune with the severity and self-sacrifice which was to characterize much of Irish monasticism.

It is significant that in placing himself under the direction of Comgall in Bangor, Columban was joining the most austere branch of Irish monastic training. Bangor, like all the most notable Irish foundations of the period, was far closer to the primitive monastic settlements of the Nile Valley than to a later St Gallen or Clairvaux. It consisted of a collection of round wooden huts within an enclosure, with only a few communal buildings: the church, refectory, scriptorium and library. The daily fare was bread, vegetables and water. The dress was a long white tunic with a coarse hooded outer garment and sandals. The monks assembled frequently in the church by day and night for the canonical hours. They engaged in all the necessary agricultural labours from the sowing to the harvest. Their learning was centred on the Sacred Scripture, but Bangor was one of the Irish abbeys where a high standard of Latin learning was attained and per-haps a smattering of Greek as well. Fasting, silence, corporal punishment, reduction of sleep, repeated genuflections and prolonged prayer with outstretched arms were normal forms of mortification to be imposed for breaches of the rule. It was an ascetic yet happy milieu, 'the good Rule of Bangor, upright, divine' in which Columban spent many years of his young manhood until the day came when with twelve companions reluctantly released by Comgall he took leave of Ireland. It was probably 591, although Jonas's reference to the King of Austrasia and Burgundy as Sigebert (d.575) has induced some modern scholars to place it twenty years earlier.

Columban and his companions were well received by the king, who implored them to search for a secluded spot within his own territory. Their choice fell on an old Roman fort in the Vosges destroyed by Attila and his Huns over a century earlier. The ruined temple of Diana was repaired to serve as a church and thus the monastery of Annegray arose on the site of an earlier Roman settlement.

Here we see for the first time what became a well-established feature of Columban's monastic foundations later – the tendency to choose a site which had religious significance for the Romans in an earlier era. Columban did the same thing later in founding Luxeuil and Bregenz. He also searched the forests around Annegray for a secluded spot to which he could retire from time to time to be alone with God, an inevitable consequence of the fame which each of his foundations would one day achieve.

The number of monks grew so quickly that Annegray could no longer hold them. Eight miles to the west lay the ruins of another former Roman fort at Luxovium, its thermal springs stagnant among the broken columns since Attila came that way in 451. The ruins were transformed into the monastery of Luxeuil which was destined one day to outstrip its elder sister in importance and to win undying fame through the splendour of its monastic school. As the community continued to increase, a third, smaller foundation was made at Fontaine, three miles north of Luxeuil. According to Jonas the community there ultimately numbered sixty, hence the total in the three houses probably came to over 200.

By that time the dozen Irish monks were a very small minority in the three communities. We have no evidence that other recruits came from Ireland, hence the majority of the monks were recruited locally, many of them the sons of Frankish nobles. For them Columban wrote his *Regula Monachorum* which inculcated silence, prayer and fasting, broken only by one scant meal of vegetables, porridge, beans and bread in the evening. Apart from one long chapter laying down detailed regulations for the recitation of the Divine Office, the Rule is mainly concerned with the interior dispositions of the monk and the general principles of monasticism. It is thus entirely dissimilar to the detailed regulations laid down in the Rule of St Benedict. For an Irish monk obedience was everything and the details of community life could be safely left to the decisions of a wise and inspiring abbot.

For the same or another of his communities Columban drew up his *Regula Coenobialis*, which provides a more detailed commentary on the daily life of an early Irish monk than any other source. Yet even here one gets the flavour of a series of punishments for breaches of discipline rather than a systematic effort to order the monk's day towards a life of prayer, austerity and the praise of God. A fixed number of slaps, varying from six to a dozen, is laid down for such simple faults as omitting grace before meals, going astray in the chant or laughing during prayers. For graver faults like telling idle stories, striking the altar, starting a dispute or shouting loudly, fifty blows were prescribed. The most interesting feature of this Rule is the emphasis on personal confession of faults.

Columban's monks were obliged to confess their sins, mortal and venial, twice a day, and an appropriate penance was laid down for each. When the Columban monasteries applied this system to the laity as well, the abbot composed his *Penitential*, modelled on the earliest Irish Penitential of Finnian, composed a generation earlier.

Láporte has shown that the Columban document falls into three parts, one for monks, one for the secular clergy and one for the laity. To our way of thinking the penances seem long and severe – restitution followed by 120 days on bread and water for the theft of a domestic animal, three years on bread and water in exile followed by two further years of abstinence from wine and meat for perjury, a week on bread and water for drunkenness or gluttony.

Yet compared with the stern penalty of perpetual excommunication for some crimes which had gone before, both clergy and laity welcomed the Irish system as offering a hope of reconciliation and readmission to Holy Communion as soon as the period of penance was over. Like many of the great monastic founders from Basil to Finnian, Columban tried to overcome sin by prescribing the practice of the opposite virtue: 'The talkative is to be punished with silence, the restless with the practice of gentleness, the gluttonous with

fasting, the sleepy with watching, the proud with imprison-
ment, the deserter with expulsion . . . ' Mechanical as the
listing of sins and their appropriate penances may now seem,
they were used by the Irish monks to change the whole
penitential discipline of the Church in Western Europe.

Columban's independence and especially his observance
of Easter according to the Irish calculation were resented by
many of the bishops of Gaul. These were already preparing
to move against him on the Easter issue in 600, when he
bypassed them by writing a strong letter in defence of the
Irish system to Pope Gregory the Great. He declined the sum-
mons to appear before the Council of Châlons-sûr-Saône in
603, but sent a written communication in which he pleaded
for charity towards all without distinction of race, 'for we
are members of one body, whether Gauls or Britons or Irish
or whatever our race . . .'

It was Columban's refusal to condone the evil life of the
young King of Burgundy, Thierry, that ultimately led to his
expulsion from France in 610. Urged on by the Queen Mother,
Brunhilde, the King had all the Irish and British monks driven
from Luxeuil and brought under guard to Nantes to be sent
home to Ireland. But a storm blew the ship aground at the
mouth of the Loire and the captain, taking this as a sign that
God did not approve of the expulsion, allowed Columban and
his companions to go free.

The wandering of the Irish monks across Northern France
until they finally reached the Rhine was responsible for sowing the seeds of new foundations in this area in the next
generation. It brought Columban into Switzerland and Austria and led to a 2-3 year sojourn in Bregenz on the eastern
shore of Lake Constance. Once more the uncompromising
opposition of the Irish monks to anything less than full
commitment led to their expulsion, but this time Columban's
best-known disciple, Gall, refused to follow his master across
the Alps. Not for the first time Columban punished disobedi-
ence with a sanction which we today would find unduly
severe, for he ordered Gall never again to celebrate Mass
during his (Columban's) lifetime. After more than twenty
years together since they had left Bangor, they now took
their separate ways, Gall to find a place of retreat along the

Steinach which would one day bear his name (d. c.630), Columban to traverse the plain of Lombardy and found his last monastery at Bobbio (where he died within a few years, on 23 November 615). Courageous, outspoken, scholarly, unyielding, quick to enter an argument, severe on his fellow monks and on himself, he could also show tenderness and write lyric poetry of a high quality. His writings provide nearly all the evidence that exists for the study of the Latin classics in Irish monastic schools at so early a period.

Of all the Irish *peregrini* on the Continent there can scarcely be any doubt that Columban had the most widespread and most lasting impact. Within a generation France was dotted with monasteries, founded by men who had been trained in Luxeuil. Most of their founders were natives of France, hence Prinz describes the movement as Hiberno-Frankish rather than Irish. Columban supplied the inspiration, the Franks supplied the personnel.

Yet despite his pent-up energy and power to attract recruits, Columban seemed satisfied to allow his own example and leadership to be the rule of life for his followers rather than a detailed Code of Regulations. This meant that even during his lifetime the Columbanian houses never had the same orderly and balanced system as the Benedictines. After his death one after another of the daughter houses of Luxeuil adopted Benedict's Rule until finally even Bobbio and Luxeuil made it their own.

Picardy and Flanders

The spread of monasticism in Northern France and Flanders in the generation after St Columban owed much to the inspiration of the saint and the training afforded by Luxeuil. St Amand, the 'Apostle of Belgium', was trained in the Columban Rule. Under its influence the nobleman Richarius abandoned secular life and founded the abbey which became famous under his name – St Riquier. St Fara of Meaux, blessed together with her father by Columban, founded the convent which was later called Faramoutiers in her memory. Rebais, Jumièges and Corbie all owed their foundation to Luxeuil.

Bercharius, founder of Montier-en-Der, was trained there. No wonder his biographer remarks with admiration: 'What place what city does not rejoice to have a bishop or abbot who was trained under the rule of that holy man?' (Columban).

A few of the new monastic founders were Irishmen who had come to Gaul with Columban and remained after his expulsion. One was Deicolus, who founded Lure not far from Luxeuil. Perhaps his Gaelic name was Dicuil. Another was Rouin or Roding, abbot of Beaulieu in the Argonne.

In contrast to these Irish monks who set up new religious houses in the generation after Columban, a few arrived in the north of France to pursue the life of a recluse. The best-known of these was Fiachra who arrived in the Brie district around Meaux about 630 and was welcomed into his diocese by Faro, Bishop of Meaux. The latter gave him a site for a hermitage in the forest of Breuil, where he erected his cell and an oratory dedicated to Our Lady. Unfortunately his *Vita* is a late (twelfth-century) unreliable production. It is probably correct, however, in stating that Fiachra built the first hostel for Irish pilgrims on the Continent and planted a vegetable garden to provide food for them. In that respect St Fiachra is always depicted with a spade and has become patron of gardeners. He died about 670.

The priory of St Fiacre arose in medieval times around the cell of the Irish saint and it became one of the most notable pilgrimage places of France. The saint's bones were enshrined in 1234 and brought to Meaux cathedral for safety in 1568 during the religious wars. Kings Louis XIII and Louis XIV, Richelieu and St Vincent de Paul were among the distinguished pilgrims to the shrine of St Fiacre during the seventeenth century. Hundreds of chapels in his honour are still to be found throughout Northern France, especially in Brittany and the Ile-de-France. His name came to be associated with the horse-cab because such vehicles used to be available for hire at the Hôtel Saint-Fiacre in the rue Saint-Martin in Paris.

The centenary of St Fiachra's death in 1970 was celebrated with great enthusiasm both in France and Ireland. It is not certain, of course, that the St Fiachra of Kilfeery, Co. Kilkenny is the same as the hermit who went to France; but the identity of their feastdays suggests that they are identical. On the other hand, the Fiachra commemorated at Ullard near Graguenamanagh is probably quite different. Many pilgrims from the Meaux area came to Ireland in 1970 to visit these two places associated with a saint named Fiachra, and the centenary reached its climax in September 1970 when Cardinal Conway was chief concelebrant at the open-air Mass beside the original hermitage of the Irish saint.

Bishop Faro of Meaux patronized a further Irish hermit named Kilian who settled in Aubigny year Arras in the mid-seventh century. Although his *Vita* contains much that is absurd, its use of the form Chillenus suggests that some parts of it must go back to the seventh century.

Another Irish recluse and a contemporary of St Fiachra bore the strongly Irish name of Gobán ('little mouth'). The town of Saint-Gobain, famous for nearly three centuries for the manufacture of glassware, still preserves his name in the region where he settled. Saint-Gobain is nearly 20km west of Laon and preserves the skull of the Irish hermit in its parish church. Local tradition still points out the site of his hermitage in the forest known as *La Forêt de Saint Gobain*. He was murdered on 20 June 670.

Much less is known about the Irish hermit Ronán, whose tomb is preserved in the church of Locronan, about 15km north-west of Quimper in Brittany. The church was erected in the fifteenth – sixteenth centuries with a separate chapel for the saint's tomb. The saint's fifteenth-century statue is one of the oldest artistic works in *kersanton*, the hard granite-like stone used in many of the Brittany calvaries. According to the skimpy evidence available Ronán came from Ireland in the seventh century.

One must wait till near the middle of the seventh century before a new wave of Irish monastic founders is active in northern Gaul. Among them St Fursey attained unique fame because of his visions. He was born, according to his *Vita Prima*, along the shores of Lough Corrib in the modern Co. Galway, but districts in Co. Louth and Co. Kerry can also lay some claim on him. After preaching in Ireland for ten years he crossed to Britain where his first foundation was at Cnoberesburg in East Anglia – the impressive Roman fortification of Burgh Castle near Great Yarmouth marks the site today and is adjacent to an ancient church dedicated to St Fursey. About 644-5, when the pagan King Penda of Mercia threatened attack, he left his brother Faelán in charge of the monastery and journeyed to France where he was kindly received by Clovis, King of the Franks, and Erchinoald, Mayor of the Palace of Neustria. Fursey founded a new monastery at Lagny on the Marne, about 20km east of Paris. He died in 649-50 at Mézerolles, where two local villages, Frohens-le-Grand and Frohens-le-Petit, are said to have got their names through a corruption of his own.

Fursey's reputation for sanctity and his visions of the other world made a deep impression on his contemporaries. Bede in his *Ecclesiastical History* pays a generous tribute to him: 'renowned among his people according to worldly standards, yet more eminent because of the heavenly gift of grace'. Hence it was not surprising that despite some efforts to hold on to Fursey's corpse in the district in which he died, Erchninoald took possession of it for the new church which he was just completing in Péronne.

Fursey's tomb in Péronne attracted many Irish pilgrims in subsequent centuries. First to come were his two brothers, Faelán and Ultan, who were expelled from Cnoberesburg with their community by King Penda about 650. Both of them held the abbacy of Péronne in turn. A later abbot, Cellan (d.706), poet and correspondent of the English scholar Aldhelm, was also Irish by birth, and it is possible that Péronne remained an Irish monastery until its destruction by the Northmen in 880.

Whether under Irish control or ruled by friendly Franks, 'Perrona Scottorum', as it came to be designated, remained an important link between Ireland and the Continent for several centuries. It must have kept in close touch with some monasteries in Ireland, as the obits of monks who died in *Cathair Fhursa* (Fursey's city) found their way into various bodies of Irish annals. Devotion to St Patrick spread to Péronne at latest during the second half of the seventh century, the era in which Armagh was making its first great effort to collect the traditions of the saint at home. I believe that family links between some of the Péronne monks and the church of Louth facilitated the introduction of the cult of St Patrick. The monastery possessed relics of the saint, possibly brought to France by Fursey himself; it also provided itself with an early copy of Patrick's *Confessio* and *Epistola* from which the other Continental manuscripts of these texts are probably descended. Péronne became both a *Monasterium Scottorum* and a *Hospitale Scottorum*, i.e. a place where Irish monastic recruits and penitents could retire from the world and where Irish pilgrims en route to Rome or the Holy Land or any other European sanctuary could get lodgings.

Closely linked with Péronne was the monastery of Fosses (the town is now called Fosse-la-Ville) in the south of modern Belgium, founded by Fursey's younger brother, Faelán. When his East Anglian monastery at Cnoberesburg had been over-run, Faelán narrowly missed execution. He led his community to Péronne where Erchinoald suggested that they seek another patron. Like other wandering Irish monks of the mid-seventh century they travelled to Nivelles where Itta, widow of Pipin I, was abbess of a renowned convent following the Irish rule, whose community included also her daughter Gertrude. The two pious ladies welcomed Faelán and his companions, and together with Itta's brother, Grimoald, Mayor of the Palace of Austrasia, founded for them the monastery of Fosses, probably in 651.

Faelán did not live to see his new foundation grow and flourish. Only about four years later, on 31 October 655 according to the close reasoning of Paul Grosjean SJ, the outstanding Bollandist scholar, he was murdered with three companions by robbers at the present-day village of Le Roeulx. The bodies were terribly mutilated and buried under a piggery. But a widespread and prolonged search was carried out on the initiative of Gertrude, who backed it up with fasts and unceasing prayer. Finally, on the feast of St Fursey, 16 January 656, the four bodies were discovered and brought back by night to Nivelles in a procession of honour. Some relics were left with the nuns and the remainder of the bodies were brought to Fosses. Excavations carried out in 1951-2 have shown that the church attached to the *Monasterium Scottorum* at Fosses was a wooden building, erected on the site of an earlier Roman villa, and that a small wooden oratory was added to the church to receive the body of St Faelán. The first stone church was not erected on the site until about 800 AD.

The third brother, Ultan, succeeded Faelán, first as abbot of Péronne and later as abbot of Fosses. We are not certain of the year of his death, but as he is said to have told St Gertrude of Nivelles on 16 March 659 that she would die on the following day, this provides a *terminus post quem* for the death of Ultan. While still commemorated by a special 'chapelle de St Ultain' in the Collégiale Saint-Feuillen in Fosse-la-Ville, it is his elder brother who caused Fosses to become an outstanding place of pilgrimage in medieval times. Every seventh year the shrine of St Feuillen is still brought around the countryside in the *Marche de St Feuillen*, a colourful procession of uniformed and armed marchers, viewed by thousands of spectators.

The hermit Kilian of Aubigny near Arras has already been referred to. Another St Kilian from Ireland (who latinized his name as Quintilianus) founded in the first half of the eighth century the monastery of Moutiers-en-Puisaye, near Saint Fargeau, about 45km from Auxerre. It was placed under the patronage of Our Blessed Lady and St Germanus of Auxerre. Many Irish monks and scholars were active in the diocese of Auxerre from the eighth to the tenth century and this monastery was presumably their headquarters. In the middle ages it was a strongly fortified monastery; the ruined walls and traces of the outer enclosures may still be seen. A manuscript written in Moutiers about 800 is now preserved in the Chapter Library in Cracow. It contains addresses given to the monks and some medical prescriptions. One interesting feature is that the abbot is called the *princeps*, just as he is given this title in the Irish annals of the same period. The manuscript is dedicated to Bishop Aaron and the only bishop of this name in France in the early middle ages was an Irishman who ruled in Auxerre from 794 to 808.

Kilian of Moutiers-en-Puisaye may be completely unknown today outside the immediate neighbourhood of the monastery founded by him. Yet he is more certainly of Irish origin than some of the popular saints of Northern France and Belgium whose supposed Irish birth has been taken for granted for centuries. One such is St Dympna, patroness of Gheel near Antwerp. Though reputed to have lived in the seventh century, her *Vita* was not compiled until the thirteenth century. It has little historical value but considerable folklore interest. Dympna has been venerated for centuries as protectress against insanity, something which goes back to the tradition recounted in her life that she was slain by her father, a prince of Oriel, because she refused his advances. It is possible that the local tradition concerning her Irish birth was accurate.

Less likely to be correct is the theory that St Rumold or Rombaut of Malines, who was murdered about 775, was Irish. His earliest *Vita*, written by Thierry of St Trond about 1100, makes him bishop of Dublin, although Dublin did not become an episcopal see until the eleventh century. While the illustrious Franciscan hagiographer, Fr Hugh Ward, went to great lengths in the seventeenth century to defend his Irish origin, recent research suggests that this is very doubtful. Another supposed Irish saint who must be surrendered by Ireland is Livinus or Liéven of Ghent. His eleventh-century biographer makes him an Irish missionary who suffered martyrdom in Flanders in the seventh century. Since the end of the nineteenth century, however, scholars are inclined to question his very existence and to argue that he is a doublet of the Anglo-Saxon missionary St Liafwin or Lebuin (d.773) of Deventer in Holland, the Apostle of the Friesians.

The names of about a dozen other Irish saints who worked in Northern France and Belgium have been preserved as objects of popular local cults. Some of them, like Éloque, the successor of Fursey as abbot of Lagny, and Monon, a hermit who was murdered by robbers in the forest of Ardenne, and Maugille, companion of Fursey, whose relics are preserved in St Riquier, were, I believe, genuinely Irish. Many of the others must be pronounced at least doubtful. They provide additional proof, however, if further proof were needed, of the tendency on the part of medieval hagiographers to assume an Irish origin for people of an earlier age who had left a reputation for sanctity and whose place of origin was unknown.

Doctissimi Magistri

The Carolingian Renaissance brought a new type of Irish exile to the Continent. For more than a century after the reign of Charlemagne the typical Irishman to be met in the schools and courts of Europe was more of a 'scholar' than a 'saint'. Under the Emperor himself but particularly during the reigns of his son, Louis the Pious (d.840) and his grandson, Charles the Bald (d.877), Irish scholars played no small part in the integration of classical learning and a higher standard of education into the organization of the Christian Church. The Irish no longer came primarily as *peregrini pro Christi nomine* but rather as scholars attracted to the new centres of learning. Perhaps it is more than a coincidence that the exodus of the scholars coincided with the Viking attacks on the Irish monasteries at home. The *repos des savants* was no longer available on Irish soil. They swarmed to the Continent with their manuscripts written in the distinctive Irish script which was to prove the longest-lived script in the history of Western writing.

Yet we must not exaggerate the influence of the first generation of Irish scholars. As Dr Bieler puts it: 'In this cultural movement the Irish played an important, though not a decisive, role. Individually, some of them, for example Sedulius and Iohannes Scottus, are among the greatest scholars of that age. The inauguration of the new movement, however, owes little or nothing to the Irish'. Let us add that they had no-one as influential as Alcuin of York or Theodulf of Orléans. Individual scholars – apart from the two mentioned above – left little trace of their personality on their writings, and historians can therefore still argue about how many Dungals or Dicuils were to be found among the Irish exiles. Some of their European contemporaries like Theodulf looked on them as upstarts, while Einhard felt that the Emperor allowed them to become too heavy a burden on Charlemagne's court.

The account given in the *Gesta Caroli Magni* of the arrival of the first two Irish scholars at the Emperor's court is well known. They arrived in Gaul in the company of British merchants. Crowds gathered to purchase their wares and as the

Irishmen had no goods to sell, they kept on shouting: 'If anyone is desirous of wisdom, let him come to us and acquire it, for we have it for sale'. The hearers, partly because of the strangeness of the event and partly because they thought the two Irishmen were mad, reported the incident to the Emperor, who called them to his presence. They explained that all they requested for their teaching was food and clothing. The Emperor kept them at his court for a while, but when he had to go to war he appointed one of them, Clement by name, as teacher of a large number of boys in Gaul, and sent the other (perhaps Dungal was meant) as a teacher to Italy.

These ninth-century Irish *savants* were a remarkably versatile group – scholars and poets, philosophers and biblical commentators, geographers and cosmographers, grammarians and philologists and lexicographers. They liked to show off their learning, to parade their knowledge of Greek (which was sometimes fairly elementary), to indulge in fanciful speculation, to take part in loud unending disputations. Some of them found their way to Aachen when Charlemagne was still alive, but as the focus of learning moved further west under his successors, they are more actively involved in the episcopal sees of Gaul – Laon and Soissons and Rheims and Cambrai and Liège, even as far west as Paris.

Alcuin's links with Ireland might have been what first attracted them to Aachen but these have never been fully explained. Colcu his 'master', whom he addresses in one of his letters, has been identified with a Clonmacnois scholar of that name who died in 796, but he could equally have been an Irish teacher in York. Similarly the Irish scholar Joseph, whom Alcuin refers to as his 'son', may have studied in York. Alcuin's acquaintance with the abbot, bishop and monks of the Northumbrian foundation of Mayo suggests a visit to Ireland on his part but cannot prove this on its own. All we can say with certainty is that he was friendly with some Irish scholars and churchmen and may have introduced some Irish practices into the Frankish liturgy. But the scholars needed no invitation from Alcuin to bring them to Aachen.

We can do little more than list the most notable of the Irish scholars during the first half of the ninth century – Joseph, poet and commentator on Isaias, author of acrostic verses addressed to the Emperor and of other riddles and puzzles; Clement, who probably succeeded Alcuin as Master of the Palace School, author of the *Ars Grammatica*; Dungal of St Denis and Dungal of Pavia, poets and controversialists (perhaps one and the same scholar at two different points of his career); Muiredach of St-Michiel on the Meuse who translated his Gaelic name into Smaragdus and was author of a number of monastic rules; Dicuil who wrote the best geography to come from the new empire, *Liber de Mensura Orbis Terrae*; Thomas who taught in the Palace School and composed a series of puzzles to test his colleagues; finally Cruinmael who compiled a famous treatise on metrics.

With the last-mentioned we have reached the middle of the ninth century when Donatus the Irish bishop of Fiesole near Florence composed his life of St Brigid in Latin hexameters. His two contemporaries north of the Alps, Sedulius Scottus in Liège and Johannes Scottus Eriugena in Laon, marked the apex of Irish learning on the Continent and were unequalled for their brilliance in many fields.

Sedulius was an all-round scholar, a priest-poet, a combination of *savant* and humanist. After his arrival on the Continent about 848 Bishop Hartgar of Liège appointed him *scholasticus* and the Irishman repaid him with a rich harvest of writings – commentaries on the psalms, notes on versions in Greek and Latin of St Paul's Epistles, grammatical tracts and a handbook for Christian princes – *De Rectoribus Christianis*. He was familiar with classical authors like Horace and Ovid. The Greek Psalter in Ms. 807 in Bibliothèque de l'Arsenal, Paris, may be in his hand.

At times Sedulius forsook serious scholarly research for some light-hearted whimsical banter with the bishop or other friends in verse. More than eighty of his poems have survived, some of them professional pieces in gratitude to a benefactor, others on serious topics like death, but the most attractive are highly sophisticated personal lyrics complaining like all scholars of the difficulty in making ends meet and asking the bishop gently for some extra food and drink. Professor James Carney captures well the spirit of the originals:

The crops are green and fields are all in flower,
budding the vine – the year now has its hour;
gay-painted songbirds fill the air with glee,
there's smile on land and sky and laughs the sea.

Of mirth-provoking sap I too have need,
some beer, or Bacchus' gift, or perhaps some mead;
and then there's meat, produce of earth and sky,
and I have none, but ask the reason why.

But, says Helen Waddell, 'the Bacchanalian verse is only
the blown spray of a profound and serious scholarship'.
Sedulius always bore his learning lightly. Probably his best-
known poem is his mock-lament for a ram which the bishop
had promised him but which was torn to pieces by a dog. It
never spoke an idle word, he recalls; it said nothing during its
life but *bah* and *béh*, drank no wine or beer, and died among
thieves like the Lamb of God:

Adieu good chief of gleaming herd – alas
I see you not a-feeding on my grass . . .

You have I loved and love your widow too,
mother I love, and brothers all – Adieu.
(English translation by J. Carney)

Like most poets in the Gaelic tradition, down to Blind
Raftery, Sedulius composed a Confession in verse in which
he begged pardon for his sins:

I read and write and teach, philosophy peruse,
I eat and freely drink, with rhymes invoke the muse,
. . .
And sin and fault inform the life I plan:
Ah! Christ and Mary pity this miserable man.
(English translation by J. Carney)

Some literary critics have suggested that it was the Irish
who introduced rhyme into Latin verse. The manuscripts
connected with the Circle of Sedulius which have survived
preserve the names of many of the Irish scholarly fraternity in Liège – Dongus, Dubthach, Comgan, Cathasach,
Suadbar and so on. Sedulius eulogizes particularly the four

Irishmen whom he calls 'the fourspan of the Lord, the glory of the Irish race' – Fergus, Blandus, Marcus and Beuchell. Unfortunately, apart from an epic in praise of Charles the Bald by Fergus, their writings have not been identified.

While Sedulius was a priest, we are fairly certain that Eriugena was a layman. He was a teacher, probably master, in the Palace School of Charles the Bald which at that time was located in Laon.

But Eriugena stood head and shoulders over all his contemporaries. He was the only speculative philosopher and theologian of his era. In his controversies with Gottschalk concerning Predestination he frightened even his supporters by his daring. 'While his contemporaries were only lisping in philosophy', wrote Maurice de Wulf, historian of medieval philosophy, 'Eriugena in the ninth century worked out a complete philosophical synthesis'.

His translation into Latin of the supposed Greek writings of Denis the Areopagite brought him into the field of neo-Platonism. This led directly to his best-known work *De Divisione Naturae*, in which he stressed the claims of philosophy as an independent science. It has often been pronounced pantheistic but Eriugena would have been the last to admit any departure from orthodoxy. However, when some thirteenth-century scholars taught an explicit pantheism and claimed Eriugena as their source, his work was condemned by the Pope in 1225.

Eriugena was very proud of his knowledge of Greek, which was superior to that of any contemporary European scholar. Yet his Greek composition was weak, though he could translate difficult Greek texts into Latin. Scholars have argued interminably as to whether he brought his knowledge of Greek from Ireland or acquired it on the Continent. His most recent biographer, Dom Cappuyns of Louvain, is inclined to reduce the input from Ireland. Yet no scholar has yet disproved Traube's challenging statement that 'whoever on the continent in the days of Charles the Bald knew Greek was an Irishman, or at least his knowledge was transmitted to him by an Irishman . . . '

Eriugena was a much more original thinker than Sedulius and surpassed him in the range of his interests and in his knowledge of Greek. But in one respect Sedulius was his master. As a poet Eriugena was heavy, overly learned and lacked the light touch of his contemporary. He tended to lace his Latin poems with Greek words and phrases. Indeed, his best-known poem is the savage two-line epigram he wrote on Archbishop Hincmar of Rheims who had upbraided his nephew, the bishop of Laon, for wasting his time trying to learn Irish from the Irish colony in that city:

Hic jacet Hincmarus cleptes vehementer avarus,
Hoc solum gessit nobile, quod periit.
(Here lies Hincmar, a rogue they say,
His one great deed – he passed away.)

Eriugena had obviously a sharp tongue, something which is recalled by the story of his retort to Emperor Charles the Bald as they faced each other across the table well-stocked with wine. *Quid distat inter sottum et Scottum*, asked the Emperor, intending to make fun of Eriugena's Scottic name. *Tabula tantum*, replied the Irishman. It has been called the best *bon mot* of the middle ages. ('What separates a fool [sottum] from an Irishman [Scottum]' was the Emperor's fun-making attempt at a pun. 'Only the table', was the reply.

This short account of Eriugena will have to stand for the other members of is circle in Laon – Martin, the best Irish Grecian after Eriugena and Sedulius, who composed a Greek-Latin glossary which still exists in Laon in his own hand, Aldelm, who is called the brother of Johannes Scottus and from whom a few scraps still survive, Elias, bishop of Angoulême in the middle of the ninth century, where another Irishman Toimene had been bishop two centuries earlier.

In the same way the Laon group of scholars will have to represent a few stray Irish scholars who were active in the eighth – ninth centuries in a number of other cathedral cities and for whom we have no space. One such was to be found in Rheims, a certain Donnchadh who taught in the monastery of San Remi and wrote a commentary on Martianus Capella. Another was in Soissons, which had an Irish Archbishop named Abel in the eighth century. An Irish monk whose name is unknown composed some stray verses there about

858 and copied them into his manuscript of Priscian's grammar which is now in the University Library of Leyden. The final centre which should be mentioned is Cambrai, where in a manuscript of canons compiled for Bishop Albericus (763-90) portion of a homily in Irish has been surprisingly copied. Still preserved in the public library in Cambrai, it now forms the earliest piece of continuous prose which exists in the Irish language. One of its themes is the martyrdom of exile and it thus forms an appropriate epitaph for the work of so many Irish scholars abroad.

We occasionally find Irish pilgrims, on their way to or from Rome, deciding to settle down at one of the shrines en route. Such was the case of Donatus, bishop of Fiesole from about 826 to about 877, who wrote a famous metrical life of St Brigid. In 850 he granted to the monastery of Bobbio a church in Piacenza and afterwards added a hospice for Irish pilgrims there, the forerunner of the present well-known church of St Brigid in Piacenza. Another traveller who settled down en route was Moengal, probably the former Abbot of Bangor, who with his uncle, Bishop Marcus, and a few Irish servants, remained in St Gallen on a return journey from Rome. Moengal was later put in charge of the monastic school and was teacher of Notker Balbulus, the famous composer of sequences. We still have evidence of his skill as a scribe in charters which survive from the 850s. He died on 30 September 871.

After the brilliance of the ninth-century scholars the tenth century is dull by comparison. An Irish priest named Israel was appointed bishop of Aix (in Provence) in the middle of the century. He was both poet and grammarian, an outstanding scholar, who had Bruno the future Archbishop of Cologne as one of his students. After the destruction of Aix by the Saracens he became a monk in the monastery of St Maximin, Trier. The oldest manuscript containing the *Navigatio Sancti Brendani* was once in this monastery and it is now considered likely that this epic of the early Irish Church was put into literary form by none other than Bishop Israel. It caught the imagination of the German peoples especially along the Baltic coast, and in this strange way St Brendan 'the navigator' had his name affixed to the area around Berlin under the form

Brandenburg. Another Irish poet Moriuht (Muiredach?) is found in Northern France in the second half of the tenth century. He was the subject of a rude satire written by Garnier, a monk of St Ouen of Rouen. None of his own compositions seems to have survived.

An Indian Summer in Germany

While continuous ecclesiastical links between Ireland and the German-speaking parts of Europe were not forged until after the institution of the Ottonian Empire in the tenth century, individual Irish missionaries found their way there much earlier. The alleged Irish origin of the earliest two, Fridolin and Wendelin, however, must be regarded as somewhat dubious. Their names seem Teutonic rather than Celtic. Their *floruits* in the sixth century would place them in the generation before St Columban. But the popular cult of these two saints, Fridolin founder of the monastery of Säckingen on the Rhine, and Wendelin, hermit in the diocese of Trier, whose relics are honoured in the town of St Wendel, is among the most widespread in Germany.

From the seventh century on we are on surer ground, though many of the supposed Irish saints are still doubtful. What we do know for certain is that Luxeuil sent missionaries to Bavaria not long after the death of Columban (615) and both Franks and Irish were involved in the conversion of Bavaria. Hence some of the local saints still honoured as Irish in Southern Germany could have arrived there as part of this mission.

In the past it was believed that St Rupert of Salzburg and St Erhard of Regensburg were Irish by birth. In 774 Rupert's remains were brought by a genuine Irishman, Virgilius, to his newly erected cathedral in Salzburg, and subsequently Rupert was identified as an Irishman and continued to be celebrated liturgically by the Irish Church until recent years. It is now accepted that he was a Frank by birth and came to Bavaria at the end of the seventh century from the district of Worms. Erhard's *Vita* contains the puzzling phrase *Narbonensis gentilitate, Nervus civilitate, genere Scoticus fuit.* Whatever about his ancestry, he was probably born in Narbonne. During excavations in the Niedermünster of Regensburg (1964-8) the grave of St Albart was found beside that of St Erhard. According to his *Vita* he had been Archbishop of Cashel in Ireland, and arrived in Regensburg shortly after the death of Erhard, i.e. *post* 700. While his title is an obvious anachronism, his possible Irish origin cannot be completely ruled out. The same would apply to his contemporary, St Disibod, after whom the monastery of Disibodenberg in the diocese of Mainz was named.

It is only when we come to St Kilian in the latter part of the seventh century that we meet an indisputable Irish missionary in Germany. According to Irish tradition he was a native of Mullagh near the Cavan-Meath border and had only preached in Franconia for a few years when he was martyred with two companion, Totnan and Kolonat, in Würzburg in 689. Preparations are afoot at the time of writing for the celebration of his centenary in 1989.

The relics of the 'Apostles of Franconia' were placed in the first cathedral of Würzburg in 752 and numerous pilgrims from Ireland came to pray at Kilian's tomb. Clement Scottus, formerly Master of the Palace School, died there in the middle of the ninth century. The famous St Paul Codex with its copious glosses in Irish and other manuscripts from Ireland were probably brought by Irish visitors in the ninth century. The chronicler Maelbríde was ordained priest there, as he tells us himself, on 13 March 1059. Shortly afterwards we have evidence for a community of Irish monks resident in Würzburg.

Roughly contemporary with St Kilian were two other martyr-missionaries from Ireland in Southern Germany, Sts Anian and Marin, who have been completely forgotten in their native land. Bishop Marin was put to death with great cruelty at Wilparting (just off the autobahn from Munich to Salzburg) on 15 November 697 and his deacon Anian died a natural death on the same day. Within half a century Bishop Arbeo of Freising, who was present when their remains were taken from the grave, wrote a valuable account of their deaths. Their remains are still entombed before the high altar in Wilparting church, while their cult is also alive in the church of Alb nearby and in the beautiful rococo church of Rott am Inn.

Moving into the eighth century we encounter many alleged Irish missionaries in the region around Munich. St Korbinian of Freising, whose relics are preserved in the crypt of Freising cathedral, began his missionary work in this area about 715. His name and the interest which Virgilius later showed in having his life written suggest an Irish origin. In 764 Bishop Arbeo transferred his bones to his new cathedral in Freising and wrote his life, which states that he was born *in regione Melitonensi*, wherever that may have been.

A question mark must also be placed before St Magnus or Mang, patron of the Allgau. We know that he came to the area with two companions from the monastery of St Gall about 744, that he founded the church of Füssen and died there on 6 September 770. A third doubtful Irish missionary, this time north of Munich, is St Alto, after whom Altomünster near Dachau is named. It is surmised that he may have come to the area in the entourage of Virgilius in the 740s and he received a grant of land from Pipin on which to build a monastery, now the only Bridgettine convent on German soil. The final doubtful Irish saint who will be mentioned in this group is St Pirmin, founder of Reichenau in 724. Most scholars now favour Spain as his birthplace. During the abbacy of Strabo (838-49) it became a great calling-place for Irish monks. In it was probably written the poem Pangur Bán.

After so many doubtful Irish saints it is a relief to come upon a missionary whose Irish credentials cannot be gainsaid. Virgil of Salzburg was probably a native of the Trim area in Co. Meath. His Irish name was Fergil. He may or may not have been the same as the Fergil who was abbot of Aghaboe in Laois. There is some evidence that he was a monk of Iona before departing for France where we find him at Quiercy, the court of Pipin, about 743. He was keenly interested in cosmography and the Irish Annals call him 'Virgil the geographer'. Heinz Löwe has argued strongly that he was the author of the cosmography of Aethicus Ister.

Pipin sent him on a mission to Duke Odilo of Bavaria, who appointed him to rule the vacant see of Salzburg as abbot of St Peter's. In imitation of Irish practice he did not receive episcopal orders but employed an Irish bishop of the neighbourhood, Dubhdáchrích of Chiemsee, to administer those sacraments for which episcopal orders were required. After Boniface's death he was consecrated bishop of Salzburg in 767.

On several issues Virgil was at loggerheads with St Boniface, who suspected his orthodoxy and delated him to Rome. The Pope supported him on the validity of baptism administered with a trinitarian formula lacking grammatical accuracy and also, more guardedly, on the existence of the antipodes. Virgil built the first great cathedral of Salzburg in 767-74 and evangelized the Slavs of Carinthia. The *Verbrüderungsbuch* which is still preserved in St Peter's, Salzburg, shows that he remained in close touch with Iona. He died on 29 November 784 and he was canonized in 1233, the only one of the early Irish missionaries to be raised to the altars by Rome.

Nearly a century after St Fergil came St Fintan of Rheinau. He is said in his ninth-century biography to have been carried off by Viking raiders to the Orkneys. He escaped from there to the Continent and went on pilgrimage to Rome. On the return journey to Ireland he visited the island of Rheinau in the Rhine near the Falls of Schaffhausen, and was so attracted by the religious life that he spent more than a quarter of a century there. He died there about 878. A Rheinau manuscript, now in the University Library of Zürich, is sometimes called the Fintan-Martyrologium. It contains portions of a Gelsasian sacramentary and missal and is thought to have been brought to Rheinau by St Fintan but the script is Continental.

With the setting-up of the reconstructed German empire in 962 the movement of Irish monks into the empire was intensified. Weisgerber speaks of *Eine Irenwelle an Maas, Mosel und Rhein* (An Irish wave on the Meuse, Moselle and Rhine). The new wave produced excellent religious and eager reformers, but with the decline of learning in the monasteries at home because of the Viking attacks and the increased secularization, it produce few scholars.

Even before he became Emperor, Otto I granted a charter to the monastery of Waulsort (now in southern Belgium) in 946.

It stated that Waulsort had been founded for pilgrims from Ireland who wished to live under the rule of St Benedict and that the abbot should always be an Irishman as long as there was one in the community. The first five abbots were all Irish – Maelchalainn, Cadroe (born in the Irish colony in Scotland and educated in Armagh), Godfrey, Immon and Forannan (967-82). Waulsort marked the culmination of the big swing-over, among the Irish *peregrini*, from Celtic to Benedictine monasticism.

It was the era of the Cluniac Reform of the Benedictines and Irish monks played a big part in its progress. Maelchalainn became abbot of St Michel in Thiérache till his death in 978 and sent a group of his monks in 961 to reform St Vincent's monastery in Laon. Cadroe moved to St Clement's, Metz in 953 for the purposes of reform. After his death in 978 he was succeeded by another Irish abbot Fingen who reformed St Vannes in Verdun in the 980s. Emperor Otto III granted a second monastery in Metz – San Symphorian – to the Irish in 992. 'to receive Irish monks as far as possible but if the Irish are lacking, the number of monks will always be kept up with recruits from other nations'. After Fingen's death Sirianus succeeded as abbot of the two Irish communities. The Irish then lost San Symphorian, but three further Irish abbots – Haymo, Widelo and Hagano, to give them the Germanized forms of their names – kept the Irish in control of St Clement's until 1057.

In Cologne the Irish also got possession of two churches in the tenth century. The famous monastery of Gross Sankt Martin, between the Cathedral and the Rhine, was presented to them in 975 and Minnbairenn became its first abbot. His successor Kilian became abbot also of St Pantaleon's, another of the renowned Romanesque churches of the city. The third abbot, Ailill (Elias), from Muckno in Co. Monaghan, met strong opposition and seems to have lost St Pantaleon's. His obit occurs in the *Annals of Ulster*, 1042: 'Ailill Mucnoma, cenn mhanach na nGoeidhel, in Colonia quievit', as do the obits of other Irishmen of the same period who died in the Cologne monastery. At least two further Irish abbots, Faelán and Alcaldus – perhaps more – maintained Irish control of St Martin's until the early twelfth century.

The three Irish Benedictine groups in Waulsort, Metz and Cologne must be allowed to represent also the Irish monks at Toul where they were supported by Bishop Gerard (963-94), and the Irish communities of Trier, Mainz and Würzburg which appeared during the eleventh century. A somewhat unique figure about whom scarcely anything is known was the saintly bishop John of Mecklenburg, who came from Ireland and was martyred in northern Germany in 1066.

The overthrow of the Vikings in Ireland from the beginning of the eleventh century on was a further step in reopening the Continental mainland to Irish pilgrims and monks. A royal pilgrim on his way to the Holy Land, named Colman, was hanged as a spy at Stockerau near Vienna on 17 July 1012. According to Irish tradition he was son of Maelseachlainn Mór and grandson of Brian Boru, two high-kings. His body was brought to Melk and around his tomb the great Benedictine Abbey arose from 1089 on. St Koloman(n) is now one of the patron saints of Austria and at least a score of Austrian churches and chapels are dedicated to him as well as nearly forty others in Bavaria and several in Jugo-Slavia and Hungary. In fact a number of villages have been called after him in Southern Germany and Northern Italy. Colman was unfortunate among Irish pilgrims, for more than half a dozen Irish kings reached Rome safely on pilgrimage in the eleventh century and the tomb of Brian Boru's son, Donnchadh, who died there in 1064, is still identifiable in Santo Stefano in Rotundo. Before the end of that century a permanent Irish Benedictine community was in residence in Rome.

Side by side with Rome and Jerusalem, Germany strongly attracted Irish pilgrims in the eleventh century. Among the *inclusi* who led lives of prayer and penance, walled up in their cells beside some well-known monastery, one must mention Animchad (d.1043) in Fulda, Paternus (d.1058) in Paderborn and, of course, Maelbríde who was placed under the penance of perpetual exile in Movilla in 1056 and spent three years in Cologne, ten years in Fulda and thirteen years in Mainz, where he died on 11 January 1082/3. His famous chronicle is now in the Vatican Library.

Maelbríde was known in Germany as Marianus Scottus, and it is therefore necessary to distinguish him carefully from another Irish priest of that name who founded the Irish Benedictine community of Regensburg. The latter was presumably a Donegal man and bore the family name of Muiredach Mac Robhartaigh. When he reached Regensburg with a few companions en route to Rome on pilgrimage in 1067, he was persuaded by an Irish *inclusus* there named Muirchertach to settle down in that city. The Benedictine nuns in 1076 gave the group the old church of Weih-Sankt-Peter outside the city walls, where Marianus continued his avocation of scribe until his death about 1080. At least two of his manuscripts still survive, St Paul's Epistles (1079) in the State Library in Vienna and Patristic notes (1080) in Fort Augustus Monastery in Scotland.

With many new recruits the *Scotti* of Regensburg decided to build a new church and monastery which were dedicated to St James in 1111. They sought the protection of Wratislaw, King of Bohemia, for their roving representatives in Poland, and even sent a monk on a bear-hunting expedition to Kiev in order to provide funds for the roof. The King and his nobles sent them back with bear-skins worth one hundred marks. The third abbot, Giolla Críost Mac Carthaigh, came to Ireland on a collecting tour about 1150 and the O'Brien and Mac Carthy princes of Munster presented him with two hundred marks, an enormous sum for that era, worth about 0,000 in today's money. Two small priories, one in Rosscarbery and one near Cashel, were set up as novitiates for the Regensburg Benedictines.

St James's Abbey became the mother-house of eight new Irish houses in the German-speaking part of Europe – Würzburg (1134-9), Nürnberg (1140?), Konstanz (1142), Vienna (1156) and Erfurt (end of twelfth century) as abbeys and Memmingen (1161), Eichstätt (1183) and Kelheim (1230s) as priories. They were usually called *Schottenklöster* and were all linked together as a separate branch of the Benedictine order with the abbot of St James, Regensburg as superior. Monks from Vienna made a foundation in Kiev at the end of the century, mainly for Vienna merchants who had settled there as traders, but they were forced to withdraw by the Mongol invasions in 1241. It was the most easterly foundation of the *Scotti*.

The setting-up of the Schottenklöster in the twelfth century gave Ireland an extra bridge to Europe. Henceforth the traffic was two-way. European influences poured into Ireland with the Cistercians and Augustinian Canons (and in the next century the new religious orders), the institution of the Irish dioceses and parishes, the reforming synods, the appointment of Papal Legates. Irish clerics in turn were frequently travellers to Europe – *ad limina* visits to Rome, journeys there for the pallium and the Lateran Councils. Inevitably some Irish churchmen died on the Continent with a reputation for sanctity – Malachy in Clairvaux in 1148, Conchobhar Mac Conchoille in Chambéry in 1175, Lorcan O'Toole in Eu in 1180.

For centuries the Schottenklöster struggled on, and many of their inmates reached a high standard of sanctity and learning. In Etting near Ingolstadt and in Griesstetten near Dietfort there is a strong local cult of two groups of saints – the *Drei Elende Heiligen* – the three 'miserable' or pilgrim saints. As the Eichstätt Schottenklöster had a hospice in Etting, and St James, Regensburg had land in Griesstetten, it is thought that the six saintly figures may have been Irish Benedictine monks. The Schottenklöster in Vienna gave at least two rectors to the University there and had a fine library and scriptorium. Nürnberg, Regensburg and probably Vienna had their own schools.

But gradually lack of recruits and funds caught up with the Schottenklöster. At the same time the growing chauvinism of some of the German States found it harder to accept that foreigners should hold large estates and fine religious houses in their midst. Many allegations began to be made against the Irish monks – ignorance, neglect of their spiritual duties, drunkenness, immorality. One after another the houses were taken over by German Benedictine communities: Memmingen shortly after 1400, Nürnberg and Vienna in 1418, Würzburg in 1497, Eichstätt before 1500. Only three communities were left after 1500 – Regensburg, Erfurt and Konstanz – and their end came in 1515 when the civil government and Rome were both persuaded by Scottish priests that *they* were the genuine *Scotti* and the Irish were usurpers. Hence the last Irish monks were expelled and their former monasteries handed over to the Scotch. Würzburg was also granted to the Scotch in 1595, but all the houses were secularized during the Napoleonic period. The Scotch made a final attempt to save Regensburg in the nineteenth century by turning it into a seminary for training secular priests for Scotland, but since 1862 it has been the Major Seminary for the diocese of Regensburg.

Epilogue

The story of the Irish monks on the Continent is an inspiring one and needs no embellishment. The exaggerations of some writers in the past have now given way to a more balanced and more accurate appraisal. A considerable amount of new material has been brought to light in recent decades. Commemorations such as those of St Columban in Luxeuil in 1950, St Fiachra in Meaux in 1970, St Fergil in Salzburg in 1984 were accompanied by scholarly lectures and discussions, whose publication added enormously to our knowledge of these three Irish saints and several of their contemporaries. A vast amount of research on the Schottenklöster has been carried out during the past few decades, particularly in Germany. The Europa-Zentrum in Tübingen has organized three notable *Colloquia*, one in Tübingen in 1979, the others in Dublin in 1981 and 1984, and has thereby been enabled to publish a series of splendid volumes on various aspects of Irish-Continental relations. A scholarly *vue d'ensemble*, which would take account of all the recent research, is now required. It may surprise many to learn that the most recent overview of the whole subject has been published during 1987 in Polish. It still awaits translation into other languages.

Despite recent research many problems remain unsolved. I mention only a few to whet the appetite. One thing which is bound to strike all students of the subject is the smallness of the female contribution. Apart from St Dympna of Gheel, whose Irish origin is not certain and whose departure from her native area took place in unique circumstances, no other nun figures prominently among the Irish saints honoured on the Continent. It is true that communities of nuns do not seem to have been very numerous in early Christian Ireland. Yet St Patrick himself mentions some of his converts who became 'virgins for Christ'. One would have expected later that some of the daughters of St Brigid, St Moninne, St Ita or St Samthann would have joined their brothers in exile. Double monasteries on the model of Kildare were not unknown on the Continent, and Nivelles, the royal convent, was much frequented by Irish priests. The circle of Sedulius at Liège, judged by manuscripts written there, was particularly devoted to St Brigid. Churches in honour of the saint still stand or once stood in Fosse, Liège, Cologne, Henndorf (near Salzburg), Piacenza and throughout Brittany. Pilgrimages in her honour are still held in Fosse and Amay in Belgium. As recently as 1977 a seventh-century sarcophagus with Celtic ornamentation showing a female figure carrying a crozier and bearing the name *Sta Chrodoara* was discovered during excavations in the Church of Amay. All this suggests that we may yet discover evidence for some group of Irish female missionaries on the Continent.

Another surprising feature of the work of the *Scotti Peregrini* is that, wherever they went, language difficulties never seem to have caused them a problem. Columban was equally at home in Luxeuil, Bregenz and Bobbio, although three distinct languages, at least in embryonic form, must have been spoken there. Gall's acquaintance with the language of the Alemanni served him in good stead around Lake Constance. Some of the missionaries were so fluent in Latin and Irish that they could write very sophisticated poetry in either language. Their learning made them the first to introduce the writings of Isidore of Seville to the learned classes of France and Germany and probably the first to give the names Caspar, Melchior and Balthasar to the Magi. But what language did they use in preaching to the uneducated masses?

A third problem arises in connexion with the continuity of the Irish mission to the Continent. While not suggesting that the fervour of its members always glowed with the intensity of a Columban or a Fergil, I hope I have made it clear that there was no period from the sixth to the sixteenth century in which a group of *Scotti Peregrini* was not active somewhere on the European mainland. In the sixteenth century the Reformation ensured that the Schottenklöster would be followed by more than thirty 'Irish Colleges' throughout Spain, France, Belgium and Italy, which maintained an Irish religious presence on the Continental mainland until Napoleonic times and beyond. One has to ask, therefore, if some element of the *Wanderlust* always associated with the Irish people did not contribute to the exodus of Irish monks and scholars from the beginning. *Gratia perficit naturam* seems to sum up the position rather well. A nation which was in all centuries prepared for foreign travel, adventure and self-improvement was never without individuals who were raised to a supernatural level by God's grace and the desire to abandon all worldly things for Christ. In God's design they were enabled to produce what was surely the greatest achievement of the Irish Church and people.

Bibliography

Barry, P.J., *Die Zustände im Wiener Schottenkloster vor der Reform des Jahres 1418*, Aichach 1927.
'Irish Benedictines in Nuremberg', in *Studies*, Dublin, 21-22, 1932-3.
Bauerreiss, R., *Kirchengeschichte Bayerns*, 6 vols, St Ottilien, 1949-56.
Berardis, V., *Italy and Ireland in the Middle Ages*, Dublin, 1950.
Bieler, L., *Irland, Wegbereiter des Mittalters*, Olten-Lausanne-Frieiburg, 1962 (Eng. trans.: *Ireland, Harbinger of the Middle Ages*, London-Oxford-New York, 1963).
Binchy, D., 'The Irish Benedictine Congregation in Medieval Germany', in *Studies*, Dublin, 18, 1929.
Bischoff, B., 'Muridach doctissimus plebis, ein irischer Grammatiker des 9. Jhs', in *Celtica*, Dublin, 5, 1960.
'Il Monachesimo irlandese nei suoi rapporti col continente', in *Mittelalterichen Studien*, Stuttgart, 1, 1966.
'Irische Schreiber im Karolingerreich', in *Jean Scot Érigène et l'histoire de la philosophie*, Paris, 1977.
Breatnach, P.A. (ed.), *Die Regensburger Schottenlegende*, Munich, 1977.

'The Origins of the Irish Monastic Tradition at Ratisbon (Regensburg)', in *Celtica*, Dublin, 13, 1980.

Cappuyns, M., *Jean Scot Érigène, sa vie, son oeuvre, sa penséee*, Louvain-Paris, 1933.

Carney, J., 'Sedulius Scottus', in *Old Ireland*, Dublin, 1965.

Clark, J.M., *The Abbey of St Gall as a Centre of Literature and Art*, Cambridge, 1926.

Colgrave, B. and Mynors, R.A.B., *Bede's Ecclesiastical History of the English People*, Oxford, 1969.

Daniel-Rops (ed.), *Le Miracle irlandais*, Paris, 1956. (Eng. trans.: *The Miracle of Ireland*, Dublin, 1959).

David, P., 'Un recueil de conferences . . . MS.43 . . . de Cracovie', in *Revue Bénédictine*, 49, 1937.

Desbordes, J.M. (ed.), XIIᵉ Centenaire de Saint Fiacre: Actes du Congrès, Meaux, 1970.

Dienemann, J., *Der Kult des hl. Kilian im 8. und 9. Jahrhundert*, Würzburg, 1955.

Dilworth, M., 'Marianus Scotus, Scribe and Monastic Founder', in *Scottish Gaelic Studies*, Aberdeen, 10, 1965.
The Scots in Franconia, Edinburgh, 1974.

Dopsch, H., and Juffinger, R. (eds), *Virgil von Salzburg, Missionar und Gelehrter*, Salzburg, 1985.

Doyle, E.G. (ed.), *Sedulius Scottus: On Christian Rulers; and the Poems* (Eng. trans.), Binghamton (New York), 1983.

Dubois, M.M. (ed.), *Mélanges Colombaniens*, Paris, 1950.

Duft, J., 'Iromanie-Irophobie', in *Zeitsch. für Schweiz. Kirchengeschichte*, 50, 1956.
'Irland und der irische Einfluss auf das Festland', ibid, 51, 1957.
'Irische Einflüsse auf St Gallen und alemannien', in *Mönchtum, Episkopat und Adel zur Gründungszeit des Klosters Reichenau*, Sigmaringen, 1974.

Esposito, M., 'A Bibliography of the Latin Writers of Medieval Ireland', in *Studies*, Dublin, 2, 1913.
'An Irish Teacher at the Carolingian Court: Dicuil', in *Studies*, Dublin, 3, 1914.
'Notes on Latin Learning and Literature in Medieval Ireland', in *Hermathena*, Dublin, 45-50, 1930-37.

Fuhrmann, J., *Irish Medieval Monasteries on the Continent*, Washington, 1927.

Gougaud, L., *Gaelic Pioneers of Christianity*, Dublin, 1923.

Christianity in Celtic Lands, London, 1932.

Les Saints irlandais hors d'Irlande, Louvain-Oxford, 1936.

Grosjean, P., 'Notes d'hagiographie celtique: Chronologie de S. Feuillen', in *Anal. Bolland*, Brussels, 1957.

'Virgile de Salzbourg en Irlande', in *Anal. Bolland*, Brussels, 78, 1960.

Gwynn, A., 'Ireland and Würzburg in the Middle Ages', in *Ir. Eccles. Rec.*, Dublin, 1952.

'The Continuity of the Irish Tradition at Würzburg', in *Herbipolis Jubilans*, Würzburg, 1952.

'Ireland and the Continent in the Eleventh Century', in *Ir. Hist. Studies*, Dublin, March, 1953.

'Some Notes on the History of the Irish and Scottish Benedictine Monasteries in Germany', in *Innes Review*, 1954.

'New Light on St Kilian', in *Ir. Eccles. Rec.*, Dublin, 1957.

Hammermayer, L., 'Die irischen Benedictiner Schotten-klöster in Deutschland . . . vom 12. bis 16. Jarhrhundert', in *Stud. u. Mitt. Ben. Ord.*, 87, 1976.

Hellmann, S., *Sedulius Scottus*, Munich, 1906.

Hughes, K., 'The Changing Theory and Practice of Irish Pilgrimage', in *Jnl. of Eccles. Hist.*, 1960.

Joynt, M., *The Life of St Gall*, London, 1927.

Kelly, J.F., 'The Decline of Irish Monasticism', in *Amer. Ben. Rev.*, 31, 1980.

Kenney, J.F., *The Sources for the Early History of Ireland: Ecclesiastical. An Introduction and Guide*, New York, 1929 (updated 1979).

Koch, M., *Sankt Fridolin und sein Biograph Balther*, Zurich, 1959.

Krusch, B. (ed.), 'Ionae Vitae Sanctorum Columbani, etc.', in MGH SS. rer. Germ. 37, Hannover-Leipzig, 1905.

Laporte, J. (ed.), *Le Penitentiel de Saint Columban*, Tournai-Paris, 1958.

Levison, W., 'Die Iren und die Fränkische Kirche', in *Hist. Zeitsch.*, 109, 1912.

Löwe, H. (ed.), *Die Iren und Europa im früheren Mittelalter*, 2 vols, Stuttgart, 1982.

Maestri, A., *Il culto di San Colombano in Italia*, Piacenza, 1955.

Mai, P., 'Das Schottenkloster St Jakob zu Regensburg im Wandel der Zeiten', in *100 Jahre Priesterseminar in St Jakob zu Regensburg 1872-1972*, Regensburg, 1972.

Marnell, W.H., *Light from the West: The Irish Mission and the Emergence of Modern Europe*, New York, 1978.

Meyer-Sickendiek, I., *Gottes gelehrte Vaganten*, Stuttgart, 1980.

Murphy, G., 'Scotti Peregrini', in *Studies*, Dublin, 1928.

Ní Chatháin, P. and Richter, M., *Irland und Europa: Die Kirche im Frühmittelalter*, Stuttgart, 1984.

Ó Briain, F., 'The Expansion of Irish Christianity to 1200', in *Irish Hist. Studies*, September 1944.

Ó Cuív, B., 'Medieval Irish Scholars and Classical Literature', in *Proc. R.I.A.*, Dublin, 81C9, 1981.

Ó Fiaich, T., *Irish Cultural Influence in Europe, VIth to XIIth Century*, Dublin, 1967.

Columbanus in his Own Words, Dublin, 1974.

Gaelscrínte san Eoraip, Dublin, 1986.

O'Meara, J.J., *Eriugena*, Cork, 1969.

O'Meara, J.J. and Bieler, L., *The Mind of Eriugena*, Dublin, 1973.

O'Neill, P., 'The Background to the Cambrai Homily', in *Ériu*, Dublin, 32, 1981.

Ó Riain-Raedel, D., 'Aspects of the Promotion of Irish Saints' Cults in Medieval Germany', in *Zeitsch. für Celt. Phil.*, 1982.

Prinz, F., *Frühes Mönchtum in Frankénreich*, Munich-Vienna, 1965.

Rapf, C.R., *Das Schottenstift* (Vienna), Vienna-Hamburg, 1974.

Ryan J., *Irish Monks in the Golden Age*, Dublin, 1963.

Scholle, J., *Das Erfurter Schottenkloster*, Düsseldorf, 1932.

Schreiber, G., *Irland im deutschen und abendländischen Sakraltum*, Cologne-Opladen, 1956.

Selmer, C. (ed.), *Navigatio Sancti Brendani abbatis*, Univ. Notre Dame, 1959.

Sheldon-Williams, I.P. (ed.), *Scotti Eriugenae Periphyseon (De Divisione Naturae)*, Dublin, 1968 on.

Smit, J.W., *Studies on the Language and Style of Columba the Younger (Columbanus)*, Amsterdam, 1971.

Snieders, I., 'L'hagiographie irlandaise', in *Revue d'Hist. Ecc.*, Louvain, 1928.

Stockmeier, P., *Bischof Korbinian von Freising*, Bayer. Bistumspatrone, 1966.

Stokes, M., *Six Months in the Apennines in Search of Vestiges of the Irish Saints in Italy*, London, 1892.

Three Months in the Forests of France: A Pilgrimage in Search of Vestiges of Irish Saints, London, 1895.

Strzelczyk, J., *Iroszkoci w Kulturze Sredniowiecznej Europy*, Warsaw, 1987.

Tierney, J.J. (ed.), *Liber de Mensura Orbis Terrae* (Dicuil), Dublin, 1967.

Tommasini, A.A. *I Santi irlandesi in Italia*, Milan, 1932. (Eng. trans., *The Irish Saints in Italy*, London, 1937.

Tosi, M. (ed.), *Vita Columbani et discipulorum ejus*, Piacenza, 1965.

Traube, L., *Perrona Scotorum*, Munich, 1920.

Van der Essen, L., *Étude critique et littéraire sur les Vitae des saints mérovingiens de l'ancienne Belgique*, Louvain-Paris, 1907.

Waddell, H., *The Wandering Scholars*, London, 1927.

Walker, G.Ś.M. (ed.), *Sancti Columbani Opera*, Dublin, 1957.

Wattenbach, W., 'Die Kongregation der Schottenklöster in Deutschland' in *Zeitsch. für Christ. Arch. und Kunst*, 1859. (Eng. trans. in *Ulster Jnl. of Arch.*, 1859).

Weisgerber, L., 'Die Spuren der irischen Mission in der Entwicklung der deutschen Sprache', in *Rhein. Vierteljahrsbl.*, 1952.

'Eine Irenwelle an Maas, Mosel und Rhein in Ottonischer Zeit?', in *Aus Geschichte und Landeskunde*, Bonn, 1960.

Wendehorst, A., 'Die heiligen Kilian, Kolonat und Totnan', in *Bavaria Sancta*, Regensburg, 1, 1970.

Whitelock, D., etc. (ed.), *Ireland in Early Medieval Europe: Studies in Memory of Kathleen Hughes*, Cambridge, 1982.

Wittstadt, K., *Sankt Kilian, Leben-Martyrium-Wirkung*, Würzburg, 1984.

Zimmer, H., *The Irish Element in Mediaeval Culture*, New York-London, 1891.

Celtic Monks and the Culdee Reform

Peter O'Dwyer

Christianity had become the dominant religion in Ireland round the middle of the sixth century. It was structured round bishops and clergy. Gradually a change developed as leadership passed from bishops to abbots of large monasteries. In time the offices of bishop and abbot were divided. Colum Cille, one of the most famous of the monastic founders, was an abbot but not a bishop. This development from an episcopal to a monastic organisation may be attributed to a certain Welsh influence due to monks like David and Cadoc who were highly respected in Ireland, to the generosity of Irish rulers in bestowing land on men like Ciaran of Clonmacnoise, and possibly also to the influence of men like Augustine of Hippo and Martin of Tours who lived a communal life with their clergy. By the year 600 abbots were commemorated more frequently in the Annals than bishops.[1]

Columbanus, the first great Irish missionary abbot to Europe, sums up the monastic daily round in the advice 'Pray daily, fast daily, study daily, work daily'. The abbot was

---

[1]   Patrick J. Corish, *The Irish Catholic Experience* (Dublin, 1985), 4-6.

assisted by a *secnab* (second in command), a bursar, cook, scribe, cellarer and various grades of workmen. Large monasteries had a bishop who was highly respected and conferred Orders on some members of the community. Anchorites, who were often scribes, tended to a more eremitical life of prayer and study. A great number of monasteries developed in the sixth and seventh centuries, with some very large ones at Armagh, Clonard, Clonmacnoise, Kildare, Emly, Lismore and Iona. These monasteries had a deep influence on the country as a whole but especially on the people who lived near them.

It is an unwritten law in monastic history that Orders need a reform at least every two centuries. This would account for the culdee (*céle dé*) reform, the early stages of which may be dated to the second quarter of the eighth century when Maelruain, who was the real father of the movement, was a young student in Darinis, Co. Waterford. *Céle dé* means 'servant of God', and we shall look at Irish monasticism through the literature of the reform movement which eventually took this title for its own name.

This movement, which resulted in the foundation of the monastery of Tallaght (AD 774) by Maelruain, was clearly aimed at enforcing strict observance among the members who adhered to it. An examination of the literature of the reform[2] throws little light on its precise nature, but it does show that its scope was to counterbalance a tendency towards laxity in the older churches. We notice a certain enmity between Maeldithruib, a disciple of Maelruain

---

[2]   These are four sources: a) the Franciscan transcript of an older document probably written in the Early Irish period. It was made by John Colgan OFM and is an early modern Irish paraphrase which is published by E.J. Gwynn in *Hermathena*, XLIV, Sec.Vol. Supplement. I refer to it as F. b) 'The Rule of the Céli Dé, *Hermathena* XLIV. Supplement. I refer to it as C. c) 'The Monastery of Tallaght', *Proceedings of the Royal Irish Academy* (PRIA) XXIX Sect.C. no.5 pp.115-179. The language is Early Irish. I refer to it as T. d) 'The Penitential' edited by E.J. Gwynn, *Ériu* VII, 121-195. I call it Pen. 'The Irish Penitentials' (*Scriptores Latini Hiberniae V*) edited by L. Bieler has an Appendix by D.A. Binchy which gives a more recent translation of this Penitential. Binchy has also published 'The Old-Irish Table of Penitential Commutations, (*Ériu* XIX, 47-72) and has included a translation in 'The Irish Penitentials', 277-283 and adds that it is almost certain that the Table was compiled in Tallaght or possibly in Terryglass in the eighth century.

from Terryglass, Co. Tipperary, and members of the older churches who had not performed their duties properly.[3] We do not know whether these duties were the personal obligations of the religious to his monastery or of clergy to the laity. In these documents we notice the use of the words *fír-clérech*[4] (true-cleric) and *fír-manach*[5] (true monk), possibly to distinguish them from their laxer brethren.

It is interesting to note that other similar reforms were introduced elsewhere in the eighth century. Bede, in his letter of 734 to Egbert, metropolitan of York, complains of lack of celibacy among the priests, of the ignorance of the people and of unattended country-folk. He also complains of lack of chastity in monasteries, many of which were ruled by noblemen or soldiers who sought to increase their possessions.[6] Chrodegang, bishop of Metz, composed a Rule c.755. His main purpose was to regularize groups of canons into a community to serve his cathedral. To my mind this Rule had little influence on Irish monasticism.[7] Kathleen Hughes would relate the culdee reform with that of St Benedict of Aniane. The latter founded his monastery (of Aniane) in 784, the fourth year of his religious life.[8] But Maelruain, who was considered to be the head of the reform in Ireland, had moved from Darinis, on the Blackwater near Youghal, to Tallaght in 774,[9] and since he died in 792[10] his influence must have been at its highest when Benedict was a mere stripling.

The origin of this eighth-century reform is, then, to be sought in Ireland. The leaders, Maelruain and Dublittir, abbot

[3]   F.4. F.35
[4]   F.62. T.13.
[5]   Pen. *De Gula* 150, 13. Binchy translates as 'regular monk'. *Ir. Pen.* 261, 15. In Whitley Stokes *Félire Oengusso* (London, 1905) (henceforth FO) it us used in connection with Fothad na Canóine, p.4 and in Charles Plummer *Irish Litanies* (London, 1925) (henceforth Ir.Lit.), p.60.
[6]   *Patrologia Latina* (ed. J.P. Migne) 95, cols 657-668.
[7]   Peter.O'Dwyer, *Céle Dé* (Dublin, 1981) (henceforth CD), 2-3.
[8]   Kathleen Hughes, *The Church in Early Irish Society* (London, 1966) (henceforth CEIS), 179-180.
[9]   *The Annals of the Four Masters* (O'Donovan, Dublin, 1851) (henceforth FM) 769.
[10]   *The Annals of Ulster* (Hennessy, Dublin, 1887) (henceforth AU) 791. FM 787 calls him a bishop, as do the *Annals of Innisfallen* (MacAirt, Dublin, 1951) (henceforth AI) 792. v. also CD 31 n.2.

of Finglas, were obviously inspired by the spirit which they found in religious such as Ferdácrích, abbot of Darinis (747),[11] Mac Oige of Lismore, Co. Waterford (753)[12] and Samhthann, abbess of Clonbroney, Co. Meath (739),[13] who are treated as models in the documents of the reform.

One notes that the Annals indicate that there was a considerable increase in violence, the murder of abbots and bishops, and the burning of churches, in the eighth century.[14] While it is true that the annalists begin to expand the number and content of entries round the middle of that century, the following century does show a very notable increase in violence. The eighth century also saw the introduction of the hereditary abbot. Among the early instances was Moenach abbot of Slane, who was son of Colman, who had been abbot of the same monastery.[15] This practice tended to increase and naturally had an adverse effect on monastic life. The reform aimed at restoring monastic studies to their rightful place. It also insisted very strongly on poverty and forbade members of the reform to hoard goods. It is well to bear in mind that at this period the church elsewhere was experiencing similar difficulties with local rulers and that the Papacy itself was later dominated by Italian family interests.

Origin and Diffusion of the *Céle Dé* Reform

In its broad sense the term *céle dé* is the equivalent of *servus Dei* and was convertible with the term *manach* (monk). But in the Milan gloss 30ᶜ3, dated c.800, we find a more precise meaning. 'He whom anyone loves and helps is thrown afterwards into the possession of the man who helps him, as it is said, that man is a servant of God (*céle dé*)'. This gloss helps us to get a good idea òf the fundamental meaning of the term

---

[11]   AU 746.
[12]   ibid. 752.
[13]   ibid. 738.
[14]   CD 5-6.
[15]   AU 772. FM 768.

which is total self-abandonment to the loving providence of God.

While Maelruain was the principal leader of the reform, its initial inspiration began in the south of Ireland in the district round Darinis – Lismore – Daire na bhFlann (near Cashel), probably in the second quarter of the eighth century. The canonical collection known as the *Hibernensis* had Ruben of Darinis and Cucuimhne of Iona as its compilers. Though non-official in origin it had come to be held in high favour before long. It is a compilation of aphorisms and enactments, each subdivided into a number of chapters, and it deals with matters pertaining to Christian discipline, the religious life and the care of souls. Its material is drawn chiefly from Scripture, from the decisions of foreign and local councils and from the works of the Fathers.

This work, which provided for the spiritual and canonical direction of ecclesiastics and laity and is the most canonical collection of Celtic origin of the eighth century,[16] must have been well known to Ferdácrích, Maelruain's tutor and uncle from Daire Eidnech, or Daire na bhFlann as it is later called.[17] The reform documents look back with great respect to him as abbot of Darinis, to Mac Oige, to Mocholmóc Ua Liatháin of Lismore and to Caencomhrac, who was also from this district. Obviously they were noted for their sincerity and wisdom in spiritual matters.

Oentú Maelruain (Maelruain's Union)

An *oentú* or unity was a close relationship between communities or between particular persons. The 'unity' of Maelruain in the *Book of Leinster* consists of twelve names in addition to Maelruain's, which comes at the head. Maeltuile is second on the list. The fact that the latter had a *dísert* (hermitage) is

[16] *Christianity in Celtic Lands* (Gougaud, London, 1932) (henceforth CCL, 278-281.
[17] *Vitae Sanctorum Hiberniae* (Plummer, Oxford, 1910) (henceforth VSH), II, 250. It was at this site that the Derrynavlan chalice was found.

significant, as Kenney rightly points out that both *dísert* and anchorite typify this reform.[18] We know practically nothing about Maeltuile except that his *dísert* was near Lough Ennell in Co. Westmeath. Maelanfaidh, abbot of Darinis, is next on the list. He lived more than a century before Maelruain and is included probably because the latter had special reverence for him. Flann Mac Faircheallaigh (825) is contemporaneous with the reform movement. He was abbot of Lismore, Emly and Cork.[19] Flann Mac Duibthuinne is most likely the Flann Duibhchenna who appears in the Tallaght documents and in common with his namesake hails from Daire na bhFlann, which probably owes its change of name from Daire Eidnech to Daire na bhFlann to them. The next, Flannan, may be from Cill Áird, Co. Clare. He died in 778[20] or he may be a Flann possibly connected with Daire na bhFlann if we follow the second version of the *oentú* in the *Book of Leinster*. We know a good deal about the next member, Maeldithruib, since he lived in the Tallaght community for a period under the direction of the master and returned later to Terryglass. We owe much of the information about Tallaght in Maelruain's time to him.[21] He was a young, enthusiastic and eager questioner who had great respect for his 'hero'. He wished to have access to all the sacred writings which had come to Ireland, to serve in the most perfect community, to discuss matters with Maelruain and to earn the blessing of his community. These wishes, more or less, contain the central idea of the movement. He died anchorite and *suí* (wise man) of Terryglass in 840.[22] Dalbach, who died c.800, belonged to Cúl Collainge, near Castlelyons, Co. Cork.[23] The next member of the 'unity' is a rather strange character, Feidlimid mac Crímthainn, born in 770, who became king of Cashel in 820. His marauding exploits,[24] which included the

---

[18]   *Sources of Eary Irish History* (Kenney, New York, 1929) (henceforth Kenney), 468.
[19]   AI 825.
[20]   AI 778.
[21]   FM 769.
[22]   AU 810. FM 806.
[23]   CD 40 n.6.
[24]   ibid. 41-43.

burning of monasteries, set him apart from the other members and make him a rather unlikely model, though Prof. F.J. Byrne classes him as 'a powerful champion of the céle dé.[25] Diarmait, the founder of Dísert Diarmata (Castledemermot, Co. Kildare) in 812, was probably very deeply motivated by the reform.[26] This monastic school, with its Scriptural Crosses, and the probability that Diarmait was the scribe of the Milan glosses, shows it as an important centre of Scripture studies.[27] The last name in the oentú is Oengus, a very gifted man. A considerable number of his writings still survive. It is quite probable that he received his early training in Cluain Eidnech in Co. Laois. He came to Tallaght to benefit from Maelruain's direction. He had a dísert near the river Nore in Co. Kilkenny. The story tells us that on his way to Tallaght he stopped at Cúl Beannchair, Co. Laois, where he got the idea of writing a martyrology.[28] Having arrived at Tallaght he concealed his identity and was given heavy work in the kiln. Finding one of Maelruain's pupils who could not learn his lesson, he helped the boy to such an extent and that Maelruain found out who he was and brought him into the monastery and chided him for concealing himself.[29] Maelruain and he collaborated in liturgical compositions and Oengus had great respect for his master. Some time later he returned to Cluain Eidnech, where he died on March 11th. The year is either 819, 824 or 830.[30]

The 'unity' consists of thirteen persons,[31] probably based on the grouping of Christ and the twelve apostles. The names point to a Munster origin. With the advent of Maelruain the

[25]   F.J. Byrne, *Irish Kings and High-Kings* (London, 1973), 226.
[26]   CD 43-44.
[27]   Martin MacNamara, *Psalter Text and Psalter Study in the Early Irish Church (600-1200)* PRIA. Sect.C (1973), 221-222.
[28]   FO 8-10.
[29]   ibid. 12.
[30]   CD 46 n.7.
[31]   CD 36 where it also notes that the number thirteen is frequently found in Scottish Culdee communities of a later period. For information on these, which lie outside of the scope of this chapter, v. Wm Reeves 'On the Céle Dé', RIA Trans. XXIV 27-55. D.E. Easson, *Medieval Religious Houses, Scotland* (London, 1957), 3. M.V. Haye, *A Chain of Error in Scottish History* (London, 1927), 73-75.

'unity' found a firm base in Tallaght and influenced Finglas. Maelruain attracted disciples from other parts of Tipperary, Laois, Cork and Westmeath and the 'unity' spread to Kildare, Clonmacnoise, Iona and Loch Cré, near Roscrea. Louth and Clonfert are also quoted in the Tallaght documents. It found its longest duration in Clonmacnoise, Terryglass and Armagh.[32]

The period of the reform is marked by what has been described as the anchorite movement, the aim of which was to give the monk the opportunity for solitude close to the monastery, often in the *dísert*. His life was a poor one. Prayer, work and reading and especially growth in charity were his daily occupations. The core of the anchorite rule was charity, self-denial, useful occupation and perseverance. This useful occupation took the form of intellectual labour or, frequently, of scribal work. In the ninth century we find twenty-one anchorites who were also scribes listed in the annals. Though Armagh and Clonmacnoise are the most frequently mentioned, it is obvious that the production in Tallaght of the *Martyrology of Tallaght* and the *Martyrology of Oengus*, not to mention the *Stowe Missal*, required considerable scribal activity among the members of the reform.

The *Irish Penitential*, published by E.J. Gwynn, is very probably a work of the reform.[33] Most of the document is taken up with lists of penances for various sins. The listing of sins follows the division into the seven capital sins. In addition to the list of penances to be imposed on penitents, cleric or lay, each chapter of the *Penitential* has a body of positive and very helpful teaching. Speaking of abstinence it lists its fruits as spiritual joy, decency of body, purity of soul, silence, appreciation of wisdom, increased intelligence and application to the mysteries of God. To overcome gluttony it recommends moderate fasting, remorse of heart, sparse meals, frequent self- examination, watching, feeding the poor and hungry, confinement at certain hours with a specified allowance, and finally patience. Similar positive practices

[32]   AU 921, 1164, 1479. CD 25-27.
[33]   *Ériu* 7, 122-123.

and mentalities are recommended to overcome the other vices.[34] An interesting example of the manner of spiritual direction is seen in Maelruain's statement to Maeldithruib, who came to him for guidance:

> The first year that a man comes under our guidance is treated by us as a year of purification, and you will have to spend three periods of forty days on bread and water, except for taking a drink of whey on Sundays and mixing the water with milk-whey in the Summer Lent only . . . When you put yourself under the judgment or control of another seek out the fire that will burn you fiercest (that is he who will spare you least).[35]

Study, and in particular study of the psalter, was of prime importance.[36]

> This is the most excellent of all labours, to wit, labour in piety; for the kingdom of heaven is granted to him who directs study and to him who studies, and to him who supports the pupil who is studying.[37]

Diet

Considerations of food occupy almost one-third of the Tallaght documents. Excessive mortification was discountenanced. A regular measured pittance was recommended. Each one was to regulate his own allowance. If the general diet regime was too strict the abbot was to see that the quality was improved. The daily allowance was a half-loaf of bread with a quarter of something else which is unspecified, a few ounces (selann) of butter or honey and a ration of drink. But it is difficult to get any adequate idea of what was allowed and what quantity might be taken. Pottage was permitted, as

---

[34] Pierre J. Payer has a very interesting article 'The Humanism of the Penitentials and The Continuity of the Penitential Tradition', *Medieval Studies* Vol.XLVI (1984), 340-354.
[35] F. 77.
[36] CD 66-67.
[37] C 63.

was a slice of fish, beestings, cheese, eggs and half a dozen large apples. Meat was not allowed in Tallaght, though other monasteries were allowed game, wild swine, deer or fowl. Beer was also forbidden in Tallaght, though not in Finglas. But the fasting diet, bread and wheywater, was severe.

They ate together in community and the meal was accompanied by the reading of the Gospel. The reading also included *The Rules* (of founders) and the *Miracles of the Saints* (probably early lives of Irish saints). From the maxims on which the diet regulations were based, and also from the concession made to those who had heavy work or who were sick, the rule seems to have been tempered to the individual and each man's allowance was sufficient to enable him to perform his duties. This was specially true in the case of priests who experienced difficulty in offering Mass.[38]

Closely allied to the question of food was the acceptance of gifts. The benefactors often expected easier terms of forgiveness. Monks or anchorites had doubts as to whether they should accept food from their laxer brethren. But Hilary, a reform monk in Loch Cré, received bread from the less strict monks of Roscrea and Maelruain was also of the opinion that the culdees had a right to this support. Others accepted gifts but gave them to the poor.[39]

In the matter of apartments each culdee had his own cubicle and the monastery provided facilities for taking a bath.[40] Monks were warned by Samhthann of Clonbroney to be very careful in their association with women, religious or lay.[41] Maelruain told Cornán, an anchorite and a piper on whom 'lay the grace of God', that he could not listen to his music as his 'ears are not lent to earthly music that they may be lent to the music of heaven'.[42] On the other hand there was general festivity in the paschal season and relaxation in the matter of food and vigils. The visit of a venerable ecclesiastic might also be the occasion for a more wholesome repast.[43]

[38]   CD 68-81.
[39]   CD 81-82
[40]   T 15. T 45
[41]   T 61
[42]   T 10
[43]   CD 85-86.

Liturgy and the Spiritual Life

Mass was offered on Sundays, Thursdays and on great feasts. All were expected to attend and the penance for absenting oneself from Sunday Mass was the recitation of the 'three fifties' (psalms or more likely *paters*) standing with eyes shut in an enclosed house.[44] Weekly reception of the Eucharist was the norm for the *céle dé*, but this was achieved only on a gradual basis over a period of some seven years. One was expected to receive Holy Communion from one's confessor. Reception of the Eucharist was a help towards releasing souls from Purgatory. There was a difference of opinion as to whether *viaticum* should be given *in articulo mortis* to those who had lived bad lives even though at the end they did renounce their sins. The old fathers used to say that the repentance was mere dread of death. Others, notably Colcu, held that the Eucharist should given if the sorrow seemed to come from the heart. 'Let God be the judge' was his advice.[45]

In the matter of confession one must distinguish between sacramental and minor confession (*min-coibsiu*) which was made to an elder who might not be in Orders, on the lines of 'Confess your sins to one another' (James 5, 16). Maelruain wished his monks to consult their confessor (*anamarchara*) once a year at least.[46] Columbanus had advised that confession should precede the reception of the Eucharist.[47] A confessor was expected to be well versed in the rules laid down in Scripture and in the Rules of the saints.

The actual confession was very exacting and all-embracing. Bad confessions seem to have been fairly frequent, so much so that Hilary of Loch Cré abandoned the office of confessor. Many confessors were worried as to whether the penance would be performed. Frequent confession was not considered very profitable if the relapses were frequent.

---

[44] F 85. C 32 has fifty (psalms?).
[45] CD 88-90.
[46] CD 90.
[47] *Pen. Columbani* can.42. *Ir.Pen.* 106, 30. cf. also *Archiv für Celtische Lexicographie* (Stokes and Meyer 1898-1907), III, 319 n.82.

The Old-Irish Table of Penitential Commutations (*De Arreis*) which allowed for substitute penances was helpful where the sick were concerned. This document also gives valuable insights which should be taken into account when reading the *Penitential*. The final commutation 'atones for every [kind of] sin [if] accompanied by keen and heartfelt repentance . . . and heals him who transgresses against his clerical Orders provided there be keen repentance'.[48] The *min-coibsiu* was a very valuable exercise. If the confessor were not at hand it could be made to a *mac-légind* (ecclesiastic) or to a *mac-clérech* (cleric) provided the penitent performed the penance prescribed. In these documents it is very difficult at times to determine whether it is sacramental confession or a 'confession of faults'.[49]

Prayer

As Kathleen Hughes mentioned in relating the culdee reform with that of Benedict of Aniane, intensification of the life of prayer was common to both. But in any reform the various practices or rules must have as their purpose to deepen the prayer-life of the community. Columbanus had stated in his Rule that a man became a monk *uni Deo adhaerere hac in tellure* (to unite himself on this earth to the one God).[50] This is done mainly by prayer, as the culdee reform expressed it: 'three profitable things in the day: prayer, labour and study'.[51] Maeldithruib asked Maelruain how he should rule himself. 'I bid thee', said Maelruain, 'to abide always where thou art wont to be. Meddle not with worldly disputes. Go not with any man to a lawcourt . . . but continue in prayer and pondering thy reading and in teaching, if there be any that desire to receive instruction from thee'.[52] The New Testament, especially the Gospel of St John and the book of the

[50] Ed. D.A. Binchy, *Ériu* XIX (1962) p.67 par.37.
[49] CD 93-94.
[50] *Reg.Coen.* XV. (Walker, *Sancti Columbani Opera*, Dublin, 1957), 168, 12-13.
[51] C 55
[52] F 12.

apostle, which may be the Acts of the Apostles or the writings of St Paul, were their constant reading.[53] The threefold division of the spiritual life was accepted in Ireland: 'In the church the foot is those who are in the purgative way; the hand is those who are in the purgative way more than the others; the eye is those who are in the contemplative way'.[54] In the *Triads of Ireland*[55] Tallaght and Finglas are called 'the two eyes of Ireland'. We naturally think of the pure eye of asceticism or of the eye as the symbol of knowledge referred to in the Apocalypse.[56] The reference could also embrace the literary-spiritual movement stimulated by these monasteries.

It is true that the Irish character is more attracted to vocal prayer and external practices. For the monk the prayer par excellence was the divine office and in the reform it consisted of eight hours, *iarmhéirghe* (night vigil), *maiden* (morning), *anteirt* (prime), terce, sext, none, vespers and compline (*fadg*). We are fortunate that Michael Curran has given us a good description of the development of the divine office in the early Irish church.[57] Several, if not all, of these hours were accompanied by the cross-vigil (*lúirech léire*) which was a penitential manner of praying with arms outstretched.[58] The *Hymnum dicat* was said several times in the day, as was the *Benedictus* Canticle (Lk 1, 67-79). *The Canticle of the Three Youths* (Dan. 3, 57-88) was also said daily. The ferial office was said daily even if it were a feastday when the saint's office was also said.[59] The penitential touch experienced in attending the office is found in the lines

> The wind over Hog's Back moans
> It takes the trees and lays them low,
> And shivering monks o'er frozen stones
> To the twain hours of night-time go.

(That is, the wind is keen when men go to church at Glendalough for vespers and matins.)[60]

53   F 17, 80, 89.
54   J. Ryan SJ, *Irish Monasticism* (Dublin, 1963), 219 n.3.
55   CD 29 n.3.
56   Apoc. 1, 14; 2, 18; 4, 6; 5, 6.
57   *The Antiphonary of Bangor* (Dublin, 1984), Chapter 19.
58   CD 108-109.
59   ibid. 97-98.
60   *Irish Tradition* (R. Flower, Oxford, 1947), 49.

Each monk recited the psalter in private daily. Various divisions of the psalms were used by different leaders along with various postures of standing or sitting or praying them by heart or reading them. Two members kept night- vigil in the church as they recited the psalter from nightfall till matins. Special predilection was shown for Psalm 118, commonly called the *Beati* from its opening word. It was considered to have special efficacy, as was the *Magnificat* (Lk 1, 46-55).[61] Maelruain had a special devotion to St Michael known as the *cuairt coimhge Mhichil* (safe-conduct of Michael).[62] The feast of St Michael had a special celebration in Tallaght where it was treated as a Sunday.

When a member of the community was at the point of death they used to sing the *Canticle of Canticles*, thereby signifying the union of the church with the Christian soul. Prayers for the dead were frequently offered both in public and in private and penances were also performed on their behalf.[63] In reference to prayers for people still living one notes a tinge of selfishness. Thus Maelruain had the custom of praying for those who were praying for him.[64]

Vows

The reform does not mention religious profession as such, but it does lay down that the resolution to do a good deed should be vowed and proclaimed openly.[65] The ideal of perpetual chastity may easily be gauged from the severity with which breaches of it were punished. One of the offences which could not be sufficiently punished was when those in higher Orders failed in its observance.[66] It is noticeable that the

---

[61]   CD 100-101.
[62]   F. 86.
[63]   CD 102-103.
[64]   F 66. T 75.
[65]   T 83. T 21 'through a vow a man comes into the membership of God's family'.
[66]   C 38. Pen. 140, 2-4.

positive aspect of the vow is not stressed and the approach to marriage relations in the documents is very negative and limited.[67] Needless to say great stress was laid on poverty: 'As for him who desires to reach the pitch of perfection, he distributes all he has to the poor and goes on pilgrimage or lives in a communal church until he goes to heaven'.[68] Obedience is taken as a matter of course throughout the documents. Monks came to Maelruain or to Dublittir to follow their direction. It corresponded to white martyrdom for them. Their sincerity is obvious from the questions these monks asked their abbot and from their eagerness to follow his wishes.

Penitential Practices

The penitential aspect of Celtic spirituality has always been specially noted. The cross-vigil, i.e. praying with out-stretched hands for a considerable period of time, was a common practice. Genuflections were also much in vogue. Dublittir genuflected after each of the hundred and fifty psalms.[69] Castigation was regularly practised. Among the culdees it was inflicted by another member and was never performed on a Sunday. Standing in cold water might be undertaken to crush evil desires or as a labour of piety. Penances were inflicted for breaches of discipline or for carelessness especially if waste resulted from it. But excessive penance was not encouraged. Normally monks were not to perform more than two hundred prostrations in the day. An anchorite in Clonard was accustomed to genuflect seven hundred times in the day. The matter was reported to Maelruain and he said that a day would come when the anchorite would not be able to genuflect. His words proved true because in time the man became a cripple. The external practices of penance were, to their minds, a vital condition

[67] CD 106.
[68] *Ériu* VII, 154 n.6.
[69] F 101-102.

for attaining God's friendship and indicated that they were sincerely contrite for their offences.[70]

Pilgrimage was also an important aspect of early Celtic spirituality. It was an ascetic exercise to part from home and friends for the love of Christ in order to bear witness to the Gospel values. Among the pilgrim saints one readily recalls Colum Cille's pilgrimage to Iona with its effects on Scottish Christianity and the conversion of the northeastern region of England, and Columban's missionary journeys through France, Switzerland and Italy founding monasteries, especially Bobbio where he was finally laid to rest. But by the eighth century the practice of leaving Ireland on pilgrimage was being criticized probably because some were more wanderers (vagabundi) than pilgrims. Samhthann of Clonbroney had firm ideas on the subject.

> A certain teacher named Dairchellach came to the virgin and said to her: 'I propose to lay aside study and give myself to prayer'. To whom she replied: 'What then can give your mind stability that it wander not, if you neglect spiritual study?' The teacher continued, 'I wish to go across the sea on pilgrimage', he said. She replied: 'If God could not be found on this side of the sea we would indeed journey across. Since, however, God is nigh unto all who call upon Him, we are under no obligation to cross the sea. The kingdom of heaven can be reached from every land'.[71]

Maelruain gives the general opinion of the elders that anyone who journeyed outside Ireland was 'a denier of Patrick in heaven and of the faith in Erin'. But he was quite favourable to going on pilgrimage within Ireland.[72] Mac Oige of Lismore was once asked what was the best point in the clerical character and he replied steadiness (foss). 'Whatever task a man has set his hand to, it is best for him to persevere in it'.[73]

---

[70]   CD 110-111.
[71]   VSH II, 260, xxiv.
[72]   C 64.
[73]   T 76 but also CD 113 for Fursa's reply 'perseverance in holiness' and Molua's 'stabilitas in servitio'.

Feasts

There must have been a great number of feastdays celebrated in Tallaght. The work of Oengus and Maelruain in the Martyrologies ensured that! In addition to St Michael, Patrick and Colm Cille were great patrons and Cainnech of Finglas was held in special reverence.[74] Needless to say Christmas, the Epiphany, Low Sunday and Pentecost were the basic liturgical feasts.[75] Sermons must have been preached frequently to try to maintain the spirit of the reform. Sunday was the normal day for this. On Maundy Thursday there were two sermons, one after the washing of the feet, the other on the Eucharistic Supper.[76] Great respect was shown to the altar because of the sacrifice of the Body and Blood of Christ.[77] There was a very interesting point with regard to the ceremonies of baptism. If a pregnant woman became sick so that she was in danger of death, the baptismal service was read aloud over a vessel of water. The woman made confession (of faith) on behalf of the unborn child. She then drank the water which passed over the child and baptized it.[78] Respect for the observance of Sunday was, to say the least, strict. A journey of more than a thousand paces whether it was to visit the sick, to bring viaticum, to celebrate Mass or hear a sermon was discountenanced. It was even forbidden to lift an apple from the ground. Sunday was to be a day of prayer and rest.[79] Sundays and feastdays had special celebrations, some of which lasted even three days. Parts of the year, such as the three Lents, were marked by fasting and cross-vigils, while others, such as Eastertide and Christmastide, were marked by corresponding relaxation. In general the monks' lives may be summed up in the words: 'They sang in secret and paid the debts of sinners',[80] by their spirit of praise and penance.

---

[74]   F 72.
[75]   CD 88.
[76]   F 25. F 26 remarks that no sermon was preached at the Litanies which might suggest that a sermon was part of the ordinary liturgy.
[77]   F 16.
[78]   C 49.
[79]   CD 116.
[80]   F 18. CD 120.

Though we cannot call the documents mentioned at the beginning of this section a rule in the strict sense of the word, since they are neither formulated nor complete, they give us a very interesting, if incomplete, picture of the monastic life in eighth- and ninth-century Ireland. Though the life is strict, and though some of the practices are strange to our way of thinking, still the general observance is not unduly harsh if we except the modern aversion to castigation – an aversion which would have been quite alien to the European mind a thousand or even four hundred years ago. It is, to my knowledge, the most detailed picture that we can get of life in any period of early Celtic monasticism, and so serves not only for its own period but also helps to fill in for earlier or later periods in its history.

The Rules

An ancient tradition tells us that Oengus, author of the *Félire* showed his completed Martyrology to a monk named Fothad na Canóine of Fahan, Co. Donegal (818), and that the latter showed his work in turn to Oengus.[81] Our chief interest here is in a metrical Rule attributed to Fothad. It is also attributed to Mochuta of Lismore (636). The language of the Rule is very probably ninth-century. It is composed of a set of regulations and divided into sections for different members of the community. The introduction treats of the general duties of all the members. It enunciates the great principle of Christian life, namely the love of God and of one's neighbour, and then outlines the Commandments very briefly. One section deals with the duties of the culdee, or, as he is also called, 'the cleric of the prayer-cell,'. He would seem to be the equivalent of the anchorite. It was his duty to celebrate each canonical hour. On hearing the call of the bell he should raise his heart to heaven and cast his eyes down to earth. Then he said a *Pater* and *Gloria* to ward off sadness and made the sign of the Cross. At the church he prostrated himself three times.

[81] FO 5.

It was his duty to pray the Hours, to keep vigil, read and pray till Terce. Between Terce and None each member went to his particular duties – those in Orders to celebrate Mass, professors to teach, youths to practise the labours of humility. The unlettered were to perform manual labour under the direction of a wise and holy cleric. Before celebrating the Hours they prostrated three times and they repeated these prostrations three times also at the conclusion. Deceit, murmuring and mutual rivalry should give place to silence, fervour and amiability. The Rule also treats of the duties of the bishop, the abbot, the priest, the *anamchara* (spiritual director), the monk and of the king; but our interest lies in the section dealing with the culdee.[82]

Several other Rules e.g. *The Rule of Colm Cille* in its present form dates from the ninth century and it promotes the anchoretical ideal,[83] *The Rule of Cormac Mac Cuillenain*, king-bishop of Cashel (908)[84] may be authentic since Cormac had received his education in Dísert Diarmata and Diarmaid was one of the *oentú Maelruain. The Rule of Ailbe of Emly*[85] also belongs to this period. They all have points of similarity with the life of the *célí dé*. Granted that many of the practices were probably general the Rules cannot be considered as a direct outcome of the reform, but taking into account both the date and the considerable number of points of resemblance, and also the fact that Emly is not very far from Daire na bhFlann, a certain amount of influence is likely. The fact that there are contemporary or updated Rules may be due to the spirit of reform being felt especially in the south and east of the country.

The poem entitled *Anmcháirdes Mancháin Léith* (The Spiritual Direction of Manchán Liath)[86] also derives from this period, and its subject-matter would indicate that it is partly influenced by Mochuta's Rule. The section of the latter's

---

[82]   v. n.47 Arch.Celt.Lex. III, 312-320. v. also CD 124-132.
[83]   *Zeitschrift für Celtische Philologie* (Halle, 1897-) (henceforth ZCP) III, 28-30 and Primate Colton's *Visitation of the Diocese of Derry* (Dublin, 1850), 109-112.
[84]   *Ériu* II, 62-68. CD 133.
[85]   *Ériu* III, 93 ff. CD 134-135.
[86]   ZCP VII, 310-312. CD 136-137.

Rule prescribing the duties of the culdee – the triple prostra-
tion on entering choir, the duty of celebrating each hour and
the general tenor of the poem – show a certain similarity with
culdean practice. It has also quite a number of points of resemblance with the Tallaght documents – concealment of sins,
prudence in regulating daily labour and food and the avoidance of idle gossip. It also points out that the profitable way to
spend one's time is working, reading and praying. The poem,
Dúthracar, a maic Dé bí (I wish, O Son of the Living God),[87]
which describes the natural and supernatural recompenses
of the anchorite life, mentions the ideal number for a monastic community as thirteen. Another poem, *Ceilebram, léighim,
lubrum* (We celebrate Mass, we read, we work),[88] echoes parts
of the Tallaght documents and Mochuta's Rule. The first duty
of the monk is to pray. Reading and work must occupy a
goodly portion of his day. Superfluity is to be avoided 'as
the culdees are content without superfluity, with no excess,
without importunate requests for food, without a life of comfort, without wealth, without cattle'. It seems to have a strong
connection with the movement.

The *Rule of Fothad*, or Mochuta, is, to my mind, the best rule
in the Irish language both as to order and content. The writer
begins with the two great precepts of the Law and a brief summary of the Decalogue as the introduction. Then he treats of
the duties of the different persons in the monastery and gives
each a general rule of life with some particular applications. It
must be borne in mind that each monastery had its own set of
customs. The author knew this and concentrated on giving
more of the theory underlying their religious observances,
thus helping their interior development. The Irish idea seems
to have been that a Rule was designed to regulate the interior
life. Custom regulated external practices. The Rule emphasized the fundamental principles and custom, interpreted by
the abbot, fixed the external observance. Thus the combination of Mochuta's Rule and the teaching and practices of the
Tallaght documents are the best approximation that one can

---

[87] *Early Irish Lyrics* (G. Murphy, Oxford, 1956) (henceforth EIL), pp.28-31.
[88] ZCP VIII, 231.

find to form a picture of the interior and exterior aspects of the reform.[89]

The Influence of the Movement on Irish Literature

The Rule attributed to Fothad or Mochuta is metrical. We shall shortly see reference to Oengus's Félire being sung, and mention has been made of some poems in the last section. This raises the large issue of the influence of the Irish monks on Celtic literature, and perhaps the even larger issue of the influence of the traditional Celtic preference for poetry (spoken, at first, rather than written) for the preservation of all that was of deep significance in life. We must confine our attention here to some examples of the literary claims that can be made for, and some of the more obvious literary content of, the literature connected with the culdee movement.

Liturgical and Exegetical Literature

Two Martyrologies from the monastery of Tallaght have been preserved for us. *The Martyrology of Tallaght*[90] is contemporaneous with *The Stowe Missal*[91] and was compiled towards the end of the eighth century or the beginning of the ninth. The second is The Martyrology or *Félire of Oengus*.[92] The former is ascribed to Maelruain and Oengus as joint authors.[93] Both provide lists of saints' feasts. *The Martyrology of Tallaght* gives a list of Roman saints and one of Irish saints for each day except for some six weeks which are missing. *Félire Oengusso* has a stanza for each day commemorating the saint(s) of the day. It was composed between 797-807[94] but it has some later additions. Dr J. Hennig suggests that *The Martyrology of Tallaght* was read during the Canon of the Mass and that

---

89 CD 138-139.
90 R.I. Best and H.J. Lawlor (London, 1931) (henceforth *Mart.Tall.*).
91 ed. G.F. Warner (London, 1906).
92 ed. W. Stokes (London, 1906).
93 *Mart.Tall.* x. CD 139 n.2.

the *Félire* was read in the chapter-room.[95] Oengus' work is more a composition for private devotion. He tells us that he searched earlier martyrologies and 'Ireland's host of books'.[96] There are varying judgments on the literary merit of the work. Stokes held that it has 'not a trace of imaginative power or observation of nature and human life as they really are'.[97] David Greene agrees with Stokes but admits of 'an occasional flash of inspiration' in the *Félire* itself; but he rightly points out that the Prologue and Epilogue have 'deep religious feeling' and technical virtuosity.[98] On the other hand Hennig writes that the *Félire* is the largest and most highly developed work of early Irish religious poetry.[99] Oengus divides his work into three parts, the Prologue, the *Félire* proper and the Epilogue, or as Oengus entitles it the 'final Prologue'. The whole work being in metrical form could be memorized and sung.

In the Prologue he has some reflections on the vanity of earthly power and of rulers as compared with the love of Christ:

> The might of the world is a lie
> To all who within it live;
> This is the [true] strength –
> Great love of Mary's Son.[100]

Tara has perished while Armagh remains with her host of Christian champions. Loeguire's glory has vanished but Patrick's name lives on. Here and there some beautiful stanzas break a long list of comparisons which tend to become wearisome.

> Naught is dearer to you than God's love
> If you can win it –
> Adoration of the King of the clouds
> Does not bring sadness with it.[101]

[100]   ZCP VI, 6.
[95]   *Medieval Studies* XXVI, 325.
[96]   FO Epil. lines 141-142. CD 143.
[97]   David Greene, 'The Religious Epic', *Early Irish Poetry* (ed. James Carney, Cork, 1969), 75-77.
[98]   ibid.
[99]   *Medieval Studies*, XVII, 219.
[100]   FO Prol. lines 145-148.
[101]   ibid. 185-188.

The forgotten fame of pagan chieftains is contrasted with the abiding glory of the native saints:

> Donnchadh the wrathful one, ruddy, chosen
> Or victorious Bran of the Barrow,
> Visiting their tombs
> Dispels not my weary weakness.[102]

> Maelruain after his pious service
> The great sun of Meath's south plain –
> [Visiting] his grave with purity
> Heals the sighs of my heart.[103]

Oengus gives voice to his praise of Jesus and prays for the success of his work:

> Let our will be firm
> Let us strive after what is dearest
> Since this is the noblest
> Let us all love Jesus.[104]

In the actual *Félire* the entries normally name the saint(s) adding a phrase or stock epithet about the person. On February 13th he notes the tradition of the introduction of bees into Ireland.[105]

This part of the Martyrology is copiously annotated with poems and marginal notes, partly mystical, partly hagiographical or partly historical. This tends to show that Oengus, while in Tallaght, had a large collection of these materials. At the conclusion comes the Epilogue. Having acknowledged Christ's help in compiling the Calendar he prays for eternal life in union with the saints whom he has commemorated. Significant are the lines

---

102   ibid. 221-224.
103   ibid. 225-228.
104   ibid. 261-264.
105   ibid. 269-272

May the copious blessing of the King
With His beautiful hosts
Descend over your assemblies
On Maelruain before all men.
May my tutor bring me unto Christ
Dear beyond affection
By his pure blessing
with his heart's desire.[106]

An indication of the wide use of the *Félire* is seen in the lines 'every group sings it to ascertain the feasts'.[107] In keeping with his predecessors, like Blathmac in his poem on Our Lady, Oengus promises that whoever sings his *Félire* will be attended by these saints on his deathbed and the 'dew of the grave will heal'.[108] Hennig has the interesting remark that 'this whole idea originated from the fundamental conception of the precariousness of life without the assistance of the saints, or, conversely, is expressive of an extremely realist conception of the efficacy of the intercession of the saints'.[109] Here and there in the Epilogue Oengus reveals his inner self to us and one is struck by his humility and his intense desire to be united with those whom he has commemorated.

Hear Thou, O Jesus, Thy feeble exile
To leave the world I would rather than stay.[110]

If you possess charity in good measure
You may exercise it meetly on this poor deserving wretch.[111]

If you be compassionate your succour is timely,
Here is one of the loneliest, a weakling of Jesus.[112]

[106] FO Epil. lines 65-68.
[107] ibid. line 80.
[108] ibid. lines 221-224.
[109] *Medieval Studies* XXVI, 324.
[110] il. lines 365-368.
[111] ibid. 389-392.
[112] ibid. 393-396.

Hearken Thou, O Jesus, Whose servant (céle) I am,
Mayest Thou grant every prayer of each son of piety.[113]

The poem ends with the entreaty that the saints may carry us to our haven of peace.

One of the most important products of the reform was *The Stowe Missal* which contains extracts from St John's Gospel, the Ordinary of the Mass, followed by three special Masses, one for saints, one for living penitents and one for the dead. It has the order for baptism with the rite of Communion for the newly-baptized, the rite of the visitation of the sick, Extreme Unction and Viaticum, a short treatise in Irish on the Mass and three short spells in Irish. It is dated c.800.[114] The order of the visitation of the sick is the longest of the four surviving versions of this rite in the early Irish church. The manuscript also contains a unique tract on the Mass written in Old Irish c.800. It is a symbolic or mystical explanation. The triad of thought, word and deed as causes of sin and ways of repentance, which seems to be of Irish origin,[115] is mentioned. But the Easter and Christmas confraction of the Eucharist is most interesting being in the form of a Cross and a circle.[116] I doubt if it was actually used but it certainly is based on the notion of the mystical body, or church universal – bishops, priests sub-grades in Orders, anchorites, innocent children, penitents, married folk and first communicants. The tract lacks unity and is more a series of excellent thoughts without any close connecting link. But it does manifest the keen desire to relish the mystery of the Eucharist and to conform the communicant to Christ on the Cross.

The reform movement manifested a keen interest in the Scriptures and exegetical studies. Thus the *Book of Dimma*, a manuscript of the four Gospels, which belonged to

---

[113]   ibid. 425-428.
[114]   CD 152.
[115]   Patrick Sims-Williams, 'Thought, Word and Deed, An Irish Triad', *Ériu* XXIX (1978), 108-111.
[116]   v. CD 156-158 for an effort at reconstructing the confraction.

Roscrea,[117] may be the work of Dimma, who died c.800, who may be the Dimmán of Ara, Co. Tipperary, a member of the *oentú* Maelruain. Binchy and Bergin suggest that Diarmait of Dísert Diarmata, another member of the *oentú*, is the scribe of the Milan and Turin glosses on the Scriptures. Mailgaimrid, who is also cited as an authority on Scripture, is 'almost certainly to be identified with *Mailgaimrid scriba optimus et anchorita, abbas Bennchair*' who died in 839 and with the Mailgaimrid cited in the Notes to the *Félire*.[118]

Françoise Henry held that there was a connection between the Scripture Crosses and the reform movement. When one considers the location of these Crosses, mainly east of a line between Carrick-on-Suir/Lismore and Lorrha/Clonmacnoise, this is the area frequently mentioned in the reform literature. Moreover, the Scripture Crosses at Castledermot give a direct link. But I am dubious about her detailed linking of the iconography of the Crosses with the ideas of the reform spirituality.[119] The remarkable poem, entitled *Saltair na Rann* (Psalter of the Quatrains), written by Oengus, *céle dé*, is generally dated as the end of the tenth century. Prof. James Carney gave me his opinion that it should be dated c.870-900. Obviously it is not the Oengus of the *Félire* who is the author. The poem consists of one hundred and fifty smaller poems which treat of incidents from the Old and New Testaments and takes ideas also from the apocryphal gospels. David Greene, referring to it, says that while it can be remarkably obscure 'the psalter has a native charm all of its own. It is full of native colour, which gives the Bible an unmistakably Irish touch . . . it is just the sort of literature, christian in subject and Irish in treatment, that the *Célí dé* school aimed at but seldom achieved.[120]

Fr Grosjean SJ has suggested that at least part of the Vatican manuscript 49 of Reginensis, an exegetical and catechetical work, may be a product of the movement. As scholars are

[117] CD 159-160.
[118] O.J. Bergin and D.A. Binchy, *A Grammar of Old Irish* (Dublin, 1946), 5.
[119] CD 162-163.
[120] cf. n.97, *Early Irish Poetry* (ed. J. Carney), 80.

at the moment studying and editing the complete manuscript, one awaits their findings to ascertain how plausible Grosjean's opinion may be.[121]

Hagiography

In the *Book of Leinster* the text of the *Martyrology of Tallaght* is followed by much hagiographical material concerning the saints of Ireland. This is followed by the *oentú Maelruain*. Flower has suggested that this material derives from the work done in Tallaght and, to my mind, this is highly probable. A period of about twenty-five years produced two marytrologies and Oengus says that he did not use all the material that lay at his dispoasl.[122] Dr Hennig remarks that 'in the western church no country has made a contribution as wide, as systematic or as varied to the development of the basic pattern of devotion to all the saints as has Ireland. The preoccupation of the old Irish church with the subject of the choirs of the saints can be pursued in the Irish tradition of hagiography and private devotion right through the middle ages'.[123]

Though the *Lives* of the Irish saints as we have them today date from the twelfth to the fourteenth century, there are earlier strata in them e.g. in the Life of Samhthann, Ciaran, Ita and others which indicate that *Lives* were being written in the ninth century. Kenney suggests that in St Molua's *Life* much of the subject-matter is not later than the ninth century.[124] The saint's parting advice to his monks: 'Let there be stability among you . . . always open yourselves to prayer in the morning, then to reading, afterwards work till evening prayer'[125] stresses perseverance, prayer, study and

[121] *Analecta Bollandiana* LIV, 119-136.
[122] FO Epil. line 75 and lines 121-4.
[123] J. Hennig, 'Studies in Early Western Devotion to the Choirs of the Saints', *Studia Patristica* 8(2) (1966), 247.
[124] *Sources for the Early History of Ireland (Ecclesiastical)* (New York, 1929, Reprint Ó Táilliúir, Dublin, 1979), 398.
[125] V.S.H. II, 223, 1i.

work. This is the common doctrine and at times the actual words which lay at the centre of the reform. The *Rules and the Miracles of the Saints* were read in the refectory by the culdees.[126]

Devotional Literature

The *Scuab Crábaid* may be the work of Airerán, the successor of Maelruain, or more probably that of Colcu mentioned in the Tallaght documents.[127] It is in the form of a litany which falls into two parts. The second part begins with a number of beautiful invocations of Christ: 'O holy Jesu, O gentle friend . . . O Son of the merciful Father without mother in heaven, O true and loving Brother'. He beseeches Him to hear the prayer of a poor weak man on behalf of all the Christian churches and on his own behalf, for the sake of His kindliness, love and mercy, for the sake of His merciful Father, for the sake of His own divinity, for the sake of His humanity conceived of the Virgin Mary of the Holy Spirit, so that he may reach the unity of the Trinity in heaven.[128] It is in such texts that we find some distinctive characteristics of Irish spirituality more so than in the liturgical prayers. One is struck by the constant repetition and by the sincere outpourings of trust, self-abandonment and love which mark the earnest desire for union with God in heaven. The *Triads*, dated c.850-900,[129] note Lismore as the monastery which specialized in litanies. One wonders if the devotion to the Irish saints began in Lismore and found its way to Tallaght to return once again to Lismore.[130] The work *Apgitir Crábaid* (Alphabet of Piety) is ascribed to Colmán maccu Beógnae. I have put forward reasons for identifying him with Mocholmóc Ua Liatháin, mentioned in the Tallaght documents, who died in 730 entitled *religionis doctor*.[131] The

---

[126] F 80. C. 31.
[127] CD 173.
[128] ibid. 174-175.
[129] *Analecta Bollandiana* LXXVII, 310.
[130] CD 175-178.
[131] Vernam Hull, *Celtica* VIII, 44-89. CD 177-181.

fact that the tract is found in eighteen manuscripts indicates its popularity. The treatise recommends prudent holiness for clerics, avoidance of boasting and other vices. While it does not outline an *itinerarium* for sanctity in the strict sense of the word, it is a work well-suited to train beginners in a reform movement: 'Four things to be fulfilled – duty to God, kindness to man, devotedness to all, thought of death . . . Four duties of the sons of life [a term often applied to *célí dé* later) – suppression of wishes, fear of pain, love of suffering, hope of reward . . . Who is nearest God? He who meditates on Him . . . In whom does the Holy Spirit dwell? In him who is pure without sin. Then it is that a man is a vessel of the Holy Spirit when the virtues come to replace the vices. Then it is that desire for God increases when desire for the world withers'.[132] This is the basic doctrine of mystics like St John of the Cross. The tract *Cinti crábuid ocus gnáthuighthe scoile Sinchil so sís* (Practices of Piety in Sinchell's school) occurs among the Tallaght material in the *Book of Leinster* and is dated as eighth or ninth century. It bears a close resemblance to the *Apgitir* and is very probably a work influenced by the reform.[133]

Personal Poetry

The origin of the Irish personal lyric has been traced to the monastic movement of the seventh and eighth centuries by Prof. Gerard Murphy.[134] It is certain that it was at least influenced by it. These lyrics, expressing the poet's emotional and religious reaction to the beauties of nature, are the outcome both of Celtic sensitivity (some nature poems have no mention of God), and of the monotheistic religion which led the poets (who were often monks) to consider nature as God's handiwork. This idea is found in the psalms but nowhere is it more cogently expressed than in the *Canticle of the Three Youths*, which was said daily in Tallaght. The writer calls

---

[132]   Hull, op.cit. 77.
[133]   CD 182.
[134]   *Studies* XX, 87-102. CD 184.

on all the powers of nature sun, moon, stars, fishes, birds, animals, cold and heat and lastly on man to praise God. David Greene's option for a tenth-century origin from contemporary Latin poetry is not tenable since many of the poems are of an earlier date, not to mention other reasons.[135] They are also connected with the Tallaght movement. Little attention has been paid to a poem on the margin of the *Martyrology of Tallaght* which is dated c.800. The poet is conversant with the times of the year at which the birds begin to sing:

> The birds of the world, power without ill
> [Come] to welcome the sun,
> On January's nones, at the different hours,
> The cry of the host from the dark wood.

> On the eighth calends of noble April
> The swallows come on their pure tryst,
> [Till they depart]
> On the eighth calends of October.

> On the festival of Ruadan, no petty saying,
> their fetters are unloosed,
> On the seventeen calends of May
> The cuckoo calls from the pleasant wood.

> On the nones of July the birds cease
> To sing the music of holidays
> . . .
> for Maelruain from Tallaght.

> Melodious music the birds perform
> to the King of the heaven of the clouds,
> Praising the radiant King
> Hark from afar the choir of the birds.[136]

The notes to the Martyrologies of Tallaght and of Oengus, though sometimes difficult to date, contain some of the ninth-century poems belonging to the category of personal nature poetry. In the notes to the *Félire of Oengus*, under

[135]   CD 184 n.1.
[136]   *Mart.Tall.* 95-96.

March 31st one sees the combination of the natural and the supernatural beautifully interwoven:

> Learned in music sings the lark,
> I leave my cell to listen;
> His open beak spills music, hark!
> Where heavens bright cloudlets glisten.
> And so I'll sing my morning psalm
> That God bright heaven may give me,
> And keep me in eternal calm
> And from all sin relieve me.[137]

This translation is by Robin Flower. Though more literal translations have since been made, his verse retains the beautiful touch of the original without an undue forcing of the meaning. We are indebted to Gerard Murphy for editing and translating many of these personal poems.[138]

The Lives of the Saints have many charming narratives which reflect this beautiful sympathy with and appreciation of nature, birds and animals.[139] Such was their familiarity with and their love for their dumb friends that the writer of the *Annals of Innisfallen* noting the events of 917 says with obvious regret 'a mortality of cattle and birds such that the sound of a blackbird or a thrush was scarcely heard this year'.

Conclusion

Reform is a recurring factor in the history of the church and comes about when men ask themselves with a new urgency how they are to be sincere with God. In the middle of the eighth century a group of monks strove to live a life in full conformity with their ideal. In doing this they introduced a freshness and vigour, though somewhat austere and occasionally puritanical, into the religious life, which is always inclined to follow the easier course, an inclination often the more marked according as the body or institute is

---

[137] *Ir.Trad.* 54.
[138] *Early Irish Lyrics* (Oxford, 1956).
[139] CD 190-191.

farther removed from the time of its founder or reformer. The abuses which it was expected to counteract were at this time in their initial stages and were trifling in comparison with those which affected the life of the contemporary church on the Continent, or the life of the church in Ireland in later times. Yet these abuses developed during the succeeding centuries, and finally led to the downfall of Irish monasticism in the twelfth century. The coming of the Vikings certainly hindered this movement from having a lasting effect on the religious life of the country. The monasteries of Tallaght and Finglas so closely connected with the reform give us a detailed picture of the typical monastery of the reform. From Tallaght it spread to other monasteries throughout the country. But as Gearóid MacNiocaill has written:

> The ascetic reform had however no machinery for renewing itself. Each church attached to the reform during Maelruain's lifetime was dependent on the character of its abbot to maintain its level of asceticism. No authority existed to maintain a check on any individual monastery, to prevent it slipping from its standards The ascetic reform had indeed a future, but not an institutional one; it survived as an inspiration to small groups of ascetics and individuals.[140]

That it had a good effect on the religious life of the country is evident from the spiritual writings of these centuries, comprising Missals, Gospels, Martyrologies, sermons, Scripture studies, Lives of saints, litanies and hymns. Few events in early Irish monastic history had such a wide effect on monastic life after its first fervour had waned; few had such an effect on Irish literature as this ascetical movement. In addition to making a very important contribution to religious devotion, it developed those delicately-wrought lyrics which show us the inner depth of these monks and which are, to my mind, one of the most attractive features of the whole of Celtic literature.

---

[140] *Ireland before the Vikings* (Dublin, 1972), 151.

Protestantism and Scottish Highland Culture

Terence P. McCaughey

Almost every aspect of highland studies has at some time suffered from the fact that the highlands have been regarded merely as a peripheral culture, only ever to be understood in terms of what was deemed to be the cultural and political centre. That centre was most often considered to be Edinburgh and the lowlands: with reference to the state of religion in the period immediately before and immediately after the sixteenth-century Reformation, this has often meant such things as the following:

(i) the idea that the highlands were 'remote' and therefore peculiar;

(ii) the idea that reforming ideas were essentially alien to the highlands;

(iii) the idea that, in contrast with the situation obtaining prior to 1560, the Reformed Church was neglectful in the provision of the means of grace, with the consequence that the people 'were left severely alone, to pray and believe as they wished, without priest or minister'.[1]

---

[1] ed. C. Giblin, *Irish Franciscan Mission to Scotland, 1619-1646*, Dublin 1964, vii.

James Kirk, in an article published in 1986,[2] has done something to right the balance in respect of (i). He points out that Dornoch is only marginally more distant from Rome than Dundee or Glasgow. Furthermore, if one disregards the fact that the highlands do not seem to have shared in the late medieval expansion of the major religious orders, the church in the highlands conformed in every respect to the patterns which prevailed elsewhere in Scotland.[3] A high proportion of the higher clergy were lowlanders and those who were highlanders had in any case studied in one of the lowland universities or on the Continent – in either case through the medium of Latin – and all this kept the doors of communication open for that particular class.

With reference to (ii), it is doubtless important that we do not import notions derived from a reading (sometimes a superficial one!) of Irish church history of the same period.[4] The sources do not throw a great deal of light on the extent to which reforming ideas were beginning to enter the consciousness of highland nobility and clergy. But we do note that in 1534 Roderick Maclean, who was to be bishop of the Isles for most of the 1540s,[5] set off to study in Wittenberg where no doubt he listened to lectures on Scripture from Martin Luther himself. In the previous decade Cardinal Beaton had given authority to the bishop of Ross to move against the heretics in his diocese. Patrick Hamilton, who was burned for heresy in 1529, had spent a lot of time on his penultimate trip back to Scotland at St Leonard's College, where he is reported to have made a strong appeal to the younger canons.[6] He financed his studies in France from the emoluments of Fearn Abbey in Easter Ross, of which he was nominally abbot. Many of

[2] James Kirk, 'The Jacobean Church in the Highlands, 1567-1625' in *The Seventeenth Century in the Highlands*, Inverness Field Club, Inverness 1986, 24-51.
[3] James Kirk, loc.cit., 25.
[4] A study of early seventeenth-century Irish diocesan visitations reveals a much higher percentage of Gaelic names among ministers, reading ministers and even bishops than has sometimes been assumed.
[5] J. Wormald, *Court, Kirk, Community, Scotland 1470-1625 (The New History of Scotland 4)*, London 1981, 63.
[6] J. Wormald (1981), 103.

the higher clergy of the highlands in the first half of the sixteenth century were educated in St Andrews and it is into that town that Wolsey's agents report that a number of Tyndale New Testaments exceeding even the number going to Edinburgh or Leith, were being imported. No student in the two or three decades prior to 1560 could be untouched by the disputes engendered. In the years after Patrick Hamilton's death, a number of friars left their houses, some with Gaelic names. John McDowall, prior of the Wigtown Dominicans, left for Germany in 1540. John McAlpine, Dominican prior of Perth, fled Scotland in the 1530s, after a stay in Salisbury in England, took a doctorate in Wittenberg and eventually became a professor of theology in Copenhagen. In 1556 Colin Campbell of Glenurchy heard John Knox preach at Inveraray and was sufficiently impressed to urge the Earl of Argyll to retain him there. By 1559 that same Colin Campbell had joined the Lords of the Congregation and, by 1561, he had his own chaplain installed as minister at Kenmore at the east end of Loch Tay and provided with stipend, manse and glebe in return for 'teching and preching sinceirly the Word of God and mynistairing of the sacramentis to the glory of God and instructione of the pepill'.[7] Some time earlier the 4th Earl of Argyll himself had defied the opposition of the Archbishop of St Andrews by appointing John Douglas, a young man with reforming ideas, as his chaplain.[8]

In the light of these examples, it is not surprising to find the young notary Eoin Carsuel within a year of graduating MA (1544) at St Andrews, throwing his weight on the side of the Earl of Lennox. Lennox was supporting the attempt of Domhnall Dubh to regain the Lordship of the Isles and this was to be effected through the good offices of Henry VIII of England. Both Lennox and the young graduate of St Andrews, who was to seek ordination a couple of years later, fully appreciated the significance an alliance with

[7] James Kirk, loc.cit., 28.
[8] R.L. Thomson (ed.), *Foirm na n-Urrnuidheadh*, Scottish Gaelic Texts Society, Edinburgh 1970, lxii.

Henry and against the French connection had for church reform. Lennox's brother, Robert Stewart, temporarily lost the see of Caithness in punishment for his involvement in the same political action, but he survived to regain it and be one of three pre-Reformation bishops who undertook to continue service in the Reformed Church, *post*-1560. There is no evidence to suggest that they were mere time-servers, ignorant of disputes that were shaking the whole of Europe or uncommitted to the movement for change and reform.

Carsuel is of course an unusually well-documented case: his family had been henchmen of Campbell of Argyll for generations and constables or captains of Carnassary Castle in the parish of Kilmartin a few miles south-west of Loch Awe where he was born. He belonged to the class of *uaislean* who were used to administering for the chief, raising troops and tribute: it is therefore no surprise to find that oral tradition remembers him as punctilious if not grasping (presumably in demanding payment of church teinds). Thus Argyll tradition remembered, . . . *tha dhroll mar dhruinnein na curra 's a sgròban lom, gionach farsaing* (his rump is like the back of a crane/ and his empty maw greedy and rapacious). He graduated BA in 1542 and MA in 1544 at St Andrews so, assuming that he went to university aged about 15 years, we may assume him to have been born not later than 1525. He specifically makes no claim to have been educated formally and professionally in Classical Gaelic, but his translation of the Book of Common Order (which must have been done fairly quickly, since it came out just over six years after the Reformation) has only very few slips into the vernacular dialect and shows very considerable skill in the deployment of varying styles and registers in the classical literary language.[9] So he must have acquired this literacy in the classical form of his native language before the age of fifteen when he left home for university, for he would not have acquired it there. When he says that he 'did not acquire learning in Gaelic any greater than any person of the ordinary people', the people he has in mind are ordinary people of his own class – not the lower orders! If he could

---

[9]   R.L. Thomson (1970), lxix-lxxii.

have found someone trained in the poetic school to undertake the work he says himself he would have employed him.
Faut de mieux he must do it himself. At a time long before the
Bible itself was available in Gaelic, he produced a book, as he
says himself, which gives the 'form of prayers and the holy
sacraments' in the Gaelic language. Carsuel translated the
Book of Common Order largely as it stood; however, we may
assume that any alterations he did make are deliberate and
significant. The most important are as follows:

(a) those which no doubt reflect the pastoral experience of
the early years as Superintendent of the Isles, e.g. 1. 2111, the
insistence on monthly celebration of the Lord's Supper; 1.
751, the omission of a phrase from the original which has the
effect of allowing the minister to act without the elders but
not the other way round; 1. 704, the procedure for election
of ministers and, 1. 777, the form of the mid-week meeting.
See further R.L. Thomson (1970) lxvii;

(b) the decision not to attempt to produce the psalms in Common Metre, a metre wholly strange to Gaelic tradition, which
was to prove a formidable task in the following century;

(c) the shortening of the graces – no doubt in the interests
of realism; the interesting addition of a form of blessing of
a ship going to sea, 1. 3879-3903. See further R.L. Thomson
(1970) lxvii f;

(d) for Calvin's large catechism in his exemplar, Carsuel
substituted a catechism of his own. It represents some 500
lines of R.L. Thomson's edition, and gives the reader the
opportunity to note the theological mind of Carsuel at work.
This catechism was clearly composed with Calvin's little
catechism to hand, but it shows real sensitivity to the differences in the situation of a Genevan catechumen living in
an established Reformed city and the Gaelic catechumen
surrounded by older people with only an imperfect grasp
of Reformed faith and practice. It is therefore much more
polemical, sharply contrasting the old teaching and the new
– so, when the *discipulus* is asked what means are used in
baptism, it is not enough to say the Word of God and water.
He must go on to rule out 'the other things which were used
hitherto in the Papist Church', op.cit., 1. 3748-9. Except for
the absence of any stress on communication in both kinds,

the emphases of the Catechism are predictable, but they are certainly emphases which Carsuel has appropriated after study and experience.

What complicated the situation in the highlands in the sixteenth and seventeenth centuries is the fact that the progress of the Reformed church in the highlands was inextricably linked with a process which had been set in motion well before the Reformed church came into existence: that is to say, the endeavour to create in Scotland a single nation, unified in terms of law, religion and language, exactly like the other emergent nation-states of Europe. James IV, who has been described as the first Renaissance monarch in Scotland, was criticized (as was his successor in Scotland and their counterparts elsewhere in Europe) for advancing persons of the merchant or burgher class who then became directly beholden and responsible to the Crown. Such persons were to be prepared in a Reformed or new school and university system for service and administration of the State. It is no accident that the bull founding King's College Aberdeen (a) provides for a law school and (b) provides for laity as well as clergy. We might note also that of Aberdeen it is said 'quae insulis borealibus et montibus praedictis satis vicina est'. James's Education Act of 1496 laid down that all barons and freeholders in the country should 'put their eldest sonnis and airis to the sculis quhill [= until] thai be competentlie foundit and ha perfyte Latyne, and thereftir to remane thre yeris at the sculis of art and jure' (i.e. at university). This provision was to be followed, with particular attention to the highlands, by the Statutes of Iona (1609), and the Education Act of 1616.[10] In these cases, of course, the goal is to provide for competence in English, and they are aimed at the upper stratum of the highlands' patriarchal society.

But the highlands (with the exception of small pockets of lowland influence like Inverness) had no merchant class,

---

[10] Gordon Donaldson, *Scottish Historical Documents*, Edinburgh and London 1970, 171-175, 178-9.

no rising bourgeoisie anxious to have their say in city and church affairs, such as were attracted to Calvinism in France and Switzerland. Nor did it have a multitude of angry peasants as did parts of Germany. If reforming ideas were to gain ground and if the Reformed church was to be organized in the highlands, that had to depend on the same forces as had always controlled highland society. The implementation of the law would be effected through the nobility or not at all: and certainly church reformation could not (and did not) mean the liberation of or the acquisition of power by any new class of persons, as it had in various ways in Basel or Zürich or the south of England. The warrior class who hitherto had controlled everything else as well would run the new church as they had the old. It was only the terms on which they did so that had altered slightly.

After all, Eoin Carsuel was a scion of the family who had been constables of Carnassary Castle for generations in the Campbell interest. Nor was this untypical: Maighstir Fearchar,[11] minister of Kintail in Wester Ross from 1618 until his death in January 1662 at the age of 82, was presented to the parish and simultaneously made constable of the strategically important Eilean Donan castle at the mouth of Loch Duich. His predecessor had also held both positions. In the castle he lived[12] 'in an opulent and flourishing condition, much given to hospitality and charity'. According to the same source, Colin, Earl of Seaforth, would come to Eilean Donan from time to time on extended visits with between 300 and 500 men. During his stay the Earl would sometimes be visited by other clan chiefs of the West, arriving in their galleys – Maclean of Duart, Clanranald from South Uist, Macleod of Raasay and Mackinnon from Strath in Skye, and there be entertained to 'the wine and other liquors that were brought from Fortrose in the Earl's train'. After their departure it was

---

[11]   Alexander Macrae, *History of the Clan Macrae, with genealogies*, Dingwall 1899.
[12]   The source here is the ms history of the clan, written by the Revd John Macrae (Mgr Iain) of Dingwall, brother of Donnchadh nam pìos and grandson of Mgr Fearchar, and referred to as a source by Alexander Macrae, see note 11 above, in his Preface.

the Earl's custom to hold a great hunt[13] with all the principal tacksmen of Kintail, Lochalsh and Lochcarron to the forest of Monar. Earl George, who succeeded his brother in 1633, did Maighstir Fearchar the honour of placing his son, Coinneach Mór, under fosterage with Mgr Fearchar, and we are told that 'the sons of neighbouring gentlemen were brought to keep him company'.[14]

Mgr Fearchar himself had been sent to school for four or five years in Perth twenty years (it should be noted) before the Statutes of Iona. Thence he had proceeded to the new university in Edinburgh, where he did so well at his studies that it seems he was unanimously chosen to succeed his teacher, James Reid, as Regent. He did not take that up, however, for the Earl of Seaforth intervened, took him back to Easter Ross and appointed him to take charge of the Grammar School of Fortrose. Fifteen months later he resigned and was ordained.

His is a spectacular and large-scale career, but a study of the *Fasti Ecclesiae Scoticanae* shows that in seventeenth- and eighteenth-century Scotland it was in certain respects typical. The majority of ministers whose ancestry can be checked turn out to be either sons of the manse[15] or the sons of tacksmen. Most were graduates and therefore bilingual. Given their background it is scarcely surprising to find that by the mid-eighteenth century very many of them (especially those who had not been touched by the 'moderate evangelicalism' of the time) were regarded as somewhat worldly by their contemporaries, often justifiably though sometimes unfairly so.[16]

John Skeldoch, minister of Farr in Sutherland (d.1753), translated thither from Kilmonivaig in 1732, is a case in point. He came to be thought of more as a drover than as a pastor.

---

[13]   Such hunts are well documented and could involve several hundred beaters. The Earl of Mar mustered forces for the beginning of 1715 under the guise of gathering for a hunt.
[14]   D. Thomson (ed.), *Companion to Gaelic Scotland*, Oxford 1983, 64, 148, 220.
[15]   *Fasti Ecclesiae Scoticanae* vols I-VIII, Edinburgh 1915-50.
[16]   R. Macleod, 'Ministearan an arain? *Transactions of the Gaelic Society of Inverness* 52, 243-69.

When complaints were brought to the presbytery against him in 1737, his colleagues stood by him. But ten years later a man he had sent south with the cattle of a number of small tenants disappeared, and the money with him. This time the presbytery had no alternative but to suspend him for a time. Nevertheless, ministerial solidarity was sufficiently strong for a motion to depose him to be defeated in presbytery.[17] John Skeldoch belonged to the very presbytery and is the very kind of minister Rob Donn holds up to view in his song to the presbytery.[18]

(i)

Fhuair sinn fir mar luchd préisgidh,
Tha oil-bheumach 'n an cleachdadh,
'S nach 'eil crìoch ac' nì 's airde.
Fa uiread chràbhaidh 's a phasas;
O 'n tha 'n teagasg neo-spéiseil,
D'fhas luch-éisdeachd mì-fheartal,
'S e meas Ministeir sgìreachd,
A bhi 'n a Chrìosdaidh mar fhasan.

(ii)

Ach ma ghabhas sinn beachd orr'
do réir an cleachdaidhean sanntach,
's an tha tomult luchd-teagaisg
a thachair againn 's an am so,
mar tha sligean na caislinn,
bhith 'n a' cosnadh 's an t-samhradh,
gheibh thu fichead dhiu falamh,
mu 'n aon anns bi neamhnuid.

(iii)

Falbh 'n an cuideachd 's 'n an comhradh,
is gheabh thu móran do 'n mhac ud.
dhéanadh ceannaich no seòl'dair,
dhéanadh dróbhair no factoir,
dhéanadh tuathanach críonnda,
dhéanadh stiúbhard neo-chaithteach,
's mach o 'n cheàrd air 'n do mhionnaich iad,
tha na huile nì gasd' 'ac.

---

[17] I. Grimble, *The World of Rob Donn*, Edinburgh 1979, 104-6, 149, 193.
[18] Hew Morrison (ed.), *Songs and Poems in the Gaelic language by Rob Donn*, Edinburgh 1899, 75-7.

(iv)

Cha 'n ann leamsa is ionghnadh,
(ged robh lìonmhoireachd neònach)
gu'm bheil an cuideachd na bhacadh
gu bhi 'g aidmheil na còrach.
ged nach 'eil e mar leithsgeul
droch eisimpleir an òlaich,
có a dh' itheadh gu sunndach
am bîadh a dhiùltadh an cócair?

(i) We have now as preachers men who are mighty in their conduct and have no higher aim than just what piety will pass muster. Since their preaching is unenthusiastic, the hearers have ceased to heed and the reputation of the parish minister is that he is a Christian by fashion.

(ii) But if we judge them according to their acquisitive ways, then the majority of ministers we come across these days are like the shells on the shore which we gather in the summer – you'll find twenty of them empty for every one that has a pearl in it.

(iii) If you join their company and conversation you'll find plenty of that pack who'd make a merchant or a sailor, a drover or a factor, a prudent farmer or a canny steward – indeed, except for the calling they took vows for they're fine.

(iv) Certainly I'm not surprised (though the number of them is amazing) that their company is a stumbling-block to the confession of the right. Even though the bad example of the host is no excuse, nevertheless who would happily eat food which the cook refuses?

We gain insight into the mind and consciousness of at least some highland Protestant gentlemen by looking at the contents of the Fernaig manuscript.[19] The manuscript may be thought of as the commonplace book of Donnchadh nam pìos (Duncan Macrae of Inverinate, nr Kintail, Wester Ross), reflecting in large measure his own tastes and loyalties. It bears the date 1689 and contains some lines of verse roughly one quarter of which is by the scribe and owner himself. Most

[19]   C. Mac Phàrlain, *Dorlach Laoidhean*/ M. Mac Farlane, *A Handful of Lays*, Dundee 1923. See also D.S. Thomson (1983) 71-2.

of the rest is either by relatives of his own or his wife's – his maternal great-grandfather, his father-in-law and his brother – or by members of the Mackenzie family of Achilty whose relationship to the Earls of Seaforth was similar to that of his own people. A few poems are by others associated with Ross-shire or the North-west. A good deal of it is religious and has some bearing on the concerns of this paper.

Donnchadh's own verse shows him to be a Gaelic-speaking Jacobite Protestant who would prefer to see the church run by bishops than by presbytery, in every way typical of many of his class. His religious verse does bear some of the marks of Reformed theology, as in the following with its emphasis on *sola fide/sola gratia*:[20]

> An gealladh sin do thug mo Rìgh,
> dhòirt fhuil gu fìor air chrann,
> cha chuirear e leis a dhìth
> air gach tì a chreideas ann.
> Creidim-s' ann am Mac mo Dhé,
> slánuighear nan léigh 's nam fann,
> an nì ta dh'easbhuidh air mo chreud
> meudaich féin is cuir 'na cheann . . .
> Dòirt orm' bho nèamh a nuas
> le huile luath's tuilleadh gràis
> dh'fhàgas m'aithridh gu buan
> gu m' fhuasgladh as gach aon chàs[21]

(That promise which my God gave – he who truly spilled his blood on the cross – that he will not suffer one who trusts in him to fall.
I believe in the Son of God, the saviour of the weak: whatever may be lacking in my faith increase it and supply.
Make haste to pour down further grace on me which will make my repentance of lasting avail and free me in every peril.)

His own compositions include an exercise in metrical paraphrase of Scripture, a popular contemporary genre,[22] and the *crosanachd*/flyting between body and soul is concerned, in characteristically Protestant fashion, with the keeping of

---

[20] Sola fide/by faith alone.
[21] The emphasis here is on the grace of a 'repentance unto life'.
[22] Millar Patrick, *Four Centuries of Scottish Psalmody*, Oxford 1949, 209-11.

the Lord's Day.[23] But otherwise the most characteristically and overtly Protestant verses in tone and expression are those of MacCulloch of Park (*Fear na Pàirce*), maternal great-grandfather of the scribe. Alasdair Munro *fear teagaisg a bha an Srath Nàbhair* (a minister who was in Strathnaver) and by Sir John Stewart of Appin. These three belong to an earlier generation and, as such, are worthy examples of what Ian Grimble[24] has called 'the pious gentry which had played such a dominant role in planting the reformed church in the lowlands and highlands alike'.

Sir John Stewart's litany of prototypical heroes of faith, drawn from the Old Testament – Noah, Moses, David, Shadrach Meshach and Abednego, Susanna, Daniel and Manasseh – are, of course, favourites of reformed homiletics. Also Reformed is the unmistakable emphasis on God's Word, as made effectual by the operation of the Spirit, e.g.:

> (a) O Dhé, mi teagaisg le fìor-chreideamh . . .

(Teach me, O God, through true faith . . .)

> (b) Déan le spionnadh treun do spioraid,
> Dhé mo philleadh is m' iompadh!
> Ath-nuadhaich 's ùraich mo chridh-dhùilean
> 's gum faighinn sùilean sìor-dhiadhaidh.

(By the great power of your Spirit, O God, effect my repentance and conversion: renew and refresh my affection, that I may receive godly eyes.)[25]

> (c) Ge tàim lochdte, O Rìgh shochraidh [?]
> le brìgh t'fhocail dìon mi . . . [26]

(though I am sinful O God, shelter me by the power of your Word.)

---

[23] Sabbatarianism became a distinctive mark of Protestantism throughout Europe, but it did not become as strict as it has since become until the late eighteenth and early nineteenth centuries.
[24] Ian Grimble (1979), 28.
[25] C. MacPhàrlain (1923), 37. The poem is by Alasdair Munro; on whom see Ian Grimble (1979), 25-6, 28.
[26] Ms reads *ge taimb loighti o ri hoghri*.

The quality of the serious and religious verse of Donnchadh mac Ruairi[27] or of Alasdair mac Mhurchaidh[28] and his son Murchadh mac 'ic Mhurchaidh is not in question, either in terms of form or of content. But, except for the fact that they invoke neither the saints nor the Virgin Mary, they show in general no specifically Protestant characteristics. It is as though there was a kind of time-lag: they might have been written in the classical language in the immediately preceding centuries. All the great commonplaces of medieval religious verse are there. Gille-bhrìde in his *crosanachd* employs the *ubi sunt?* form: he asks where is the strength of Samson or of Cù Chulainn now or the labours of Hercules, the beauty of Absolom or Aristotle's mind. The *sic transit* theme occurs over and over: it receives delicate and restrained expression in the following by Sir John Stewart:

> Mar an dealt ri latha ciùin
> no' n sneachd is dlùithe bhios geal;
> toradh nan duill' air a' chrann
> nì mhair daoine sionn ach seal.

> An rós is cumhra no'n lili,
> am plumas no 'n siridh dearg,
> gur gearr a bhitheas iad fo bhlàth:
> siud meadhair an tsluaigh gu dearbh.[29]

(Like the dew on a calm day or like the snow lying packed and white, the growth of leaves on the tree: people stay here for but a little time.
The most fragrant rose or lily, the plum or the red cherry: only for a little they are in bloom: and so it is with the mirth of Man.)

---

[27] Ms *donochig mc ryrie* probably to be identified with Donnchadh mac Raoiridh who died c.1630 and was bard to MacDonald of Sleat.
[28] Died 1642. See S. Maclean, 'Alasdair mac Mhurchaidh', in *Transactions of the Gaelic Society of Inverness*, 41. Alasdair was fourth chief of the Mackenzies of Achilty. His son, Murchadh mac' ic Mhurchaidh, who died about 1689 having succeeded his father in the chieftainship and acted as chamberlain for Mackenzie of Seaforth in Lewis, was also a very fine poet. See W. Matheson, 'Further gleanings from the Dornie Manuscript', *Transactions of the Gaelic Society of Inverness*, 45.
[29] C. MacPhàrlain (1923), 45.

Later in the same poem this theme is interwoven with that of the soul's battle against (in this case) the world, greed and the flesh – a theme which, in one form or another, occurs several times in the Fernaig collection. That conflict achieves a refined expression in what Sorley Maclean has called 'the restrained, economical ironic and paradoxical' poems of Alasdair mac Mhurchaidh concerned, as they mostly are, 'with the battle over the very mixed soul' of the poet. Even the abrupt final stanza of his poem *Is tursach dhuinne ri port* in which, after lamenting friends and patrons now dead, and hours spent sailing on the Minch, and comparing it with today's inactivity and (in a stanza omitted by W.J. Watson from *Bàrdachd Gàidhlig*) impotence,[30] he turns to the 'holy book', is characteristic of much medieval European verse. The same could be said of Donnchadh mac Raoiri, who is probably to be identified as the bard to Macdonald of Sleat of the same name.[31]

These gentlemen were in charge of their world: but they were not involved in theological polemics. They had no need stridently to reiterate the theological emphases of the Reformation.

What did move the gentlemen of this class increasingly as the seventeenth century wore on, was the control of the church and questions about that and other matters raised by the war between Charles I and the Estates, the Restoration and the deposing of King James VII. It could, indeed, be argued that the most specifically 'protestant' verse in the Fearnaig ms is not theological or devotional at all, but political. It is certainly the liveliest: and this is not surprising for, to a man like Donnchadh nam pios (Protestant, Episcopalian, Jacobite chief of the Macraes of Kintail under Seaforth) a lot was at stake. After all, in the years after 1688 some 500 non-juring ministers were to lose parishes without compensation,[32] all of them presented to those parishes by people like Donnchadh nam pios. The Williamite settlement

---

[30] *Op.cit.* 230-2. Cf. C. MacPhàrlain (1923), 147, stanza 19.
[31] Cf. note 27 above.
[32] Bruce Lenman, *The Jacobite Risings in Britain 1689-1746*, London 1980, 55 ff.

threatened to disturb – not so much Reformed doctrine, as the structures of control over the church.

In a song he composed just after the exile of King James, Donnchadh says in a rather melancholy vein:

> Ge bu mhór a shaibhreas 's a mhùirn,
> a staoighle fòs 's a dhà chrùn,
> a shlóghraidh uile 's a threis
> d'fhògradh leo e gu mìdheis.

> Ge bu mhór a thabhairt 's a dhuais
> dà chomhairle agus dà shluagh,
> do dh'ìoc iad fhéile le tais:
> éiteach an sgeul ri h-aithris.

> Mac a pheathar – fàth an euchd -
> comhcheangailt' ris air dhà ghleus;
> a chliamhain, fheòil agus fhuil.
> chaidh da dheòin 'ga dhì-chrùnadh dhuinn.[33]

(Though great was his wealth and his hospitality, his 'style' and his two crowns, all his host and his might, he was banished unjustly by them. Though great his giving and his rewards to his council and his host, they repaid him coldly: it is a melancholy story to tell. His sister's son related to him in two ways: his son-in-law, his flesh and blood, went against him to dethrone him for us.)

In a second song, composed at the same time, Donnchadh traces present trouble back to the beheading of Charles I:

> Bho'n latha mhurt sibh Rìgh Seurlas
> tha fhuil-san aig éigheachd gu teann:
> 'Gabh aithridh a t'eucoir!
> Thoir dhachaidh Rìgh Seumas
> no thig sgiùrsadh bho Dhé ort a nall!'[34]

(Ever since you murdered King Charles, his blood is crying out: 'Repent of your misdeed! Bring home King James, or scourging from God will come upon you')

and, in a poem which is anonymous with the ms, the well-worn parallel between David/Absolom and James/William is

---

[33] C. MacPhàrlain (1923) 170-2.
[34] C. MacPhàrlain (1923) 186-7.

neatly worked out. For God it will be no problem to send William and Mary home.

> ach réir's mar thachair a Dhàibhidh,
> 's a mhac àluinn da shìorruith,
> thig Rìgh Seumas gu àite
> dh'ainneoin cràbhadh Phreisbìtri.[35]

(. . . but just as happened to David when his lovely son Absolom was pursuing him continually, King James will come into his own in spite of the devotion of Presbytery.)

An anonymous poem contains a stanza which gives a vivid and gloating impression of the Covenanters dead and dying on the battlefield at Killicrankie when the conflict was over:

> Bu lìonmhor 'san uair ud
> corp a' gluasad 's e leòinte:
> cinn, aid agus gruagan,
> fir gun chluasan, gun chomhradh;
> cha chluinnt' ann a dh'éibh ach
> 'Alas!' agus 'Woe 's me!'
> 'Quarters for Jesus!'/
> bu bheurla dhaibh 'n comhnuidh.[36]

(Many's the wounded body moving there at that time – heads, hats and hair, men with no ears, without words. And all you would hear would be 'Alas!' and 'Woe is me!' 'Quarters for Jesus!' was their continual English.)

In all the above we have been dealing, of course, with the thoughts, conflicts and loyalties of the *uaislean*, the upper stratum of highland society, insofar as evidence permits us to do so. The common people have left us no manuscripts. What they thought, what the more or less syncretistic religion they practised was like, is not open to our unobstructed view. Only painstaking and methodologically hazardous research into the oral material collected since the time of Alexander Carmichael[37] and the careful sifting of such evidence as has been gathered into the archives of the School of Scottish

[35] C. MacPhàrlain (1923) 176-7.
[36] C. MacPhàrlain (1923) 196-9. The title is *Soraidh a chaidh a chur am meadarachd dàin dh'ionnsaigh nan uaislean Gàidhealach a bha ar latha Raoin Ruaraidh.*
[37] Alexander Carmichael (1832-1912), the great nineteenth-century collector of oral material, the greater part of whose collection has appeared in *Carmina Gadelica* I-VI, on which see D.S. Thomson (1983), 36.

Studies at the University of Edinburgh can begin to enlighten us. But there can be little doubt that the position varied from place to place and from time to time during the whole of this period. No doubt can exist either that, even before 1560, especially those people who lived in inaccessible places were often cut off from ordinances, catachesis and discipline of the Church for extended periods of time. The experience of Mgr Fearchar[38] in 1610 on his visit to Lewis with Coinneach the laird of Kintail, when the latter was trying finally to bring the island under his authority, probably was different only in degree from that of pre-Reformation priests from time to time. According to Kintail tradition still current at the turn of the last century, Mgr Fearchar married people who had been cohabiting for years, baptized people of 50 years of age and even had to sprinkle at random with a heather those seeking baptism, so great were their numbers.

Martin Martin tells of people in Lewis sacrificing to Shony who appears to be a sea-spirit, and evidence points to St Maol Rubha having turned into a numen of some kind inhabiting an island in the middle of Loch Maree in Ross-shire. Customs too numerous to mention, particularly those associated with the great seasonal festivals, and no doubt associated with the old pre-Christian religion, long survived the introduction of Christianity and were in time baptized into it.

They appear to have survived a reformation which was initially an upper-class affair and which affected the lives of ordinary clanspeople very little indeed. Certainly by the time John McSwan was giving evidence to the Napier Commission in Skye (where very few had any first-hand acquaintance with Roman Catholics) it was very easy to identify what he had heard of Catholicism with idolatry, paganism and the worldly pastimes which the godly were expected to turn away from.

In the Napier Commission Report on Skye[39] Fraser-MacKintosh, one of the Commissioners, is quoted as asking McSwan,

---

[38]   Alexander Macrae (1899).

[39]   *Report of Her Majesty's Commissioners of Inquiry into the condition of the crofters and cotters in the Highlands and Islands of Scotland*, 1884 (British Parliamentary Papers) Query 7360.

one of those giving evidence from the parish of Diurinish, for an explanation for the decrease in pipe-playing. John McSwan replied: 'My opinion is that they were looking more to the Pope than they are to-day and I believe it is the Gospel that has done away with the pipe'.

In all this, however, it is important to consider that the evidence from the rest of contemporary Europe confirms that, even where there was an energetic clerical presence, Christian and pagan belief and practice could persistently co-exist.[40]

The large corpus of waulking songs sung by women at the fulling of the cloth scarcely adverts to matters of faith and practice, but the songs do mention religion at one point where it impinged most forcibly on their lives, i.e. the discipline of the church in the punishment of fornicators and adulterers. In one poignant song a young woman who has been raped by her brother ends this way:

'S mi màireach dol dha'n tseisein.
Gur h-ainneamh ann luchd mo leithsgeil.
Gura lìonair luchd mo leatrom;
Bidh am ministear ann 'na sheasamh.
Galair 'na cheann, gé b'e an teasach;
's gun e dh'éirigh as am feasda![41]

(Tomorrow I go before the session: there will be few to take my part and many more to do me injury. The minister will be standing there. Sickness take him – even if it be the fever and he never rises again!)

Significantly, in the light of what we will be noting below about the poetry and song of the evangelicals, it is not till the nineteenth century that religious themes enter the corpus of what was sung at the waulking board. That was when the converted jibbed at singing the traditional words and provided godly ones to take their place.[42]

[40] Calum I. Maclean (1915-60), the first collector and research worker in the School of Scottish Studies, himself born and reared in the largely Free Presbyterian island of Raasay, refers to this phenomenon in his native island in his book, *The Highlands*, London 1959, 129-30.

[41] K.C. Craig (ed.), *Òrain luaidh*, Glasgow 1949, 26.

[42] See Mórag Macleod's notes to the waulking songs on the cassette *Harris Tweed, Òrain luaidh/waulking songs*, Clò Mór 1986.

We have already referred to the worldliness of many of the eighteenth-century ministers. The spectacular *trahison des clercs* committed by many of them when they failed to defend the people against clearance, and in some cases even went so far as to suggest that forced emigration came upon them as a punishment for sin, has been well documented. What is less often spoken of is the ministers, both 'moderate' and 'evangelical', who sustained the culture of the parish and in their own manses, though Dr John MacInnes[43] and the Revd R. Macleod[44] in recent articles have done a lot to right the balance in this respect. They have drawn attention to the skill as piper and fiddler of Maighstir Morchadh (the Revd Murdoch Macdonald of Durness, Rob Donn's minister) and the fact that his sons, Joseph and the Revd Patrick, were the author or publisher respectively of a study of *pìobaireachd* and the first collection of highland airs.

One also thinks of the great ms collection of song made by the Rev James Maclagan of Blair Atholl and the Revd Donald MacNicol of Lismore.[45] And, whatever about the last-mentioned, Maighstir Morchadh must (on the evidence of what survives of his diary) be accounted an evangelical of great earnestness. In the light of the almost manichean puritanism of the nineteenth century, it is worthy of note that even in the manse of the Revd Donald MacDonald the 'Apostle of the North' there was known on occasion to be dancing.

Still less often spoken of is the manifest effectiveness of the evangelicalism which moulded a man like Rob Don (1714-1778). As a young boy Rob Donn was taken on to be a cowherd with Iain mac Eachainn, the tacksman of Strathmore.[46] In due course, he accompanied his master

---

[43]   J. MacInnes, 'Religion in the Highlands', *Transactions of the Gaelic Society of Inverness*, 52, 222-42.
[44]   R. Macleod, 'Ministearan an arain' TGSI 52, 243-69.
[45]   D.S. Thomson (ed.) (1983), 179, 188.
[46]   Ian Grimble (1979), *passim*.

on a long trek southwards to sell the black cattle in the markets of Falkirk, Crieff and even perhaps Carlisle. Though he was the child of musical parents, he was not born into a bardic family. His songs do inherit some of the tradition of rhetoric of the professional panegyrists, but the cast of mind has changed radically. He has no parallel in Ireland and, coming as he does just before the patriarchal social system was swept away by 'Improvement' and clearance, he has no exact parallel in Scotland either, if it comes to that. The old panegyric started with a 'mould' into which the composer (as it were) poured the individual. Rob Donn begins with the individual, whom he then proceeds to assess in terms of a set of expectations and standards which transcend those of aristocracy and clan solidarity, though he would not have imagined that those standards were in any way threatened by them.

Quite the contrary: when Rob Donn came to lament Iain mac Eachainn, who had so long been his employer but who had also been, to all intents and purposes, his foster-father, he ends by saying what the elegist of an earlier time could not truthfully have said:

> Ach ged bhithinn-sa air mo mhionnan
> do'n Tì tha cumail nan dùl rium,
> cha do luaidh mi mu'n duine-sa
> ach buaidh a chunnaic mo shùil air.[47]

(Though I should be on my oath to the One who sustains me, I have not mentioned any quality in this man which I did not see with my own eyes.)

The praise of generosity and hospitality, the full table with shining cups and plates, the provision of music and dancing, are commonplaces of traditional praise, and Rob Donn does not forget them. Following Iain mac Eachainn's death he says: 'I see the musician no longer honoured and the loss of his talent for want of practice' (Chì mi an ceolair gun mhios air,/ call a ghibht do chion cleachdaidh).[48] But Rob

---

[47] W.J. Watson, *Bàrdachd Gàidhlig*, Stirling (1959), 85.
[48] ibid. 85.

Donn's theme is different: his moral framework is concern for the responsibilities that go along with land and wealth and, against this framework, he praises Iain and weighs the new landholders who are interested only in profit, and finds them wanting:

> Leis an lethonoir riataich-s'
> tha na ceudan diubh faomadh,
> leis an fheàrr bhith am fiachaibh
> fada aig Dia na aig daoinibh . . .[49]

(To this semi-honour hundreds of them are inclined, who much prefer to be in debt to God than to men . . . .)

Rob Donn is so familiar with the Bible that he can cite or paraphrase in a quite unforced and natural way, as in the following:

> Fhir nach d'ith mìr le taitneas
> nam b'eòl duit acrach san tsaoghal;
> fhir nach faiceadh am feumnach
> gun an éigh aige chluintinn;
> b'fheàrr leat punnd de do chuid uat
> na unnsa chudtrom air t'intinn:
> thilg thu t'aran air uisgeach'
> is gheibh do shliochd iomadh-fillt' e.[50]

(You who could not eat a bite so long as you knew there was a hungry person in the world; you who could not see the needy person without hearing his cry; you would rather miss a pound of your money than have an ounce weighing on your conscience: you cast your bread upon the waters and your offspring will get it back many times over.)

Rob Donn's verse is saturated with the Calvinist ethic, giving him an ethical context which often engenders courage though it should be said that from time to time it degenerates into an unattractive self-righteousness. What is significant from the point of view of this article is that Rob Donn did not come from a family of *filidhean*, nor was he of aristocratic birth like such bards of the previous century as Eachann Bacach

---

[49]   ibid. 83.
[50]   ibid. 84.

or Iain Lom. He could claim no immunity.[51] When he turned on Lady Reay for trying to marry to a local young man one of her maids who had become pregnant (by a gentleman close to Lady Reay?), Rob Donn stands alone, armed only with that morality to which he believes all must submit. This is something new in Gaelic poetry, and comes from a new direction: Protestantism has found a voice in the cowherd drover.

The traumatic events of 1745-6; the penal legislation which followed and was applied across the board without regard to what side people had in fact taken in the Rising; the dramatic rise in rents which led to emigration by tacksmen and sub-tenants to Carolina;[52] the clearance of thousands of poor people by their own clan chiefs, often with the acquiescence of their ministers, undoubtedly led to a loss of confidence, a widespread bewilderment and sense of anxiety and often inarticulate resentment among those who were left. In such a situation the new evangelicalism made a pronounced appeal.

(a) In the face of military defeat, penal legislation and further serious attack on the language and culture of the highlands,[53] it offered the sword of the spirit and the helmet of salvation, religious experience and personal relationship with the Lord of a kind that was more pietistic than it was Calvinist. Not long after the '45 in which one poet had spoken of the Jacobite cause as being *soisgeul nan Garbhchrìoch*, 'the Gospel of the highlands', Dùghall Bochanan the Rannoch teacher wrote this:

[51] Speaking of a case against Neil Morrison the Pabbay bard brought before the Sheriff by a woman whom Neil had attacked in a poem, an old Harris woman told Neil Macdonald (TGSI 53, 229) that the bard was in an awkward position because his 'name was not in the Book of the Bards' (Cha robh ainm ann an Leabhar nam Bard). When the case came up, Sheriff Shaw who was a Gaelic speaker said: 'Bheil Niall Moireasdan, Bard Phabbaidh an làthair?/Is Neil Morrison the Pabbay bard present?' Without further delay, as Neil came forward the Sheriff asked, 'Có ghoir bàrd dhìot?/Who said you were a bard?' to which he replied, 'A' Siorram Seadha/Sheriff Shaw.' And since he had been classified as a bard, apparently that was the end of the matter. The 'Book of the Bards' is of course a fictional notion, but it reflects what must be an ancient notion of bardic immunity.
[52] Cf. W. Matheson, *The Songs of John MacCodrum*, Edinburgh 1938, 314 ff.
[53] C.W.J. Withers, *Gaelic in Scotland 1698-1981*, Edinburgh 1984, *passim*.

Cha bu ghaisgeach Alasdair Mór,
no Caesar thug an Ròimh gu géill;
oir ged a thug iad buaidh air càch,
dh'fhan iad 'nan tràill' d'am miannaibh féin.

Cha ghaisge an nì bhith liodart dhaoin',
's cha chliù bhith ann an caonnaig tric;
chan uaisle intinn àrdan borb
's cha treubhantas bhith garg gun iochd.

Ach 's gaisgeach esan a bheir buaidh
air eagal beatha 's uamhunn bàis,
's a chomhlaicheas le misnich cridh,
a huile nì ata dha 'n dàn.[54]

(Alexander the Great was no hero, nor was Caesar though he
vanquished Rome; for even though they conquered others
they remained slaves to their own desires. To be wounding
people is not heroism nor is it glorious frequently to fight.
Nobility does not come from haughty pride nor is it valour
mercilessly to fight. A hero is one who has overcome the
fears of life and terror of death and who encounters what lies
in store for him with courageous heart.)

The greatest battle is the battle within, and here Buchanan
paraphrases and adapts Paul (Phil. 6 12-16), but see in what
attitude the battle is won:

A nàmh cha choisinn air gu bràth
ged gheibh e sàrachadh ri huair;
's e neart 's a shlàinte cridhe bruit',
is air a ghlùinibh bheir e buaidh.[55]

(His foe will not ever overcome him, even though he may
sometimes be exhausted; his strength and his health are a
bruised spirit, and he shall conquer on his knees.)

Buchanan goes on (stanza 17) to speak of overcoming the
passions in order to subdue a kingdom in the self, but the
shape of a dualism to come can be descried in the following
stanza even though, at first sight, it seems merely to echo
Isaiah 40:

[54] *Dàin Spioradail le Dùghall Bochanan/Spiritual Songs of Dugald Buchanan*,
Glasgow 1946, 37.
[55] Dùghall Bochanan, *op.cit.* 38.

Biodh t'intinn ard os cionn nan speur,
chan eil fo'n ghréin ach pòrsan truagh;
mar tholman ùire faic an saogh'l,
is daoin' mar sheangain air mun cuairt.[56]

(Let your mind be set above the skies, for this world's portion
is but poor, like little hillock behold the world with men like
ants around it crawling.)

Certainly, a new *Innerlichkeit*, 'foes without and fears within,
by Satan sorely pressed', with the hint of anxiety of a sexual
character, has entered the scene by Buchanan's time.

Also new (though it has parallels from other times and
places) is a preoccupation with the sufferings of the Saviour which becomes unwholesome when it is entertained
at the expense of concern for the sufferings of those he
came to save. This tendency in highland devotion with its
attendant political supineness has often been castigated, but
never more eloquently than by Sorley Maclean in his poem
Calvary or in *Highland Woman*:

Chan eil mo shùil air Chalbharraigh
no air Betlehem an àigh
ach air cùil ghrod an Glaschu
far bheil an lobhadh fàis,
agus air seòmar an Dùn-éideann,
seòmar bochdainn 's cràidh,
far a bheil an naoidhean creuchdach
ri aonagraich gu bhàs.[57]

(My eye is not on Calvary nor on Bethlehem the Blessed, but
on a foul-smelling backland in Glasgow, where life rots as
it grows; and on a room in Edinburgh, a room of poverty
and pain, where the diseased infant writhes and wallows till
death.)

While the justice of this and other criticism must be
acknowledged, it should perhaps also be said that the
individualism and pietism which came sometimes to very
beautiful expression, also indicate the way in which evangelical Protestantism was capable of giving a sense of value and

[56]   Dùghall Bochanan, *op.cit.* 39.
[57]   S. MacGilleàin, *Reothairt is contraigh*, Dùn Éideann 1977, 85. 'Ban-
Ghàidheal/Highland Woman' is on p.77.

self-respect to people who saw very little evidence elsewhere in their lives that they mattered at all. So, while it is true that what Sorley Maclean, with irony, called Christ's 'gentle' church often only compounded the highland woman's suffering by speaking of her 'lost soul' before committing her to the grey sleep of death, another highland woman, Anna Mic Ealair, would sing:

'S ann a thug thu dhomh do ghaol
fo dhubhar craobh an aiteil;
a's comh-chomunn do rùin
ann an gàradh nan ubhall.

Is millse leam do ghaol na'm fion –
seadh, am fion nuair is treis' e –
's nuair a thug thu dhomh do ghràdh
's ann a dh'fhàilnich mo phearsa.

'S ann a thug thu dhomh do ghràdh
gusan d'fhàilnich mo phearsa;
's gusam b'éigin dhomh a ràdh
'Cum air do làimh, a charaid'.

'S ann a dh'éirich thu le buaidh
as an uaigh suas le cabhaig,
amhluidh dhùisgeas do shluagh
suas le buaidh anns a' mhadainn.

'S chaidh thu suas air ionad ard
dh'ullach' àite do m'anam;
's tha thu 'g ràdh gun tig thu rìs
a choimh-lìonadh do gheallaidh.[58]

(You gave me your love in the shade of the juniper and the companionship of your love in the garden of apples. Sweeter to me than wine is your love – yes, than the strongest of wine and when you gave me your love my body melted away. When you gave me your love, my body melted away, and I had to say 'Friend, restrain your hand.' You rose victoriously from the tomb and so also will your people awake victorious in the morning. And you went up to a high place to prepare a place

58   Gilleasbuig Mac na Ceàrdadh, *An t-Òranaiche*, Glasgow 1889, 425-6.

for my soul, and you say you will come again to fulfil your promise.)

Even highland ministers who cannot be dismissed as Moderates were often deeply suspicious of preaching which appeared to give too prominent a place to the individual's experience, whether in terms of their conviction of sin or their conversion. Everything in their Calvinist rearing, not least the double predestination of the *Westminster Confession* and the *Shorter Catechism*, reacted against such an emphasis. One might preach (particularly at evening services when they were introduced in the nineteenth century) for conversions, but orthodox preachers in the highlands knew perfectly well that this was done in the context of the *rùintean sìorraidh*, the eternal decrees of God whereby for His own good pleasure he had foreordained whatsoever comes to pass.[59] The call was directed towards confirmation of one's election (2 Peter 10-11) – no less and certainly no more – and it was an awesome call. But it did serve to keep even the best preaching in perspective: it was itself no more and no less than the voice for that effectual call of God to those whom He had elected from all eternity. This acknowledgment of the sovereignty of God could (and often did/does) lead to a certain gloominess in the face of so inscrutable a deity, as men and women sought to 'confirm their election' or to discern the signs of it in themselves and others. To this Ruaraidh Mac Thòmais bears a kind of grudging testimony in his great poem, *Am Bodach Ròcais/The Scarecrow*:

> . . . sguab e 'n teine a meadhon an làir
> 's chuir e 'n turlach loisgeach 'nar broillichean.[60]

(. . . he swept the fire from the centre of the floor, and set a scaring bonfire in our breast.)

Sometimes this sense of God's sovereignty gives rise to a largely passive but no doubt very profound sense of satisfaction tinged a little with fear, as on the occasion of the storm in 1887, when Fraser of Kilmuir's great house was swept away by

[59] Shorter Catechism Q.
[60] Domhnall Mac Amhlaigh (deas.), *Nua-bhàrdachd Ghàidhlig*, Dùn Éideann 1976.

the flood. Writing of the end of the 1870s and the early 1880s, Donald Meek rightly says:

> There was from the beginning a very close connection between the movement for land reform and popular evangelical Presbyterianism. The view that God gave the land to the people is either implicit or explicit in numerous poems, since it helped to reinforce the claim to land based on clan tradition. This was the argument consistently developed by the Revd. Donald MacCallum who was quick to discover that a fusion of biblical allusion and anti-landlord propaganda evoked a powerful response from a devout audience with many personal grievances. It was also something of a comfort to remember that a just God would ultimately punish the cruel landlord whether by divine retribution in this life or at the Judgement.[61]

From time to time during the nineteenth century the sense of God's sovereignty certainly led, not to fatalism or inactivity as one passed through this vale of tears, but to anger and action.

Certainly there is anger in some of the songs of Dr John MacLachlan of Rahoy in Morvern.[62] Dr MacLachlan's practice included most of Morvern and Ardnamurchan. He was the son of a tacksman whose tack had long gone, but who now maintained himself in a prestigious position in his native place by the practice of medicine. He despised many of those who bought up the surrounding estates (including the infamous Patrick Sellar), bound to the country only by financial considerations. He was not a radical: but there is in his songs an element of *ressentiment*, informed with a biblical sense of justice and clear distinction between ownership and occupation of the land. Addressing himself to one who had acquired leases to several townships in Ardnamurchan to the satisfaction of the people but had then proceeded to clear the people off them, he asks in language which echoes Matthew's gospel:

---

[61]   D.E. Meek, 'Gaelic Poets of the Land Agitation', TGSI 49, 326.
[62]   A collection of his poems was published in 1869 in Glasgow under the title *Dàin agus Òrain*, and a number were reprinted in *An t-Òranaiche* (1889). See above, note 58.

Bheil thu 'n dùil gum faigh thu saorsainn
leis na caoirich 's do chuid bhuailtean?
B'fheàrr dhut beannachdan an fheumnaich
d'an tugadh tu 'n déirc' an uaigneas.[63]

(Do you expect to gain salvation with your sheep and booleys?
Better off you would be with the blessings of the needy to
whom you gave alms in secret.)

Much closer to action, however, was Iain Mac a' Ghobhainn
of Iarshader in Lewis (1848-81), who addresses himself to
those who by the 1870s were coming to regard the highlands
as nothing more than a playground for hunting, shooting and
fishing during a few months of the year. He compares their
sport, thoughtlessly enjoyed at the expense of others' liveli-
hood, with the sporting in the ocean of the mythical beast,
Leviathan:

Mar gharbh-leibhìatan nan cuantan,
is fìor-chulaidh-uamhais ri spors e:
faodaidh aon bhuille de èarra
dochann is bàs thoirt air móran.[64]

(Like great Leviathan of the oceans, he's a terror for sport:
one blow from his tail can bring destruction and death to
thousands.)

He then goes on, in language which echoes Isaiah and
the Psalms (e.g. Ps. 104.26) and no doubt the lengthy Gaelic
sermons which were rarely written down:

'N Tì shocraich bun-daingean na talmhainn
's a thug am muir gailbheach gu ordugh,
'n Tì shuidhich bundaingean nan àrdbheann
's a dh'àrdaich am barr gu na neòil orr,
'n Tì chuir ùir air an aigeal
's a sgaoil brat maiseach an fheòir air—
nuair a chunnaic E 'n domhain so crìochnaicht',

---

[63] Matthew 6 3-4: Ach an uair a bheir thusa déirce, na biodh fios air do
làimh chlè ciod a tha do làmh dheas a dhéanamh; chum gu'm bi *do dhéirc'
an uaignidheas*.
[64] D.S. Thomson (1983), 158. His poems appear in I.N. MacLeoid, *Bàrdachd
Leódhais*, Glasgow 1916, 67-131.

dh'iarr E gun lìonte le slòigh e.

(The One who settled the foundation of the earth and brought the restless sea to order; the One who established the base of the high mountains and raised their tops to the clouds; the One who put soil on the abyss and spread a beautiful mantle of grass on it – when He saw this world completed, *He ordered that it should be filled with people.*)

Apparently He does not will it to be denuded of them!

In the moral vacuum created by the aftermath of the '45, emigration, clearance and the *trahison des clercs*, there emerged a modified social structure and a new moral leadership. The 'Men' (*na Daoine*) were a divinely-elected leadership raised up from among the people for such a time as this. Ministers like Mgr Ruairi who, even before 1843, had begun to purge the communion roll and to refuse baptism to the children of the lukewarm, were encouraged to go further.[65] Communicant membership came to be restricted to a small group of (mostly older) people upon whom the *cùram* had come.

The sense that Christians have been called out of the 'world' while still in it and the sense that this is an uneasy calling, is often given most beautiful expression in the hymns of the movement. No-one who has ever heard Murdina Macdonald sing can forget the impact of the song *Smuaintean aonarach*:

> 'S lìonmhor trioblaid is cruaidh chàs 's an fhàsach aig do shluagh-sa
> chuile neach le éigin féin ag éibheach airson fuasgladh
> Cha bhi trioblaid ac' na bròn, nach obraich sòlas buan dhaibh
> Cha bhi cuimhn' air gleann an deòir, bidh crùn na glòir mar dhuais ac'.

> O nach cianail bhios Do shluagh, air uairean anns a' ghleann seo
> Nuair a dh'fhalaicheas Tu go ghnùis orr' 's dumhlaidh bhios an oidhch' ac'

65   R. Macleod, 'The Bishop of Skye' TGSI 53, 180 ff.

Cha déan comh'urtachd bho dhaoine sìth a thoirt dha'n
inntinn
Bidh iad mar ghealbhonn beag 'na aonar 's fear an gaol
air chall orr'.[66]

(Many's the trouble and affliction your people go through
in the desert: each one with their own need crying out for
deliverance. They have no trouble or sorrow that will not
work an everlasting solace for them. They will not remember
the vale of tears: they will have a crown of glory as reward.
How miserable your people are sometimes in this glen, when
you hide your face from them the night is very dark for them.
No human comfort can bring peace to their minds: they are
like the little sparrow on its own and the one they love, lost.)

They are God's people, the remnant and in the desert/vale
of tears/wilderness/darkness they are comforted by what He
has done for them in Christ. What he has done for them in
Christ has its point of origin in the eternal purpose of God
from before all time and is not to be unfolded till the end of
time. This hymn gives expression to that objective aspect of
salvation with simple sensitivity:

'S e crùn daor Ìosa a ghaol, a gheibh na naoimh an uair
od
Choisinn E air a' chrann-cheus, 'nuair dh'éibh E 'Tha e
crìochnaicht'
Chrìochnaich E an obair mhór thug Athair dha ri
dhéanamh
'S siod an duais a bha 'na rùn, na bha 's na rùintean
sìorruidh.

Thug Thu buaidh air bàs is uaigh 's le luathghair rinn thu
éirigh
Chuir Thu cath bha cruaidh ri Sàtan, 's b'éigin dhà-san
géilleadh
Bha Do nàdur-sa cho naomh 's nach gabhadh sgeulachd
breug air
Cha b'e siod do dh' Eubh 's do dh' Adha bh'ann an
Gàrradh Éden.

(His love is the dearly-bought crown which the saints will
get then, which he won on the cross when he cried out, 'It

[66] Miss Murdina MacDonald, Barvas, Lewis, in *Scottish Tradition 2, Music from the Western Isles*, TNGM 110, Side 2: Band 6.

is finished'. He finished the great work his Father gave him and that is the reward that was meant for them – all that was in the eternal decrees.
You gained the victory over death and the grave, and with joy you arose. You gave battle to Satan and he had to yield. Your nature was so holy that no lie could be told about it – not like Eve and Adam in the garden of Eden.)

Side by side with that is something much more subjective, which has its origins in the preaching of those influenced by the Haldanes and others – the fear of a fading vision, an irrecoverable experience. Those who heard the call of the evangelicals emerged either from the moralism of the Moderates or the gloomy fatalism of double predestination. No wonder they spoke of it as 'blessedness' or 'liberation'. No wonder they feared, like Cowper and Newton, to lose the blessedness they knew 'when first they met the Lord':

> Cha bheag an àmhghair th'aig Do shluagh, cridh cruaidh
> is inntinn shaoghalt
> 'Na' smuaintean dh'iarradh iad bhith suas, bho measg
> plaosgan fuar' an t- saoghail
> Chan' eil iad faighinn mar bu mhiann leo, beo do Chrìosd
> 'na ghaol-san
> 'S ann shaoileas iad aig iomadh uair gum bheil an cuan
> air traoghadh.

(Your people have no small share of adversity – hard hearts and worldliness. In their thoughts they would be up and away from the cold husks of the world. They do not get, as they would like, to be alive to Christ in his love – indeed they often think that the tide has ebbed.)

This hymn steers fairly safely between the subjective and objective – perhaps because 'experience' is spoken of not in terms of the first person singular but of the third person plural.

Such hymns are not sung in church services, of course. In church the Psalms of David only are permitted: in the singing of them the individual has a certain freedom of movement, though all the time joined with the rest of the congregation in a corporate praise. It could be argued that this mode of singing gives as eloquent an expression to the creative tension between pietist individualism and Calvinist objectivity as any sermon ever did.[67]

It can hardly be denied that there was now to be seen everywhere a new earnestness: in the homes of adherents, as much as in those of members, family worship came to be a matter of course, and serious efforts were made to control excessive drinking etc. But sometimes, it would appear, ordinary people were taken aback by the excessive puritanism, particularly associated as it was with sabbatarianism and with negative attitudes towards 'worldly songs', story-telling and piping. A lovely story is told of the Dall Munro, the catechist of Skye (c.1773-1830), who had acted for a number of years as a catechist before he was converted by one of the Haldanes' preachers. Prior to his conversion he had always taken his fiddle with him on his rounds. Afterwards he did not, and eventually he even persuaded the people of Skye to make a great bonfire of their fiddles. Shortly after the change came over him, he visited a house in Ainort in the parish of Bracadale and a man said to him:

> 'Is tù fhéin, a Dhomhnaill, a bha grinn an uair bha thu a' tighinn a dh'Ainort a cheasnachadh agus a chluich na fidhle.' 'Nan robh mise air bàs fhaighinn an uair sin,' arsa Domhnall, 'bha mi air a dhol a dh'ifrinn.' 'Chan eil mi creidsinn guth dheth,' arsa'n duine . . . , 'bha thu cho laghach.'[68]

('You were great, Donald, when you were coming to Ainort to catechize and play the fiddle,' said the man. 'Well,' said Donald, 'If I had died then, I would have gone to Hell.' 'I don't believe a word of it,' said the man. 'You were so nice and good.')

In the event a more or less satisfactory *modus vivendi* was arrived at which lasted, with local variation, for decades. While it was understood that communicants would abandon worldly entertainments, it was accepted that those who

---

[67]   *Scottish Tradition 6, Gaelic Psalms from Lewis,* School of Scottish Studies: University of Edinburgh, TNGM 120.

[68]   Domhnall Mac Fhionghuin, *Domhnall 'Munro' an Dall,* Port Rìgh, n.d. 2.

were only adherents (i.e. the great majority) would probably engage in them. Members may to this day include in their number people who were in their youth proficient performers, singers or dancers. The increased puritanism of the nineteenth century can scarcely be detached from a desire to distance oneself as clearly as was possible within a fairly monochrome society from those one was protesting against not only theologically, but socially and politically.

The 'Men' were protesting against indifferentism, and certainly they were placed further down the social scale than the moderate ministers they were criticizing, but they were not social revolutionaries any more than the Free Church leadership in the south was.[69] Free Church ministers by the 1880s were sometimes even being criticized for fraternizing too much with the gentry. Far from occupying themselves fervently in the grievances of their parishioners, they were often as much concerned in disputes about getting a site for a Free Church building from the landlord. In all this it should be understood that what was being erected was not a new society but an alternative and purified social order parallel to the old and, for that reason, political radicalism was only very occasionally a part of it. Certainly, since the Education Act of 1872 which took Gaelic out of the school system for decades, there has been set in motion a slow but tragically accelerating movement towards identifying Christianity and respectability. Against this tide the very best people in the highlands (whether communicants or adherents) have always fought.

Today highland Calvinism is at risk; what is at stake and even who exactly is involved in the conflict would require another study by another person. Suffice to say, in conclusion to this article, that its survival is probably more closely linked with that of the language than is always openly admitted, though tacitly (one suspects) it is widely conceded. Church services are certainly still the most important activity in which Gaelic gets pride of place. However, another view is gaining ground,

69   D.S. Thomson (1983), 86-89.

even in the Free Church of Scotland, which recognizes that the Church cannot be tied to a particular culture or language. This is, of course, quite true, and the expression of it is timely. However, it is also true to say that Christian faith and practice can only come to expression within some cultural context or another.

An outsider may perhaps be permitted to ask whether it is the Gaelic language (which has been the vehicle of expression for a variety of cultures since it arrived in Scotland a millennium and a half ago) which is shackling highland Protestantism so that it becomes a *Kulturchristentum*. Is it not rather the dogged attempt to recapture and petrify the experience of the evangelicals that is doing the damage, forgetting that that experience was new and liberating once too? The language can open up to view the plurality of experience of the people who have lived over centuries in the highlands and islands. The evangelicals were offering a coherent vision in the face of social trauma and they selected certain practices and signs of witness (which included strict sabbatarianism) to give expression to this. No honour is done to them by pretending that we are living in the eighteenth or nineteenth centuries or are faced with the same threats. (The imperfect sabbatarianism of the House of Windsor is probably not the most serious threat to the moral health of the nation). The fact that the evangelicals either were ignorant of the historical-critical method or set their faces against it, does not mean that twentieth-century highland ministers should do so. In fact a historical approach to Scripture could itself liberate people from an anachronistic and slavish relationship to their own past.

Those who select the language as the most appropriate element of the past to say farewell to, necessarily opt for another culture. A de-Calvinized, de-Gaelicized highland Protestantism would seem set fair to be no more than the Hebridean branch of an English-speaking mid-Atlantic pietism, unmonitored by those emphases within Calvinism which, at their best, always distrusted 'religious experience' as being potentially just another attempt to walk by sight.

Medieval Wales and the Reformation

Glanmor Williams

Christianity, it hardly needs saying, formed no part of the original Celtic heritage of the Welsh. It was first brought to Britain by Roman merchants and soldiers and, during the era of imperial rule, remained very much a religion of the towns and the civilian settlements, of which there were relatively few in Wales. When the legions finally departed, Christianity undoubtedly survived, as may be gleaned from the archaeological record of a Roman town like Caerwent or the Roman villa at Llantwit Major, and also from the accounts of missions by St Germanus of Auxerre, who came to Britain in the fifth century AD and combated with devastating success such followers of the British-born heretic, Pelagius, as he found there. Furthermore, the sixth-century writings of Gildas, the only contemporary native author whose work survives, make it plain that he was addressing an audience that had long been mainly Christian, even if some of them – notably their rulers – were outrageously sinful and near-pagan in their practice.[1]

---

[1] For the early church history of Britain and Wales, see L. Alcock, *Arthur's Britain* (1971); M.W. Barley and R.P.C. Hanson, *Christianity in Britain, 300-700* (1968); J.E. Lloyd, *A History of Wales* (1948).

Nevertheless, one of the most striking and long-lived features of the religious history of the Welsh was the profound impact made upon them by 'Celtic Christianity'. This was the legacy of the activities of the 'Celtic saints' among them from the fifth to the seventh-eighth centuries AD.[2] These enthusiastic, peripatetic evangelizers, mainly monks, were associated with a number of lands which then spoke Celtic languages – Ireland, western Scotland and the Isles, the Isle of Man, parts of northern England, Wales, Cornwall and Brittany – and most of which we still think of as the Celtic countries and regions. It was the impetus given by these monks as itinerant preachers and missionaries which did a great deal to extend and strengthen Christian belief and worship among the population. They not only inherited the existing Christian tradition but were candescently inspired by the infusion into their midst of the ascetic ideals of Eastern Christianity, which spread into Britain via France; a religious and cultural importation that seems to be confirmed by archaeological finds of high-quality pottery of eastern Mediterranean origin. Their ranks may also have been augmented by the arrival among them of Christian compatriots moving westwards from those parts of Britain which were coming under pressure from pagan Anglo-Saxons. Certainly, there survived long afterwards an intense awareness of what the Britons believed to be their Christian superiority over the pagan and barbarian origins of the Anglo-Saxons.

Information concerning the Celtic saints is sparse and uncertain. Most of those *vitae* which purport to recount their deeds, with one or two rare exceptions like the seventh-century life of St Samson of Dol in Brittany, were not committed to writing until five or six hundred years after their lifetime.[3] Though, like the Life of St David by Rhigyfarch (1056-1099), they may contain fragments of early material

---

[2]   E.G. Bowen, *The Settlements of the Celtic Saints in Wales* (1954); *Saints, Seaways, and Settlements in Celtic Lands* (1977); N.K. Chadwick, *The Age of the Saints in the Early Celtic Church* (1961); G.H. Doble, *The Lives of the Welsh Saints* (1971); Siân Victory, *The Celtic Church in Wales* (1977).
[3]   S.G. Baring-Gould and J. Fisher, *The Lives of the British Saints* (1907-13); A.W. Wade-Evans, *Vitae Sanctorum Britanniae et Genealogiae* (1944); *Welsh Christian Origins* (1934).

transmitted down the centuries by oral tradition, they are interspersed with so many legends, miraculous stories, and hagiographical myths, that it becomes extremely difficult to establish the truth concerning the genuine deeds of the saints. Some, especially those of south-east Wales, such as Illtud or Dubricius, were associated with traditions of learning. A few, like Cadog or David, were well-known, widely venerated, and have a number of churches dedicated to them in more than one Celtic country. Others were much more localized in their appeal and are remembered in no more than a single dedication, like Crallo, recalled now only at Llangrallo (Coychurch). But the widespread general appeal of these saints is impressively borne out by the large number of ancient Welsh place-names which are made up of the element *Llan* (meaning church) together with the name of the saint to whom it is dedicated, e.g. Llandeilo ('the church of Teilo'), or Llantrisant ('the church of three saints'). Not all of these names go back as far as the lifetime of the saint(s) whose name is preserved, and many of these churches were dedicated to them after they themselves were dead – saintly dedications being somewhat unstable in the Middle Ages. But all the same the nomenclature brings out the popular attraction of the saints; a popularity which survived throughout the Middle Ages and well beyond. Though they were not formally canonized, these saints acquired for themselves an illustrious reputation as men of exceptional sanctity on the basis of their dedicated leadership, their moral qualities, and their power to work miracles.[4]

Many of them had chosen the monastic way of life. Reliable evidence exists to show that there were men living according to the monastic rule from the fifth century onwards. The number of monastic foundations appears to have increased substantially between c.550 and 650 AD and that period was distinguished by an increased impetus to travel abroad and found new churches in fresh territories. Some devotees went as far as to live a life of unworldly holiness in eremitical isolation or in the company of a small select group of associates,

---

[4] Wendy Davies, *Wales in the Early Middle Ages* (1982).

often on island sites such as Caldey off the Pembrokeshire coast or St Seiriol's Island off Anglesey. Testimony from early sources right down to Rhigyfarch's eleventh-century Life of St David suggests that many of these men, whether living in community or not, set great store by austerity and self-renunciation. The ascetic ideals of these early monks, and especially of the hermits, were held up for centuries afterwards as the very mirror of Christian perfection. There is no doubt, either, that for a long period after the fifth and sixth centuries, the monastery had a more important and prominent role in the Welsh Church, even if it was less significant than it was in Ireland, than was usual in many other countries.

In spite of the importance of the monastic element, however, there remained considerable scope for the influence and authority of bishops also. Some of the leading monasteries, like St David's or Llandeilo Fawr, housed a bishop as well as an abbot. 'There was no incongruity in placing the seat of a bishopric in a monastery', says Dr Wendy Davies, 'no distinction of type was seen between the two communities; and there may have been no actual distinction between the two, particularly by the ninth and tenth centuries.'[5] From the bishops downwards, it was usual for the clergy to take wives, and the practice of clerical marriage remained widespread in Wales right down to the Reformation, when legislation permitted it again. Among the Welsh clergy, before the Norman Conquest it was common enough for sons to succeed to their fathers' benefices by hereditary right, although it is also only fair to recall that remarkable gifts of learning and character might be transmitted in some clerical families along with ecclesiastical position and material possessions; as such gifted bodies of men as the family of Bishop Sulien (1011-1091) of St David's, or the family of Llancarfan in the diocese of Llandaff, remind us.[6]

---

[5] Davies, Early Middle Ages, p.149.
[6] J.E. Lloyd, 'Bishop Sulien and his Family', National Library of Wales Journal, II (1941-2), 1-6; J. Conway Davies, Episcopal Acts relating to Welsh Dioceses, 1066-1272 (Hist. Soc. Church in Wales, 1946-8).

The administration and jurisdiction exercised by these bishops are not easily determined. Neither is the number of pre-Conquest dioceses; there may have been as many as seven bishops' seats in south Wales, including centres like Llandeilo Fawr and Llanbadarn, as well as St David's and Llandaff, though only two – Bangor and Llanelwy (St Asaph) – have been traced in the north. The bishops of St David's may have enjoyed a place of some pre-eminence among their brethren, judging by some slight indications in the writings of Asser and elsewhere; but it is almost certain that this did not constitute an institutionalized archbishopric but was merely a recognition of greater prestige and distinction. Over most of the pre-Norman period the links between the bishops and those clergy who recognized their authority took the form of an association between 'mother' churches, founded mostly by major saints, and 'daughter' churches, founded later by the same saint or one of his followers and acknowledging a state of 'filial' dependence on the 'mother' churches. Thus, for instance, many churches in Glamorgan regarded Illtud's foundation at Llantwit Major as their mother church; others in mid-Wales looked to Padarn's church at Llanbadarn; while those of the north-west were dependent on Beuno's foundation at Clynnog. Nevertheless, by the end of the 'Celtic' period, i.e. the tenth and eleventh centuries, there are signs of a gradual shift towards a more territorial organization of diocesan arrangements. A number of monasteries continued to exist, but all were under the overarching authority of bishops.

Some of the larger and better-known churches exercised extensive privileges of protection (*nawdd*) over those who fled to them for sanctuary. They zealously upheld and guarded such powers, since they were among the most efficacious weapons they had at their disposal when contending with lay powers. The Life of St David, for example, went to the length of claiming that all the bishops of the British Church acknowledged that David's protection 'should apply to every ravisher and homicide and sinner, and to every person flying from place to place in every kingdom and each region where there may be land consecrated to holy David'. And, it added, 'let no kings or elders or governors or even bishops, abbots, and saints dare to grant protection in priority to holy David'.[7] Closely associated with such moral authority was the formidable talent for cursing their enemies attributed to some of the Celtic saints; Cadog, for one, was credited with having caused robbers to be swallowed by the earth and King Rhun and his followers to be blinded.

Comparatively little can be established with certainly concerning the extent to which the Church was able to maintain its tradition of learning and scholarship during the Dark Ages. But there are pointers indicating that some of its achievements in this field were well kept up in spite of all the detrimental pressures from ignorant laymen and the savage onslaughts of Scandinavian raiders, whose attacks wrought havoc on many leading churches from the eighth to the eleventh century.[8] Early on in the period, the erudite Illtud (475-c.525) had founded a famous school at Llanilltud Fawr (Llantwit Major) in that part of south-east Wales which had come under the most pervasive civilizing influences of Rome. Illtud was reputed to have a profounder knowledge than any other Briton of the Old and New Testament and of every other kind of scholarship and art, and he succeeded in attracting to his academy disciples from far and near, including St Samson of Dol (c.485-565), Gildas (*flor.* sixth century), and possibly even the redoubtable Maelgwn Gwynedd (d. c.547), prince of north Wales. The churches and monasteries of south-west Wales, on the other hand, do not seem to have shared in this exceptional level of attainment. Even so, it ought not to be forgotten that it was a man from west Wales, Asser (d.909), a son of the diocese of St David's, whom Alfred the Great chose to summon to his court to raise the standards of learning there. Similarly, the clergy of Gwynedd in the north-west maintained close contacts with scholars in Ireland and on the Continent.[9] The intellectual achievements of a distinguished family like that of Bishop Sulien (1011-1091) provide further impressive evidence of how brilliantly the best clerics of

[7] Davies, *Early Middle Ages*, p.167.
[8] Glanmor Williams, chap. 1 in J.L. Williams and G.R. Hughes, *The History of Education in Wales* (1978); H.R. Loyn, *The Vikings in Wales* (1976).
[9] N.K. Chadwick, *Studies in the Early British Church* (1958).

the age succeeded in keeping alive the highest traditions of ecclesiastical learning in spite of all the difficulties and discouragements. Not surprisingly, there were close links between the Church and literature – in Latin and in Welsh. Among the very earliest writing in the Welsh language which has survived to us are the *englynion* (quatrains) penned by a Welsh cleric in honour of the Trinity on the tenth-century Juvencus manuscript. Again, the ancient Welsh prophetic poem of the tenth century, *Arymes Prydain* ('Presage of Britain'), presents St David as the focus of patriotic unity and religious zeal for his compatriots.[10] Illustrated manuscripts and other early examples of early Christian art are comparatively rare, though the Gospel of St Chad, now at Lichfield, has undoubted connections with Wales. Much the most important survivals of this kind are the 450-500 stone monuments of the early Christian period (fifth to the eleventh century AD). The earlier ones, dating from the fifth and sixth centuries, show the influences of the Latin alphabet and Roman styles of writing, but some are in the Ogam alphabet and Irish style. The later monuments of the ninth to the eleventh centuries are magnificent examples of tall, sculptured stone crosses revealing a Celtic fondness for geometrical patterns and elaborate stone carving, though they are not uninfluenced by Hiberno-Saxon models.[11]

The nature of Christian belief and practice among the population at large is not at all easy to determine in the light of the scanty evidence available to us. Over the centuries emphases may no doubt have changed significantly. It is also possible that there were marked differences of approach as between one region of Wales and another; south-east Wales, for instance, was inclined to maintain much more intimate contact than other parts of the country with neighbouring regions of England, whereas Gwynedd tended to preserve closer links with Ireland and Irish clerics. However, insofar as it is possible to generalize on the subject of Christian faith and custom, we may perhaps be justified in singling out for special emphasis the following traits.

It seems probable that the most enticing attraction held out by the Christian Church was its promise to the faithful, beset by the hardships and uncertainties of brief existence on earth, of the reward of life eternal. In this respect, the Juvencus *englynion* provide us with a vivid evocation of the power of God as mediated through His Church:

> The world cannot express in song bright and melodious, even though the grass and trees should sing, all thy glories, O true Lord . . . He who made the wonder of the world will save us, has saved us. It is not too great toil to praise the Trinity.[12]

Those moral qualities which ought to typify the true Christian were increasingly emphasized. Among them were resistance to the deadly sins prompted by the three cardinal enemies of mankind – the world, the flesh and the devil – and adoption of the central Christian virtues of commitment, humility and charity. By the time that the lives of the saints came to be written, these were pre-eminently the merits which those heroes of the faith were said to have manifested. The same qualities would also be heavily underscored in the later literature of the court poets of the twelfth and thirteenth centuries and the *cywydd* poets from the fourteenth to the sixteenth century.

The saints themselves tended to dominate popular religion. Although the more famous figures in the Christian pantheon such as the BVM, or Peter, or Michael, were as well-known in Wales as in other European countries, the saints who loomed particularly large in the people's mind were the home-grown variety like David or Beuno or Cadog and many other saints, little-known or even unknown outside their own particular locale. In an age which set such enormous store by secular heroes and demigods and attributed to them superhuman qualities on which the leadership and security of the country depended, it was hardly to be wondered at that the Christian Church should produce its own champions, on especially

---

[12] Ifor Williams, transl. by Rachel Bromwich, *The Beginnings of Welsh Poetry* (1972), p.101.

favoured terms with the Almighty and endowed by Him with miraculous authority. The saints were normally the scions of royal or aristocratic lines, possessing the same characteristics of leadership, fortitude, and determination being shown by their secular brethren in this formative age when the future of the Welsh people was being shaped out of the débris of the Roman Empire. The saints had the added advantage over laymen of being willing to place their talents unreservedly at the disposal of the King of Heaven. When, in return, He showed them marks of His special regard, it was thought only natural that in the exercise of their God-given attributes they would remember particularly their own people who held them in such high regard.

Long after a saint was dead, his *mana* was firmly believed to live on in the place(s) he had adorned with his holy life. Relics associated with him became the objects of intense pride and veneration in those localities where they were preserved. The bones of a saint were especially highly regarded. Cadog's were attributed with far-reaching powers of being able to perform miracles, expel demons, and procure abundance and fertility. A saint's bones were not only the 'spiritual title-deeds' of a church but also represented his 'continuing presence and the protection which he afforded to his community and its possessions'.[13] From at least as early as the sixth century, as we know from Gildas's testimony, shrines were constructed so as fittingly to contain and protect the saintly remains, and such shrines became of greater consequence than the churches associated with them. Not surprisingly, many ordinary men and women wished to be buried as near as possible to the aura of the saint in the hope of benefiting from his favour after death. Some of the excavations of early sites, carried out at places like Arfryn near Bodedern in Anglesey, have revealed a large number of burials concentrated around a central focus. Nor were the bones of a saint the only objects held in honour. Other possessions closely linked with him, such as bells, croziers,

---

[13]   J.K. Knight, chap. IX in H.N. Savory (ed.), *Glamorgan County History* II (1984). *Prehistory and Early History* on p.368.

altars, wells, or even books, were also treasured. Cadog's bell, said to have been made by Gildas, was preserved at Llancarfan, as was another, also reputedly made by Gildas, at Llantwit Major, and both had supernatural properties attributed to them. The brass head of a crozier, preserved at Baglan, was commended to Edward Lhuyd as late as 1690 as a 'sacred relic which had wonderful effects on the sick'.[14] Holy wells associated with the saints were, for centuries, resorted to by those seeking a cure for physical ailments, and some, like Winifred's Well at Holywell, still command the loyalty of present-day pilgrims.[15]

Such places sanctified by connections with saints and their relics naturally attracted a large concourse of those who came to venerate the holy men's memory, or to seek health for their own bodies and souls, or even from more mundane motives of curiosity and a desire to see wonders. Journeys by Welsh votaries to foci of Christian remembrance as distant and celebrated as Jerusalem or Rome were not uncommon; traditionally, one of David's most famous peregrinations was his visit to Jerusalem, where he was believed to have been created archbishop by the patriarch. But there were other revered shrines within easier reach for would-be worshippers, like St David's, or Bardsey, hallowed as the burial-place of thousands of saints, which attracted large numbers of pilgrims.[16]

Parishes do not seem to have been carved out in Wales until the twelfth century, after the coming of the Normans. It may well be, however, that in the lowland and more populous areas of Wales, as in Cornwall, there were a considerable number of churches and chapels founded in the pre-Norman period and probably transformed into full-scale parishes in the twelfth century. Of the relationship between priests who served these churches and their people during the earlier period it is difficult to pronounce with any certainty. Little has survived to show that there was much in the way of close pastoral or instructional contact between them or to

---

[14] Knight, *Glam. County Hist.*, II, 373.
[15] Francis Jones, *The Holy Wells of Wales* (1954).
[16] G. Hartwell Jones, *Celtic Britain and the Pilgrim Movement* (1912).

indicate how frequently or regularly the populace attended for worship at church services. Care does appear to have been taken, however, to ensure that infants were baptized by the clergy and the dead buried by them – two aspects of the priestly function to which we might have expected singular importance to be attached. There also seems to have been considerable emphasis on the need for giving alms and doing penance. But in general, as might be anticipated amid a population that was small, scattered, poor and illiterate, and subject to frequent internal wars and raids as well as invasions and attacks from outside, the people were, as far as can be judged, 'collective Christians'. That is to say, they reposed their trust in the prowess of their saints and in the ritual performed by their clergy to do all that was necessary to safeguard them from evil and ensure their salvation in the world to come.

There are some other prevailing attitudes in the Celtic Church in Wales on which attention should be focused. First, the Welsh cherished unqualified pride in what they held to be their early conversion in apostolic times and the independent origin of their Christianity, regarding both as tokens of the signal approval bestowed on the early British by God. Second, they believed strongly in the superiority of their own indigenous British tradition, as contrasted with that of the Anglo-Saxons who had for so long been pagan barbarians. Third, they associated with their distinctive past the glorious achievements of their own native saints, accounts of whose holiness and supernatural feats were firmly interwoven into the history, folklore and legends of the various regions of Wales. Fourth, they were unshakably convinced of their orthodoxy and loyalty to the faith throughout their history; they believed themselves to have been proof against Roman persecution, Pelagian and other heresies, and pressure from Anglo-Saxon oppressors and Scandinavian raiders. Finally, they continued to harbour a hope that, as a people, they had been preserved by the hand of God to carry out some major sacred mission which He had in store for them. In the centuries following the Norman Conquest all these convictions were to be subjected to severe erosive forces; but, although in some respects weakened or changed, they continued to survive, buckled but unbroken, to the end of the Middle Ages and beyond.

The Norman Conquest and the Medieval Church[17]

When, from the end of the eleventh century onwards, the Normans began to encroach on parts of Wales, it was inevitable that they should seek to exercise control over the Church in the interests of their own expansion. What they found was an ecclesiastical polity still markedly Celtic in character; its discipline and institutions differing widely from those with which they were familiar. This constituted a state of affairs which the intruders would tolerate no longer than they had to. Accustomed to a church ruled over by warrior-aristocrat bishops of Norman origin and upper-class abbots of Latin-style monasteries which had come under the inspiration of a reforming Papacy, the Normans were pious according to their lights, as well as practical. Brutal and worldly as they often were, they could cloak their pugnacious instincts and their political need to control the Church with an agreeable sense of a mission to introduce ecclesiastical reform. Individual Norman lords carried out their conquest of the south and east – the 'Marches' of Wales – in piecemeal fashion; but they were not the only ones to appreciate the need for getting their hands on the Church. Behind them stood the Norman kings of England and their archbishops of Canterbury, who were at least as aware of the strategic importance of bringing the Welsh Church under their sway.

One of the first steps in the process of subordination, from which complete subjection might be expected to follow, was to gain direction over the choice of bishops and secure their allegiance to the archbishop of Canterbury. Hitherto, bishops in Wales had been independent of his authority; but in 1107 Urban, the first Norman bishop of Llandaff, was induced to

---

[17]   For the medieval church, see J. Conway Davies, *Episcopal Acts*; R.R. Davies, *Conquest, Coexistence and Change: Wales, 1063-1415* (1987); Glanmor Williams, *The Welsh Church from Conquest to Reformation* (1976).

make the initial profession of obedience to the primate of England. It was a decisive step which set the pattern for the future. By the middle of the twelfth century the bishops of all four Welsh dioceses had been pressurized into making a similar profession. Thus had the first and crucial step for bringing the Church under the control of king and archbishop been accomplished. It was a shift pregnant with consequences for Church and people, not incomparable in scope and magnitude with those later to be brought about by the Protestant Reformation and the Methodist Revival.

The new-style prelates introduced far-reaching modifications into the organization, possessions and discipline of their dioceses. They replaced authority exercised on the basis of 'mother' and 'daughter' affiliation with a pattern of territorially-demarcated dioceses having fixed geographical boundaries; a tactic not carried through without fierce disputes and controversies over possessions and jurisdiction between rival bishops. Within the newly-defined territorial bishoprics other ecclesiastical boundaries were also mapped out for the first time. Rural deaneries and archdeaconries came into being; the former based on civil administrative units, the commote (*cwmwd*) or cantref; the latter on earlier kingdoms or provinces like Meirionnydd (Merioneth) or Brycheiniog (Brecknock). Parishes were carved out, too – a slow and complicated procedure, not completed in north Wales until well into the fourteenth century. For the maintenance of the clergy in these parishes, tithes were introduced on a regular basis for the first time.

In this process of reconstruction and reorganization, some of the most distinctive features of the life of the Celtic Church were rudely thrust aside. The Normans found dedications to Celtic saints strange and unacceptable and proceeded to eradicate them and rededicate the churches to saints with whom they were familiar. The old Celtic *clas*, or body of canons, usually hereditary and attached to a mother church, was destroyed wherever possible. Its endowments were then transferred to monasteries in England or on the Continent which found favour with the conquerors. Churches in southeast Wales, which came early under Norman rule, suffered especially badly, and by this process the venerable *clasau* founded by Illtud at Llantwit Major and by Cadog at Llancarfan were suppressed and their possessions handed over to the abbeys of Tewkesbury and Gloucester.

Closely connected with the steps taken to break up the *clasau* was the introduction of Latin-style monasteries into Wales.[18] The first to be founded were daughter priories of English or Continental houses approved of by the Normans. Planted only along the Normanized fringes and built in the shadow of Norman castles in lordship capitals like Chepstow, Monmouth, Brecon or Cardiff, they were almost as much an instrument of conquest as the castle or the borough. Not one Benedictine house flourished in those parts of Wales held for any length of time by the Welsh princes. Throughout the Middle Ages the Black Monks' houses were alien colonies, recruiting their members from a non-Welsh population.

Another of the purposes of the new territorial organization was to pave the way for the introduction of stricter canons of ecclesiastical discipline, in the enforcement of which arch-deacons and rural deans were to be the key officers. These officials were normally men of Welsh origin and in close touch with priests and people. But theirs was no easy task; progress was slow, and compromise and failures inevitable. A notorious stumbling-block was the celibacy of the clergy. Many of the Welsh priests in accordance with time-honoured custom and in defiance of canon law, continued to take wives right down to the Reformation. Such notable sixteenth-century bishops as the Catholic William Glynn (1555-1558) or the Protestant Richard Davies (1560-1581) were both sons of married priests.

One of the more beneficial consequences of the Norman Conquest was that it ended the tendency on the part of the Welsh Church to be somewhat isolated from the Church in general; the price of earlier autonomy had been the peril of stagnation. The advent of the Normans helped decisively in throwing the Welsh Church open to fresh and invigorating streams of reform flowing briskly from the Continent. One of the most momentous consequences of this was to bring

[18]   F.G. Cowley, *The Monastic Order in South Wales, 1066-1349* (1977).

clerics in Wales into a more intimate relationship with the
fountain-head of medieval religion, the reformed Papacy. To
Rome the most active and zealous clerics, Welsh and Norman
alike, turned for leadership and guidance; from Rome came
much of the driving force underlying the transformation of
ecclesiastical organization and government.

Yet, profound and far-ranging as were the changes
brought about by the Normans, they did not by any
means completely submerge earlier characteristics. Older
ways were tenaciously defended and novelties stubbornly
resisted. The overlordship of Canterbury, for instance, was
not accepted without tense and embittered struggles to
uphold the autonomy previously enjoyed by Welsh prelates.
In the northern principality of Gwynedd the princes, following a precedent set by Owain Gwynedd (1137-70), regarded
the diocese of Bangor as their own preserve, and were unwilling to allow the authority of Canterbury to be extended over
the see. In south Wales the claims of St David's to be regarded
as an archbishopric were an even more crucial source of
controversy. Gerald of Wales, himself three parts a Norman,
was to stand forth as the most vigorous of all champions of St
David's alleged rights to be considered the metropolitical see
of Wales. For a quarter of a century, from 1176 onwards, he
fought a desperate though ultimately vain campaign to have
those pretensions upheld, pleading his case in season and
out of season, in St David's and in England, at royal court
and papal curia, amid the clergy and the laity, with all the
resources of one of the swiftest pens and most fluent tongues
known to the Middle Ages.[19]

Moreover, however much the Normans might dominate
some of the upper echelons of the hierarchy, they were simply too few in number to be able to dispense with the option
of having to make extensive use of native-born clergy at the
grass-roots level and also on some of the more exalted planes
within the Church. Many Welshmen were not unwilling to
participate in changes which they recognized as being in the

[19] Davies, *Episcopal Acts*; M. Richter, *Giraldus Cambrensis. The Growth of the Welsh Nation* (1972).

best interests of religion. Among other things they accepted papal leadership readily, and in due course were success-ful in enlisting papal support for Welsh claims to more sympathetic treatment. In 1274, for example, seven Welsh Cistercian abbots wrote to Pope Gregory X seeking, with some success, his sympathy on behalf of Prince Llywelyn ap Gruffydd.[20]

Again, in the face of the Norman intention to drive out or downgrade dedications to Welsh saints, the Welsh contrived to cling on to them with rare and dogged determination. St Andrew might have been introduced by the Normans to a place alongside St David in the dedications of the lat-ter's cathedral, but it was Welsh Dewi who survived as the magnet for popular pilgrimage and patriotic loyalty, almost completely eclipsing St Andrew in the people's devotion. Similarly, at Llandaff – the cathedral and see which came most completely under Norman domination – the shrine which proved to be its most specific and enduring attrac-tion was that of the three Welsh saints: Teilo, Dyfrig and Euddogwy.

Not even in the sphere of Latin-type monasteries did the Normans have it all their own way. In contrast with the fail-ure of the Norman-sponsored Benedictines, the Cistercian order was conspicuously successful among the Welsh. Admittedly, the White Monks were first introduced into Wales under the Norman aegis, and a small minority of their houses, like Tintern or Basingwerk, always remained Anglo-Norman in sympathy. But as an order the Cistercians were not associated in Welsh minds with alien conquest. Far from being the timid henchmen of the conquerors who clung to the skirts of castle and borough, the sons of Cîteaux sought out the undeveloped solitudes of mountain and moor-land, especially in *pura Wallia*, i.e. the area not encroached upon by the Normans. Their emphasis on retreat into the wilderness, manual labour, austere discipline, and rigorous self-renunciation, seemed to reincarnate the pristine ideals of the monastic life of the Celtic saints. Their adoption of pastoral

20   Williams, *Welsh Church*, p.10.

ways of farming on the whole fitted smoothly into prevalent agrarian patterns in Wales, though there was more friction between them and the native population in this context than has often been recognized. Cistercian houses became havens of ordered prayer and worship, cradles of learning, patrons of literature, literary chroniclers and active agents of historic and patriotic aspiration, pioneers in the arts of agriculture and stock-breeding, flock management and wool production, and even embryonic industry and metal-working. Contributions of this kind won them a unique place in the affections of prince and people. The names of their houses – Strata Florida, Aberconway, Valle Crucis, Margam or Hendygwyn-ar-Daf – are among the most hallowed in the history of religion in medieval Wales.[21]

The newer religious orders of Franciscan and Dominican friars were likewise taken warmly to the Welsh bosom when they appeared in the thirteenth century. From their ranks sprang some of the foremost scholars and bishops of the age. Typical of them was the Dominican, Anian Ddu, bishop of St Asaph (1268-1293). Scion of a royal line of princes and warriors, he was prepared to proclaim his rights as a prince of the Church against Welsh abbots or English bishops, King Edward I or Prince Llywelyn the Last.[22] Another leading friar, John Wallensis, was an outstanding Franciscan regent-master at Oxford and Paris, a prolific author whose sermon collections were among the most popular compendia of their kind in medieval Europe. John was one of a number of young Welsh clerics fired with an insatiable thirst for learning. Members of the religious orders and secular clergy alike, they found their way in growing numbers to the universities, particularly to Oxford.

The learning of the clerics was not confined to the small and highly-educated élite who were at ease in the Latin language and literature. One of the most striking achievements

[21]   J.F. O'Sullivan, *Cistercian Settlements in Wales and Monmouthshire, 1140-1540* (1947); D.H. Williams, *The Welsh Cistercians* (1983, 1985).
[22]   R.C. Easterling, 'The Friars in Wales', *Archaeologia Cambrensis*, 6th ser., XIV (1914), 323-56.

of the medieval Welsh Church was to produce a substantial body of literature in the vernacular, which the less-educated clergy and laity might understand.[23] Parts of the Bible were translated into Welsh; so were the Creed, the more popular hymns and prayers, the lives of the saints, and works of devotion and mysticism. These prose recensions were well-known to the bards of Wales and left a pronounced impress on their verse, much of which was devoted to religious subjects. Their themes were few and simple, recurring again and again. Chief among them were praise of the Trinity, especially the sufferings of Christ, and terror at the prospect of the last Judgment and Hell – this was, perhaps, the most persistent and awe-inspiring motif. It was accompanied by unrelenting insistence on the brevity and brittleness of human life and the vanity of men's preoccupation with worldly honour and possessions, the need for regular confession of sins, and the merit of devotion to the BVM and the saints. All of these are refrains which serve to demonstrate the marked continuity between the values of the medieval era and those commented upon earlier in considering the mentality of the Celtic Church.

The Last Phase of the Medieval Church[24]

From the fourteenth century until well on into the fifteenth, the Church passed through a prolonged series of upheavals which had detrimental consequences for it. Some of the most important causes of this 'time of troubles' affected the western Church as a whole and can be mentioned only briefly in passing. Among the most serious were the decline in the moral, spiritual and practical authority of the Papacy as a result of the Babylonish Captivity and the Great Schism; the break-up of the thirteenth-century synthesis of philosophy and religion and the emergence of deeply divisive

---

[23] J.E.C. Williams, 'Welsh Religious Prose', *Procs. Inter. Congress Celtic Studies 1963* (1966), pp.65-97; *Canu Crefyddol y Gogynfeirdd* (1977).
[24] or the late-medieval phase, see Williams, *Welsh Church*; and *Recovery, Reorientation, and Reform: Wales, 1415-1642* (1987).

controversies and heresies; the cooling ardour of the religious orders; and the economic and social disruption caused by demographic crisis and economic decline.

Other causes affected England and Wales more immediately. First among them was the final conquest of Wales, effected by Edward I in 1282-3. The tendency thereafter – much speeded up in the fourteenth century – was to subordinate the interests of the Welsh Church to those of the English State even more intensively than before. In the fourteenth century the king of England recruited virtually all his leading civil servants from among the clergy. He rewarded them with bishoprics and other valuable preferment in the Church. This tended to turn them more and more into administrators and politicians, absent from their sees and incapable of giving them pastoral care and direction. In Wales the deficiency was made all the worse by the king's exclusion of Welsh clerics from the most lucrative benefices there. For a time, the Papacy sought to protect native interest by promoting Welshmen by means of papal provisions. But before the end of the fourteenth century papal influence had been effectively negated in practice, though not in name, as a result of the Pope's need to placate the English monarchy in order to gain its support during the Schism. This exclusion of Welsh clerics from the upper ranks of the hierarchy built up a strong sense of resentment and frustration which was to find expression in the Glyndŵr Rebellion (1400-c.1415).

Another major source of upset was the seemingly interminable campaigns of the Hundred Years' War with France. They led the king to exploit clerical appointments and tap the financial resources of the Church still more thoroughly in the interests of the State. The wars also had a damaging effect on the leading religious order in Wales, the Cistercians, who were now cut off from their mother house in France for long periods and whose discipline and standards suffered in consequence.

To add still further to the woes of the Church came the Black Death (1348-50) and a number of subsequent visitations of epidemic disease in 1361, 1369 and later. Landed possessions and income of the clergy were hit hard. Even more serious, the numbers of the clergy were sharply reduced and

the replacements hastily drafted in were of very mixed quality. The religious orders suffered extremely badly and, as the
numbers of monks and friars fell drastically and afterwards
remained well below their former levels, their contributions
to scholarship and literature slumped markedly.

All these disasters could not but aggravate the severe
economic difficulties of the age. By the end of the fourteenth
century the Church and its clergy had become much poorer,
and there is widespread evidence of the acute financial problems and reduced resources confronting them. To adjust
to their added liabilities and diminished income they were
obliged to resort to a variety of devices, most of which
were not in the best interests of the Church even if they
temporarily palliated economic embarrassment. Pluralism
and non-residence became increasingly common among the
secular clergy, while the monasteries resorted to acquiring
appropriations of parishes and leasing out rectories and
temporal estates, as well as deliberately restricting their
intake of monks. Clergy of all kinds found it increasingly
necessary to depend upon the more unrestricted sale of
indulgences to make ends meet. Like the laity, they found
themselves under grinding pressure from deteriorating social
and economic circumstances. Many of the Welsh clergy
were in as bitter and rebellious mood as their lay kinsfolk and
were inclined, like them, to attribute their problems almost
wholly to their English overlords. It needed only a spark to
touch off rebellion.

That spark came when Owain Glyndŵr raised the standard
of revolt in September 1400.[25] In his approach to the problems
of the Church as well as those of the State, Owain could
appeal to age-old and elemental layers of patriotism among
the clergy as well as the laity. In his 'Pennal Programme' of
1406 he resurrected the immemorial claim to the autonomy
of the Welsh Church and the role of a Welsh archbishop of
St David's, independent of Canterbury and controlling all the
higher clerical appointments in the interests of Wales -and, of
course, its independent prince! He also sought to re-establish

[25]   J.E. Lloyd, *Owen Glendower* (1931).

earlier Welsh links with a sympathetic Papacy – in his case the pontiff at Avignon – to use it as an ally against England in the creation of a separate province and two independent Welsh university institutions. He succeeded, moreover, in harnessing the patriotic energies and ambitions of a variety of Welsh clerics in the interests of his principality. The success of his appeal to his principal allies bound all the recognized upholders of the Welsh heritage to him: higher clergy like Bishop John Trefor and Gruffydd Young, along with many of the parish and lesser clergy and students, and their counterparts among the Cistercian and Franciscan orders. He even managed to secure support from that notable Lollard critic of the English establishment, Walter Brut.

For a brief, intoxicating year or two it looked as if Glyndwr's heady and high-flying prospectus for an independent State and autonomous Church might be implemented; but by 1408-9, at the latest, his whole ambitious enterprise could be seen to be unravelling fast into ignominious failure. Meantime, in the course of his insurgency the Church had suffered untold losses. Its buildings and estates were severely damaged, in some instances destroyed; worship was badly disrupted and discipline shattered; learning and literature were at their lowest ebb. The monastery of Margam was in 1412 described as 'utterly destroyed so that abbot and convent were obliged to go about like vagabonds'.[26] Such destitution was not untypical of much of the life of the Church when the Rebellion ended. Even a century and a half later, in the preface to the first Welsh New Testament of 1567, its appalling consequences were still remembered. Bishop Richard Davies could deplore in tones of deep distress the damage caused by Glyndwr and his enemies: 'What destruction of books (i.e. manuscripts) Wales suffered . . . from the townships, bishops' houses, monasteries and churches that were burnt throughout all Wales at that time'.[27]

And yet, painful and devastating as had been the troubles of the fourteenth century, and especially those of the fifteenth, the Church was able to stage a remarkable recovery. By 1500 the process of material recuperation was largely complete. Income from clerical possession was more or less back to normal, and the adjustments needed to meet a changing age, already begun in the fourteenth century, had been taken much further. It was now normal for the higher clergy to hold a number of preferments simultaneously and for most of them to be non-Welsh and non-resident. Monasteries were content to lease out most of their temporal and spiritual assets and live in comfortable and relaxed fashion on the proceeds. Their charitable functions – care of the sick and elderly, hospitality for travellers, and alms-giving to the poor – though still undertaken, were sharply diminished in scale. Friars tended to be far more confined to their houses and much less concerned with itinerant preaching than they had earlier been.

The revived material fortunes of the Church were visible, too, in the great wave of church-building, in the shape of extensions, refurbishing and embellishments which characterized the period from the second half of the fifteenth century down to the Reformation. This was an age of building new Lady chapels, aisles and towers; extending and glazing windows; and erecting new images and, especially, graceful and elaborate rood screens and lofts. Much of this activity was connected with and financed by fresh or revived activity in encouraging devotees to resort to the new attractions set up in the churches. Famous roods, like the ones at Tremeirchion or Brecon, or images such as that of the BVM at Pen-rhys in the Rhondda or of Gwenfrewi at Holywell, developed into sources of magnetic appeal for worshippers from far and near.

Another symptom of contemporary recovery was the upsurge of religious verse and prose, which constituted a striking feature of the efflorescence of literature in general. Although earlier concepts of the Deity as a remote, majestic and omnipotent ruler and judge of the universe are not absent from this literature, greater emphasis is now being placed on the humanity of the Second Person in the Trinity and the agony of his sufferings on behalf of sinful and frequently ungrateful mankind. The same human touch may also be seen in the approach to the BVM, whose womanly qualities of tenderness and affection, and her compassion for sinners at the Last Judgment, are prominently highlighted. As much to the fore as ever, also, are the *mana* of the saints and sacred places, especially those of Welsh origin, and their continuing capacity to work miracles on behalf of their votaries and shower blessings upon them. Along with these familiar motifs goes an increased emphasis on the need to resist the insidious temptations of wealth and self-indulgence and to eschew the grosser sins of carnality, pride and sensuality; all of which are unsparingly denounced after the fashion of those versified medieval sermons made so popular by Siôn Cent (?1367-?1430), the poet of puritanical restraint, austerity and other-worldliness, and his many followers.[28] Attendance at church, regular payment of tithes, and respect for the sacraments, are also warmly advocated. But perhaps the most persistent refrain of all is still the overwhelming concern with the four last things – Death, Judgment, Heaven and Hell – and the ineradicable dread of the possibility of an eternity spent in indescribable torment as punishment for sins unpardoned.

On the threshold of the Reformation, although to outward appearances the Church had recovered well from the trials and tribulations of the fourteenth and fifteenth centuries, there were aspects of its condition which left it in vulnerable state. First, there were manifest weaknesses among its clergy. Almost all the bishops in Welsh dioceses and a majority of the higher clergy were servants or favourites of the Crown, owing their preferment to royal goodwill, and men who would hesitate to act in opposition to the king's commands and wishes, whatever they might be. Customarily not Welsh by origin and absent from Wales, most were graduates in law, not theology, and administrators rather than pastors of souls. Between them and most of the parish clergy, as well as between them and the native population, yawned a wide gap of wealth, interest, attitude, culture and language. Oversight of the dioceses, with their poor, thinly-populated, dispersed and inaccessible parishes, was fitful and inadequate. Nor was the state of belief and morals amid the largely illiterate and

---

[28] Williams, *Welsh Church*, pp.239-41.

monoglot Welsh-speaking population improved by the presence among them of an ill-educated and badly-remunerated
lower clergy, scarcely capable of setting a moral example or
imparting doctrinal instruction to their parishioners. It was
hardly to be wondered at that in his preface to the first
Welsh printed book of 1546, *Yny Lhyvyr Hwnn* the devout
and learned Erasmian humanist, Sir John Price of Brecon,
should pointedly denounce the Welsh clergy for their failure
to teach their charges even the rudiments of religious belief; a
state of affairs which had made it necessary for him to publish
his primer.[29]

Shortcomings in Church life such as these occasioned
by the indifferent quality of the secular clergy were further
aggravated as a result of the reduced state of the religious
orders, once the spearheads of devotion and learning. Friars, formerly so active in preaching, hearing confession
and promulgating Latin and Welsh literature, were now
much more inert and less effective. The monks, also, for
a century or more stringently reduced in numbers, had lost
most of the zeal and vitality which had fired their orders in
earlier centuries, and appeared content to lead the leisurely,
comfortable, quiescent life of *rentiers*. Neither they nor the
friars seemed any longer desirous or capable of awakening
religious enthusiasm or offering a conspicuous example to
the laity. In view of this lack of vision and dynamism among
the clergy much of the creative drive in religious life and
literature seemed to have passed from them to a minority of
educated and pious laymen.

As far as popular belief and devotion were in question,
there was a disturbing dependence on the externalities of the
means of grace, many of which appeared to be divorced from
considerations of morality and genuine understanding. Men
and women depended on practices like the multiplication of
Masses, lifeless repetition of prayers, unthinking veneration
of the saints and quasi-idolatrous addiction to their relics,
participation in pilgrimages and commercial transactions in
indulgences, rather than to a more committed adherence to

---

[29] Sir John Price, *Yny Lhyvyr Hwnn . . .* ed. J.H. Davies (1902).

Christian behaviour and belief, to save them from the consequences of their misdeeds. The more enlightened trends of
contemporary piety, like the *devotio moderna*, or Catholic
humanism, or reformed monastic life, found little echo in
Wales. The overwhelming majority of its population remained
collective Christians, content to leave it to the priesthood,
many of whose members were no better than the laity, to
minister the sacraments and perform the ritual on their
behalf. Religion consisted for most of a body of traditional
practices and assumptions, unquestioningly accepted but
dimly apprehended. Habit, not conviction, was the strongest
element in their faith, as it had been down the centuries. It
left them nearly as ill-prepared to defend the old as to accept
the new in the face of the Reformation storm soon to break
on them.

The Reformation

When the Reformation came to Wales, it fell into two distinct
phases, separated by the five-year intermission (1553-1558)
of the Catholic Mary's reign. The first phase, from c.1527
to 1553, witnessed the innovations introduced into the life
of the Church during the reigns of Henry VIII and Edward
VI, while the second, from 1558 to 1603, ensured that the
Reformation was secured on a lasting basis by Elizabeth I.[30]

Widely-ranging and weighty in consequence for the future
as Henry VIII's policies were – insofar as they destroyed the
links binding England and Wales to the Papacy, established
the king as Supreme Head of the Church, dissolved the
monasteries, broke up many of the centres of pilgrim devotion, and tentatively introduced some cautious measures of
religious and doctrinal reform – on the whole they made
surprisingly little difference to the everyday practice of religion. Medieval rite continued largely intact, conducted in
Latin by a priesthood still celibate in theory. It could almost

---

[30]   L. Thomas, *The Reformation in the Old Diocese of Llandaff* (1930); Glanmor
Williams, *Welsh Reformation Essays* (1967).

be said to be Papism without the Pope. In Wales, Henry was a strong and popular king, his actions were acceptable to the gentry, and by and large met with very little opposition. Even such conservative poets as Siôn Brwynog, later to attack the Reformation with vehemence, greeted Henry's changes with some approval.

The same could not be said of the Edwardian changes, which proceeded more radically in several directions. First, they swept away much that was accustomed and dearly loved in the fabric and appearance of parish churches. Altars, images, shrines, vestments, ornaments, treasures, rood lofts and screens, chantries, guilds, fraternities, candles and incense, now disappeared, leaving the churches cold and bare, 'like barns', as one indignant poet protested. Customary practices, such as the veneration of the saints, carrying rosaries, kneeling at Mass and beating the breast, praying for the dead, or 'creeping to the Cross' on Good Fridays, and other similar observances, were forbidden. Second, medieval services were replaced by the Reformed rites embodied in the transitional Prayer Book of 1549 and the even more distinctly Protestant services of the Book of 1552. The fact that English was the language of the Prayer Books gave added offence in Wales, where over most of the country it was no more intelligible than Latin and far less revered. The Welsh, having always prided themselves on their loyalty to the Church, now believed that they were being turned by *force majeure* into heretics, and English heretics at that. *Ffydd Saeson* – 'faith of Saxons' – was how one poet contemptuously dismissed the hated new régime.[31] Third, the clergy were officially allowed to take wives, though formal permission to do so may have made very little practical difference in Wales, where many were already accustomed to maintain wives, or at least 'hearth companions'.

Edward's reign had brought about nothing less than a religious revolution. It was a transformation that proved to be deeply unpopular in Wales, where a number of poets

[31] Glanmor Williams (ed.), *Glamorgan County History. IV. Early Modern Glamorgan* (1974), pp.218-19.

voiced uncompromising opposition to the innovations as they affected churches and their furnishings, clergy, altars, saints, the language of worship, and other alterations in celebration and practice. The Protestant bishop of St David's, Robert Ferrar (1548-1554), was only one of those who commented on the adherence of the people to their old ways and their impenitent resistance to rapid and brusque change. He feared that what he called 'the grudge of the people' was so impassioned that it might irrupt into open rebellion.[32] A minority, admittedly, accepted the new fashion; but the greater number by far appeared to welcome the return to the papal fold led by their royal shepherd, Queen Mary, in 1554.

For much of Elizabeth's long tenure of power, too, a mass of conservatism and time-serving was reported to be obstinately lingering on. Right down to the end of her reign, and even after, there were eloquent comments by Protestant observers on the people's ignorance, lack of conviction and reluctance to abandon ingrained habits. The Welsh clergyman and Protestant author, Huw Lewys, could comment as late as 1595 that many of his fellow-clergymen had been 'like bells without clappers or a candle under a bushel', with the result that even old people of sixty and upwards could give no more account of their faith than newborn children.[33] Nevertheless, it is also true that the Elizabethan Church made a more profound and lasting impact, especially on the literate sectors of the population, than has usually been acknowledged. It succeeded for a number of reasons. Some of these were political and social and depended on its appeal to the ruling élite, the landed gentry; but, important as they were, we shall not pursue them here.[34] For our particular purpose, more relevant are the two chief religious and cultural considerations: the reinterpretation of Welsh religious history put forward by the Reformers;[35] and the translation of the Bible and Prayer Book into Welsh.[36]

---

[32] Williams, *Welsh Reformation Essays*, pp.124-35.
[33] *Perl mewn Adfyd*, ed. W.J. Gruffydd (1929), p.xxi.
[34] Williams, *Wales 1415-1642*, chap. 13 for fuller discussion.
[35] Glanmor Williams, *Reformation Views of Church History* (1970).
[36] J. Ballinger, *The Bible in Wales* (1906); A.O. Evans, *A Memorandum on the Legality of the Welsh Bible* (1925); Isaac Thomas, *Y Testament Newydd Cymraeg, 1551-1620* (1976).

The most complete and skilful revision of Welsh history was the version of it outlined by Bishop Richard Davies in his highly influential 'Letter to the Welsh Nation' (*Epistol at y Cembru*), with which he prefaced the first translation into Welsh of the New Testament (1567), undertaken by William Salesbury, Thomas Huet and himself. The 'Letter' was an imaginative adaptation to the particular needs of Wales of the general tenor of Reformation historiography. Like Reformers elsewhere, Davies was convinced that the Reformation was no new-fangled heresy but that it represented a return to that purity of teaching and worship established by Jesus Christ and his immediate followers in the early Church and unsullied by corruptions later introduced by the Papacy and its agents. As far as Wales was concerned, he rehearsed a number of firmly-held convictions but gave them a strongly Protestant twist. He referred lovingly to the belief that Britain had first been converted to Christianity by Joseph of Arimathea, who had planted the faith in all its gospel immaculacy. This had subsequently been maintained by the people of Wales intact and uncontaminated in spite of Roman persecution, the heresies of Pelagius and others, Anglo-Saxon paganism and – most crucial of all – in face of that brand of Christianity tainted by papal superstition which Augustine of Canterbury had brought to England as the emissary of Rome. Only as a result of being forced to accept the adulterated Papism of England at the point of the sword had the Welsh eventually been dragged down into the mire of Roman superstition and idolatry. Now, after centuries of benighted ignorance and idolatrous superstition, Davies argued, by virtue of what he called 'the second flowering of the Gospel', they were being led back to the realm of truth and light. His reconstruction of history proved to be compellingly influential and appealing among many of his fellow-countrymen on three counts. It bonded the Reformation to some of the oldest and most venerable themes of Welsh history. It bluntly refuted the commonly-made suggestion that Reformation teaching was a neoteric, upstart heresy, lacking roots in earlier faith and history, and sought to show, on the contrary, that it was grounded in the earliest and most glorious phase of Christianity in Britain. Finally, it met, head-on, the criticism that Reformed teaching was an alien, English creed, imposed on the Welsh by the insensitive *diktat* of an unsympathetic government; in Davies' book it was *Papist* beliefs which had originally been forced on the Welsh by their Saxon enemies. Implicit in all that he wrote was the idea that it was the Reformation that was the great purpose for which God had preserved the Welsh people and their language.[37]

The potential seductiveness for the Welsh of this revamping of their history was not lost on defenders of Catholicism. The anonymous author of *Y Drych Cristnogawl* (1585), the most notable Catholic book to be published in Welsh during Elizabeth's reign,[38] was not slow to repay Davies in his own coin. He directed his efforts to showing how all earlier Christian history in Wales had been betrayed by the treachery of the Reformation. He agreed that one of the most memorable aspects of the past had been the early conversion by Joseph of Arimathea. But he proceeded to point out also that another early pioneer in Britain had been King Lucius son of Coel, who had sent to the *Pope* for missionaries to come to Britain to convert the people. In addition, the first Christian emperor of Rome, Constantine, had been a Briton, who had been received into the faith by the Pope. He then went on to show how the early saints of the Welsh, in whom they took such justifiable pride, had all been firmly in the Catholic tradition. Such had been the glorious state of Wales in the past. Alas! how dramatically circumstances had been changed for the worse by the 1580s, when there were whole shires in Wales where some of the inhabitants lived like animals, knowing little more of Christ and his religion than brute beasts. So much for the Reformers' concept of the great things for which the Welsh had been preserved! Literary duels like this one between Davies and his anonymous antagonist make it plain that the two sides viewed the battle for the soul of Wales past as an integral part of the struggle for its soul present.

[37] Williams, *Welsh Reformation Essays*, chap. ix.
[38] The whole text of the work appeared only in manuscript. Part of it was, however, clandestinely printed in a cave on the Little Orme near Llandudno. Before it could be completed, the press was detected and the printers scattered.

One of the central contentions of the Reformers was that the faith of the early Britons had been unshakably founded on scriptural authority and that a vernacular Bible had been an essential and much-loved possession among them. To restore a Welsh version of the Scriptures was their first priority. In the first decade of Elizabeth's reign Richard Davies and William Salesbury exerted themselves with unresting vigour and purpose to secure a new translation for their people. An Act of Parliament of 1563 laid down that the Bible and Prayer Book should be translated into Welsh by 1567 and thereafter used in public worship in all those parishes where Welsh was the language normally used by the inhabitants. Translations of the New Testament and Prayer Book were duly published in 1567. Twenty-one years later William Morgan produced his classic version of the whole Bible. These translations represented an epoch-making triumph for the Reformation and, in the long term, proved to be of incalculable worth to the life of Wales. In the religious sphere, they gave meaning and reality to Reformation doctrine and worship for the largely monoglot population of Wales. As for the Welsh language, they accomplished more than any other single factor in keeping the language alive and vigorous into the twentieth century. Welsh literature, too, benefited just as much from being provided with a standard and model on which to base itself in the future. Bible and Prayer Book contributed no less powerfully to buttressing the sense of a separate and distinctive nationality in Wales.[39]

Scriptural translation, as in other countries, proved to be the key to the success of the Reformation in Wales. At the end of the sixteenth century it had a long way to go but was now firmly on the road to its ultimate triumph. The Reformers had, with brilliant success, grafted their ideals into the ancient stock of patriotic instincts and emphasized the essential continuity of the Reformation with all that was earliest, best and most specific to Wales. They had appealed

---

[39] Glanmor Williams, 'Religion and Welsh Literature in the Age of the Reformation', *Proceedings of the British Academy*, LXIX (1983), 371-408.

to the belief in its links with the earliest roots of Christianity in the country. They confirmed that the Reformation, like the initial conversion, was a renewed token of God's continuing favour. They underlined that the Reformation meant a return to the pristine purity of Christianity based on scriptural authority. They upheld the autonomy of the early Celtic Church and the virtues of its leading figures. They stressed the long-standing belief in the purpose which God had had in reserve for the Welsh and confidently implied that its fulfilment had been the 'second flowering of the Gospel' in their own tongue; a translation authorized by the restored British (i.e. Welsh) kingship of the Tudor dynasty. It was here, if anywhere, and now, if at all, that the true rebirth of the ancient glories of the British race was taking place. It was a striking and, on the whole, successful revitalization of Celtic ideals, and one eagerly taken to heart by many of the educated classes; not least because it merged so smoothly into the political stance of loyalty to the Tudor dynasty and State being encouraged by the monarchy. Yet, as we have seen, there was little in all this that could not have been given an equally convincing Catholic adaptation and complexion by those Catholic reformers determined to work through the vernacular tongue as well as Latin, or by a Catholic political régime desirous of winning over Welsh loyalty. What has subsequently made the Protestant version look 'inevitable' has been the continued existence down the centuries of a Protestant establishment in Church and State.

The Evangelical Revival in Wales: A Study in Spirituality

R. Tudur Jones

The Evangelical Revival in Wales was a spiritual awakening of astonishing power that was eventually to affect in some way or other every aspect of the nation's life.[1] In introducing its leaders, the men with whom we shall be chiefly concerned, pride of place must be given to Howel Harris (1714-1773). He was born at Trefeca-fach, near Talgarth, in Breconshire[2] and educated locally. After his conversion in 1735, he began to evangelize amongst his neighbours but as his sphere of influence extended he became an itinerant preacher whose journeys took him all over Wales as well as London and many places in southern England. Despite opposition from hostile mobs and people of influence, he proved himself a man of indomitable spirit. He proclaimed his evangelical message at

[1] For the Revival in general, *v.* G.M.. Roberts, *Hanes Methodistiaeth Galfinaidd Cymru* I (1973); D. Llwyd Morgan, *Y Diwygiad Mawr* (1981); Geraint H. Jenkins, *Literature, Religion and Society in Wales 1660-1730* (1980); J.M. Jones and W. Morgan, *Y Tadau Methodistaidd* I (1895); T. Rees, *History of Protestant Nonconformity in Wales* (2nd ed. 1883); R.T. Jenkins, *Hanes Cymru yn y Ddeunawfed Ganrif* (1928); biographies in *Dictionary of National Biography* (*D.N.B.*) and *Dictionary of Welsh Biography* (*D.W.B.*).
[2] 'Trefeca' is the Welsh spelling; 'Trevecka', the anglicized form, is often used. The old Breconshire is now part of the new county of Powys.

great physical and mental cost to himself but with a directness and passion that brought thousands to conversion. And it was his organizing ability that was mainly responsible for welding these converts into a coherent movement. He left an indelible mark on his people and it has been said of him, not without justification, that he was the greatest Welshman of the eighteenth century.[3]

His colleague, Daniel Rowland (1713-1790), was the son of the incumbent of Nantgwnlle and Llangeitho, Cardiganshire (now part of Dyfed). He was ordained deacon in 1734 and priest in 1735. Like Harris, he was converted in 1735, and he too was transformed into an assiduous evangelist. Sad to say, the Church had no sympathy with his enthusiasm. He was never granted a living but ministered as a curate until he was deprived of his licence in 1763. But he was not inhibited thereby. He, like Harris, made preaching journeys from time to time, but preferred to concentrate his energies on his work at Llangeitho and the neighbourhood. He was an intensely powerful preacher and people came in their thousands to enjoy his ministry there. He had joined forces with Harris in 1737 and the two co-operated as leaders of the movement until disagreements led to disruption in 1750. The bulk of the Methodist societies abandoned Harris and acknowledged Rowland as their leader. From then until his death on 16 October 1790 he remained the undisputed head of the Welsh Methodists, although the breach between him and Harris was healed in 1763.[4]

In his contribution to Evangelical spirituality, William Williams (1717-1791) holds a unique position. He was born

---

[3] For Harris, v. *D.W.B.*; *D.N.B.*; (ed.) Benjamin La Trobe, *Brief Account of the Life of Howell Harris Esq.* (1971); G.M. Roberts, *Portread o Ddiwygiwr* (1969); Hugh J. Hughes, *Life of Howell Harris* (1892); Eifion Evans, *Howel Harris, Evangelist* (1974); G.F. Nuttall, *Howel Harris: the Last Enthusiast* (1965); G.T. Roberts, *Howell Harris* (1951); H. Elvet Lewis, *Howell Harris and the Welsh Revivalists* (1911); R.T. Jenkins, *Yng Nghysgod Trefeca* (1968); Richard Bennett, *The Early Life of Howell Harris* (1962). And, of course, for our whole study an essential source is the Journal of the Historical Society of the Calvinistic Methodist Church of Wales – *Cylchgrawn Cymdeithas Hanes Eglwys Methodistiaid Calfinaidd Cymru (C.C.H.M.C)*

[4] For Rowland, v. *D.N.B.*; *D.W.B.*; Eifion Evans, *Daniel Rowland and the Great Evangelical Awakening in Wales* (1985); (in Welsh) D.J. Odwyn Jones, *Daniel Rowland Llangeitho* (1938).

at Cefn-coed, in the parish of Llanfair-ar-y-bryn, Carmarthenshire (now Dyfed) and was brought up a Congregationalist. He was one of Howel Harris's early converts. He was ordained deacon in the Church of England in 1740 but was refused ordination as a priest. After serving for a brief time as a curate he threw himself into the activities of the Methodist movement. After his marriage in 1748 he went to live in his mother's home, a farm called Pantycelyn – hence the tradition of calling him 'Williams Pantycelyn'. He was a man of rich culture and profound religious experience. What makes his contribution to spirituality unique is his gifts as an author. He stands in the front rank of European hymn-writers and at his best he expresses in an incomparable way the richness of the spiritual life fostered by the Evangelical Revival. His significance extends beyond his hymns. He published some ninety titles during his career and his prose works and epic poems add considerably to our understanding of eighteenth-century Evangelicalism. Precisely because he was such an accomplished author, his published works have continued to contribute to the religious life of the Welsh people. Even today the collections of hymns used by the churches contain more contributions by him than by any other hymn-writer.[5]

It is appropriate in a study of this kind to recall also the contribution of Griffith Jones (1683-1761). From 1716 until his death he was rector of Llanddowror, Carmarthenshire. The Methodist leaders turned to him frequently for advice, although as the years passed by he became more critical of some of their methods. But he was one of the living links between the older piety of the Puritan type and the spirituality of the Evangelical Revival. He is best-remembered for his work as an educationist whose circulating schools brought literacy within the reach of thousands. But his motivation

[5] For Williams, v. D.N.B.; D.W.B.; G.M. Roberts, Y Per Ganiedydd I (1949), II (1958); J. Gwilym Jones, William Williams Pantycelyn (1969) – bilingual); Glyn Tegai Hughes, Williams Pantycelyn (1983 – English); Derec Llwyd Morgan, Williams Pantycelyn (1983); J.M. Jones and W. Morgan, Y Tadau Methodistaidd I (1895).

was entirely religious and his labours made no small contribution to the spread of the Revival.[6]

There are some preliminary observations that need to be made before entering on the main subject of our study.

First of all, we are concerned with a spirituality that found expression through the medium of the Welsh language. By the Act of Union (1536) the Welsh language was banned from public and legal use, and that prohibition remained virtually unchanged until the present century. But there was one surprising modification of this policy. In 1563 an Act of Parliament was passed 'for the translating of the Bible and the Divine Service into the Welsh Tongue', and it enacted also that a copy of the Bible in Welsh and of the Book of Common Prayer, as well as the corresponding English versions, should be placed 'in every Church throughout WALES'.[7] This legislation, by enforcing a bilingual policy upon the Church of England in Wales, ensured that the Welsh language would continue to be a vehicle for the expression of the nation's spirituality. Over the years a succession of writers enriched that tradition and the Evangelicals made a substantial contribution to it. This meant on the one hand that there was a firm link between the idiom of spirituality in the eighteenth century and that used by former generations. On the other hand, if the language which we use to express our deeper thoughts and most moving experiences qualifies and colours our image of the spiritual (as well as the material) world in which we live, one would expect to discover that there are subtleties of emphasis and emotion that are not fully appreciated without a knowledge of the language. The vast majority of the population of Wales in the eighteenth century knew no language but Welsh, and in consequence the revivalists in their public work and in their published books rarely used English. This was true of Howel Harris as regards his preaching in Wales, but the language of

---

[6]   For Jones, v. D.N.B.; D.W.B.; D. Jones, Life . . . (1902); D. Ambrose Jones, Griffith Jones (1928); F.A. Cavanagh, Life and Work of Griffith Jones (1930); M.G. Jones, The Charity School Movement (1938); Geraint H. Jenkins, Hen Filwr dros Grist (1983).

[7]   For the Act, v. I. Bowen, The Statutes of Wales (1908), 149-51.

his private spirituality, insofar as it is conveyed to us through his diary, was English. That was surely exceptional. The main point still stands, that Welsh was the language of the Methodist Revival.

Secondly, there is a social consideration. The Welsh Evangelists were devoted to the task of elaborating a spirituality to meet the needs of an unlettered and disadvantaged community. This consideration, of course, had not escaped the attention of their Puritan and Anglican forbears who worked to publish 'good books' for the edification of the Christian public no matter what their social status might be. But one of the striking characteristics of the Evangelical Revival was its success in penetrating to social strata that had barely been touched by previous promoters of piety. Thus, Williams Pantycelyn felt that it was a special proof of God's graciousness that the underprivileged were being converted:

> Tis obvious to all that observes that the Lord is for exalting free grace – for tis ye poor ignorant people in the worlds account the Lord owns to the wise and the betterlearned Doctors of this world . . .[8]

The same social fact was used by the satirists to pour scorn on the revivalists. For example, in an 'interlude' published in 1745, the author mocks a Methodist exhorter by attributing to him a fatuous sermon in which he says, amongst many other things,

> . . . you have heard of Methodism, that is, the new faith that has come amongst the illiterate people of the Llŷn country.[9]

---

[8] Letter to Howel Harris, 7 December 1745, printed in G.M. Roberts, *Y Per Ganiedydd*, 83-5.

[9] *Interlude . . . Morgan y Gogrwr a'r Cariadogs neu Ffrewyll y Methodistiaid yn dair act* (R. Lathrobe, Shrewsbury, 1945) quoted by Bob Owen in *Y Cofiadur* (1950), 46-51. The author was William Roberts, the sexton of the parish of Llannor, for which *v. D.W.B.* Some of the local gentry at a meeting at the mansion of Bodfel made him a present of £52/10/0 for composing it. 'Morgan y Gogrwr' was the much-persecuted Methodist exhorter, Morgan Griffith, for whom *v.* G.P. Owen, *Methodistiaeth Llŷn ac Eifionydd* (1978), 40-1. An 'interlude' was a morality play.

A spirituality that was to play a meaningful part in the life of such poor people could not presuppose that they had parlours or private bedrooms in which it would be practised. The tiny crofts and cottages in which they lived possessed no such amenities. Hence the strong communal element that was characteristic of it – a point to be discussed later.

Thirdly, it is necessary to explain the theological presuppositions of Welsh Evangelical spirituality. It was rooted in the Federal Theology of the Calvinist tradition. Systematic Theology was not Howel Harris's strong point, and the details of his credo developed and changed through his contacts with a variety of people and his own intense personal experience. Nevertheless, he moved consistently within the orbit of Calvinism. Thus, when writing to James Erskine, 19 February 1745, he was able to say,

> I think we all agree with ye Good old orthodox Reformers & Puritans; I have their works in great Esteem . . .[10]

Thus, during his visits to London in 1739 and 1740, he records in his diary that he had read Thomas Shepheard (d.1646), *The Sincere Convert* on 1 May 1739; Jeremiah Burroughs, *The Rare Jewel of Christian Contentment* on 2 May; selections from *The Complete Works* (1674) of Isaac Ambrose (1624-1664) on 5 May; John Cotton's *Treatise of the Covenant of Grace* (1671), one of Harris's favourite books, on 6 May; Ralph Venning (d.1663), *A Discourse on Regeneration* (1689) on 13 May 1740; and on 2 June 1739 he was perusing Thomas Wilcocks (1622-1687), *A Choice Drop of Honey from the Rock Christ*. And at various other times he studied John Bunyan, Dr John Owen, Vavasor Powell, Thomas Doolittle, Edmund Calamy and John Calvin himself.[11]

Williams Pantycelyn had a passionate concern for theological orthodoxy. He insisted that the Welsh Methodists stood

---

[10]   G.M. Roberts, *Selected Trevecka Letters 1742-1747* (1956), 166.
[11]   John Thickens in *Howel Harris yn Llundain* (1934) takes careful note of Harris's reading during his visits to London, 1739-40, and provides full bibliographical details of the books mentioned on pp.108, 110-11, 119, 121, 159, 289-90, 299-301. For further treatment of the topic, *v.* Eifion Evans, *Howel Harris* (1974), 18.

squarely in the tradition of the early ecumenical creeds, the Protestant Reformers and Puritan Calvinism. In 1756 we find him criticizing certain unsound views about the relation between the Person of Christ and his Work and asserting,

> Such a teaching does not agree with the Articles of the Church of England, nor with the views of any of its distinguished writers, nor with the Westminster Catechism; nor with the Puritan writers of the last hundred and forty years.[12]

He still acknowledged the same standards of orthodoxy thirty-four years later when he wrote to Thomas Charles of Bala that

> the Articles of the Church of England, the Nicean, and Athanasian Creeds, the lesser and larger Catechisms of the Assembly with their confession of faith are some of the grandest and most Illustrious beauties of the reformation . . .[13]

In his very last letter to Charles, written 1 January 1791, just a few days before he died, Williams is more specific about his debt to the Puritans. After listing the main doctrines of his personal creed, he says that 'the books of Dr. Goodwin, Dr. Owen, Dr. Gill, Marshal, Hervey, Usher and others helped to sharpen my understanding of these great truths'.[14] It is quite clear, then, where Williams stood as regards his Theology.

---

[12] From the Preface to the first edition of his long poem, *Golwg ar Deyrnas Crist*, dated 5 June 1756. The original in Welsh.
[13] The original, in English, is in G.M. Roberts, *Y Per Ganiedydd* I, 167-8. For Charles (1755-1814), the most influential Methodist leader after the deaths of Rowland and Williams, *v. D.N.B.*, *D.W.B.* and the three-volume English biography, *Thomas Charles of Bala* by D.E. Jenkins.
[14] G.M. Roberts, *Y Per Ganiedydd* I, 171. Dr Thomas Goodwin (1600-1680), Dr John Owen (1616-1683), Dr John Gill (1698-1771), James Hervey (1714-1758) and James Ussher (1581-1656) are all in *D.N.B.* Who was 'Marshal'? Probably not Stephen Marshall (1594?-1655), the leader of the Presbyterians at the Westminster Assembly. More likely he was Walter Marshal (1628-1680), the author of the popular volume, *The Gospel Mystery of Sanctification* (1692), whose ideas were exactly those of Williams. The volume, by the way, is extensively quoted (in Welsh) by John Griffiths, Glandŵr (1731-1811) in his *Stafell Gyfaill* (1791). For Griffiths, *v. D.W.B.*

Daniel Rowland was at one with Williams in his theological convictions. Dr Eifion Evans's conclusion is that he follows 'the mainline Calvinist treatment of the plan of salvation' while adhering to the classical ecumenical creeds in his understanding of the doctrines of the Trinity and of the Person of Christ as Prophet, Priest and King.[15]

Having dealt with these preliminaries, we can now come to our main topic – the spirituality of the Evangelical Revival in Wales. It is appropriate to start with Howel Harris. That would have pleased him because he always insisted that he enjoyed a certain precedence over Rowland, Whitefield and the Wesleys because he was the first to be 'awakened'. In his Diary for 7 October 1743, for example, he speaks 'Of God's peculiar love to me in calling me first of all and sending me by myself'.[16]

Dr Geoffrey F. Nuttall in his perceptive study of Harris draws the conclusion that 'No other leader of the Evangelical Revival was so predominantly an enthusiast'.[17] Harris's spirituality was that of an enthusiast. The flame of enthusiasm was kindled in his heart by the shattering experience of his conversion in 1735. So significant was it for him that he frequently celebrates the annual return of the happy day in his Diary. It was not his own doing – 'At 21 I was called by divine grace'.[18] Throughout his life he adhered to the conviction that conversion was God's sovereign act. Although he looked upon Whitsunday, 25 May 1735, as his spiritual birthday, he saw it as the crucial point in a series of providentially

---

[15] Eifion Evans, *Daniel Rowland*, 370-3.

[16] This and numerous similar references are listed by Tom Beynon in *Howell Harris, Reformer and Soldier* (1958), 5[8]

[17] *Howel Harris, 1714-1773* . . . (1965), 8. Most historians when dealing with Harris's Diary have been primarily interested in extracting factual material from it, and in reproducing it they have tended to omit those substantial passages which have to do with his spirituality. A notable exception is John Thickens. His fine study of Harris's visits to London, *Howel Harris yn Llundain*, is very helpful in the material it provides about Harris's piety. Thus the three chapters, 'Bitter and Pleasant Experiences', pp.179-241, are especially enlightening. And his substantial quotations from the Diary are accurate translations into Welsh of the diarist's original English.

[18] Diary, 23 October 1761, quoted by Tom Beynon, *Howell Harris, Reformer and Soldier*, 123.

controlled events. This is one example of the way in which he
reviewed the new birth in his own experience:

> The various steps unsought for – conviction from the ser-
> mon March 30, the conviction at the sacrament April 6,
> the conviction from the 'Whole Duty of Man' April 20, my
> pardon at the Sacrament and what was previous to it my
> giving myself to the Lord; the Temptation that followed and
> my deliverance from it May 25, all 1735. My being sealed June
> 18 by the word, 'I change not' confirmed about my mission to
> preach . . . [19]

Obviously it was implicit in the experience that Divine Grace
had elected to use a variety of means. The Bible, an extempor-
ary address by Pryce Davies, the Vicar of Talgarth, a 'good
book', the Sacrament of the Lord's Supper and even temptation. This analysis also shows how the Evangelicals paid
close attention to the details of personal experiences, to the
intricacies of God's dealings with the sinful heart. Although
the experiences were understood within a general theological framework, the actions of the Holy Spirit were not to be
restricted to a rigid psychological pattern.

  Holy Communion had played a dramatic part in his conversion and his respect for the sacrament never diminished. He
communicated at every possible opportunity. He explained
his attitude in a letter to Griffith Jones in 1742:

> Since the Lord was pleased to work on my Soul, now above
> Seven Years ago, I have been a constant Communicant in our
> Church, and thought it my Duty whenever the Ordinance was
> there, to communicate in our own Parish Church, receiving it
> every where else, where it Should be administered . . . and I
> trust I can in truth say, that I have never been there without
> meeting the Lord, more or less every where I received . . .

He goes on to say, 'had most Good' when he went 'looking
most to Christ and least to the man administring' and he
found attendance a means of blessing even 'tho' I could not

---

[19] *Ibid.* For a detailed story of his conversion, *v.* Eifion Evans, *Howel Harris*,
5-10; G.M. Roberts, *Portread o Ddiwygiwr*, 18-23.

benefit by the Preaching'.[20] Clearly, the significance of the sacrament for him rested not so much in the rite as such, still less in the elements themselves, but rather in the fact that it proved in his experience a place to meet the Lord.

One of the characteristics of the Evangelical Revival which most strikes the student of the eighteenth century, whether he is studying Harris or Rowland or Williams or Whitefield or the Wesleys, is the way in which a massive current of spiritual energy released by conversion was directed specifically towards evangelization. It was so with Harris. His conversion was not only his entrance into the Christian faith, it was also his call to become an exhorter. As he put it, 'My being sealed June 18 by the word, "I change not" confirmed about my mission to preach'.[21]

This 'sealing' was by the Holy Spirit during a period of private prayer at the church of Llangasty Tal-y-llyn. 'I felt suddenly my heart melting within me like wax before the fire with love to God my Saviour.' He could not refrain from calling God his father and acknowledging himself to be God's child. Shortly after this profoundly moving experience, he lost his temper with one of the pupils in his school and feared that he might forfeit the spiritual blessing he had received. But 'God pitied me, and soon sent that word home to my soul, I CHANGE NOT, Mal. 3.6.' He did not immediately appreciate what the word had to do with his condition, but 'light broke in upon my soul, to show me that my salvation did not depend on my own faithfulness, but on the faithfulness of Jesus Christ'.[22] He took this to imply at the same time that his own weakness should not discourage him from preaching. It was his personal commission to be God's emissary. This

[20]   Harris to G. Jones, from Llangeitho, 24 May 1742, G.M. Roberts, *Selected Trevecka Letters 1742-1747*, 24. A. Talfan Davies when arguing that the Methodist Revival was rooted in the Lord's Supper is overdoing the obvious fact that Harris's experience of conversion was closely intertwined with his attendance at Communion in Talgarth Church, *Tell Wales* (1964), 4. V. also Eifion Evans's observations on the point in *Howel Harris*, 5. Dr Evans may not be doing full justice to the distinction between Sacrament and Preaching as exemplified in the above letter.
[21]   23 October 1761.
[22]   Benjamin La Trobe, *Brief Account of the Life of Howell Harris, Esq.* (1791), 15-17.

was a sufficient validation for his life's mission and the fact that his four applications for ordination were refused did not in the least undermine his confidence that he had been called as effectively as any priest in Holy Orders. In this way a charismatic ministry emerged within the Church of England in Wales. It was, of course unsanctioned by the episcopate, but as the Revival spread a host of other exhorters were similarly called and provided the Methodist movement with a surprising number of local leaders. So for Harris, the call to evangelize was an integral part of his conversion. As he put it in his brief autobiography, the 'fire of God' burned in his bones and the sad spiritual condition of people round about him caused him intense distress. 'I felt some insatiable desires after the salvation of poor sinners; my heart longed for their being convinced of their sins and misery.' So he began to hold domestic worship in his mother's house and then to visit his neighbours, pleading with them to repent. His friends were embarrassed by such behaviour and they hoped, says Harris, that 'I should be . . . cured of my Enthusiasm (as they called it) but the Lord Jesus had now got possession of me . . .'[23]

The influence of the Holy Spirit pervaded his experience. He had great faith in immediate inspiration. ''Tis the presence of the Spirit that is my all to preach,' he wrote.[24] As a result, he did not open his discourses by referring to a specific text, 'but discoursed freely as the Lord gave me utterance.' The topic to be discussed 'was all given unto me in an extraordinary manner, without the least premeditation.'[25] This was a typical mark of Methodist enthusiasm. It was all very puzzling to a dry old Dissenter like Philip David who noted sadly in his diary for 17 November 1774, 'heard Thomas Saunders . . . his way of preaching is like ye Methodists, observing no order but rambling. What will become of such things I know not.'

Two aspects of the influence of the Holy Spirit which were of crucial importance to the revivalists were 'power'

[23] *Ibid.*, 20-22.
[24] Tom Beynon, *Howell Harris's Visits to London* (1960), 46.
[25] La Trobe, *op.cit.*, 22. 25.

and 'authority'. Thus Harris, in his Diary on 24 July 1743, reports a sermon by Howell Davies and comments, 'O! the power that was there.'[26] And again on 27 November 1743, he notes that Davies 'preached with vast power'. When Williams Pantycelyn preached on 2 December 1743 on Exodus 15.25, 'There came very great power indeed, and there was great crying out.' It is instructive that Harris, when speaking of his own public work, describes this power as though it were something quite objective. On 18 December 1742, he preached at St Kennox 'with uncommon power, so sweet that I was obliged to cry – the best wine is reserved to the last.' Obviously, he did not consider this access of power as in any way the product of his own efforts. On the same day as the sermon at St Kennox he preached two miles away at Llwyndryrys and he says in his Diary (not without a touch of irony), 'Discoursed with no power at all on the Spirit.' The 'power', then, was God's gift and could not be commanded. The power was closely associated in Harris's mind with 'authority'. Of his visit to Wolf's Castle on 1 March 1741 he writes, 'Discoursed on John 5.25. with authority. Tandem the power came, which continued near 4 hours . . . ' If at St Kennox the power came with sweetness, it was different at Llanrhian on 2 March 1741. There he addressed about 5,000 people with 'vast authority, most dreadful to cut such as won't come to Christ, exposing all the gaiety, sports, dancing, &c.' At Cwm, near Llechryd, 4 February 1745, he noted that he had 'great authority to cut and condemn their cruelty, rapine' and readiness to plunder wrecked ships and participate in smuggling. Another word which he uses in connection with 'power' and 'authority' is 'freedom'. During his twenty-sixth visit to Pembrokeshire, October 1750, he enjoyed 'especial freedom'.[27] For him these influences were manifestations of the presence of Jesus. Of his visit to Jeffreyson, 13 February 1748, he wrote, 'Discoursed on Zech. 13.1. The Lord came down and melted us all to

---

[26] For Davies (c.1716-1770), one of Harris's converts, a Methodist clergyman, and the leader of the movement in Pembrokeshire, v. D.W.B.
[27] T. Beynon, *Howell Harris's Visits to Pembrokeshire*, 179-187.

love and sweetness.' In Harris's vocabulary, 'melting' and 'sweetness' are often used to describe the effects of the divine presence. For the preacher that meant 'light, liberty, unction from above' and 'sound heart-searching Preaching'.[28]

What did all this mean to the congregations? It did mean, of course, that the Biblical message either smote their conscience or filled their hearts with tokens of God's blessing. Only the presence of the Spirit could bring life to a service. Harris once asked Griffith Jones, 'What is the Bible but a dead letter to us till we do experience the work of the Holy Spirit in us, not one or other separately, but both together?'

The power of the Holy Spirit was emotionally apprehensible. The spiritual excitement produced by the divine presence can be exemplified by quoting a letter written to Harris by one of the exhorters, William John, on 10 September 1743. He first describes a Communion Service led by Howell Davies at Capel Ifan. The text of Davies's sermon was Jeremiah 31.2:

> I never heard the covenant of grace so clearly preached and with so much power, the communion was there and our d^r Immanuel was there in truth; of my part I can say y^t my eyes ever seen or my ears ever heard such amazing things as there at a sacram^t, such cries and Joys, they were melted down y^t scarcely they could receive ye elements Mr Davies were melted y^t he could not speak ye words of ye Institution. I never felt such power coming with these words before my hard heart among others were melted with uncommon sweetness . . .

It is striking that the vocabulary he uses is precisely that used by Harris to describe similar experiences. William John then goes on to write of a service which he himself conducted:

> y^t ev^g I was to be at Llanddarog . . . I Discoursed out by ye house and ye presence of our Dear redeemer was with us and much power to speak to those y^t were without and to feed ye D^r lambs and ye fire of gods love burning on ye alters of our hearts, praised be his name . . . [29]

[28] G.M. Roberts, *Selected Trevecka Letters 1742-1747*, 21.
[29] For the letter (which is somewhat mutilated), see G.M. Roberts, *Selected Trevecka Letters 1742-1747*, 102-3. William John (d.1776), lived at Glancothi, parish of Llanegwad, Carmarthenshire.

One senses from this letter the emotional dynamism of the Evangelical awakening. Clearly people were transported into ecstasies reminiscent of those described in the classical literature of mysticism. At the same time it must be admitted that this aspect of the spirituality often caused offence. To some observers it was a subject for mockery as, for example, in the words of one observer who wrote,

> They have a sort of rustic dance in their public worship, which they call religious dancing, in imitation of David's dancing before the ark.[30]

This was the kind of ill-informed comment which made it possible for the *Oxford Dictionary of the Christian Church* to inform us that 'Welsh Jumpers' was a synonym for Methodists. Yet it is remarkable that these words find an echo, quite accidental no doubt, in the account of the 1762 Revival written by Robert Jones of Rhos-lan (1745-1829):

> There was a great difference between this revival and the one that started first of all through Mr. Harris: that one . . . was sharp and full of thunder. But this one, as once in the house of Cornelius, saw large crowds praising God and unable to desist, and sometimes jumping for joy like David before the ark . . . [31]

Even religious leaders who had some sympathy with the Methodists found this pentecostalist element disturbing. Griffith Jones, for example, 'was offended with the screamings and crying out under the Word', and that, by the way, was in 1755.[32] Thomas Morgan (1729-1799) was not very far apart from the revivalists in his Calvinistic theology, but was appalled at the manifestations of emotion in Caernarfonshire during the 1762 Revival when he said of the Methodists,

---

[30]   *Lloyd's Evening Post and British Chronicle* (27-9 June 1763).
[31]   (ed.) Glyn Ashton, *Drych yr Amseroedd*, 84-5. It was originally published in 1820. For Robert Jones, *v. D.W.B.*
[32]   Howel Harris, Diary, 13 October 1745.

it appears to all true and serious Christians that they are stark mad, and given up to a spirit of delusion, to the great disgrace and scandal of Christianity . . . [33]

And Morgan's friend, David Lloyd (1724-1779), the learned Arian minister of Llwynrhydowen, is unable to conceal his contempt when he says of the Methodists on 27 April 1764,

Their worships of the day being over, they have kept together in the place whole nights, singing, capering, bawling, fainting, thumping and a variety of other exercises . . . [34]

By this time such scenes were also to be witnessed amongst Dissenters. In 1763 the Justices of the Peace in Anglesey refused to grant a licence for a new meeting house erected by Congregationalists – in contravention of the Act of Toleration. The matter was brought to the attention of the Dissenting Deputies in London, and when they discussed the affair with the Bishop of Bangor, he sided with the magistrates and one of the reasons he gave for refusing the licence was 'That the said House had been used by Enthusiasts of the Wildest sort who striped themselves in their Worship'.[35]

For the participants in these highly emotional services, however, the experience was deeply significant. Quite early in the story of the Revival, on 1 March 1743, Harris wrote to George Whitefield giving a long description of what he had seen at Llangeitho:

I was last Sunday at the Ordinance with Brother Rowlands where I saw, felt and heard such things as I cant send on Paper any Idea of. The Power that continues with Him is uncommon. Such crying out and Heart breaking Groans, Silent Weeping and Holy Joy, and shouts of Rejoicing I never saw . . . Tis very common when He preaches for Scores to fall down by the Power of the Word, pierced and wounded

---

[33] R.T. Jenkins, *Yng Nghysgod Trefeca* (1968), 48. Morgan ended his career as the Congregational minister of Morley, Yorkshire, *v. D.W.B.*

[34] (ed.) G. Eyre Evans, *Lloyd Letters (1754-1796)* (1908), 52. For Lloyd, *v. D.W.B.*

[35] Guildhall MS 3083/1, Minutes of the Dissenting Deputies, 9 November 1732 – 25 February 1767, f. 486 under date 13 February 1765. These Minutes are housed in the Guildhall, London.

or overcom'd by the Love of God and Sights of the Beauty and Excellency of Jesus, and lie on the Ground . . . Some lye there for Hours. Some praising and admiring Jesus, free Grace, Distinguishing Grace, others wanting words to utter . . .[36]

The Methodist leaders were not unaware of the dangers that accompany high emotionalism. And it was Williams Pantycelyn who provided a typically discriminating answer to the critics. He did so in two little pamphlets, *Llythyr Martha Philopur* (1762) and *Ateb Philo-Evangelius* (1763). He readily admits that in revivals dross can be mixed with gold. Wherever the Holy Spirit is at work, there Satan is busy too. Enthusiasm can provoke hypocrites to produce spurious emotions. But when all exceptions have been made, it is still true that there are times of blessing when people's hearts are filled to overflowing by the Holy Spirit. The sinner's terror and the believer's joy are so overwhelming that they can only be expressed in extraordinary ways. The Spirit of God has to do with the whole personality, and it would be very strange if He affected the mind and the will but left the feelings untouched. Grace works on the heart, too.[37]

For the revivalists, 'heart-religion' was of the essence of their spirituality. They found it lacking in the existing churches, hence their constant complaints about their 'deadness'. In the early years especially Harris drew a sharp contrast between the religion of the head and the religion of the heart. Thus he wrote to Whitefield, 30 April 1742,

I have now observed that every where these are the most simple, humble, watchful, and most full of faith, that have least Head knowledge from Books, but grow in an inward solid Acquaintance with their own Hearts, and with the Lord Jesus . . .[38]

[36] G.M. Roberts, *Selected Trevecka Letters 1742-1747*, 81-2.
[37] For the whole topic, *v.* the excellent discussion by Dr R. Geraint Gruffydd, 'Diwygiad 1762 a William Willliams o Bantycelyn', *Journal of the Calvinistic Methodist Historical Society (C.C.H.M.C)*, liv (1969), 68-75; lv (1970), 4-13; *v.* also J.H. Davies, 'Daniel Rowland: contemporary descriptions (1746 and 1835)', *ibid.*, i (1916), 54.
[38] G.M. Roberts, *op.cit.*, 12. *Cf.* his discourse at Garn's Mill where 'he shewed the danger of head knowledge', Tom Beynon, *Howell Harris's Visits to Pembrokeshire*, Diary, 5 May 1741.

Later on he had reason to modify his views. By the time he wrote his letter of 28 April 1744 to Whitefield, the Methodist Association had decided to arrange regular meetings for catechizing in the societies and to use Griffith Jones's exposition of the Church Catechism (*Hyfforddiad i Wybodaeth Jachusol* (London, 1741)). He wrote,

> . . . tis incredibil ye Ignorance of many y^t have a sound work begun on their heart, but utterly unable to give a Rational and Scriptural account of their Hopes . . .

He admits that he had been sceptical about catechezing for 'fear of making them head wise: but now I have surmounted y^t ye L^d will take care'.[39] Even so, it seems that Harris found it difficult to refrain from making caustic remarks about books because Griffith Jones in 1746 urged him and his colleagues not 'to speak against head knowledge'. Harris, however, sought to excuse himself by saying, 'I was for grace and knowledge together proportionately'.[40] And that was the attitude of his fellow-workers, Rowland and Williams.

Mention of 'heart-religion' leads naturally to a consideration of the crucial part played by experience in the spirituality of the Evangelicals. Sincere Christian commitment meant (to use William John's telling phrase already quoted) the fire of God's love burning on the altars of their hearts. It was a profoundly personal experience but never private. It penetrated the recesses of the personality but was intended to find social expression. So the most important instrument for the promotion of this piety was the Society (*y Seiat*), corresponding to the English class-meeting. Its rules were first published in 1742.[41] In the Preface the members are warned against spiritual pride and the temptation to give the impression that they are better or more mature than others. They should also be on their guard against covetousness, sloth, flippancy, as well as double-dealing in business. Let

---

[39] G.M. Roberts, *op.cit.*, 138.
[40] Tom Beynon, *op.cit.*, 119-20.
[41] *Sail, Dibenion, a Rheolau y Cymdeithasau neu y Cyfarfodydd Neilltuol* . . . (Bristol: Printed by Felix Farley in Castle Green, MDCCXLII).

them be conscious at all times that they are in the presence of God. They should encourage one another's growth in meekness, gentleness and true humility, with unfeigned love towards the family of faith and true compassion towards the sins of other people. The Rules which follow show clearly the social character of this spiritual and moral discipline. The members must open their hearts to one another. That must be done with perfect frankness with no attempt to conceal one's private sins. In rehearsing God's goodness to them, the members should not think of it as a means to enhance their own reputation: the glory must be given to God. The members should also be perfectly open in expressing any suspicious they have about each other. The offender should be reproved but always in the spirit of love.

We have here something that is especially characteristic of the Methodist movement. Self-examination is an ancient practice amongst Christian. In the Methodist societies this discipline is given a public provenance. Public self-examination, combined with mutual heart-searching, is also seen as a means of grace. Because this discipline was exercised in public, it is not very helpful to see it as the Catholic confessional revived. After all, confession in Catholic practice is very private and confidential. Howel Harris was insistent about the value of complete frankness. He finds fault with one of his early supporters, Edmund Jones, on this score. At a meeting of ministers, he writes, 'we proposed to open our whole Hearts to each other, and to bring to Light all our evil surmisings' but 'He was the first that opposed . . . '[42] But then, he was a Congregationalist and despite his admiration for Harris, he still shared some of the reticence that characterized the older Dissenter. But Harris blamed him for it. In a couple of weeks he was complaining about Jones that although he was 'a Dear Child of God' and 'An Enemy to Sin and Satan', he was not 'deep enough in bringing to Light the Wiles of Satan, and the hidden Abominations of the Heart'.[43]

[42] G.M. Roberts, *Selected Trevecka Letters 1742-1747*, 14, in a letter, 30 April 1742, to Whitefield. For Edmund Jones (1702-1793) of Pontypool, Gwent, *v.* D.W.B.
[43] *Ibid.*, 18, letter to Thomas Price, 15 May 1742.

But Edmund Jones was not alone. In his Diary, 5 May 1741, Harris claim that Presbyterians, Baptists and Churchmen are against him 'For talking about experience and opening the heart', amongst other things. Nevertheless, Harris insisted that if the work of God's grace is visible anywhere, it is visible in the hearts and lives of believers and sharing their experience was an effective way to deepen their spirituality and strengthen faith. However, this 'opening of hearts' is not to be seen as a rather primitive form of psychoanalysis. It is dependent upon divine guidance. As Harris wrote in 1746, 'I am more & more daily convinced here that it is out of our own power to understand each other unless y[e] Holy Spirit gives even y[t] unto us.'[44]

Frank talking, however, could very easily deteriorate into bickering. Harris himself could be extremely rude in dealing with his closest friends, although it must be admitted that he was the first to apologize when brought to book. One does get the impression that one of the factors in producing the Disruption was unbridled loquacity. The one who had mastered the craft of conducting society meetings was Williams Pantycelyn.[45] It was Thomas Charles who wrote of him that 'his eye was sharp and penetrating, with many heavenly influences on his spirit when he ministered publicly and in his conversations with people about the state of their souls in the private societies.'[46] It was after long years of experience in the work that he published his *Templum Experientae apertum: Neu, Ddrws y Society Profiad* (1777). It is a wise and mature guide to organizing and conducting society meetings. Williams had long realized the value of reticence. There are things that are better left unsaid publicly. Discernment is needed in separating those experiences that are helpful to

---

[44] *Ibid.*, 200, letter to Thomas Adams, one of Whitefield's preachers at the Tabernacle, 6 September 1746. Harris describes a 'Band' or 'Society' as 'a friendly or Christianly meeting together to confer ab[t] y[e] state of our souls to unburthen our minds to consult together ab[t]our growth in Grace – to Pray and Sing & open our Hearts together accord[g] to y[e] ozanner of the children of God in y[e] old & new Testamen[t]', *ibid.*, 86, letter to Daniel Rowland, 9 March 1743.
[45] For which *v.* G.M. Roberts, *Y Per Ganiedydd* I, 205-9.
[46] *Ibid.*, 208.

others and those that merely put temptation in the way of the immature or which merely titillate the emotions. Those who conduct the meetings need to be men of sound conviction whose own experience is mature enough to enable them to put appropriate questions to the society members. At all costs mere inquisitiveness or a hankering after scandal must firmly be set aside. The society meetings, after all, are meant to be a means of edification to all.[47]

In considering Harris's spirituality, we have been able to gather information from his Diary and his letters. Through these sources it is possible to get very close indeed to the man's heart. We are privileged to tread very private ground. With William Williams the case is different. No diary of his has survived. What we do have is the considerable corpus of his published work. Although there is obviously a close connection between his writing on spiritual themes and his own private experience, and also with the experiences of the people whom he cross-examined in the societies. it is not possible to be more precise. Thus, in the preface to the 1758 edition of his collection of hymns, *Aleluia*, he admits that his earlier hymns were too triumphalistic and that he now sought to remedy that defect in order to make it easier for new converts to sing them.[48] This shows how he felt it necessary to modify his hymns in order to make them suitable vehicles for expressing other people's experiences. Even so, as his mastery over his poetic craft improved and his own spiritual life became richer, his hymns become magnificent expressions of very personal experiences that are of untold value to all who seek to deepen their own spiritual life.

Williams's vision of the Christian life is cosmic in scale. This is because there is in his work an unremitting Christological concentration. This is seen in his epic poem, 'A View of Christ's Kingdom' (*Golwg ar Deyrnas Crist*).[49] It reviews the

---

[48] English translation, *The Experience Meeting* (1973).
[49] It is reprinted in N. Cynhafal Jones, *Gweithiau Williams Pantycelyn*, II, 22-3.
[49] The second edition (1764) runs to 1366 verses and is the version printed under the auspices of the Board of Celtic Studies, edited by G.M. Roberts, *Gweithiau William Williams Pantycelyn* I (1964), 3-191.

mighty acts of God in Creation, Providence, Salvation and ultimate triumph in their relationship to Jesus Christ. This is the objective setting of Williams's spirituality. In his other epic poem, *Theomemphus* (1764), he presents a dramatic and penetrating study of the Christian's pilgrimage from the slavery of sin to glory.[50] Here we are guided through the subjective experiences of the Christian believer. It is typical of Williams that both these poems taken together provide us with a clear view of the balance he seeks to maintain between the universe's dependence upon Christ and the saving work of the Redeemer in the individual soul.

In order to appreciate the quality of Williams's spirituality it is necessary at this point to outline his understanding of the pattern of salvation and to remind ourselves of his debt to the Puritans. One of his key convictions was, that to be converted is to be brought into union with Jesus Christ. As a Calvinist, he did not belittle the significance of God's eternal decree, but the experiential content of that decree for the believer was the personal union with the Redeemer. And to be so united brought to the Christian untold riches. He would have endorsed Thomas Brooks's statement, 'It is our marriage union with Christ that gives us a right and title to all the promises of Christ'.[51] Similarly, as so many of his hymns show, he heartily agreed with Dr John Owen, one of his favourite authors, when he wrote,

> Christ gives himself to the *soul*, with all his *excellencies*, righteousness, preciousness, graces, and eminencies, to be its Saviour, head, and husband, for ever to dwell with it in this holy relation.[52]

It was Dr Gordon S. Wakefield who pressed the point that in Puritan mystical theology 'the normative dogma is Union

---

[50] For a discussion of the poem, *v.* D. Llwyd Morgan, *Williams Pantycelyn* (1983), 27-44 and (in English), G. Tegai Hughes, *Williams Pantycelyn* (1983), 22-42; D. Gwenallt Jones in (ed.) Dynfnallt Morgan, *Gwŷr Llen y Ddeunawfed Ganrif* (1966), 93-5.

[51] *A Cabinet of Jewels* in *Works* (1886) III, 256. There is a biography of Brooks (c.1608-80) in Volume I.

[52] *Of Communion with the Son Jesus Christ* (1657) in *Works* II, 56.

with Christ by Faith'.[53] The Welsh Evangelicals also adopted this view. This was especially true of both Harris and Williams but it was also true of Griffith Jones. In his Catechism he deals in detail with the meaning of union with Christ. 'The greatest mercy in the world,' he wrote, 'is for a man to be converted and to be united with Christ because that is the occasion when salvation enters his soul.' It is to enjoy 'all the graces of the Spirit of Christ' and to have 'a sure claim on all that God has promised to give' and to have Christ as 'our Wisdom, our Righteousness, our Sanctification and our Redemption'.[54]

This enables us to appreciate the Christological emphasis in Williams's mystical theology, as well as his intense interest in conversion. That day in Talgarth churchyard when he became a captive of grace was, for Williams, 'The ever-memorable morning, when I too heard the heavenly voice; I was arrested by a heavenly warrant.'[55] But important as that event was as a turning-point in his life, he, no more than his colleagues, believed that Christianity could be nurtured on the memory of it. Saunders Lewis argued,

> That experience [of conversion] and the experiences that followed it is the raw material of all his poetry. Exploring that experience, concentrating on its effects . . . living in it and reviving it in meditation and the fervour of reminiscence . . . that is the purpose of his poetical career.[56]

This analysis involves a serious misunderstanding. Lewis was concerned to present Williams as an early pioneer of Romanticism. But we are not dealing in the manner of Wordsworth with emotion recollected in tranquillity or even in excitement. The point for Williams was that his own subjectivity had been graciously penetrated by God. And God's grace is an objective reality. And for Williams and his friends it was not sufficient to live by the memory of a bygone experience. The experience must be renewed and repeated. The divine intrusion is not a once-for-all event; it is the beginning of God's

[53] *Puritan Devotion* (1957), 5, taking up the suggestion made by T.F. Torrance in *Kingdom and Church* (1956), 100.
[54] *Hyfforddiad Cynnwys i Wybodaeth Iachusol* (1820 ed.), 100.
[55] Elegy for Howel Harris, Cynhafal Jones, *op.cit.*, I, 492.
[56] *Williams Pantycelyn* (1927), 45-6.

repeated communion with us through the spiritual union with Christ.

Williams's greatest hymns are those which concentrate upon Jesus Christ, and they are very numerous. His Incarnation is a source of wonder:

> Yn mhlith holl ryfeddodau'r nef
> Hwn yw y mwyaf Un,
> I wel'd anfeidrol, ddwyfol Fod
> Yn gwisgo natur dyn; . . .[57]

(Amongst the wonders of heaven
The greatest of them all,
Is to see an eternal, divine Being,
Wearing human nature).

In His Person, Christ is the Rose of Sharon and the Lily of the Valley; the treasures of His Name surpass the wealth of India; amongst all who have been and who will be, there is none to compare with Him; he is all-sufficient.

The work of redemption reached its climax in the death on the Cross. Again and again, Williams brings us back to contemplate the agony, the mystery, the glory and the infinite significance of that victory on Calvary – and all for our sakes:

> Iesu ei Hunan yw fy mywyd,
> Iesu'n hongian ar y groes;
> Y trysorau mwyaf feddaf
> Yw ei chwerw angau loes;
> Gwagder annherfynol ydyw
> Meddu daear, da na dyn,
> Colled enill pob peth arall
> Os na 'nillir Di dy Hun.

(Jesus Himself is my life,
Jesus hanging on the cross;
The richest treasure I possess
Is the bitter anguish of his death;
It is infinite emptiness
To have earth, goods or man,
To gain all else is loss
Unless Thou Thyself be gained).

---

[57] Cynhafal Jones, op.cit., II, 377.

It is a thankless task to try to give any hint of the power and magic of a verse like this in a lame literal translation. But some attempt must be made to convey the substance of his poetry. Calvary was not an event buried in the dead past; every sinner must make his personal pilgrimage to the foot of the cross:

> Deued pechaduriaid truain
> Yn finteioedd mawr yn nghyd,
> Doed ynysoedd pell y moroedd
> I gael gweld dy wynebpryd;
> Cloffion, deillion, gwywedigion,
> O bob enwau, o bob gradd,
> I Galfaria un prydnawngwaith,
> I wel'd yr Oen sydd wedi ei ladd.

(Let them come, those wretched sinners,
In great legions all at once,
Distant islands of the ocean,
Come to see they lovely face;
Come the lame, the blind, the withered,
Of every kind and every class,
On that afternoon to Calvary
To see the Lamb that has been slain).

This verse enunciates in striking language the universal evangelical appeal of the Revival and then, in the next verse, we have the global scope of Williams's vision:

> Dacw'r nefoedd fawr ei hunan,
> 'N awr yn dyoddef' angeu loes,
> Dacw obaith yr holl ddaear
> Heddyw'n hongian ar y groes;
> Dacw noddfa pechaduriaid,
> Dacw'r Meddyg, dacw'r fan
> Caf fi wella'r holl archollion
> Dyfnion sy ar fy enaid gwan.[58]

(There is mighty heaven itself
Suffering the anguish of death,
There's the hope of all the planet
Hanging now upon the cross;
There we find the sinner's sanctuary,
There's the physician, there's the place,
Where I can heal the deep wounds
That afflict my feeble soul).

[58] Cynhafal Jones, op.cit., II, 215.

Did the Christological concentration in this form of devotion lead to a form of 'Jesusolatry'? By no means. Both Rowland and Williams were sensitive on this point. They insisted upon the fullness of the divine nature of the Redeemer. He is fully God – hence Williams's readiness in some of his hymns to address him as 'my God'. And doubtless this was in part a reaction against the Arianism and Deism of the eighteenth century. But for them union with Christ was the only avenue to union with God the Father. As we have seen, Williams himself adhered strictly to the classical ecumenical creeds in his doctrine of God. Consequently his hymns provide ample proof of the Trinitarian basis of his spirituality.

One of the striking things about the devotion of these men was its spiritual realism. One aspect of this realism is seen in Harris's reference to his prayers. Virtually every aspect of everyday life could be a subject for prayer. Nothing was too trivial to be brought to the throne of grace. Naturally, his journeys demanded God's approval. In his Diary on 4 January 1744 he notes, 'cry^g as to go to Lond^n. L^d shew me if Thou sendest me.' He believed God was interested in his plans for the garden at Trevecka, for on 6 July 1746 he wrote, 'I had freedom to ask again about setting fir trees att home & ye Lord shewd me again He would have them set there.' And the same subject was pressing on his mind three and a half years later: 'I had free access to God & to know His will about buying some young trees . . . ' (31 January 1750). Sometimes the minutiae of the building work that was in progress at Trevecka found a place in his prayers, as on 23 January 1753, when he noted:

asking ye Lords will about ye outside work of ye cold bath, whether it should be . . . divided into panel & whether each side should be 2 or 3 panel . . . whether ye rough cast should be white & ye Panels blue & I think I was answered about each . . .

Even more unexpected is that he should consult God about his wife's clothes, as on 4 September 1745:

I had nearness to ye Lord & on asking about buying a stays to my dear wife I had a sight in spirit of ye vanity of all Cloaths . . .

Again, he enjoyed 'nearness to ye Lord' on 16 March 1748 when he consulted 'ye mind of ye L^d about cloaths to my wife'. But one may be excused for feeling that Harris was a little presumptuous on 1 August 1744 when he made the following entry,

> in asking about having a Clock if tis His will i should have one that then I should be sure He would send money to pay for it . . .[59]

Modern readers may feel that such petitions are amusing if not ludicrous. But when one considers recent writing about 'holy worldliness' and the experiments in composing prayers as a means of penetrating through the world to God (as in Michel Quoist's *Prayers of Life* (1963), for example), it is not unfair to comment that Harris was already doing that. In addition, one can see that for him prayer was supremely relevant, and in a most realistic way, to everyday living.

There is a spiritual realism of a rather different kind that deserves attention. Union with Christ did not mean the beginning of a life of spiritual ease. On the contrary, a Christian is subject to the ills and misfortunes of life just like others. But in addition, union with Christ is a taking up of the cross. Discipleship means trials, stresses and temptations that the worldling knows nothing of. Howell Harris through his Diary permits us to taste the violent oscillations of mood which afflicted him. He records for us the horrible temptations that brought him to the edge of despair as well as the moments of intense exaltation in the divine presence that he enjoyed. There is no better illustration of this than the spiritual struggle in which he was engaged between 25 April and 2 June 1739 and which has been analyzed with such care by John Thickens.[60] At many points it is reminiscent of Martin Luther's 'Tower Experience' for it centred on the role of good works in salvation and whether faith alone in Christ alone was

---

[59] I am indebted to my son, the Revd Geraint Tudur of Cardiff, for drawing my attention to the above entries in Harris's Diary and for allowing me to use his transcript. See his article on Harris in *A Dictionary of Christian Spirituality* (1983).

[60] *Howel Harris yn Llundain*, 179-241.

sufficient. The assault brought Harris to within an inch of the conviction that he was damned, but divine grace came to his rescue. But that did not mean that he enjoyed unbroken peace thereafter. Throughout the years he was assailed by doubts and questions, by untoward circumstances and by the strength of his own lusts. And yet he was supported and revived by renewed pledges of the divine favour.

The same is true of Williams Pantycelyn's hymns. It was not a case of providing sentimental lyrics for those who hoped to go to heaven in a rocking-chair. They assume that the Christian is a fighting man. The metaphors which recur in his hymns are suggestive. We are surrounded by enemies but we can take heart for Jesus rides victoriously across the field of battle. The Christian is a footsore pilgrim:

> Guide me, O thou great Jehovah,
> Pilgrim through this barren land;
> I am weak, but thou art mighty,
> Hold me with thy pow'rful hand;
> Bread of heaven,
> Feed me 'till I want no more.[61]

He is a seafarer, sailing amidst mighty waves, but buoyed up by the hope that his Father's house is not far away. He is a mountaineer, climbing steep slopes, but sustained by grace to persevere. The believer is deafened by the raucous sounds of the world but he can call on Jesus, whose presence brings a dread silence to the whole of creation. The Christian is assailed by clouds of pessimism, but let him trust God's promises:

---

[61] Strictly speaking, this verse, usually attributed to Williams in modern collections, was not composed by him. It was composed by Peter Williams (1723-1796), an Evangelical clergyman, for whom *v. D.W.B.* He had translated Williams's Welsh hymn, 'Arglwydd, arwain trwy'r anialwch . . .' in three verses which he published in *Hymns on Various Subjects* (12 pp., Carmarthen, 1771). Then Williams decided to make his own translation but adopted Peter Williams's rendering of the first verse, adding to it three other verses, 'Open thou the crystal fountain'; 'When I tread the verge of Jordan'; and 'Musing on my habitation'. This version first appeared in Whitefield's 1774 collection. For further details, *v.* G.M. Roberts, *Bywyd a Gwaith Peter Williams* (1943), 184-5.

O'er those gloomy hills of darkness
Look, my soul, be still and gaze;
All the promises do travail
With a glorious day of grace.
Blessed jubil,
Let thy glorious morning dawn.

There is no evading tribulations but at the same time the Saviour's presence is the Christian's release from them:

Saviour, look on Thy beloved,
Triumph over all my foes;
Turn to happy joy my mourning,
Turn to gladness all my woes;

Live or die, or work or suffer,
Let my weary soul abide,
In all changes whatsoever,
Sure and steadfast by Thy side.

And in all our woes, the presence of God gives us a foretaste of heaven:

Mount up, my soul, and humbly seek
The bliss of saints above,
Communion with the God of Peace,
Immortal joy and love.

The world, its pleasure and its wealth,
Without Him are but dross;
All these to gain, and Him to want,
Is but the greatest loss . . .

Thy love is all I wish, I want,
Thy love is all I crave;
Thy love my only food and health,
Yea, all that I would have.[62]

William Williams devoted himself to the task of nurturing the spirituality of people, most of them poor and disadvantaged, who were only too familiar with the sombre side of eighteenth-century life. And he did not fail them.

[62] William Williams's English hymns are printed in N. Cynhafal Jones, *Gweithiau Williams Pantycelyn* II, 394-445. For a useful treatment, *v.* Stephen J. Turner, 'Theological Themes in the English Works of Williams, Pantycelyn' (unpublished M.Th. thesis, University of Wales, 1981).

Of course, Williams meant his hymns to be sung. Manuals of devotion and histories of spirituality do not always pay serious attention to music. Soon after the beginning of the Evangelical Revival, hymn-singing became an inspiring and creative element in Welsh spirituality. It is true that the highly disciplined singing in four voices did not come to full flower until the second half of the Victorian age, but its influence began before then.

To sum up. We have been examining the spirituality of the Welsh Evangelicals of the eighteenth century. It understood itself in the light of Protestant orthodoxy. In due course it was to overflow from its original Anglican setting to penetrate deeply into the life of the older Dissenting churches. Its focal point was union with Christ through faith. It saw conversion as a new birth which enlightened the mind, strengthened the will for moral action and melted the heart. It was realistically conscious of the tragic power of sin but even more so of the transforming love of God displayed in the sacrifice of the Redeemer and applied to the condemned soul by the Holy Spirit. The spirituality was subjectively appropriated by the individual but communally strengthened and enriched in society meetings and by hymn-singing. It did not offer believers a secluded refuge from the troubles of everyday life, but rather inspired them to face temptations and tribulations with courage and hope. It drew fresh inspiration from the pentecostal enthusiasm that was a sincere reaction to God's renewed intervention in the life of the fellowship. It was a tough, militant, vigorous and dynamic spirituality, and that it proved relevant to the needs of people was proved by the fact that thousands in Wales embraced it. And its effectiveness in bringing people together in the bonds of a close fellowship was to be the spearhead of the remarkable advance of Christianity amongst the uprooted proletariat that thronged the Welsh valleys when the Industrial Revolution came.

Two points remain to be mentioned.

The first has to do with the relation between Evangelical spirituality and Catholic spirituality. St Bonaventure (1221-1274), the 'Prince of Mystics', in the *Threefold Way*, had written of the three stages of the spiritual pilgrimage as the Way of Purification, the Way of Illumination and the Way of

Union 'in which the Bridegroom is received'. St John of the Cross (1542-1581) had written at length in his *Dark Night of the Soul* of that desolate experience of abandonment which the believer suffers before achieving union with God. And these stages have long been the model for Catholic understanding of the mystic experience. Saunders Lewis sought to expound Williams Pantycelyn in the terms of this framework. His book was a brilliant piece of special pleading but quite misguided.[63] It is only too obvious that the Welsh Evangelical saw the crucial stages of the spiritual life as marked by Creation, the Fall into sin, Redemption through Jesus Christ and union with Him in the Holy Spirit, Sanctification and Glory. This is not an absorptionist spirituality in which the believer is in any way absorbed into the divine. Rather is it a covenantal relation with God through Christ. If the term 'mysticism' is to be used of it at all, it must be in this sense. And the way in which the Evangelicals understood the Dark Night of the Soul is instructive. Certainly, they understood that conversion is preceded by acute spiritual anguish, as Williams shows in his *Theomemphus*. But during the Christian's life, dark night often alternates with the brightness of day until death brings final release into light eternal. So there are significant differences between Catholic and Evangelical spirituality. In what way they can be reconciled, if at all, is a subject for much more detailed study.

The second point has to do with the question whether we have in Welsh Evangelicalism a distinctive Celtic spirituality. A.M. Allchin and Esther de Waal in their fascinating anthology, *Threshold of Light* (1986), have made some helpful suggestions. They ask, 'Is there any special quality of vision or understanding which characterizes the spirituality of the Celtic peoples?' They make three suggestions. 'First, there is an astonishing confidence that this world is God's world, that nature and grace belong together.' This point is fully vindicated if only by reference to Williams Pantycelyn's

---

[63] *Williams Pantycelyn* (1927). I have ventured a critique of his argument in my Henry Lewis Memorial Lecture, *Saunders Lewis a Williams Pantycelyn* (University College, Swansea, 1987).

epic, 'A View of the Kingdom of Christ', in which he celebrates the Redeemer's kingship over the universe and amply demonstrates his fascination with the realm of nature. At the same time his hymns show how sensitive he was to the allurement of created things and how they can come between the believer and God. Hence the need for the Redeemer. The second point is that the 'love of the natural world . . . does not make these people blind to the reality of evil, to the need for a radical repentance'. And that is eminently true of the Spirituality we have been considering.

The third point is 'a powerful sense of the closeness of eternity to the things of every day'. And we have been able to illustrate that point too, especially from Howel Harris's Diary.

One could go a step further. Professor R.M. Jones in his meticulous analysis of the theological and philosophical presuppositions of Welsh literature has concluded that 'Augustinian theology (at least with the exception of its ideas about the nature of the Church) has provided the main highway for Welsh thought . . . from the time when Welsh literature was born across thirteen hundred years until the middle of the nineteenth century'.[64] This suggestion takes us right back to the Age of the Saints in Celtic Christianity. Welsh Evangelical spirituality certainly belonged to this theological succession. We ought not to minimize the theological differences that have developed in the Celtic countries in the meantime, but it is not surprising if Welsh Evangelical spirituality echoes at many points a very old Christian tradition. Their communal spiritual discipline, as well as their devotion to itinerant preaching and the warmth of their dedication to the service of God, is reminiscent of the enthusiasm of those Celtic saints of long ago who commuted with such energy between Ireland, Scotland, Cornwall, Brittany and Wales.

[64] *Llên Cymru a Chrefydd* (1977), 176.

Prayers and Hymns in the Vernacular

Diarmuid O'Laoghaire

If you have ever listened to the Irish radio or television service (RTÉ), you may have noted such welcoming or parting greetings as these from some of the newsreaders: 'Go mbeannaí Dia dhaoibh', 'Bail ó Dhia oraibh', 'Beannacht Dé libh' (all meaning, with various nuances, 'May God bless you'), 'Cumhdach Dé oraibh', 'Go gcumhdaí Dia sibh' (May God protect you). Those are clearly prayers, and perhaps rather unique as greetings, not least over the airwaves, in a secular age when God's name is more often used as a swear-word.

There is quite a large body of traditional prayers in Irish and Scots Gaelic. In Manx there is but an echo of what must once have been there. There is nothing extant in Cornish, although we are fortunate in possessing the medieval miracle plays. Oddly, perhaps, there are no living traditional prayers in Welsh, although there is some evidence of their existence. As regards Brittany, no full collection of prayers has been made. A small number may be found in the *Revue Celtique* of a hundred and more years ago. Of course, Brittany is rich in the religious *kantikoù*, as Wales is in hymns, but they form a different category from the traditional matter with which we are concerned here. We will have occasion to cite some of the Breton prayers.

Ireland and Scotland

When we talk of traditional prayer in Scotland and Ireland there come immediately to mind the great collection, *Carmina Gadelica*, made by Alexander Carmichael in the Highlands and Islands of Scotland in the latter half of the last century, and *The Religious Songs of Connacht* published by Douglas Hyde in the beginning of the last century – inspired perhaps by Carmichael's work.[1] Since then, especially through the organized collecting of folklore, which started over sixty years ago in Ireland and a good deal later in Scotland, many traditional prayers have been gathered. On Raidió na Gaeltachta in Ireland one can often hear such, as well as the kindred blessings and greetings. We may remark that very few of those prayers found their way into English.

For many centuries after the introduction of Gaelic into Scotland it could be said that, to all intents and purposes, Ireland and Scotland were one country. References in Scottish Gaelic poetry, even in relatively modern times, to places in Ireland, required no gloss. There is a notable similarity in the prayers of the two countries.

Most of the traditional prayers in both countries are in verse and were passed on orally, although we have a fair number also written in manuscripts, especially in Ireland

[1] The following are the main collections used in the chapter with their abbreviations:
Alexander Carmichael: *Carmina Gadelica*, Oliver and Boyd, Edinburgh, 1928- (CG).
Douglas Hyde: *Religious Songs of Connacht*, Gill, Dublin, 1906 (RSC).
Diarmuid Óaoghaire, SJ: *Ár bPaidreacha Dúchais*, Foilseacháin Ábhair Spioradálta, Baile Áa Cliath, 1975 (APD).
M. Sheehan: *Cnó Coilleadh Craobhaighe*, Gill, Dublin, 1907 (CCC).
W. Stokes and J. Strachan: *Thesaurus Palaeohibernicus* II, Cambridge University Press, 1903, p.306 (TP).
L.-F. Sauvé: 'Formulettes et Traditions Diverses da la Bas-Bretagnè', in *Revue Celtique*, Vieweg, Paris, 1881-3, vol. V (RC).

and in the eighteenth and nineteenth centuries. Naturally, what is passed on orally tends at times to undergo corruption, particularly in the matter of proper names. Even so, a new prayer can evolve through the very corruption. Another characteristic of the prayers is that they often alternate, more especially in the Irish prayers, between singular and plural, a prayer commencing in one and continuing in the other, more often singular at first and then plural. I think it can be said that the vast majority of the prayers were community or communal prayers. Further, whatever about their origins, they were prayers of the laity, representing a lay spirituality. The family features very much in them. It is enough to mention the occasions of some of them: the family waking and rising in the morning and going to bed at night, grace before and after meals, going to Mass, putting on and off the light, putting a child asleep, lighting the fire, making bread, prayers for mother and father, many night prayers around the rosary, prayers for a happy death, etc.

When we speak of these prayers as traditional we speak very truly. We have many echoes from Scripture in them, not least from that most 'prayable' part of Scripture, the psalms. When we find God or Christ spoken of or addressed as 'Ardrìgh' (High-King), we realize that we are speaking with the ancient voice of our Gaelic ancestors. It occurs as frequently in the Scottish prayers as in the Irish, if indeed not more so in the former. That points to the antiquity of the Scottish prayers, since there were no High-Kings in Scotland. Once again the common heritage. In all our prayers, and this dates back from ancient times, the commonest title for God or Christ is 'Rìgh' (King), and we must remember that for the Gael, although a term of respect, it was not by any means one signifying remoteness, for the king in the small states or *tuatha* of ancient Ireland (of which at times there were more than a hundred) was related to many of the people, and even if the ruler, was also very much one of the people. So in these prayers, as well as terms that could date from pagan times, such as 'Rìgh nan dùl, Rìgh na gréine, Rìgh na reula, Rìgh na speura' (King of the elements, of the sun, of the stars, of the sky), there are many others completely Christian, some of which occur commonly still in conversation, for instance,

'Rìgh nan gràs, Rìgh na glòire, Rìgh nam feart, Rìgh na féile, Rìgh nan aingeal, Rìgh nam buadh' (King of grace of glory, of wonders, of generosity, of the angels, of victories). A very distinctly Gaelic use of the term is, in Scotland and Ireland, 'Rí an Domhnaigh' (King of Sunday). It occurs for the first time, as far as I have evidence, in a fifteenth-century poem by Risteard Buitléir: 'Rí an Domhnaigh mo dhochtúir-si' (The King of Sunday is my doctor) (*Éigse* vol. IX, p.89). Here is one of the many examples in Irish:

Míle fáilte romhat, a Rí an Domhnaigh,
a Mhic na hÓighe a rinne an Aiséirí.

(A thousand welcomes, King of Sunday, Son of the Virgin who has risen from the dead). (APD 60)

We have an example from Scotland:

Chan 'eil ar muir no 'm fonn
Na bheir air Rìgh an Domhnuich.

(There is not in sea nor on land that can overcome the King of Sunday). (CG I, pp.58-9).

A few excerpts will show with what affection the King was regarded and addressed:

O Ìos gun lochd,
A Rìgh nam bochd,
A chiosadh gort
Fo bhinn nan olc,
Dìon-s' an nochd
bho Iudas mi.

(O Jesu without sin,/King of the poor,/Who wert sorely subdued/Under ban of the wicked,/Shield thou me this night/From Judas) (CG I, pp.76-7).

Sìth Dhé dhomh, sìth dhaoine,
Sìth Chaluim Chille chaomha,
Sìth Mhoire mhìn na gaoldachd,
Sìth Chriosda Rìgh na daondachd,
Sìth Chriosda Rìgh na daondachd.

(The peace of God, the peace of men,/The peace of Columba kindly,/The peace of Mary mild, the loving,/The peace of Christ, King of tenderness,/The peace of Christ, King of tenderness) (CG III, pp.264-5).

Mo ghrá-sa mo Dhia, mo gharda, mo lia,
mo ghrá geal mo Thiarna tróc'reach,
mo ghrá milis Críost agus gráim uile a chroí,
mo ghrá ar fad tú, a Rí na glóire. (APD 384)

(My God is my love, my guard, my healing one,/my bright love is my merciful Lord,/my sweet love is Christ, his heart is my delight,/all my love are you, O king of glory)

Tháinig an dall le cupa 's é líonta lán
de nimh 's de dhomlas, go gcuirfí é 'un báis;
bhuail sé 'n tsleá thríd an chroí ina lár.
Dá gcluineadh sibh an osna a rinne Rí na ngrás! (APD 399)

(The blind man came with a cup full of venom and gall to put him to death; he sent a spear through the midst of his heart. Could you but hear the sigh that came from the King of grace!).

In other Irish prayers Christ is addressed as 'Rí na truamhéala' (King of pity). Longinus, as the legend has it, was the soldier who pierced the Lord's side. He was called 'an dall', the blind man; perhaps his spiritual blindness was cured by the blood of Christ that came out of the wound he caused.

It is interesting to note that there are prayers in Scotland lacking or almost lacking in Ireland and vice versa. However, one can never argue from silence, and it could well be that the missing prayers, as it were, have not been collected or that they went out of use. We remark that prayers celebrating the new moon, blessings of animals, Christmas prayers or hymns and certain baptismal prayers, to mention some examples, are commoner in Scotland than in Ireland. The varying circumstances in the two countries account for some of the differences. For instance, in regard to what is called in Irish 'Baisteadh urláir', lay baptism, there are several fine baptismal prayers in Scotland. This is one prayer with its introductory words: 'Dar a thig an naoidhean a steach dh'an t-saoghal tha a' bhean-ghlùin a' cur trì braona burn air clàr-ung an leanabain bhig bhrònaich a thàinig thugainn dhachaidh bho uchd an Athar shìorraidh. Agus tha am boireannach 'ga dhèanamh seo ann an ainm agus ann an urram na Trianaide chaoimh chumhachdaich, agus ag ràdh mar seo:– (When the child comes into the world, the knee-woman puts three drops of water on the forehead of the poor little infant, who has come home to us from the bosom of the everlasting Father. And the woman does this in the name and in the reverence of the kind and powerful Trinity, and says thus:–)

An ainm Dhé	(In name of God,
An ainm Íos,	In name of Jesus,
An ainm Spioraid,	In name of Spirit,
Triùir innich nam buadh.	The perfect Three of power.
Braon beag an Athar	The little drop of the Father
Dha do bhathais bhig, a luaidh.	On thy little forehead, beloved one
Braon beag an Mhic	The little drop of the Son
Dha do bhathais bhig, a luaidh.	On thy little forehead, beloved one
Braon beag an Spioraid	The little drop of the Spirit
Dha do bhathais bhig, a luaidh.	On thy little forehead, beloved one
Dha do chomhnadh, dha do chaithris,	To aid thee, to guard thee,
Dha do chaimeadh, dha do chuairt.	To shield, to surround thee.
Dha do chumail o'n a sìodh,	To keep thee from the fays,
Dha do dhìonadh o'n a sluagh.	to shield thee from the host.
Dha do choisrig o'n a frìd,	To sain thee from the gnome,
Dha do librig o'n a fuath.	To deliver thee from the spectre.
Braon beag an Trì	The little drop of the Three
Dha do dhìonadh o'n a truaigh.	To shield thee from the sorrow.
Braon beag nan Trì	The little drop of the Three
Dha do lionadh le an suairc.	To fill thee with Their gladness.
Braon beag nan Trì	The little drop of the Three
Dha do lionadh le am buaidh	To fill thee with Their virtue
O braon beag nan Trì	O the little drop of the Three
Dha do lionadh le am buaidh.	To fill thee with Their virtue.)
	(CG III, pp.16-19).

When we realize that in the year 1679, as a typical example, there were only four Catholic priests, three of them from Ireland, in the Highlands and Islands, and that these prayers came from the Catholic parts, we can appreciate that lay baptism had become common and had developed its own ritual, perhaps at times unorthodox. Such a situation, in general, did not arise in Ireland, although priests might be on the run. Earlier than that, in 1596, the General Assembly of the Church of Scotland reported that apart from the kirks in Argyll and the Isles there were four hundred parishes in Scotland without ministers.

There are many prayers in *Carmina Gadelica* celebrating the new moon and a few for the sun. There are not so many extant in Ireland. They come from a people in very close contact with nature, both on land and sea and with animal and plant life, and who had a keen realization of how much they depended for their material and spiritual existence on all these elements. Their life had little of artificiality about it. It would not be correct to say that they worshipped the moon or the sun. Alexander Carmichael says of them that they were 'sympathetic and synthetic, unable to see and careless to know where the secular began and the religious ended' and that 'religion, pagan or Christian, or both combined, permeated everything – blending and shading into one another like the iridiscent colours of the rainbow' (CG I, p. xxxiii). One might not agree entirely with that judgment, for undoubtedly it was always understood that all was the work of the Creator. Here is one of these prayers on seeing the new moon:

> Siod, siod, a' ghealach ùr!
> I Rìgh nan dùl d'a gealadh dùinn;
> Bitheadh agamsa deagh rún
> Do gach sùil a sheallas dhi.

> Bitheadh mo shùil an aird
> Ri Athair àigh nam beannachdan,
> Is bitheadh mo chridhe bhàn
> Do Chrìosda ghràidh a cheannaich mi.

Bitheadh mo ghlùin a sìos
Do rìoghainn na maisealachd;
bitheadh mi ghuth a nìos
Don Tì a rinn 's a bheannaich i.

(There, there, the new moon!
The King of life making he bright for us;
Be mine a good intent
Toward all who look on her.

Be mine eye upward
To the gracious Father of blessings,
And be my heart below
To the dear Christ who purchased me.

Be my knee bent down
To the queen of loveliness;
Be my voice raised up
To him who made and blessed her). (CG III, pp.296-7)

There are a couple of explicit references to the Creator:

Gloir dhuit féin, Dhé nan dùl,
Air son lòchran iùil a' chuain

(Glory be to thee, O God of life
For the guiding lamp of ocean). (CG III, p.281)

Am fear a chruthaich thusa
Chruthaich e mise os barr.

(He who created thee
Created me likewise). (CG III, pp.304-5)

The three great patrons, Patrick, Brigid and Colm Cille, figure prominently in the prayers, especially in Scotland. As in ancient Irish tradition Brigid is referred to as 'muime Chrìosda', foster mother of Christ. Other saints too figure, unknown in Irish prayers – Carmac, Carbre, Maolribhe, Odhràn, Brèanainn, Torrann (Tiarnán), Maodhàn, Donnàn, Moluag, Maolruain, Connàn, Adhamhnàn.

On the other hand, there are various prayers in the Irish tradition that figure hardly, or not at all, in the Scottish tradition. Such are the rosaries, prayers connected with and during Mass, scapular prayers, the medieval joys and sorrows of Our Lady (the absence of matter from Scotland in Angela Partridge's study of the Passion theme in the oral poetry of Ireland, *Caoineadh na dTrí Muire*, is notable. The theme figures greatly in Irish poetry, and many examples are given in other languages and literatures in Europe).

The verbal similarity between quite a number of the Irish and Scottish prayers is quite notable. We know that the Highlands in the seventeenth century had to rely on priests from Ireland to look after the Catholics there, and among them, Fr Diarmaid Ó Dubhgáin is still remembered. In Barra we have still Bealach a' Dhugain and in South Uist a graveyard, Cladh a' Ghugain. It is possible that these priests promoted the use of these prayers, part of their own inheritance. Who knows? Here is a grace before meals:

> Beannaigh sinn, a Dhia,
> beannaigh ár mbia agus ár ndeoch;
> ós tú a cheannaigh sinn go daor,
> saor sinn ó gach olc.
> (cf APD 37)

(Bless us, O God,
bless our food and our drink;
since it is you who bought us dear,
save us from all evil.)

> Íosa beannaich is coisrig mi,
> Beannaich mo bhiadh 's mo dheoch,
> Íosa a cheannaich mi gu daor,
> Saor m'anam o gac olc.

(Jesus, bless and sanctify me,
Bless my food and my drink,
Jesus who bought me dear,
Save me soul from all evil). (*Tocher* 6, 172, p.191)

That prayer was recorded in Eriskay in 1953 from a woman who got it from an uncle who died in 1873. Eriskay was one of the islands evangelized especially by Fr Ó Dubhgáin, whose labours were very successful.

Smilarity can derive, then, either from a common source in antiquity, or from more modern 'missionaries' bearing with them once more the ancient material.

Michael and the Angels

A sure sign of antiquity in prayers common to Scotland and Ireland is the invocation of Michael the Archangel, St John the Baptist, the apostles, St Patrick, St Colm Cille, St Brigid and other ancient Scottish and Irish saints, as well as the angels in general. Michael the Archangel was always highly honoured in Ireland and we have hymns in Latin and Irish in his honour from the early days. There is a great deal of material in early Irish literature on Michael. The material in *Carmina Gadelica* is also abundant. He is renowned for his victories, *Micheal nam buadh*. In an old homily in the Irish manuscript, *An Leabhar Breac*, there are enumerated those victories. This is a portion of an item from Scotland:

'Mhìcheil nam buadh,
Cuartam fo d' dhìon,
A Mhìcheil nan steud ìgeal,
'S nan leug lanna lìomh,
Fhir buaidhaich an dreagain,
Bi féin ri mo chùl,
Fhir-chuartach nan speura,
Fhir-feachd Rìgh nan dùl,
A Mhìcheil nam buadh,
M'uaill agus m'iùil,
A Mhìcheil nam buadh,
Suamhnas mo shùl.

(Thou Michael the victorious,
I make my circuit under thy shield,
Thou Michael of the white steed
And of the bright brilliant blades,
Conqueror of the dragon,
Be thou at my back,
Thou ranger of the heavens,
Thou warrior of the King of all,
O Michael the victorious,
My pride and my guide,
O Michael the victorious,
Thou glory of mine eye). (CG I, pp.208-9).

Michael is called in these prayers 'Rìgh (or Ard Rìgh) an angeal', King or High-King of the angels (we have already referred to the terms), corresponding to the Latin, *princeps angelorum*. There is no doubt that the old Irish had much to do with propagating devotion to Michael the Archangel and the other archangels and angels. The style of many ancient Latin prayers in their honour is unmistakably Irish. There is mentioned *signifer sanctus Michael*. In another prayer in a manuscript from about the end of the eighth century Michael is called *ductor omnium animarum ad thronum altissimi* (the leader of all souls to the throne of the Most High).[2] In Irish Michael is 'maor an anama', the steward of the soul, corresponding to the Latin, *dux animae*. He was always associated with judgment and pictured as weighing souls on that day, a task we see him performing on the tenth century high cross in Monasterboice. There is in Ireland also a 'Coróin Mhichíl' or Rosary of St Michael which is for the dying: on the large beads:

> A Mhichíl, glac é (í) i d' láimh
> is déan a shíocháin le Mac Dé,
> is má tá aon namhaid ar a thí,
> cuirse Chríost idir sinn agus é

> (Michael, take him (her) in your hand
> and make his (her) peace with God's Son
> and if pursued by any enemy,
> do you place Christ between us and him). (APD. 385)

On the small beads:

> A Íosa mhilis, a Mhuire
> 's a Mhichíl, fóir orainn,
> a Íosa 'cheannaigh sinn,
> beannaigh sinn is déan
> trócaire orainn. Amen.

---

[2] Dom A. Wilmart, OSB; *Auteurs Spirituels et Textes Dévots du Moyen Age Latin*, Bloud et Gay, Paris, 1932, p.212 (AS).

(Sweet Jesus, Mary
and Michael, help us,
Jesus who redeemed us,
bless us
and have mercy on us. Amen) (APD. 338)

Here we have from Scotland *Am beannachadh bàis* (The death blessing):

Dhia, na diobair a bhean (fear)
a d'mhuinntireas,
Agus a liuth olc a rinn a corp,
Nach urr i nochd a chunntachs;
A liuth olc a rinn a corp,
Nach urr i nochd a chunntachas.

An t-anam-s' air do làimh, a Chrìosda,
A Rìgh na Cathrach Neomh.
Bho's tu, a Chrìosda, cheannaich an t-anam,
An am tomhas na meidhe,
An am tobhar na breithe,
Biodh e nis air do dheas làimh féin,
O air do dheas làimh féin.

Is biodh Naomh Mícheal, rìgh nan aingeal
Tighinn an còdhail an anama,
Is ga threorachadh dachaidh
Gu Flathas Mhic Dé.
Naomh Mìcheal, ard rìgh nan angeal
Tighinn an còdhail an anama,
Is ga threorachadh dachaidh
Gu flathas Mhic Dé.

(God, omit not this woman (man) from Thy covenant,
And the many evils which she in the body committed,
That she cannot this night enumerate.
The many evils that she in the body committed,
That she cannot this night enumerate.

Be this soul on Thine own arm, O Christ,
Thou King of the City of Heaven,
And since Thine it was, O Christ,
to buy the soul,
At the time of the balancing of
the beam,
Be it now on Thine own right hand,
Oh, on Thine own right hand.

And be the holy Michael, king of angels
Coming to meet the soul,
And leading it home
To the heaven of the Son of God.
The Holy Michael, high king of angels,
Coming to meet the soul,
And leading it home
To the heaven of the Son of God.) (CG I, pp.118-19)

There we see the archangel in his ancient traditional roles as referred to above. 'The religious functions most commonly assigned by the people here [Benbecula] to St Michael are his meeting of the souls of the elect at the moment of death, and his presiding at the balance where the soul's good and bad deeds are weighed' (Father Allan MacDonald, quoted in CG III, p.141).

Very interesting is the introduction to that prayer:

Death blessings vary in words but not in spirit. These death blessings are known by various names, as: 'Beannachadh Bàis', Death Blessing, 'Treoraich Anama', Soul Leading, 'Fois Anama', Soul Peace, and other names familiar to the people.

The soul peace is intoned, not necessarily by a cleric, over the dying, and the man or the woman who says it is called 'anama-chara', soul-friend. He or she is held in special affection by the friends of the dying person ever after. The soul peace is slowly sung – all present earnestly joining the soul-friend in beseeching the Three Persons of the Godhead and all the saints of heaven to receive the departing soul of earth. During the prayer the soul- friend makes the sign of the cross with the right thumb over the lips of the dying.

The scene is touching and striking in the extreme, and the man or woman is not to be envied who could witness unmoved the distress of these lovable people of the West taking leave of those who are near and dear to them in their pilgrimage, as they say . . .

It may well be that the lack of a priest to anoint a sick or dying person was the occasion of such a ceremony. It is significant that the priest performed the anointing by making the sign of the cross with the right thumb. It is interesting too that the ancient term, *anam-chara* or spiritual guide, should be **used in this singular and beautiful way.**

With the Archangel Michael, the other angels and especially the guardian angels, figure in prayers before going
to sleep. The Church has always invoked the angels in her
night-prayer. Sleep is brother to death, as the people say, and
darkness itself symbolized death and sin. God's protection
was then especially needed. Here we have from Scotland
and Ireland very similar night- prayers in illustration:

> Dia agus Crìosd agus Spiorad Naomh
> Is crois nan naodh aingeal fionn,
> Da m'dhìon mar Thrì is mar Aon,
> Bho chlàr mhullach m'aodhainn gu
> faobhar mo bhonn.

> (God and Christ and Spirit Holy
> And the cross of the nine white angels
> Be protecting me as Three and One,
> From the top tablet of my face to
> the soles of my feet). (CG I, pp.86-7)

> Luìm le Dia agus go luì Dia liom,
> Làmh dheas Dé fá mo cheann,
> Dhá láimh Mhuire tharam anall,
> Crois na naoi n-aingeal bhfionn
> Ó chúl mo chinn
> Go trácht mo bhonn.
> Nár luím leis an olc
> Agus nár luí an tolc liom.

> (I lie down with God, may God lie with me,
> God's right hand about my head,
> Mary's arms around me.
> The cross of the nine white angels
> From the back of my head
> To the soles of my feet.
> May I not lie down with evil
> And may evil not lie with me.) (CCC. 83)

The white angels bring us back to the twelfth century and
the same word in a verse attributed to Colm Cille in praise
of Doire (Derry):

> ar is lomlán aingel finn
> ón chinn go n-ice ar-oile.

(for it is filled with white angels/from one end to the other).

In the prayer from Scotland just quoted there is another verse corresponding to the Irish above:

> Cha laigh mi le olc,
> Cha laigh olc liom,
> Ach laighidh me le Dia
> Is laighidh Dia liom.

> (I will not lie with evil,
> Nor shall evil lie with me,
> But I will lie down with God
> And God will lie down with me).

It was believed that the nine angels were set in the form of a cross directed towards the four airts. Yet again the word 'cro(i)s' occurs so often with, not only Christ, but others, such as Moire (Mary), Michael and the saints, that I think the word came to mean 'protection', although I have not seen that meaning given to it in any dictionary. Innumerable are the sleep- or night-prayers, asking the protection of the Trinity, of the three Persons, of Mary, Michael and the angels, John the Baptist, Brigid. Here it is fitting to give some of the matter in Breton, which parallels the Gaelic matter:

> En anv Doue d'am gwele ez an,
> An tri ael mat a saludañ.
> Daou em c'halon, un all em penn,
> Jesus ha Mari em c'hrec'henn.
> A pedan da zont d'm zifenn
> Em dihun hag em c'housket.

> (In the name of God to my bed I go,
> The three good angels I salute.
> Two in my heart, another in my head,
> Jesus and Mary in my breast.
> I pray them to come to protect me,
> In my waking and in my sleeping). (RC V, 180)

In the Middle Ages, 'angel' could stand for God or one of the Trinity. In our prayers the three signify the Trinity. Here is another item recorded in 1987 in Brittany:

Va ael mat, kannad Doue,
Mirit va c'horf ha va ene;
Va mirit diouzh an droukspered
Ha dreist pep tra holl diouzh ar pec'hed
Me ho ped, sent ha santezed,
Ma vin ganeoc'h gwarezet;
Grit din-me kaout digant Jezuz
Ur marv mat hag evurus.

(My good angel, messenger of God,
Protect my body and my soul;
Protect me from the evil spirit
And above all else, from sin.
I pray you, saints, men and women
To protect me;
Obtain for me from Jesus
A good and happy death).

We may be sure that the invocation of God at going to bed and rising – 'Dia liom ag luí/ Día liom ag éirí'; 'Bí liom gach am,/ Ag éirigh 's a' laighe' - was not confined to the Celtic countries. 'The Brazilians are keenly aware of God's presence and action, without which nothing exists: "With God I lie down to sleep; with God I rise". These words begin and end the morning and evening prayer which the little children still learn today from their parents' lips.'[3] It is possible that such a prayer came with the evangelization of Brazil by Portuguese or other European missionaries, or was just a natural Christian development.

There is no doubt that the majority, if not the vast majority of the Scottish prayers, are of quite ancient origin or tradition, and that it is the common Gaelic tradition of Scotland and Ireland. Alexander Carmichael himself showed that there are grounds for that statement, and the same grounds would hold as well for Ireland. 'In 1860, 1861 and 1862 I took down much folk-lore from Kenneth Morrison, cotter, Trithion, Skye . . . He told me that the old men from whom he heard the poems and stories, said they had heard them from old men in their

---

[3] Anne Dumoulin, 'Popular Faith in North East Brasil', in *Lumen Vitae, International Centre for Studies in Religious Education*, Brussels, XL (1987), no. 1, p.49.

boyhood. That would carry these old men back to the first half of the seventeenth century. Certainly they could not have learnt their stories or poems from books, for neither stories nor poems were printed in their time, and even had they been, these men could not have read them.' (CG I, p.xxv) Apart from the matter itself, verbal forms in some of the Scottish prayers, forms still common in Ireland, but not now for a long time in Scotland, point in the direction of antiquity.

The Holy Trinity

We may note here some other facets of our Scottish prayers that bring us right back to our common ancient tradition: facets of the role of the Holy Trinity in the prayers.

> Tha mi lùbadh mo ghlùn
> An sùil an Athar chruthaich mi,
> An sùil a' Mhic a cheannaich mi,
> An sùil a' spioraid a ghlanaich mi
> le gràdh agus rùn.

(I am bending my knee
In the eye of the Father who created me,
In the eye of the Son who redeemed me,
In the eye of the Spirit who sanctified me
In love and desire). (CG I, pp.34-5)

> An tAthair a chruthaigh mé,
> an Mac a cheannaigh mé
> is an Spiorad Naomh a bheannaigh mé,
> go raibh sibh liom.

(The Father who created me,
the Son who redeemed me
and the Holy Spirit who blessed (consecrated) me,
may you be with me). (APD 303)

That invocation of the divine Persons occurs in numbers of prayers, but what is notable is the word 'ghlanaich' in the Scottish prayer – 'who sanctified', not 'who cleansed' (as translated in GC). In old Irish the Holy Spirit was referred to as 'In Spirat Glan' or 'In Spirat Noeb'. The latter form prevailed. It is possible that St Patrick himself or other missionaries from Britain introduced 'glan', for in Welsh the word is still used of the Holy Spirit – 'Yr Ysbryd Glan'. Hence the verb here is used of the action of sanctifying proper to the Holy Spirit. It is a testimony to the antiquity of the prayer in Scottish Gaelic. Perhaps the word was felt to be archaic in Irish and understood only in the weaker sense of 'cleansed' or 'purified' and so the more positive 'bheannaigh' was substituted. In another prayer (GC III, p.172 we have 'Dia agus Ìos agus Spiorad *Glanaidh*', as well as, in the following verse, 'Dia agus Ìos agus Spirad Naomh'.

In this next prayer there is an echo from a ninth-century Irish prayer:

> An Spiorad Naomh a bhraonadh orm
> Nuas as na flathas,
> Dha m'chomhnadh 's dha m' mhathas,
> Chun m'urnaigh chur an ceangal
> Aig cathair Rìgh nan dùl.

> (May the Holy Spirit distil on me
> Down from out of heaven,
> To aid me and to raise me,
> To bind my prayer firmly
> At the throne of the King of life.) (CG III, pp.86-7)

> For foísam Rìgh na ndúl
> comairche nachanbéra.
> In Spirut Nóeb ronbróena,
> Críst ronsóera, ronséna.

> (We) under the protection of the King of life,
> a protection which will not betray us.
> May the Holy Spirit rain on us,
> May Christ deliver us, bless us.)
> (*Thesaurus Paleohibernicus* II, 306)

What is notable there is the unique verb in the ancient and

the modern 'A bhraonadh orm', 'ronbróena' (distil on me).

This next prayer is common to Scotland and Ireland and is also found in manuscript, the earliest copy extant in a seventeenth-century Irish manuscript in Rouen (no. 1678 in the Library there):

> A Íosa a Aonmhic An Athar's a Uain,
> Thug fiorfhuil do chroí istigh
> dár gceannach go crua,
> bí i m'dhean, bí i m'choimhdeacht,
> bí i m'aice go buan,
> más luí dhom, más suí, más seasamh,
> más suan.

(Jesus, only Son of the Father and Lamb, who shed your heart's true blood, dearly to buy us, protect me, accompany me, be near me ever, as I lie, as I sit, as I stand, as I sleep. (APD 16)

> Ísligh mo dhíoltas, m'fhearg is
> m'fhuath,
> is díbir na smaointe mallaithe uaim;
> lig braon beag ó d' Naomhspiorad
> beannaithe anuas
> A chloífeas an croí seo tá 'na
> charraig le cruas.

(Lower my vengeance, my anger and my hatred, and banish my wicked thoughts from me; send down a drop from heaven of your Holy Spirit to vanquish this heart of rock of mine). (APD 151, RC 1928, XLV, 302)

> Íos! Aon-ghin mhic Dhé Athar agus
> Uan,
> Thug thu fionfhuil do bheatha
> Dha m'cheannach o'n uaigh.
> Mo Chrìosd! mo Chrìosd! mo dhìon,
> mo chuart, (2)
> Gach latha, gach oidhche, gach
> soillse, gach duar. (2)

Bi faisg dhomh, bi 'n taic dhomh,
mo thasgaidh, mo bhuaidh,
Am shìneamh, am sheasamh, am
chaithris, am shuain.
Ìos, a Mhic Mhoire! mo chobhair,
mo chuart,
Ìos, a Mhic Dhaibidh! mo dhaigneach
bhioth-bhuan;
Ìos, a Mhic Mhoire! mo chobhair,
mo chuart,
Ìos, a Mhic Dhaibhidh! mo dhaigneach
bhioth-bhuan.

(Jesu! Only-begotten Son and
Lamb of God the Father,
Thou didst give the wine-blood
of thy body to buy me
from the grave,
My Christ! my Christ! my
shield, my encircler,
Each day, each night, each
light, each dark. (2)
Be near me, uphold me, my
treasure, my triumph,
In my lying, in my standing,
in my watching, in my sleeping.
Jesu, Son of Mary! my helper,
my encircler,
Jesu, Son of David!
my strength everlasting.) (2) (CG III, pp.76-7)

In comparing Irish and Scottish prayers it is good to bear in
mind what has been justly said about Alexander Carmichael
and his work, 'whose practice seems to have been to dove-
tail different versions of traditional poems, etc. in order to
produce the best possible literary version'.[4] Even so, the
similarity between the prayers is notable. Of course also, oral
prayers can vary greatly and phrases from one prayer can

---

[4] John Lorne Campbell: *Fr Allan McDonald of Eriskay, 1859-1905*, Oliver and
Boyd, Edinburgh, 1954, p.29 (AMD).

appear in other prayers and out of context, just as happens in traditional songs. In the above prayer it appears that the oral version is more to be trusted than the manuscript version, even though that dates from the seventeenth century! In the ms. version the first line reads, 'Íosa, a Spiorad Naomh, 'Athair is 'Uain', (Jesus, Holy Spirit, Father and Lamb), which fits in ill with the following line, referring to Christ alone. Nor does it fit in with the petition in the second verse for the grace of the Holy Spirit; whereas the oral version is orthodox.

In the Scottish prayer we have a word full of meaning and of ancient origin, 'fíonfhuil', literally 'wine-blood'. In Gaelic idiom it could mean 'wine and blood'. In an eleventh-or twelfth-century homily in the Irish *Leabhar Breac* we read that Longinus with his spear 'wounded Christ in his side and split his heart in two, so that there came out from it blood and wine', 'fuil agus fíon'. The words surely have a sacramental significance. The compound word occurs in bardic poetry and elsewhere with the sense of 'noble blood'.

These two prayers illustrate very well some of the characteristics associated with these prayers. As in most of the prayers there is a plea for protection. There are many prayers of praise for God, the Trinity and each of the divine persons, for Our Lady, the angels and saints, but there is nearly always, as is common in the Church's prayer itself, the plea for help and protection. The prayers above, like so many others, remind us of the ancient breastplate prayers, seeking God's protection in every state or position. Of these breastplates, the most famous of course is the ninth-century one attributed to Saint Patrick. A common phrase in such prayers recalls the psalmist's phrase about God knowing him in his sitting and his rising (Psalm 138/139), occurring in many prayers, ancient, such as Patrick's Breastplate, and more modern. I think that Fr Seán Óuinn has expressed it well when he says that Psalm 90/91 had much influence on Celtic spirituality and had to do with the connection between the passion of Christ and our being under God's protection. We see that illustrated in the prayers just cited.[5] In the Scottish prayer above we have

---

[5] Seán Ó Duinn, OSB: *Amhra Coimrí*, Foilseacháin Ábhair Spioradálta, Baile Átha Cliath, 1979, pp.33, 86 (AC).

the very typical repetition of the last two lines of the verse. The phrase 'Gach latha, gach oidhche' has a long parentage, since it occurs in the old Hiberno-Latin prayers, for example, in a prayer very Celtic in tone among the works of Alcuin, but attributed to Pope Gregory. It is a very personal prayer to God, imploring his protection through the intercession of the great ones of the old and new testaments, and of course, Our Lady. Speaking to the Lord the writer says: *Commendo animam meam in manus potentiae tuae ut custodias eam diebus ac noctibus* . . . (PL CI 589-90) (I commend my soul into the arms of your power that you may guard it every day and night). The same words are found in the hymn of St Colmán mac Murchon in honour of St Michael: *Adiuuet me sanctus Michel diebus ac noctibus* (May Michael help me by day and night).

Dilectio Dei et Proximi in Every Ordinary Act.

There are two sayings in Irish that express well the general tenor of our prayers and tell us something of the people who made them and pray them – 'Ní maith an ghuí ghann' (Not good is a meagre prayer); 'Is cóir an ghuí a scaoileadh fairsing' (Prayer should be cast wide). When one prayed for one's own dead, one should not forget all the other dead. We have a goodly number of generous prayers. Here is a grace before meals:

Beannaigh, a Thiarna, an bia seo atáimid
chun a chaitheamh, ag iarraidh ort, a Dhia, é a
dhul chun maitheasa dúinn idir anam agus chorp,
agus má tá aon chréatúr bocht ag gabháil an
bóthar a bhfuil tart nó ocras air, go seola Dia isteach
chugainn é chun go mb'fhéidir linn an bia a roinnt
leis mar a roinneann sé na suáilcí linn go léir.

(Bless, O Lord, this food we are about to eat, and we pray you, O God, that it may be good for our body and soul, and if there is any poor creature hungry or thirsty walking the road, may God send him into us so that we can share the food with him, just as He shares his gifts with all of us). (APD 40)

This is part of a prayer said on rising in the morning:

> Iarraim ar Dhia agus ar an Maighdean Muire sinn
> féin agus ár leannaí go léir agus gach aon atá ag dul
> ar strae a chur ar a leas agus ar staid na ngrás
> agus ar shlí na fírinne, i ngrá Dé agus na gcomharsan.

(I ask God and the Virgin Mary to guide ourselves and all our children and all who are going astray on the right road and in the state of grace and on the way of truth, in love of God and of the neighbours). (APD 6)

The words 'grá Dé agus na gcomharsan' (the love of God and of the neighbours) is a commonplace in the Irish prayers as it is in the ancient Hiberno-Latin texts as *dilectio Dei et proximi*.

In the night prayers in particular, I think, we see the care for the neighbour, and the casting wide of the net of prayer. These prayers are centred around the rosary. Many of such prayers have been collected. We can give some varied examples in illustration of what we are saying:

> Ofrálaimid na hurnaithe seo le hintinn
> an Phápa agus an Teampaill Chaitlicigh, á iarraidh ar
> an Tiarna trócaireach gach ciach, trioblóid agus
> aicíd atá ag gluaiseacht a chur tharainn agus thar
> ár gcomharsana faoi mhaise; gach anam atá ar staid
> an pheaca a stiúradh agus a chur ar staid na ngrás,
> agus gach aon atá ar staid na ngrás a choiméad ar
> staid na grás. Á iarraidh ar an Tiarna bás naofa
> agus saor-bhreithiúnas a thabhairt ar pheacaigh an
> domhain agus gan a ligean dúinn ná d'éinne dár
> gcomhchréatúirí bás a fháil in aon cheann de na
> seacht bpeaca marfacha. In ainm an Athar agus an
> Mhic agus an Spioraid Naoimh. Amen

(We offer these prayers for the intentions of the Pope and the holy Catholic Church, asking the merciful Lord to spare ourselves and our neighbours from every sorrow and trouble and disease that is about and that we all flourish; that he direct every soul that is in the state of sin, and all who are in the state of grace that he keep in the state of grace. We ask the Lord to grant a holy death and a free judgment to the sinners of the world and not to permit ourselves or any of our fellow-creatures to die in any of the seven deadly sins. In the name of the Father and of the Son and of the Holy Spirit). (APD 252)

We could say that that prayer is more than ecumenical! To show that our prayers often have more than the Irish dimension – in their origins – we see in this prayer the very words spoken by Joan of Arc in her trial when she was taunted by the prosecution with not being in the state of grace: 'If I am not in the state of grace, may God make me so; if I am in the state of grace, may he keep me so.'
Another such prayer has the following:

Ofrálaim suas an Choróin Mhuire seo in onóir
agus in ainm Íosa agus in onóir na Maighdine glórmhaire
Muire a bheith rannpháirteach le híobart naofa an
Aifrinn, ar an intinn chéanna a d'ofráil ár Slánaitheoir
é féin ar chrann na croise ar ár son; le hintinn an
Phápa is an Teampail Chaitlicigh Rómhánaigh; ar son
gach anam bocht is géire agus is mó atá ag fulaingt
pianta purgadóireachta, go speisialta ár mairbh bhochta
féin. Má tá fuíoll faoistine ná dearmad Aifrinn
orthu, laghdú ar a bpianta agus méadú ar a nglóire;
lucht díchreidimh an domhain a iompú ar an staid
cheart agus iad seo atá ar an staid cheart a fhágáil
ann. Á iarraidh ar Dhia agus á chur faoi bhrí na
n-urnaithe seo.

Nár thuga Dia aon drochbhás ná gearrbhás ná
bás obann dúinn, ach dea-bhás, bás le hola agus le
haithrí, i gciall agus i gcuimhne, i ngrá agus in
eagla Dé. Corp naofa an Tiarna go raibh mar lón
síoraí ag ár n-anam bocht ag fágáil an tsaoil seo,
agus brat na Maighdine Muire mar chumbdach. Go
dtuga Dia na grásta sin dúinn. Amen

(I offer up this rosary to the honour and in the name of Jesus and in the honour of the glorious Virgin Mary, to share in the holy sacrifice of the Mass, with the same intention of the Pope and the Roman Catholic Church; for every poor soul that is

suffering most severely the pains of purgatory, especially for
our own poor dead. If they were guilty of incomplete confession or forgetfulness of Mass, may their pains be lessened,
their glory increased; may the unbelievers of the world be
converted to the right state and those who are in the right
state settled in it. We ask that of God and make our prayer
to him.

May God not permit us an evil death nor a violent or sudden
death, but a good death and a holy death in the state of grace,
a death with anointing and repentance, in possession of sense
and memory, in the love and fear of God. May the Lord's holy
body be our poor soul's final refreshment as it leaves this world
and the mantle of the Virgin Mary our protection. May God
grant us that peace. Amen). (APD 253)

It is interesting to note how such prayers agree with the
instruction given in the Constitution on the Liturgy of the
Second Vatican Council on the connection there should
be between private devotions and the Liturgy. There can
be little doubt that there is a historical reason for referring
the rosary to the Mass in Ireland. Through penal times and
down to our own day, when there was no Sunday Mass, the
custom was to say the rosary, facing towards the place or
spot where Mass would be said. So too we have the rosary
said with the same intentions as for Mass. Again we can see
the broad apostolic petitions. We are in touch again in the
Irish and Scottish tradition in asking for 'bás le hola agus
aithrí (death after anointing and repentance). The phrase is
a very frequent one in ancient times and in the annals. Here
is part of a prayer from Scotland for a happy death:

Bàs ol' agus aithreachais,
Bàs sonais agus sìth;
Bàs gràis agus mathanais.
Bàs Flathais agus beatha
le Crìosd.

(Death of anointing and repentance,
Death of joy and of peace;
Death of grace and forgiveness
Death of heaven and life with
Christ). (CG III, p.372-3)

Here are a few more random phrases from these night prayers, just to show their scope: 'Islímid anuas i láthair na Tríonóide Naofa, mar atá, an tAthair, an Mac is an Spiorad Naomh, ag guí na Maighdine glórmhaire, Máthair Dé, na naomh is na n-aspal dár gcumhdach, dár gcuibhreach, dár gcoinneáil ar dhea-staid agus ar staid na ngrás' (APD 256) (We bow in the presence of the holy Trinity, the Father, the Son and the Holy Spirit, beseeching the glorious Virgin Mother of God, the saints and the apostles to guard us, to bind us and keep us in a good state and in the state of grace). At times the connection between the rosary and the Mass is mentioned: 'Ofrálaimis suas an Choróin seo le honóir do Dhia nuair nach bhféadfaimis dul go dtí an tAifreann' (Let us offer up this rosary to God's honour, since we cannot go to Mass). A frequent petition in these prayers was 'don anam bocht nach bhfuil éinne aige a ghuífidh air' (for the poor soul – in purgatory – who has nobody to pray for him). Here is another night prayer, typical in its individuality and its communality:

Túisímid agus tionscaímid ar an urnaí seo mar a d'ordaigh ár Slánaitheoir Íosa Críost le sochar dár n-anam, a Thiarna. Cuirimid sinn féin i bhfianaise Dé agus iarraimid cuidiú an Spioraid Naoimh. A Dhia agus a Spioraid Naoimh, guím thú teacht agus seilbh a ghlacadh i m' chroí go hiomlán, mo choinsias a ghlanadh ón uile smál peaca, agus grásta a thabhairt domsa a bheith síochánta carthanach le mo chomharsa. Trí Íosa Críost ár dTiarna. Amen

(We commence this prayer as our Saviour Jesus Christ has ordained, for the good of our soul, O Lord. We put ourselves in God's presence and we ask the help of the Holy Spirit. God, Holy Spirit, I pray you to come and take full possession of my heart, cleansing my conscience from every stain of sin and grant me the grace to live at peace and in charity with my neighbour. Through Jesus Christ our Lord. Amen). (APD 251)

This is a description of these night prayers and those who recited them:

Focail bhreátha bheannaithe bhíodh acu iontu,
agus dhéanaidís iad a aithris leis an bhfíorumhlaíocht
cheart: d'ardaídís iad féin agus na daoine a bhíodh
ag éisteacht leo idir chorp agus anam suas go doirse na
bhFlaitheas.

(They had fine holy words in them and they used to recite
them with true and genuine humility: they raised themselves
and those who listened to them, body and soul, to the gates
of heaven).[6]

From (Latin) Liturgy and (Latin) Scripture

Also recited at night is the final prayer of Sunday Compline
(now said only on solemnities), *Visita quaesumus*. This brings
us to consider prayers in translation; we have such in verse in
free translation in Scotland and Ireland. There is a free version
of the *Ave Maria* (CG I, pp.110-111), a much freer version of
the *Salve Regina* (id. pp.108-9), an incomplete and free version of the *Veni Sancte Spiritus* (CG III, pp.88-9), a beautiful
and greatly expanded version of the *Memorare*, consisting
of twenty-six quatrains, the whole almost entirely in litanic
form (CG III, p.118-25). A feature of the Scottish prayers,
especially, is that so many of them end with a doxology, the
invoking of the Trinity, Father, Son and Holy Spirit, another
sign of antiquity.

Scriptural echoes are many in these prayers, pointing again
to their age. This is a prayer when one wakes in the night:

Bí trócaireach liom, a Thiarna, agus beir saor mé
ó dhorchadas agus ó scáil an bháis.
Glaoigh isteach i do sholas glórmhar mé.
Soilsigh mo dhorchadas,
a lonradh an tsolais shíoraí
a lá nach feas dó tráthnóna. (APD 314)

---

6 Pádraig Ó Cadhla, 'Sean-phaidreacha na nDaoine i bParóiste na Rinne agus
Sean-Phobal Dheugláin' in *Irisleabhar Muighe Nuadhad*, 1947, p.47 (IMN).

(Have mercy on me, Lord, and save from the dark and shadow
of death. Call me into your glorious light. Lighten my darkness, O brightness of the eternal light, O day that knows no
night).

It is a completely scriptural prayer. Phrases from the Latin
Scripture – from which without any doubt it comes – come
immediately to mind: from the psalms – *e tenebris et umbra
mortis; illuminas tenebras meas; dies quae nescit occasum*: from the
Book of Wisdom – *candor lucis aeternae;* from the first letter of St
Peter – (*qui de tenebris*) *vos vocavit in admirabile lumen suum*. In a
poem invoking the Father we have in the last verse, referring
to heaven: 'Far nach silear an deur, far nach eugar ni's mò'
(Where no tear shall be shed, where death comes no more).
A clear echo from the Apocalypse. The poem came from the
Isle of Harris.

We can notice in the prayers a making actual of scenes
from the gospel in present-day life – here is a prayer before
speaking:

> A Íosa a Mhic Dé, a bhí ciúin os comhair Pioláit, ná
> lig dúinn ár dteanga a luascadh gan smaoineamh ar
> cad
> tá againn le rá agus conas é a rá. (APD 21)

(O Jesus Son of God, who was silent before Pilate, do not allow
us to loose our tongues without thinking on what we have to
say and how we may say it).

The very same prayer we find in fifteenth-century England: Jesus Christ, God's Son, which stood still before the
judge nothing answering, withdraw my tongue till I think
what and how I shall speak that may be to thy worship.
On starting a journey: 'Leanfad thú, A Thiarna, pé áit dá
ngeobhair, de bhrí gur agatsa atá briathra na beatha síoraí
(I will follow you, O Lord, wherever you go, for you have
the words of eternal life); 'An Té a rinne fíon den uisce ar

bhainis Chána, go gcuire sé brí agus spreacadh san uisce seo (May he who made wine of water at the marriage-feast of Cana put strength and vigour into this water); 'In ainm Dé a rinne cosán de na tonnta, go dtuga sé slán sinn i ndeireadh an lae' (In the name of God who made a pathway of the waves may be bring us safely home at the end of the day); 'Glóir do Dhia go hard inniu sna Flaithis agus síocháin Dé againn ar an talamh seo' (Glory to God on high in heaven today and the peace of God with us on this earth); when blessing oneself with holy water: 'Míle fáilte roimh allas fola ár Slánaitheora Íosa Críost. In ainm an Athar agus an Mhic agus an Spioraid Naoimh' (A great welcome to the sweat and blood of our Saviour Jesus Christ. In the name of the Father and of the Son and of the Holy Spirit); a grace before meals found in many other countries:

> Bail na gcúig arán agus an dá iasc
> a roinn Dia ar an gcúig mhíle fear.
> Rath ón Rí a rinne an roinn
> go dtige sé ar ár gcuid agus ár gcomhroinn. (APD 36)

(May the blessing of the five loaves and the two fishes which God shared out among the five thousand, be ours. May the King who did the sharing bless our sharing and our co-sharing).

Such a blessing is old in Ireland as the final rhyme in the second couplet shows, and indeed we have a medieval example of it: 'Sonas Dé do rigne in roinn/go mb'é, a Choimdhe, ar mo chomhroinn' (The Blessing of God who did the sharing, may it be, O Lord, on my co-sharing). Among such blessings is one of the ninth or tenth century from Poland: *Benedic Domine, creaturam, istam panis, sicut benedixisti quinque panes in deserto ut omnes gustantes ex eo accipiant tam corporis tam animae sanitatem, Per Christum Dominum nostrum.* (Bless, O Lord, this creature bread, as you blessed the five loaves in the desert, so that all who eat it may receive health both of body and mind.

Through Christ our Lord.)[7] A psalm provides a prayer for returning home: 'Osclaígí dom doirse an chirt agus ar mo dhul isteach dom déanfaidh mé admháil don Tiarna' – *Aperite mihi portas justitiae: ingressus in eas, confitebor Domino.* We are continually reminded of the long ancestry of these prayers, and that applies to the Scottish prayers, whether collected in Catholic or Protestant parts. So in a prayer in praise of Mary (collected in Morar), we find mentioned 'Paidir is Creud', Pater and Credo. It has been demonstrated that the widespread presence of the words (or their equivalents), *cogitatione, verbo et opere* in exegetical, liturgical, devotional and penitential literature from the second half of the seventh century was due to Irish inspiration. We find it in our vernacular prayers too: '. . . Tabhair dúinn gan titim inniu i bpeaca ar leith, ach ár smaointe, ár mbriathra agus ár ngníomhartha a bheith ordaithe de réir do dhlí' (. . . Permit us not to fall into any sin today, but that our thoughts, our words and our deeds be ordered according to your law); 'Ta sinn ciontach is truaillidh, a Dhé,/Ann an spiorad, an crè is an corp,/ann an smuain, am beus' (We are guilty and polluted, O God,/In spirit, in heart and in flesh,/In thought, in act' (CG I, pp.22-3). 'Mo smuaine, mo bhriathra,/mo ghniamha, mo thoil,/Tha mi tionnsgan duit' (My thoughts, my words,/my deeds, my desires/I dedicate to thee) (CG I, pp.98-9). Christ in these prayers is often 'an léigh, an liaig', the physician, a favourite term for him in the ancient Irish Latin prayers, i.e. *medicus.*

The Rule of Life

There is another prayer, but only partially preserved, apparently in Scotland. It is rather únique in its form. It is somewhat like a rule of life. One could well imagine it being proposed to his flock by a priest, perhaps especially when his pastoral work could only be passing. The very shape of the prayer (there are a number of versions in Irish) would help

---

[7]   Marian Pisarzak, 'Les Bénédictions de la Table Pascale d'après quelques recherches effectuées en Pologne', in *Ephemerides Liturgicae* CIII (1979), p.20 (EL).

towards memorizing:

> Toil Dé go ndéanaimid,
> dlí Dé go leanaimíd,
> ár n-antoil go smachtaímid.
> De réir tola Dé go siúlaimid,
> cathuithe an diabhail go ndiúltaímid.
> Ar pháis Chríost go smaoinímid,
> le bás beannaithe go n-imímid.
> Aithrí thráthúil go ndéanimid.
> Srian lenàr dteanga go gcuirimid.
> Srian lenár mbéal go gcuirimid.
> Ag moladh 's ag gráú Dé go
> rabhaimid.

> (May we do the will of God,
> may we follow God's law,
> may we overcome our own perverse will.
> May we walk according to God's will,
> may we renounce the temptations of
> the unclean devil.
> May we meditate on Christ's passion
> may ours be a blessed death.
> May we make timely repentance.
> May we restrain our tongue.
> May we restrain our mouth.
> May we be ever praising and loving
> God.)

(APD 371-4 – lines from the various items there as corresponding, more or less to the Scottish prayer).

> Toil Dhé dhianam,
> Mo thoil féin srianam;
> Dlighe Dhé thugam,
> mo dhlighe féin thoiream;
> Slighe Dhé siubhlam
> Mo shlighe féin diultam;
> Bàs Chrìosda smaoineam,
> Mo bhàs féin cuimhneam;
> Cràdh Chrìosta meobhram,
> Aithreachas pheacaidh gabham,
> Aithreachas tràthail tagham;
> Strian ri m' theangaidh cuiream,
> Strian ri m' aigne cumam;
> Gaol Chrìosda faiream,
> Mo ghaol féin aithneam.

(God's will would I do,
My own will bridle;
God's due would I give,
My own due yield;
God's path would I travel,
My own path refuse:
Christ's death would I ponder,
My own death remember;
God's agony would I meditate,
Repentance of sin would I make,
Early repentance choose;
A bridle to my tongue I would put,
A bridle on my thoughts I would keep,
The love of Christ would I feel,
My own love know). (CG III, pp.50-1)

Actually in the Irish prayers here there are many more petitions that would justify us in calling it a rule of life. Such as:

> Insa chreideamh fíor go gcónaímid,
> ár ndóchas in Íosa go bhfaighimid,
> ar leatrom na mbocht go bhfóirimid,
> in aghaidh na locht go dtroidimid,
> as na drochbhéasa go n-éirímid,
> clú na gcomharsan go gcuidímid,
> in obair na trócaire go ngluaisimid,
> ar dhíol na trua go gcabhraímid,
> gach contúirt pheaca go sechnaímid,
> i gcarthanacht dhiaga go neartaímid,
> i dtobar ghrásta na faoistine go nímid,
> cúnamh na naomh go dtuillimid,
> cairdeas Mhuire agus Iósaef go
> bhfaighimid.

(In the true faith may we remain,
in Jesus may we find our hope,
against exploitation of the poor may we help,
against our faults may we fight,
our bad habits may we abandon,
the fame of the neighbours may we defend,
in the work of mercy may we advance,
those in misery may we help,
every danger of sin may we avoid,
in holy charity may we grow strong,
in the well of grace in confession may we wash,
may we deserve the help of the saints,
the friendship of Mary and Joseph
may we win.) (APD 373)

The following prayers show a similarity surely not accidental:

> Ìosa Mhic Mhoire éighim air th'ainm,
> Is air ainm Eoin ostail ghràdhaich
> Is air ainm gach naoimh 's a domhan dearg,
> Mo thearmad 's a chath nach tàinig. (2)
> Duair théid am beul a dhùnadh,
> Duair théid an t-sùil a dhruideadh,
> Duair sguireas an anail da struladh,
> Duair sguireas an cridhe da bhuille. (2)
> Duair théid am Breitheamh dh'an
> chathair,
> Is a théid an tagradh a shuidheach,
> Ìosa Mhic Mhoire cobhair air
> m'anam, (2)
> A Mhìcheil mhìn gobh ri mo
> shiubal. (2)

> (Jesus, thou Son of Mary, I call on thy name,
> And on the name of John the beloved,
> And on the names of all the
> saints in the wide world
> To shield me in the battle to come.
> When the mouth shall be closed,
> When the eye shall be shut,
> When the breath shall cease to rattle,
> When the heart shall cease to throb. (2)
> When the judge shall take the throne,
> And when the cause is fully pleaded,
> O Jesu Son of Mary, shield my soul (2)
> O Michael fair, receive my departure. (2) (CG I,   pp.112-3)

> A Mhic úd a bhí sa chrann
> agus a dhoirt do chuid fola ann,
> anois an t-am,
> agus ná lig an t-anam i ngeall.
> A Mhichíl naofa, glaoimse d'ainm,
> a Naomh Eoin Baite gráim thú,
> na naoimh go léir i gcabhair do
> m'anam,
> in am an chatha nár tháinig
> nuar a bheidh ár súil á dúnadh 's
> ár mbéal ar leathadh
> 's ár gciall ag imeacht chun fáin
> uainn,
> an chúis á glaoch 's an téarma caite -
> Dia lenár n-anam an lá sin.

(O Son who was on the tree
and shed your blood there,
now is the time,
and leave not the soul at risk.
Holy Michael, I call your name,
St John the Baptist, I love you,
all the saints come to the aid of my soul
at the hour of the battle to come.
When our eyes will close and our mouth be agape,
and our senses leaving us,
the case called and the term ended –
God be with our soul on that day). (APD 337)

What strikes us about these prayers and makes them one
with the ancient Irish and Hiberno-Latin prayer, in breastplate or other form, is that they reveal a constant sense of the
presence of God, in all situations and on all occasions, and
in union with each person of the Blessed Trinity, with Our
Lady, with the angels and saints and with the neighbours:

> Dia dha mo chaim,
> Dia dha mo chuairt,
> Dia dha mo chainnt,
> Dia dha mo smuain.
>
> Dia dha mo chadal,
> Dia dha mo dhùsg,
> Dia dha mo chaithris,
> Dia dha mo dhùil.
>
> Dia dha mo bheatha,
> Dia dha mo bhilibh,
> Dia dha m'anam,
> Dia dha mo chridhe.
>
> Dia dha mo riaradh,
> Dia dha mo shuain,
> Dia dha m'anam sìorraidh,
> Dia dha m' bhioth-bhuan.

(God to enfold me,
God to surround me,
God in my speaking,
God in my thinking.

God in my sleeping,
God in my waking,
God in my watching,
God in my hoping.

God in my life,
God in my lips,
God in my soul,
God in my heart.

God in my sufficing,
God in my slumber,
God in mine ever-living soul,
God in my eternity.) (CG III pp.52-3)

This sense of the presence of God paradoxically, rendered the people very human. They formed these prayers and the prayers formed them. Of course they were poor, very poor, but living in close community. We know that there flourished in Scotland and Ireland a great spirit of charity and care for one another, especially for those who were poorest. That spirit is revealed as well in the innumerable short blessings for every occasion and action, in joy and sorrow. We have a sensitivity to justice and charity to the living and the dead: 'Nár lige Dia go mbeadh aon ní de chuid na gcomharsan againn' (God forbid that we should keep anything belonging to our neighbours); 'Ba mhó Páis Chríost ná é' (The Passion of Christ was greater); 'Nar lige Dia dúinn aon bhréag a chur ar na mairbh' (God forbid that we lie about – or impute lies to -the dead). On putting on the light: 'A Shlánaitheoir, go dtuga tú soilse Flaithiunais do gach anam bocht a d'fhág an saol seo agus gach anam bocht is maith guí leis (O Saviour, may you give the light of heaven to every poor soul that has left the world and every poor soul for whom it is good to pray).

There are blessings without number, and they figure in the great occasions and the small: 'Gun dìonadh Dia dhuibh air gach bearradh,/Gun comhnadh Crìosda dhuibh air gac cadha,/Gun lìonadh Spiorad dhuibh air gach leathad,/Cnoc agus comhnard' (May God shield you on every steep, May Christ aid you on every path, May Spirit fill you on every slope, On hill and on plain). The singer is encouraged by the call 'Mac Dé leat' (The Son of God with you). One universal prayer can bring this article to a close:

> A Rí na rí, a Rí na cruinne,
> A Rí do bhí, do bheas is atá,
> go màithir dúinne agus dá bhfuil uile.
> Gabh mo ghuí, A Rí na ngrás. (APD 147)

(O King of Kings, O King of the universe, King who will be, who is, may you forgive us and every one. Accept my prayer, O King of grace).

Alexander Carmichael writes with great affection of the people who gave him their prayers. He tells of the their innate courtesy and tact and their great reverence. The same people we have met in Ireland, mostly old, possessing great calm and grace, even if living in poverty, or perhaps because living so. One could not but remark their great respect for God and his holy Mother, and yet, as shown in their prayers, their homely intimacy with them. One would see them raise their caps at the mention of the holy name or of Mary. We can leave the final word in this respect with Alexander Carmichael:

'In leaving the Isles, the writer went to say good-bye to the people who had been so good and kind, so courteous and hospitable, to him, and of whom the poorest of the poor were not the least near to his heart. When saying good-bye to me, Mór MacNeill ceased speaking and taking my hand in her two hands, kissed it and watered it with her tears, and curtseying low, said: "Agus tha sibh a nis a' falbh agus a' fàgail bhur daoine agus bhur dùthaich, a luaidh mo chridhe! O ma ta, guma slàn a bhitheas sibh agus guma h-innich a dh'éireas dhuibh gach aon taobh dh'an téid sibh, gach aon cheum dh'an siubhail sibh. Agus mo bheannachd féin leibh, agus beannachd Dhé leibh, agus beannachd Mhoire Mhàthar leibh, gach tràth dh'éireas sibh a suas agus gach uair a laigheas sibh a sìos, gus an laigh sibh a sìos an suain ann an glacaibh Ìosa Crìosda nam buadh agus nam beannachd – nam buadh agus nam beannachd! – And you are going away and leaving your people and your country, dear one of my heart! Well then, whole may you be, and well may it go with you, every way you go and every step you travel. And my own blessing go with you, and the blessing of God go with you, and the blessing of Mary the Mother go with you, every time you rise up and every time you lie down, until you lie down in sleep upon the arm of Jesus Christ of the virtues and of the blessings – of the virtues and of the blessings!" ' (CG III, p.275)

The Spiritual Upshot of *Ulysses*

Joseph S. O'Leary

What is the present value of Catholicism? Must it be defined in terms of a tried and trusted Roman model, with renewed insistence on doctrinal precision, firm assertion of hierarchical roles, rooting out of error, marshalling of all spiritual forces in a politique of global reach? Unfortunately that model does not seem to be functioning as well as it did in other days. Doctrinal precision provides only an ersatz for conviction, mongering the fetishistic archaisms that cement a sectarian retrenchment; hierocratic militancy, in the spirit of Opus Dei, seems the last bastion of reaction against democracy and sexual equality; the revival of inquisitional and excommunicatory mentalities creates not a clarification of identity but a climate of mistrust. If Catholicism is to take this course it can permit itself only one relation to the works of Joyce, namely, to burn them. But there is an alternative way, dimly envisaged by Vatican II. This is the way of dialogue, which dares to expose the Gospel to the questions of contemporary culture. The literature of Modernism has marked out the space and defined the parameters of a spiritual quest that unites believers and unbelievers, yielding a *lingua franca* more comprehensible to literate adults than any sacred scripture. Kafka, Proust, Rilke,

Woolf, Char and Celan are guides to the life of the spirit, and their works conceal the key to a contemporary unlocking of the Gospel.

Joyce, the modernist master who specifically challenges Irish Catholicism, has figured in their lore, unread, as the betrayer of religious and patriotic ideals sanctified by the suffering of generations and to which modern Ireland owes it survival. But his rejection of post-Famine nationalism and ultramontanism, now that Ulster's woes have revealed (amid much else) the dark side of those narrowing creeds, can no longer be shrugged off as Bohemian petulance and escapism, sad quirks of a maimed and embittered renegade. Instead, one might claim that, as the one who identified the strangleholds that have cauterized and paralysed us, he took the painful first step of an Irish liberation theology, and moreover that *Ulysses* (U) and *Finnegans Wake* (FW) make a major contribution to the formation of a contemporary Celtic spirituality. These works are not merely literary experiments; they are mighty apparatuses for the sounding of all the degrees of waking and sleeping consciousness. Many Irish readers prefer the rich human fare of the earlier writing, though already uneasy with its hidden patterns and tantalizing hints of symbolic significance, and their reception reaches its cut-off point somewhere in the middle of U. Yet even in its remotest reaches, Joyce's art retains some contact with its human starting-points, as John Bishop tries to show by taking seriously his claim that FW is a reconstruction of the life of a sleeping mind.[1] Moreover, the labyrinthine abstraction and reflexivity of the mature Joyce resonates with much in ancient Celtic art and thought. The monistic, cyclic, pantheistic turn of mind that drew him to Giordano Bruno, Spinoza, Vico and the Sabellian heresy can scarcely be dismissed as un-Irish if we recall the figure of John Scotus Eriugena. One could also perhaps trace in Celtic literature or psychology anticipations of the freedom of mind that allowed Joyce to indulge, on the one hand, the anarchy and laughter which cracked open the Western logos

---

[1]   John Bishop, *Joyce's Book of the Dark* (University of Wisconsin Press, 1986).

through a liberation of all the possibilities of writing, and, on the other, the unrelenting cult of form which culminated in the polyphonic superimposition of so many layers of meaning in the palimpsest of FW. For Celts to embrace Joyce's world is to embrace something of their own nature, the "uncreated conscience" of the race (*Portrait* 228).[2]

He is as Irish, and perhaps as Catholic, as we allow him to be. To embrace him means to forsake our insistence on these identities, to share that disinterestedness which, as Beckett relates, "saw no difference between the fall of a bomb and fall of a feather",[3] and which freed him to reach down beneath the feuds between Catholic and Protestant, Sassenach and Gael, which had straitened the mind of his compatriots, to a buried Ireland, older than and indifferent to these identities. This Ireland was of universal human stuff, as fit for orchestration in Hebrew and Hellenic or in the sixty languages of FW as in Celtic myths. Setting his career in counterpoint with those of his contemporaries, some cut off in the years of upheaval (Tom Kettle, Frank Sheehy-Skeffington, George Clancy), some living on through the long twilight of the Free State[4] or in exile,[5] one could say that he attained, in his airless world of words, that stranger freer Ireland envisioned in the heady talk of nationalist myth-making and the Celtic Revival, and that had failed to find adequate social or political embodiment. Working out the psychodrama of "Ireland's split little pea" in the logomochy between Shem and Shaun (himself and De Valera), he won through to an element in which Irish souls must be pickled if they would escape the "nightmare of history" (U 28) that still weighs on the brains of the living.

Conquerors create establishment language, but eloquence on the lips of the defeated is either escapist or subversive. In the Irish case language fed on itself, for want of practical outlets, either burgeoning as infectious rhetoric or picking itself

[2] *A Portrait of the Artist as a Young Man* (Grafton Books 1977).
[3] Quoted in Tom Bishop and Raymond Federman, eds, *Samuel Beckett* (Paris: l'Herne, 1976; Livre de Poche edition), p.49.
[4] See the various memoirs of Oliver St John Gogarty, and Eugene Sheehy, *May it Please the Court* (Dublin: Fallon, 1951).
[5] See John F. Byrne, *Silent Years* (New York 1953).

ironically to pieces, in either case making a plaything of the victorious tongue and asserting verbal freedoms and political defeats. Both varieties of linguistic implosion feed Joyce's prose. In contrast to this conquest in language of a wider Irish freedom, it might seem that his dealings with religion petered out in stalemate. Louis Gillet reports such remarks as "Of all of us who are seated this evening at this table, in a little time nothing will remain . . . I am unable to believe . . . We are all destined to be eaten by worms . . ."[6] Catholicism took the form in his bitter imagination of an uncanny array of ghostly authorities clutching at his soul from the depths of the ages. There is hardly a chapter in his works not troubled by the apparition of some sinister dehumanizing ecclesiastic. His style absorbs phrases from scripture, creed or liturgy, which echo emptily, bereft, or deliberately stripped, of their original significance. He could not reshape Ireland's imported religion as he transformed her imported tongue, yet his argument with it catalyzed an original original spiritual sensitivity, alert to hints of inscrutable mystery in the least of incidents and the commonest utterance. Dedalus's ambition to be a "priest of eternal imagination, transmuting the daily bread of experience into the radiant body of everliving life" (Portrait 200) is reported ironically, as the diction shows, yet it reveals the degree to which Joyce's practice of sacralizing the commonplace by the magic of words derives from his immersion in Catholic sacramentalism.

Even his agnostic gropings serve, as Beckett's do more bleakly, to light up the difficulties a contemporary adult Catholic is likely to encounter in his or her spiritual quest. Agnosticism is serene in Bloom, and almost sapiental, offering release from the fixated anticlericalism of Dedalus and Mulligan and also from the frozen priesthood of art that cuts Dedalus off from the human environment to which he vainly beckons. Agnosticism is eventually sublated in a will to celebration, which, as the obituarist in L'Osservatore Romano perhaps recognized, does not shut out faith but keeps the door open for a Catholicism commensurate with all the riddles and resources of consciousness and language. The

<hr>

[6] Jacques Aubert and Fritz Senn, eds, *James Joyce* (Paris: Cahiers de l'Herne, 1985), p.178.

simple passions behind Joyce's attitudes to religion emerge in remarks recorded by Arthur Power: "When we are living a normal life we are living a conventional one, following a pattern which has been laid out by other people in another generation, an objective pattern imposed on us by the church and state. But a writer must maintain a continual struggle against the objective: that is his function. The eternal qualities are the imagination and the sexual instinct, and the formal life tries to suppress both."[7]. The key to a Joycean transformation of Christian faith is given if for "the writer" here, one substitutes "the believer" or "the theologian".

The Assault on Convention

Spirituality in our time has to take a paradoxical, Eckhartian turn – "I pray God to deliver me from God" – for the conventional idioms of prayer, in addition to suffering the inbuilt obsolescence of all verbal constructs, have been poisoned by long abuse. "I pray writing to deliver me from language" might be the equivalent Joycean twist. He could write well only by over-writing, for he had not the natural eloquence, the *continuus motus animi* that keeps Henry James going for forty volumes of magnificence. His first drafts are flat (*Stephen Hero, Giacomo Joyce*) and as long as he remains within the bourne of conventional English pall of dulness lies on his spirit: "My soul frets in the shadow of his language" (*Portrait* 172). His awareness of the limits any convention imposed kept him trying to build a style which would be the ripe expression of his personality and in which he could be at home, for each of these concepts – "style", "personality", "home", "expression" – represented institutional foreclosures of the project first formulated as "to express myself in some mode of life or art as freely as I can and as wholly as I can" (*Portrait* 222) but later developed beyond this individualistic focus. An ironic attention to each element of speech and an elaborate process of condensation, allusion, superimposition is necessary to release from the bonds of

---

7   Quoted in Bishop, *Joyce's Book of the Dark*, pp.423-4.

language the liberating word. The finished Joycean sentence casts a withering light on the facilities it renounces.

By comic parody, focusing primarily on linguistic phenomena, U is constantly undermining definitions, identities and conventions, microcosmically those of lower-middle-class Dublin, and macrocosmically, those of Western literature, history, ideology and religion. An upshot of this process for the theological reader is insight into the conventionality of all religious discourse and the need to surpass and sublate it in a free critical word, such as that of the Gospel represented over against the religious traditions to which it alluded. The forging of such a "skilful means" (Buddhist *Upaya*) for the communication of religious insight today can draw on the resources of Joycean parody.[8] The conventionality of our speech may cease to be oppressive if we fully recognize its ludicrously makeshift texture and if we keep our use of religious words open-ended, aware that their validity has to be confirmed anew in every usage and that the play of their resonances varies with each new context.

Joyce's style, or the strategy presiding over the various styles he deploys, aims to smash all conventions, showing their relativity as delusional constructs. All identities, those of character and theme for example, or even the identity of the meaning of a word, are revealed as flawed and feeble amalgams. That is why it is a mistake for the theological reader to focus primarily on the grand thematic structure of exile and homing, Father and Son (with Molly as Spirit), or on the potential of Bloom's character as comic Messiah, for Joyce anticipates both Derrida's demonstration that thematic unities are instable surface effects of the play of rhetoric and syntax that mounts them, and Lacan's presentation of the self as a complex dialectic of heterogeneous factors, forever incomplete, conditioned and determined by the signifiers of the culture. Thus Bloom and the situations in which he figures are never allowed to attain the univocal sense they would have in a traditional narrative. The series of his meetings with Stephen constitute a tantalizing pattern, hinting at shadows of epic significance, but firmly embodying none of

[8]   See Michael Pye, *Skilful Means* (London: Duckworth, 1978).

them. Their performance of an Easter Vigil together (572-58)[9] imposes sublime patterning on trivial incidents in such a way that the effects of elevation and of bathos coexist and undermine one another.

Any establishment of meaning that claims fixity is promptly sent spinning by the text's adoption and disruption of its discourse. The doubt that nourished deep gloom in Ibsen or Kafka, fuels in Joyce a devil-may-care sporting with chaos in order to master it, transgressing norms of vocabulary, grammar, syntax, punctuation, narrative, plot, style, literary genre, to show how fragile and misleading are the conventions structuring conversation, mores, sentiment, ethics, philosophy, literary criticism and every other academic discipline, time and space, personal identity, cause and effect, consciousness, religion, patriotism, human relationships. The targets include medicine, law and theology, the traditional butts of comedy, and contemporary jargons such as that of science, whose "objectivity", in the catechism of "Ithaca", is solicited towards the sublime (the hymn of the water, 549-550) as well as towards the ridiculous ("ignition was communicated from the faggots of precombustible fuel to polyhedral masses of bituminous coal", 550), in either case dissolving into stunning verbal performance – just as the discourse of Catholicism is made to dissolve. Even the grandiose mythic patterns in the background of the story are present only as simulacra and even the established identities of character and author are deliberately undermined, as when Molly Bloom calls out to the author: "Oh Jamesy let me up out of this" (633).[10]

Verbal collapse instigates the collapse of the powers which define their claims in stable diction, and undoes all orthodoxies in their linguistic matrix. All power, for Joyce, boils down to the unquestioned sway of limiting vocabularies. The material despoliation of the poor is of less moment than the disinheritance of their minds, saturated with conventional diction, and the deprivation of lives trapped in a round of

[9] See Robert Day Adams, "Le diacre Dedalus", in Aubert and Senn, *James Joyce*, pp.309-17.
[10] All quotations are from *Ulysses: The Corrected Text. Student Edition* (Penguin, 1986).

conventional gestures. His method of attack on this bondage is not a satirical scorching of the alienating convention, but instead a send-up, elevating to new intensity the eloquence of hellfire sermons, Shakespearian scholarship, nationalistic propaganda, fashion magazines, purple prose, erotic novels, provincial journalism, scientific textbooks, usually on the basis of deliberate researches into the genre. These are the dalects to enwrap the consciousnesss of Dublin, explored as extensions of the varieties of demotic which provide the book's lowest styles. In a mimicry that aims to release the soul of the city from these governing conventions, U plays back the talk of Dublin, vamping up its brilliance and at the same time exposing its provincial delusions of grandeur. Irish enamorment of English eloquence is carried to a terrific extreme in "Oxen of the Sun", which runs through the historical gamut of prose styles in order to demonstrate a creative freedom transcending their constraints. Yet the tone of U is not one of satire nor of the Flaubertian irony of *Dubliners*. No matter how absurd or disgusting the characters, they are subjects of epic celebration and each of them makes an individual contribution to the linguistic plenitude and diversity of work.

Joyce's revolt against Catholicism, recapitulated, telescoped and distanced in *Portrait*, was the launching-pad of his resistance to the imposition of definition on the texture of life and its expression. Such definition he saw as a lie, a way of hiding oneself or hiding from oneself, and a violence, an imposition of narrow boundaries and destructive divisions. In his disenchanted view, only one versed in the arts of deception and self-deception could play well the roles expected of him or her in Catholic Ireland. He opposed to these subtle nets not another vocal gospel, but a way of seeing, a subtlety of awareness, to which he felt his way by writing and rewriting. The keynote to U's critique of Catholicism is neither the mockery of Mulligan, nor Molly's lax acceptance, nor the fretting of Stephen "Of him that walked the waves. Here also over these craven hearts his shadow lies and on the scoffer's heart and lips and on mine. It lies upon their eager faces who offered him a coin of the tribute. To Caesar what is Caesar's, to God what is God's" (22); "(he taps his brow). But in here it is I must kill the priest and the king" (481). Nor is it given by the Buñuelesque exposure of the absurdities of the clerical mind-set in Father Conmee (180-184),[11], nor even by the techniques of defamiliarization,[12] the startling juxtapositions, foregrounding of details, presentation of the domestic scene through alien eyes (those of the Jew Bloom, as much a stranger as Montesquieu's Persians when he observes the communion and funeral rites, 60-68, 85-86), whereby Joyce mounts an exhibition of religious practices which shows them as odd, archaic and vacuous.[13] The final vantage is that of the artist, who sees the terminology and symbolism of Catholicism as a heritage to be used to new end, to enrich the plot and style of the novel as a revelation of life. It is not impossible to see in this irreverent transfusion a religious purpose. Beyond its Voltairean and Flaubertian levels, Joyce's irony follows a transforming star.

The dialectic of parody deflates conventions of everyday life and converts them on the spot into literary artefacts which may recur as motifs in the unmasterably dense polyphony of the text. Paradoxically, the mockery of sacred conventions leaves over a set of comic rubrics which serve to hallow the everyday, or at least lend it aesthetic shape. Thus the scatological recycling of Robert Emmet's "Speech from the Dock" provides an apt cadence to "Sirens" (348-239), and the treatment of nationalist rhetoric in "Cyclops" and Marian effusion in "Nausicaa" coolly robs these material of their pathos and unfolds them as stylistic specimens to enrich the work's fabric. "Oxen of the Sun" displays a mastery of all styles as the reward of suspension of belief in any. This process of parodic transmutation begins in Stephen's hyperliterary stream of consciousness – "Young shouts of moneyed voices in Clive Kempthorpe's rooms.

---

[11] Kevin Sullivan misreads this episode: "Conmee, in miniature, is form and spirit, a source of existence and life" (*Joyce among the Jesuits*, Columbia University Press, 1957, p.16).

[12] For this concept see Fredric Jameson, *The Prison-House of Language* (Princeton University Press, 1972), and R.H. Stacy, *Defamiliarization in Language and Literature* (Syracuse University Press, 1977).

[13] For the element of justice here, see Cheryl Herr's examination of the sermons of the period, which reveal a mechanical and oppressive dogmatism (*Joyce's Anatomy of Culture*, University of Illinois Press, 1986, pp.222-81).

Palefaces: they hold their ribs with laughter, one clasping another. O, I shall expire!" (6) – and in the wry mimickings of Blooks – "Whispering around you. Would you like to see a priest? Then rambling and wandering. Delirium all you hid all your life. His sleep is not natural" (91). Parodic commentary allows both to integrate and master the data of experience, or perhaps to preserve the identity of their *moi* against the corrosive effect of exposure to the real. Their mental processes reflect the narcissism of the artist who finds "in the world without as actual what was in his world within as possible" (175) and this imaginary ordering is taken up into the wider patterning of the symbolic texture of the work as a whole. The saturation-level citationality of Joye's writings is already anticipated in the monologues of Stephen and Molly (even Molly has a quota of quashed quotations). Shakespeare's jokey self-quotations in *Cymbeline* (nicely emphasized in Peter Hall's recent production) explain why the close of that play is quoted at the end of "Scylla and Charybdis" (179). The triumphant order and peace felt by Stephen after his brilliant performance echoes the sense of achieved synthesis Shakespeare (unsuccessfully?) tried to communicate at the close of his first historico-tragi-comedy and anticipates an effect intended by the grand design of U as a whole.

The inner monologues are also entrusted with the first phase in the text's work of linguistic disintegration and transformation: "Angry tulips with you darling manflower punish your cactus if you don't please poor foregetmenot how I long violets to dear roses when we soon anemone met all naughty nightstalk wife Martha'a perfume" (64). Martha's letter, here parodied, is itself a parody on the author's part (63–64), as are Milly's (54), Mr Deasy's (27), H. Rumbold's (249), and every other document quoted in the course of the work, including pre-existing compositions, such as the poems of Douglas Hyde and Louis J. Walsh (153, 298: these caricature themselves, like the Sorbonne document on baptizing unborn babies, adduced by Sterne[14]). Bloom, Stephen, Molly,

---

[14]	*Tristram Shandy*, I 20.

Mulligan, Mr Dedalus are walking self-parodies, and the more two-dimensional figures caricature also the types they represent: Father Conmee as the Jesuit, Haines as the Englishman, Master Dignam as the Schoolboy, Boylan as the Bester. The parody releases the real (functions epiphanally) in the early chapters for it focuses not on general traits but on what is oddest in its targets. Later a hypertrophy of the mock-heroic, while not entirely losing sight of the events or non-events of the narrative, serves less as comic commentary than as parody of literary genres and the entire institution of literature.

Forced to reveal themselves in immediate gesture, the characters leap into unexplained life before our eyes. Bloom is always doing so in his stream of consciousness. Others we grasp from outside, and their self-manifestation is often bizarre and unexpected. The parody never blurs, but at every turn intensifies singularity, to uncover what is quirkiest in the speech and behaviour of the personae. Each of the novel's eighteen scenes subsists in its own style free of any encompassing frame or context. The effect is one of naked vividness in "Aeolus" and "Scylla and Charybdis", each character revealing his essence with concentrated vigour throughout, while the writing bends to the action, contorting into rhetorical figures (throughout "Aeolus"), or shaping itself to blank verse (167) and to dramatic dialogue (171-2). These vibrant exchanges are talk for talk's sake, the quintessence of Celtic aestheticism. Though in the total context some of the themes broached have a pseudo-structuring role (pseudo, in that the thematic web never attains structural closure), the immediate and prevalent effect is of a brilliant foregrounding of the everyday and an elimination of any ideological or conventionally realistic framework for interpreting it. If the stripping away of frames of understanding defamiliarizes the events narrated, they are subsequently enclosed in another medium which lends them their true sense: the book itself. Epiphanic realism is focused in strange and striking phrases, permitting a magical sublation of the realistic into the verbal, the enclosure of Dublin in the book. Bloom's father's book, *Thoughts of Spinoza*, (233, 582) indicates this metaphysical frame, a monism wherein the events of real life are reduced, via the phrases that light up their essence, to aspects of the absolute substance which is the book itself.[15]

Transformation

The subversive power of this writing is at the service of an effort to redeem the whole reach of banal and sordid everyday experience – by a demonstration that nothing is banal or sordid. The constantly heightened outlandishness of presentation defamiliarizes the material and increasingly the emphasis shifts to a defamiliarization of the working of words as such. There are instances, too, of what one might call defamiliarization by extreme familiarity, in cryptic notations of stray thoughts and physical sensations which the reader will recognize although no literary text had chronicled such things before. These *objets trouvés* punctuate the seamless robe of literature with the ruptures of the real.[16] Molly Bloom's monologue carries this technique to an extreme, contrasting with "Ithaca"'s extreme of suspended familiarity. The comic subversions of secure identity are reinforced by and in turn permit the emergence of the real (contingency, brute physical materiality, that which is irreducible to imaginary or symbolic recuperation).[17] U is as contaminated by the real as any text can be while still remaining literature, that is, while still overcoming the deadness and the absurdity of mere fact. "The reality of experience" (*Portrait* 228) includes many

[15]   See John Henry Raleigh, "Bloom as a Modern Epic Hero", *Critical Inquiry* 3:3, Spring 1977, pp.539-98.
[16]   In "Hades" (74), the mourners brush dried semen from the carriage seat (note Mr Dedalus's "it's the most natural thing in the world" and the diction of "the mildewed buttonless leather of the seats"). This intrusion of the real, muddy and bizarre, a piece of meaningless static in the narrative, is symbolically the white barley meal of Odyssey XI 28, and may also refer intertextually to a convention of Victorian pornography. It is one of the chapter's many images of death, close to that of cheese as "corpse of milk" (94). In "Ithaca" Bloom finds "The imprint of a human form, male, not his, some crumbs, some flakes of potted meat recooked" in his bed (600); "Penelope" gives reason to suspect euphemism here (611, ll.154-155). See Robert Adams in Clive Hart and David Hayman, eds, *James Joyce's "Ulysses"* (University of California Press, 1974), p.112.
[17]   On Jacques Lacan's notion of the real, and its interplay with the imaginary and the symbolic, see Ellie Ragland-Sullivan, *Jacques Lacan and the Philosophy of Psychoanalysis* (University of Illinois Press, 1987), pp.185-95.

realms of eloquence and fantasy, but it always carries the ballast of these grimy references. They surface throughout HCE's grandiose dream, notably in the form of the drab trappings of his public house in Chapelizod. Theology might find here a challenge to extend and deepen the incarnational principle, shattering the ecclesiastical stylization which continues to exclude the "lower", demonized dimensions of bodily being.[18] Joyce complained that traditional authors "show you a pleasant exterior but ignore the inner construction, the pathological and psychological body which our behaviour and thought depend on. Comprehension is the purpose of literature, but how can we know human beings if we continue to ignore their most vital functions."[19] Again, for "literature" substitute "theology" here. Words and the body are Joyce's two allies against fascism. Suppression of free speech and etrangement from the body have recently been singled out as the chief symptoms of renascent fascism within the Catholic Church.[20]

U espouses the commonplace to the point of seeming a compendium of useless information and stale jests. At first Bloom's mind seems only a compendium of trivia. But repeated readings increase one's appreciation not only of his moral qualities but also of his intelligence, wit, powers of observation: "Same blue serge dress she had two years ago, the nap bleaching. Seen its best days. Wispish hair over her ears. And that dowdy toque: three old grapes to take the harm out of it. Shabby genteel" (130). His value as an organ of perception and reflection is increased by an ability to make cosmic connections: "Cityful passing away, other cityful coming, passing away too: other coming on, passing on. Houses, lines of houses, streets, miles of pavements, piled up bricks, stones . . . Pyramids in sand. Built on bread and onions. Slave Chinese wall. Babylon" (135). He is one of the two major strengths of the work, the other, which also grows

---

[18] See Lindsay Tucker, *Stephen and Bloom at Life's Feast* (Ohio State University Press, 1984).
[19] Quoted in Bishop, *Joyce's Book of the Dark*, p.420.
[20] Matthew Fox, "Dear Brother Ratzinger", *National Catholic Reporter*, 4 November 1986, pp.1-30.

with familiarity (against an initial sense of opacity and over-elaborateness), is the classic radiance, the epic plenitude, of the prose, its euphony, clarity and urbanity.[21] The common-place is assumed massively into a writing that is never itself commonplace and that constantly catches the common-place at novel angles, setting it out in ironic or mock-sublime relief or finding in it an unsuspected comedy or pathos, effects partly enabled by the antiquarian character of the scenes chronicled. U freezes the life of Dublin at a point in the past in order to subject it to a treatment which, losing the flow of history and the openness of the future, becomes a retrospective danse macabre of codes and communications from the turn of the century. Not only is the movement of the characters arrested, imprisoned as they are in claustrophobic textual space, but the whole world becomes a ship in a bottle, unnaturally becalmed. This is perhaps the price that has to be paid for so thorough a conversion of life into book.

Literary dignity has always been achieved at the cost of obscurantism, imposed not by bureaucratic censors but by metaphysical principles of style. U does not flout these prin-ciples, but carefully negotiates their enlargement. A degree of homage is paid to the three unities, yet time and place are so hacked up, notably in "Ithaca" and "Wandering Rocks" (in which the place, Dublin, is itself the protagonist[22]) that this homage too results in an effraction of classical closure; as for unity of subject, it is provided by the story behind the text which the text itself deliberately fails to match, for the epiphanic parody permits the presentation of life only at odd angles, cutting across it in a series of snapshots which catch it in states of undress, and abolishing the continuity of its texture as usually represented in fiction. Still the "grand imposture" of literature (Barthes) can never allow the blunt expression of desire (deflated in any case by the impartiality of the comic medium) or disgust. It reveals only at the price of concealments. It is held in check by

---

[21] *Euphonia, sapheneia, asteiotes*, as explained by Victor Bérard, Joyce's guide to Homer (*L'Odyssée*, Paris: Belles Lettres, 1933, p.xxvii).
[22] See Clive Hart's essay in Hart and Hayman, eds, *James Joyce's "Ulysses"*.

invisible, traditional laws, with which Joyce was wrestling to the end. FW, too, for all its licence is recongizably *literature*, a still typically modernist synthesis of revolution and classicism which never cuts itself off from the tradition it subversively transforms.

But is this art transformative only in the sense of clothing ugliness and chaos in the mantle of style and form? To some extent the art is shown to have its roots in the lives of the characters. The speech of Simon Dedalus and the denizens of Dublin's pubs is revealed as crawling with puns and arresting idioms, and the more wilful inventiveness of Mulligan and Stephen lies along the same linguistic spectrum, as do the stylistic acrobatics of the entire text. Ripped from what is often an inarticulate and unimaginative context, these ephemeral fragments of speech become gems of literature. A prose which nourishes itself on the noises of the streets can be sustained only by a constant negotiation of twin dangers: while remaining open to all influence, it has to keep fighting off the banality its sources threaten to impose. This "anxiety of influence" is not stylistic only but stems from the metaphysical desire to tansmute the flatness of everyday life. The writing holds together a downward movement towards the chaos of fragmented meaningless urban existence, towards the paralysis of unproductive Dublin, city of empty talk, and an ascensional movement to an aesthetic stasis, in which the idle voices of the city are gathered into the stillness of monumental form. The reader may share in the glad descent towards life, but he will find it checked at every moment by the literary conscience which imposes form, and a certain deadness, on the exuberance of life and even of language. Each of the pearls in the literary chain is formed painfully about a piece of Dublin grit, but the grit must in every case disappear into the pearl. Yet up to the very last moment this imperative of form is resisted by the disruptive urge of fidelity to the real.

U is a tissue of imitations of others' utterances and its own, a set of variations on pre-given discourse, the earlier chapters serving as such for the later. It thus functions as a critical commentary on the whole range of human discourse, which it subjects to constant testing. In *Dubliners* the impersonal Flaubertian narrative voice was constantly exposed to contamination by the style of speech of the characters described, a contamination to which Flaubert's own use of *style indirect libre* often lent itself. The effect is one of ironic exhibition of the character's verbal universe – of the character as verbal universe. In *Portrait* this contamination is constant, as the style reflects the young man's unfolding soul, again with the ironic distance of portraiture. In U, however every authoritative narrative instance is abandoned. Deliberately clumsy devices in the opening chapter, representing "Narrative" (young),[23] include the accumulation of stock adverbs (on the first page: gently, coarsely, solemnly, gravely, coldly, smartly, briskly, gravely, quietly, gaily), a stylistic game not so obtrusive as to prevent the narrative from being young in another sense, lively and bright.[24] Once we notice the adverbal passacaglia a part of the narrative transparency of the text vanishes and we are left with opaque verbal artefacts (as when in Fellini's "E la nava va" we notice that the swelling sea is actually made of vinyl); yet the adverbs used as Dedalus recalls his mother seem more poignant because of his deliberateness; "Silently, in a dream she had come to him" (7); "A cloud began to cover the sun slowly, wholly" (8). Everywhere in Joyce's work such recurrent motifs – the heart in "Hades", wind in "Aeolus", the names of rivers in "Anna Livia Plurabelle" – can produce these discreetly beautiful effects. Utter impersonality might seem to characterize the Arranger of such effects (analed by David Hayman and Hugh Kenner), who comes obtrusively to the fore in the newspaper headlines of "Aeolus", the overture of "Sirens" and the catechism format of "Ithaca". But in fact there is no single arranger; each of these voices is a distinct comic pseudo-personality provided for this occasion. Their apparently godlike and remote personality is not the mark of omniscient intelligence but the stupefying baldness of cold print and computers, and they wield only the spurious authority of newspaper headlines or examination papers. Even these

---

[23] Karen Lawrence, *The Odyssey of Style in "Ulysses"* (Princeton University Press, 1981).
[24] See Hugh Kenner, *A Colder Eye: The Modern Irish Writers* (Allen Lane, 1983), pp.192-3.

forms of discourse, the most inimical to literature, prove pliant to comic mimicry. Again, the last stage in our acquaintance with the imposing patterns sewn into the text is the discovery that they are only gimmicks that mock themselves.

The more the narrative voices become compromised in their mimesis, the less reliable they are, but this is compensated for by the fact that the characters are very keen observers of one another, and the retention of their voices in all chapters except "Oxen of the Sun", "Eumaeus" and "Ithaca" preserves the observational focus of the work until the end. The men continue a constant commentary on one another's economic fortunes and prospects, which builds up a socio-economic portrait of Dublin more comprehensive than that of *Dubliners*. Even the adolescent Gerty MacDowell is well-versed in the secrets of her companions' lives, and the unlettered Molly spills the beans on all the people figuring in her monologue. Up to the very last sentence new information keeps flowing in, even if not with quite the novelistic valency of early sections. The chief agents of revelation in the work are the talkative characters themselves. Spinozan, again, is the conjunction of the majestic necessity of the literary patterns, the imposed styles, and the abundant randomness of the incidents and encounters they chronicle, each apparent contingency turning out to have a literary necessity. The novel exploits the properties of a small city, in which chance encounters are constantly occurring and easily fall into a pattern of karmic connections. The characters' wanderings gravitate of their own accord to ordered webs of interconnections, a principle of complication, repetition, and retrospective design on which the self-echoing texture of the work can build. "With Joyce, chance is always retrieved by law, meaning and programme, according to the overdetermination of the figures and the ruses."[25]

If Joyce is the iconoclastic reader and deconstructor of the Western literary and ideological heritage, he does not directly assault that heritage in its noblest monuments. Aristotle,

---

[25] Jacques Derrida, *Ulysse gramophone* (Paris: Galilee, 1987), p.60.

Dante, Shakespeare and St Thomas are mediated by common consciousness in the showy speech of cocky students and provincial intellectuals, or the muddled reminiscences of a travelling salesman. Even when the text seems to be reaching out into the whole history of the Western mind, above and beyond whatever the individual characters are thinking. Its Homeric parallels, its exoticisms of vocabulary, exercises in fine writing[26] and mythological machineries, do not constitute a superior authorial vantage point like that of "The Waste Land", pitting learned culture against popular inculture. The authorial vantage point is self-undermining and can offer no superior wisdom not accessible to the characters. The grandiose patterns of the encounter of Father and Son planted by the author carry no further significance than what the characters themselves provide in the day's musings on paternity and sonship. The omniscience of the "Arranger" in "Ithaca" is that of the family encyclopedia, in which Bloom seems to have become trapped. Plotinus and Spinoza would hardly find impressive the meditations on death in "Hades": "One of those chaps would make short work of a fellow. Pick the bones clean no matter who it was. Ordinary meat for them. A corpse is meat gone bad" (94). Every pretence of knowing better than the everyday mortal comes crashing on in the "reality of experience", its bits and pieces of small change which Bloom counts and recounts in his alert musings.

The artefact which absorbs and transmutes this lowly everyday world, the labyrinth of mirrors which reflect and refract, distort and enlarge, fragmentate and reassemble it from angles innumerable, opens up a play of consciousness which surpasses that of the individual, even of the author, who is more its tender or minder than its master, a catalyzing agent, whose formal, textual inventiveness kneads oral abundance to a pitch of pregnant concentration, allowing all possibilities of ambiguity, polyvalence and transformation

[26] These reflect the middle-class Irish autodidact's approach to English prose rather than the voice of the Establishment. The sources of "Oxen of the Sun" are just those the common reader might have consulted: Quiller-Couch's anthology and George Saintsbury's *History of English Prose Rhythm* (1912, reprinted Bloomington and London: Indiana University Press, 1967).

to multiply *ad infinitum*. A text in which "every word is so deep" (62) and has the maximum of interconnection with every other becomes a machinery for finding the absolute in the everyday, God as "a shout in the street" (28, 183). The author himself can no longer tell how much meaning is to be read into any given detail, a situation which prompts us to treat everything as sacred. This immanentist theological method – "I do not like that other world" (63, 94) – moves from empiricism to phenomenalism to a linguistic idealism in which language turns out to be the truth of the phenomena which it names and, in the process of naming, reveals to be constructed from itself. But each of these philosophical and theological labels indicates only the general thrust of Joyce's thinking, nor are any of them unequivocal: there are probably germs of many kinds of empiricism, phenomenalism, immanentism, idealism in Joyce, none of which provides a definitive characterization of his basic stance. To say that U is a "secular humanistic New New Testament"[27] is perhaps misleading, for the sacred keeps popping out in Joyce's secularity, humanism might suggest a cut and dried ideology which the text disallows by reason of its endlessly open-ended questioning of what it means to be human, and Joyce's affirmation of life is offered in too humorous a key to pass as a Testament. Perhaps what is most salient in Joyce's comic creed is the sacral status assumed by language as the womb in which the collective consciousness or unconscious of the race is formed.

The Autonomy of Language

Since the conventions which are the material of the text are primarily of a linguistic order, the parody of convention develops into a play of language with itself, an ever-widening gap between theme and treatment. This free play becomes absolute when the constraints of realism (but not

---

[27] Daniel R. Schwarz, *Reading Joyce's "Ulysses"* (Macmillan, 1987), p.87.

the re-emergence of the real through the disguises of the dream-work) are removed in FW's quasi-autistic combination of intense inner life and disengagement from external reality.[28] Here every word has a dreamlike life of its own and is held in check by no inelastic chain of reference. This abandonment of reference also allows an approach to the real as the chaotic dismemberment of psychosis, ready to erupt when the symbolic order breaks down. "Psychotic episodes occur when the intrinsic lack of this key phallic signifier – the Name-of-the-Father – is challenged within the Symbolic order. The confrontation topples the mental house of cards supporting the subject's identity. Imaginary relations between *moi* and others also collapse. The real ego, heretofore unsymbolized, emerges as the 'miraculous infant', looming forth with a new name, such as Christ, God, Napoleon, or any other name not the person's own, while the existential shape of synchronic relations (*je*) disappears."[29] Where the taut and, despite its density, transparent texture of U allows the sharp edges of the real to intrude vividly, the loose lapsing of FW exploits the possibilities of regression to primordial psychic chaos. The tug of war between symbolic and real (like that between social law and polymorphous perversion) in U is replaced in the later work by happier mutual accommodation under the aegis of infantile games and fantasies; the imaginary keeps both the repressive father and the threatening real at a distance, yet the strict organization of its play reflects a sane awareness of these other instances. Does the art of FW testify to an inability to assume the constraints of the symbolic order, a failure of nerve before the demands of meaning, ethics, and the transcendent? Or does Joyce, following Vico, uncover the very foundations of these orders in the primitive mind, providing a radical therapy of waking consciousness by sounding its nocturnal springs?

U plunges towards a void where only verbal echoes survive the ruin of creeds and everyday identities. These echoes

---

[28]   Kathleen Bernard in Aubert and Senn, *James Joyce*, p.493.
[29]   Ragland-Sullivan, *Jacques Lacan*, pp.198-9.

themselves seem to self-destruct; in "Oxen of the Sun" the strenuous ventriloquism finally snaps under the pressure of having constantly to give birth and collapses into incoherence: "All off for a buster armstrong, hollering down the street. Bonafides. Where you slep last night? Timothy of the battered naggin. Like ole Billyo. Any brollies or gumboots in the fambly?" (346). In this method of creation by collapse, which exposes language to every possible debauch, every lapse is retrieved by the ever-vigilant artistry of the text and made into a formal felicity. Even the gutter garrulity of the narrator of "Cyclops" becomes musical as Joyce renders it: "Arrah, bloody end to the paw he'd paw and Alf trying to keep him from tumbling off the bloody stool atop of the bloody old dog" (251).

The process whereby U allows language to deploy its own resources autonomously, both in formal devices of textuality and a free flow of orality, in growing independence from the demands of narration, is taken to its extreme in FW, which "disarticulates, rearticulates, and at the same time annuls, the maxim of linguistic, historical, mythical, and religious traces."[30] Theology can learn from this how much further it must pursue the linguistic turn, if it is to close the gap between its archaic, provincial, inaccessible linguistic world and the contemporary Babel to which Joyce, without ever deserting the gutters of Dublin, gave tongue.

In the later chapters of U the core of realistic observation and annotation is still intact, as in Bloom's inner monologue, but the foregrounded styles now dwarf substance. Retrospectively the entire earlier part of the work is seen to be effecting already, despite appearances, such a subordination of world to text. There has been from the start a gap between theme and treatment, each chapter introducing the *écarts* distinctive of a particular style. Paradoxically, the style that should introduce the least gap, that of science, creates the widest breach of all in "Ithaca". Is the gap closed in some higher significance? Efforts to see the stylistic experiments of the last chapters as subserving the book's fictional world

---

[30] Philippe Sollers, *Théorie des exceptions* (Paris: Gallimard, 1986), p.81. Sollers calls this project "an active trans-nationalism".

are unconvincing. This world indeed continues to grow, both by a massive influx of new facts and the opening of the Penelopean perspective, and by the elevation of the protagonists to mythic status. But the writing outstrips these purposes and finally frustrates the demand for closure, using style to open and keep open an abyss. The fictional world so firmly held in place in the early chapters is finally shown to be a limited, limiting construct, and we pass out beyond it into cosmic or oniric verbal spaces.

The reader is gradually initiated into the mystery that reality can take any form words choose to confer on it. In "Oxen of the Sun" a banal scene is transformed by the use of a succession of styles; in "Circe" the scenes are generated by linguistic association, by a visualization of the verbal, as when the "Halcyon days" of Bloom's musing suddenly leap into life as High School boys (447). The autonomy of language is now such that to utter a word is to create by magic what it names. "Circe" brings a replay, or "retrospective arrangement" of hundreds of key phrases and incidents, now liberated from the residual constraints of their prosaic context. Yet this is not tangential to the material of the chapter, for the melodramatic pantomime probes the guilt, intoxication, and unreality of the nightworld with considerable psychological conviction, and its phantasmagoria is spun from a core of drunken debauch mixed with sensations of shame. These sordid elements are exaggerated, however, in exuberant staginess: "On a step a gnome totting among a rubbishtip crouches to shoulder a sack of rags and bones" (351); the sense of guilt is acted out in the hallucinatory trials of Bloom (373-382) and Stephen's vision of his dead mother (473-475), which bring to a grotesque climax the unease felt by both during the day; Bloom's ambitions also attain supreme expression in his apotheosis (390-407), while the smashing of the chandelier (475) and the altercation with the soldiers and Old Gummy Granny (480-490) give Stephen's posture of revolt its most spectacular manifesta- tion. Going behind the scenes of the artifice of fiction to expose its basis in the free play of language, "Circe" exhibits the linguistic, textual substance of the events of the day; the world dissolves into textuality, climaxing in a delirious lapsing: "heart beerchops perfect fashionable house very eccentric where lots cocottes beautiful dressed much about princesses like are dancing cancan" (465). Such vertiginous slides occurred earlier in the work, but now this sliding is becoming a basic principle of composition, and is taking over as the primary form of language, language as mumbo-jumbo.

In the spells of FW, supposed to plumb and awaken the sleeping soul of humanity and of Ireland, articulate communication is balked at every turn by its pullulating simulacra, every attempt at univocal meaning seduced into the nonsensical polyvalence of dreamtalk. Already in the latter half of U, one has the sense that subversion ends by subverting itself. The evasion of convention becomes an evasion of communication. Too conscious of itself as verbal performance, mimesis is reduced to an insubstantial miming. But perhaps it is in the nature of language, when released from its bondage to the functional, to assert its autonomy and to devour itself in this way. Joyce simply let language be language, and in doing so provided an arsenal of deconstructive strategies to all who would question behind the imposingly substantial face our words present in everyday life. He shows language as a treacherous arrangement without secure foundations, spinning webs of illusion and conventional vision, which it can always dissolve again if allowed to. The dissolution never uncovers an underlying absolute, the *tathatā* (suchness) of Buddhism, but only a new weaving of the web, endlessly. FW provides a schooling in linguistic scepticism, and its readers can scarcely write the most casual sentences without an unsettling consciousness of a thousand latent ambiguities. They have learned that to speak, to write, is to involve oneself in a joke of cosmic proportion, and they are armed to find ever afterwards in the pomp of literary, scientific or religious diction occasions for incredulous amusement. Yet they themselves can enjoy no secure, superior point of vantage. This writing constantly dislodges the subject and abolishes the conveniences of perspective.[31]

---

[31] "None of the discourses which circulate in *Finnegans Wake* or *Ulysses* can master or make sense of the others and there is, therefore, no possibility of the critic articulating his or her reading as an elaboration of a dominant position within the text" (Colin MacCabe, *James Joyce and the Revolution of the Word*, Macmillan, 1978, p.14).

Comedians have always made mock of linguistic habit, but Joyce's inability to use any word except tongue in cheek threatens the very roots of sense and communication. The liberation it effects is so drastic as to be oppressive. This autonomous eruption of language could be paralleled with many other such eruptions in twentieth-century experience: the foregrounding in science of methodology at the expense of matter and the emergence of inbuilt incertitude in these methodologies; the foregrounding of critical procedures over substantive claims in philosophy; the structuralist turn in the human sciences; the various non-representational departures of painting; the prevalance of media over message in journalist and politics. FW runs ahead of every triumph of language over solid reality, and helps us find our bearings in the flux of unanchored significance. Such practice at swimming in an ocean of floating signifiers is invaluable inasmuch as the contemporary world is such an ocean.

A Brush with Nihilism

Beneath the subversive, transformative, and quasi-idealist roles of language lies a constant philosophical worry: a battle against nihilistic incertitude. This concern shows through as a jealous testing of the empirical everyday, thrown in kaleidoscopic dispersal as soon as it is written of, and as a doubt about the endless fertility of writing itself, the fear that it may be an idle game rather than an organ of revelation. Each advance of Joyce's art uncovers nihilistic possibilities, reveals that the world is "founded, . . . macro and microcosm, upon the void" (170). The wonder of verbal creation may be a tributary and offshoot of the wonder of being or it may be no more than a spume of the void. That ambivalence is not dispelled by U or FW as it is in the grand affirmation of such artists as Dante. Indeed, Joycean doubt reacts on the literary tradition and forces us to ask whether it does not all belong to the same register of trivial textual play. Can theology face up to this sense of the vacuity and jadedness of all its language, and then somehow go on to win from it a resurrection of the Logos? The resurrectional patterns of FW, a doubt-ridden myth for Joyce, might figure in a renewed kerygma that would have first undergone the experience of the fallen, falling state of all verbal performance and acquired a comic consciousness of the absurdity of all statement. The pomp of "Aeolus" . the futile brilliance of "Scylla and Charybdis" – "Folly. Persist" (152) – , the bombast of "Cyclops", the bumbling of "Eumaeus", the monotony of "Ithaca", form so many discouraging demonstrations of the impossibility of saying anything or at least of saying it in such a way as to get it taken seriously, and FW speeds up the demonstration, habitually playing on several such registers simultaneously. Is a kerygma possible after FW? Perhaps only by assuming the posture of a clown can one succeed in obliquely communicating a serious message.

The epiphanal parody of U insensibly passes over into phenomenalism; the momentary emergence of the real is preserved as a static verbal construct detached from any serious referential function, a cinema still no longer inserted in a movement of history. As U proceeds, we learn to consider each scene as primarily a text, and the comedy becomes predominantly linguistic. Even Molly's world is a fantasy spun from her flow of stray phrases. In FW any reference that promises to attain stability as an event, character or theme is dissolved, through perpetual variation, into the rise and fall, assembly and disintegration, of linguistic aggregates. What remains? A nihilistic void? A hermetically sealed soundbox? Or an opening of language beyond its habitual boundaries onto a sense of the infinite? If Henry James could find a tender of immortality in the never-ending refinements of consciousness, and the way the world seemed to meet them, as if to communicate a message,[32] Joyce's experience with language does not yield an unambiguously positive persuasion; the cycles of rebirth in FW are also cycles of decline; the buoyancy of new beginnings is shadowed by the weariness of the eternal return.

[32] See "Is there a Life after Death?" in F.O. Mathiessen, *The James Family: A Group Biography* (New York: Vintage, 1980), pp.602-614.

Joyce explodes the traditional order of Catholicism, but is it to put in its place a flat secularity? No, for secularity is itself exploded in turn. The solid floor of the secular world dissolves in the tricky and treacherous self-reflection of a text which insists on calling attention to itself as text. Is the upshot then a reduction of all reality to a mere play of words? Or does this play effect a transformation of consciousness? U might claim to convey the message of love, tolerance and human sympathy, but the upshot of FW emerges indistinctly if at all through the fog. Even in U fatalism prevails. Its characters are trapped not only in the economic circumstances of their city, but in the formalities of style which etches the bounds of their possible self-realization. The final chapters are pervaded by the rhythm of return to the womb (Bloom curling up in foetal position); creative regression is the only way forward.

In U comedy triumphs over all, but only just. The central incident of Bloom's day – his cuckolding by a brashly seductive fellow-Dubliner – is of a kind which has sometimes provided rough comic fare. But here every ounce of pain is wrung from it by the presentation through the consciousness of the husband; and like the blinding of Oedipus or the destruction of Hippolytus it is made to happen offstage. Yet the situation also corresponds to the central fantasy of Sacher-Masoch's novellas, and to the social masochism that affects most Joycean characters: the young Dedalus takes pleasure in the taste of humiliation as his family sink to ever greater depths – "He chronicled with patience what he saw, detatching himself from it and testing its mortifying flavour in secret" (*Portrait* 62) – and the characters of *Dubliners* submit themselves with the same secret gladness to the thrall of a dead past. That masochistic fatalism is the staple of Irish spirituality is suggested in "The Sisters", "Eveline" and "Clay", whose protagonists are shown succumbing to the sickly lure of self-sacrifice. Perhaps the economic and political paralysis of the nineteenth century made such masochism a survival skill. Since there is no way out for the Dubliners, they might as well enjoy their misery and their elegies for non-existent golden pasts. Some critics define this masochism as a compulsive repetition-neurosis and see Joyce's attitude to it as simply condemnatory. Thus they query Bloom's claim to heroism, see the sublime close of "The Dead" as a hymn of defeat rather than the birth of an artist's vision, and interpret Richard Rowan in *Exiles* as a figure in a "comedy of humours" rather than as the too naked embodiment of Joyce's own conflicting desires.[33] Joyce cannot sustain an attitude of comic or ironic distance towards this "taste for failure" (Sartre's definition of vice) which melts into a universal sympathy in "The Dead": "His soul swooned slowly . . ." Bloom and Gabriel Conroy do not win redemption by overcoming their masochism but by accepting it. Signs of an ideology of the triumph of failure in U include the humbling of the rebellious Dedalus, the glorification of the underdog Bloom, the fascination with debris of life, speech and writing, and the ecstasy of shame and humiliation in "Sirens", "Nausicaa" and "Circe" (continued in FW).

Bloom's suppressed agonies of jealousy could be seen as paralleling the agony of incertitude about the nature of reality which underlies so much of the writing. Other of the unseemly incidents can be construed as a proclamation of the innocence of becoming, in Nietzsche's sense. But the Boylan-Molly business allows of no insouciant integration into the comic web. If Bloom finally triumphs in the affections of his wife, that triumph does not end the oppressed and unfulfilled aspects of his life. These constitute a web that is spun out about the centre of Boylan's visit to Molly. They include his sexual inadequacy, unfulfilment, and occasional twinges of guilt, his loss of his son, the physical repellancy which gives his presentation such a tang of unmistakable bodily presence, and the contempt and mistrust of his fellow-citizens. Bloom's sorrows do not reduce him to the status of anti-hero, but rather magnify his stature as comic hero. His inner security is an antidote to the poisons of doubt and scepticism which the world that surrounds him everywhere exudes, poisons which seep into his own consciousness in

---

[33] See Edward Brandabur, *A Scrupulous Meanness* (University of Illinois Press, 1971). Brandabur's appeal to psychoanalytic orthodoxy" (p.4) cannot do justice to Joyce's exploration of perversion as a richly ambivalent resource for his art.

"Hades" and "Lestrygonians", and wherever Boylan comes to mind.

Sex can hardly be said to play an anti-nihilist role in U, with the solitary exception of Molly's, contextually mitigated, "Yes". Joyce's sexual gamut is a narrow one: his parade of perversions is bereft of poetic overtones that would lend them the finest complexity, and if he partially succeeds in working out an alliance between sex and love or life in the figures of Molly Bloom and Anna Livia, this is on a primitive level and constitutes a gospel of sexual acceptance rather than one of sexual wisdom. He places all his male characters under a cloud of sexual uneasiness – one of Bloom's first thoughts on the subject is "Who knows? Eunuch. One way out of it" (67) – and far from cultivating a philosophical theory of free mores he prefers to make fun of any attempt to take sex too seriously by a farcical exhibition of sexual detail at its most embarrassing. Molly's guiltlessness is proposed as the healthiest sexual attitude in U, but it is scarcely enough to free the others from their psychological chains. Just as the "cynical frankness" that he later regretted may have allowed the young Joyce to measure the hypocrisies of Dublin life, these chronicles of perversity play an equally crucial role in cracking open the falsifying proprieties imposed by literary forms and polite restraints on expression, to replace them with an art that shows the real without comment, challenging the reader to judgment, but baffling all efforts at conclusive judgment. Defoe's *Moll Flanders* was the model of such writing. Yet though no judgment is ever formulated, even in *Dubliners*, still the issue of judgment is never entirely dropped. Like Stanley Fish's Milton, Joyce "consciously wants to worry his reader, to force him to doubt the correctness of his responses, and to bring him to the realization that his inability to read the poem with any confidence in his own perceptions is its focus."[34] But where the puritan dogmatist aims at convicting his readers of sin and assuring them of grace, the Catholic agnostic debunks all peremptory judgment, while opening perspectives of awareness and sympathy that should give

---

[34] Stanley Fish, *Surprised by Sin* (University of California Press, 1971), p.4.

our efforts at judgment a riper quality. This gives the few moments where moral issues are explicitly raised, notably the end of "Cyclops", considerable resonance.

The triumph of Bloom as one of comic character is not the chief warrant of an overcoming of nihilism in U. What compensates for Bloom's unsatisfactory circumstances is their epiphanal notation in his resourceful inner verbalization. This is also part of a general triumph of language, one that Joyce can celebrate more originally than he can the triumph of love or goodness (just as in James the triumph of consciousness dwarfs the moral victories). Bloom's ethic of forbearance receives less emphasis than does the grace of linguistic invention shining in every line. To some extent Joyce abandons his characters, even Bloom, to their hopeless condition; the only redemption he holds out is that though the whole universe conspire to crush us, we triumph over it by the power of speech and writing. Joyce is thus himself the chief sufferer from the paralysis he excoriates, except in that one department of verbal vitality. From the start his art has signed off from any more concrete engagement with the world. His Dubliners are held fast by poverty above all, poverty which undermines not only one's physical well-being, but one's cultural and intellectual possibilities, one's human relationships and sexual life, one's freedom to differ from prevailing ideologies and social expectations. Yet Joyce never so much as breathes a hint of any liberation for his characters other than that which his absolute freedom of formulation may signify.

The dangers of radical parody are not only artistic; such writing tends to undermine the securities of creed and human understanding which shield the individual and society from chaos and despair. Joyce's comic art is never all smiles; it is an agon, a struggle for an affirmative which it barely snatches from the jaws of mere negation. His urge to test the meaning of the world by stretching the possibilities of articulation can be seen as a search for faith by one who put no trust in authoritative sources speaking from beyond experience or in poetic idealizations. Only the tried and tested real, the real manifested epiphanically, is worthy of faith, and the real is not fully tested, fully manifest, until it is put into precise words.

But at a certain point it becomes clear that the words splinter and relativize their real references, providing consciousness with a space for expansion that dwarfs what even the city of Dublin has to offer. This world of words in turn is tested by all sorts of experiments on them, in the course of which it appears that language is always testing itself, that the whole world can be grasped as a never-ending reformulation of itself. A traditional faith would surely have inhibited Joyce's attack on the frontiers of the sayable. Only writing pursued as a religion – a religion of absolute non-conformity – could break the limits of the Logos which enshrouded the consciousness not only of his race but of the West.

Irish Catholicism has flooded the world with words, most of them of a vulgar order, unworthy of the sublime verities they meant to communicate. Against an excessively rhetorical background, Joyce turned language in on itself in a searching critique, and he calls Christians to a similar linguistic self-awareness. His example shows that such a probe can lead to a re-creation, can lead perhaps much further than he was able to demonstrate. It may be that only a theology written in awareness of the Joycean questions can permit an inculturation of the Gospel in contemporary Western minds. Christian language can function as an expedient means only if reshaped in awareness of the radical relativity of all language. Joyce is a major source for the theory of that relativity. If Irish Catholicism could swallow him whole, and digest him with the necessary critical discrimination, perhaps it would find at last the contemporary adult application of its precious heritage.[35]

[35] My thanks to Ciaran Murray, George Hughes and Masaki Kondo for many stimulating comments.

Seán Ó Ríordáin:
An Existential Traditionalist

Robert Welch

From about 1907 to 1914, in Trieste, James Joyce was working on *A Portrait of the Artist as a Young Man*. The sermon on hell in this book registers an obsession with Catholic teaching and belief that never lost its grip on Joyce's mind and feelings. It conveys damnation as an imaginative reality that makes human life seem puny and worthless when set against the terrible prospect of suffering in eternity. The sermon is a turning-point in the development of Stephen Dedalus as an artist: after this he chooses the priesthood of art and with it the personal conscience of his own instinctual life (which, in Stephen's view, can include a broader more public responsibility), as distinct from the impersonal conscience of received opinion. Stephen's choice mirrors that of the priest, Father Gogarty, in George Moore's novel, *The Lake* (1905), in which the priest finds the way of life he has been confined to in his institutional role sterile, and instead he turns to the adventure of instinct and the personal conscience, but he wants to do it in the smithy of his *own* soul; and not according to the accepted norms of tradition or ritual.

This emphasis on the human, the personal and the

instinctual in Moore and Joyce corresponds to an aspect of modernism and of twentieth-century Western life in general. The Catholic Church, however, had, in nineteenth-century Ireland, acted as a cohesive and, indeed, progressive force. From O'Connell through to the Land War the Church had, reasonably consistently, allied itself to moderate social and political activism, wherever it considered that activism would lead to the improvement of living standards. It also, through this participation, acquired considerable strength as an agent of social control; and, as a symbol of unity and collective moral responsibility, it moderated some of the extreme forms of nationalism by offering the Church itself as a sign of what it meant to be Irish. In effecting this moderation it also brilliantly simplified political and cultural debate; if the Church represented Irishness, then certain appallingly difficult questions could be set aside, such as – is there such a thing as Irish cultural identity?; what does it mean for a people to lose a language?; what are the forces, economic, political and social, operating in the tangle of Anglo-Irish relations?; and, most difficult of all, how may those of the Protestant traditions be integrated with their Catholic fellow-Irishmen? Because it so effectively combined conservative and progressive impulses in Irish life (don't bite the hand that feeds you too hard but whatever you do make sure you get on) it contrived to repress difficult questions about national and indeed personal identity. And this is why modern Irish literature, if we take that to begin with, say, Yeats, Joyce, Moore, Synge and O'Casey, is so often strongly anti-clerical; and why it raises again, in a mood of total relevance, the ancient debate between Patrick and Oisín, Christian and Pagan, where the Pagan tends to win the argument. Yeats saw Synge as a kind of pre-Christian, and he himself chose Homer rather than original sin. Moore, always the comedian, renounced his own Catholicism in the *Irish Times*; and O'Casey hated crawthumpers.

By the 1950s, when Seán Ó Ríordáin, the subject of this essay, began to write, anti-clericalism had itself become something of an institution. His fellow Corkmen, Frank

O'Connor and Seán Ó Faolain, had attacked narrow Jansenist Ireland over and over again. Liam O'Flaherty had lauded the primitive instincts; Austin Clarke had chronicled the terror of Joycean damnation in obscure and tangled meditations; and Brinsley MacNamara had analyzed the restrictions of small town life in the Irish Free State. Ó Ríordáin, an individualist, and a writer of profound and subtle feeling, addressed the tradition of Irish Christianity in his own unique way.

Seán Ó Ríordáin (1916-1977) was born in Baile Bhúirne (Ballyvourney) in Co. Cork and moved to Cork City with his family when he was fifteen years of age. He went to school in the North Monastery, a Christian Brothers school on the North side of the city, and subsequently joined the staff in the City Hall, Cork, where he worked as a clerk in the Motor Taxation Department until 1967, when he retired on health grounds. He suffered from pulmonary tuberculosis for a great part of his life and was often in terrible pain. He was unmarried and lived on the outskirts of Cork City, at Iniscarra, in a small house. From 1969 he had a part-time, advisory post, attached to University College, Cork, which he obtained through the good graces of an old school-friend, Tadhg Ó Ciardha, the Registrar of U.C.C., Professor Risteárd Breatnach, Head of the Department of Irish, and Professor Seán Ó Tuama, Professor of Modern Irish Literature in the same Department. He is the greatest Irish poet since Yeats, and apart from Yeats, the greatest Irish poet since Aogán O Rathille.

And yet outside of Ireland he is virtually unknown. Even within Ireland itself he is not often widely ready, the reason being that he wrote exclusively in the Irish language. And even among his devoted band of readers, not all of his work has received full appreciation, because he is sometimes accused of abstraction and of outmoded religious feeling.

He grew up in the Ireland of Éamonn de Valera; he was twenty-one when the Irish constitution was published and he was deeply affected by the idealistic republicanism of post-Treaty, Fianna Fáil Ireland; by its adoption of a policy of detachment from many aspects of contemporary life, and by its emphasis on moral rectitude and purity. Detachment and republicanism combined in the Irish attitude towards the Second World War. Some Irish people were sympathetic to Hitler, as England's enemy; Ó Ríordáin, in some moods, shared this attitude, but for his own personal, discontented, reasons. Ó Ríordáin came to maturity during a time when Ireland was trying to make a human reality out of theoretical independence.

Ó Ríordáin's nature was primarily a religious one, if we understand that word in the simplest sense of 'binding together'. And his poetry explores the nature of binding and relationship between man and man, man and God, outer and inner, past and present. The set of his mind, the nature of his personality was such, that he sought always to experience things as fully as possible, and in this way to come to know them. This outward pulse of his mind and intelligence was complemented by a sometimes equal, sometimes unequal impulse inwards, to re-search the self, its moods, passions, hates and loves. This inward pulse is reflected in his *Diary* (*Dialann*), which he kept continuously up to his death. The *Diary* remains unpublished, and may have to for some considerable time yet because many living people are fiercely treated in it, but judging from the extracts he published in his own lifetime, and from the pieces Seán Ó Coileáin prints in his indispensable biography of the poet, the *Diary*, which is in many volumes, has a power and literary excellence of the sort we find in the *Essays* of Montaigne. There is the same merciless instinct for probing the recesses of the self, to scour out the filth of the personality, to anatomize pride and meanness; but Ó Ríordáin is without the extraordinary composure of the Renaissance Frenchman; his is the anguish and self-doubt, the fear and trembling, the deep not-knowing, of Baudelaire or Kafka:

14 August 1968, 5.35 p.m. – A fine day again, but a day of despair. As bad as yesterday was, today is worse. I am in the bottom of hell.

Rover was a stray dog. I say 'was' because maybe he is no longer with us. He was here with me first. He came to me in the winter of 1966/67 and stayed with me. And then I brought him up to Mayfield to my brother's house. He's been there since. He'd always welcome me when I'd go there. The woman of the house was getting sick of him

because he'd snap at strangers. I brought the creature to
the dog's home today. Three of the children went with me.
But the dog watcher put a halter on him and he had to go in.
I've used up so much of the welcome of the world, and the
welcome it offers you does not increase with the passing of
the years. No wonder I'm heartsore. I'm a kind of Judas.

If despair entangles itself more deeply in me I'll go mad. I lack
charity and that is why I have an emptiness in my heart.

Poor Rover was friendly and affectionate. His affection,
maybe, was what left him in the dog yard playing with his
destroyers. If he's alive yet he's waiting for death in captivity.
It was a fine summer day. I saw him playing with two children
about 2 p.m. He welcomed me. I sat in the small grassy patch
behind the house. He lay down near me, his head on my knee,
full of trust. He must have been thrown out when he was a
stray, because he was trained like a housedog.[1]

This experience lies behind one of the poems in the volume
Línte Liombó (*Lines from Limbo*) (1971), 'Tar Éis dom é Chur go
Tigh na nGadhar' ('After I took him to the Dog's Home'):

> You had a housedog's ways
> And the shyness of a stray;
> Tonight, all that remains of your
> Impulsive love's destroying my heart.[2]

Ó Ríordáin made absolute demands on himself and sometimes upon others. In many respects he is the opposite of
Yeats in his triumphal mood of self-forgiving, self-rejoicing:

> I am content to follow to its source
> Every event in action or in thought;
> Measure the lot; forgive myself the lot!
> When such as I cast out remorse
> So great a sweetness flows into the breast . . .[3]

[1] Seán Ó Coileáin, *Seán Ó Ríordáin: Beatha agus Saothar* (An Clóchomhar, Baile
Atha Cliath, 1982), pp.389-90. The translation is mine, as are all translations
in this essay. Seán Ó Tuama's study of Ó Ríordáin in *Filí faoi Sceimhle* (Oifig
an tSoláthair, Baile Atha Cliath, 1978) is essential reading.
[2] Seán Ó Ríordáin, *Línte Liombó* (Sáirséal agus Dill, Baile Atha Cliath, 1971),
p.30.
[3] W.B. Yeats *Collected Poems* (Macmillan, London, 1959), p.267.

Yeats is in his dominant, rhetorical mood here; Ó Ríordáin rarely, if ever, allows himself such triumphal claims. For him the event ramifies, expands, and may take over. It may render the personal will powerless to act: 'Bíonn clann ag gach gníomh' ('Every action has a progeny'), and there's no knowing what the progeny will be like. Of one particular action he says, in the diary for 28 June 1943:

> The accursed offspring of this action gathered round me and abused and reviled me to such an extent that I will not forget it for a long time.[4]

That action, events, things and animals should be instinct with a life, mood and personality of their own was basic to Ó Ríordáin's thought, and takes us back to the beginning of his career as a published writer.

In the long, considered preface to his first volume of poems, *Eireaball Spideoige* (*A Robin's Tail*) (1952) he outlined an aeshetic and a theology, the implications and depths of which he explored for the rest of his life. This preface is an extraordinarily coherent and shapely thing, entirely rational, perfectly clear and very disturbing. One has the impression that many who write about Ó Ríordáin do not take it entirely seriously. Drawing upon the aesthetics of Plato, Aristotle and Hopkins, the theology of St Augustine, St Thomas, the linguistic theory of Raissa Maritain, and the philosophical insights of Stephen McKenna (the translator of Plotinus who wrote in Irish), he forges a personal credo about artistic expression and its relation to being.

At the heart of this theory is the simple yet profound notion that an essential quality of poetry is the open mind of a child. Imagine, he writes, two people in a room, a child and his father, and a horse going by on the road outside:

> The father looks out and says, 'That's Mr. X's horse going to the fair'. That's telling. It appears that the father loses the horse because he remains outside it. Say that the horse is a disease. The father doesn't get that disease. The horse does

4 Seán Ó Coileáin, *op.cit.*, p.125.

not enrich the father's life. But the child – he hears the sound
of the horse. He tastes the sound of the horse, for the sound's
sake. And he listens to the sound diminishing and falling back
into the silence. And he is awed by the sound and the silence.
And he looks at the horse's hindquarters and is awed by their
authority and their antiquity. And the world fills with horse-
awe and trotting-magic. That is being, to be under another
aspect. And that, I think, is poetry . . . Poetry is being, not
telling.[5]

Poetry is the apprehension of being something else. The
word Ó Ríordáin uses is 'ionadh' – wonder, awe – for this
apprehension. To apprehend something else is to sense its
basic pattern, its form, its essential being. And each thing,
each person, each place has such a pattern, a mould, and
this pattern or mould or form, O Ríordáin says, is the prayer
that that thing, person or place, says. The child looks at the
horse, is involved with its basic pattern, strives to close the
distance between his own being and that other being, and
seeks to unite his prayer to that of the horse. Again the word
'prayer' is Ó Ríordáin's: 'Ba mhaith liom paidir a thabhairt ar
an rud duchasach, an sainrud, a thagann as an múnla.' ('I'd
like to call the traditional thing, the essential thing, that arises
from the basic pattern, a prayer'.)[6]:

> Each mortal thing does one thing and the same
> Deals out that being indoors each one dwells:
> Selves – goes itself; myself it speaks and spells:
> Crying, what I do is me; for that I came.

Ó Ríordáin cites this poem of Gerald Manley Hopkins as part
of his argument. Each thing selves itself, it 'goes' itself, and
in doing so *is*. Ó Ríordáin's idea (and ideal) is that poetry is
a reaching of the basic pattern of the poet himself towards
that form or basic pattern of the other. To accomplish this
reaching, in language, is to find the creative shape of poetic
form. And then the language itself, poetically alive, *is*. Put
down in this way, it sounds very abstract, but Ó Ríordáin

---

[5] Seán Ó Ríordáin, *Eireaball Spideoige* (Sáirséal agus Dill, Baile Atha Cliath,
1952), pp.9-11.
[6] *Ibid.*, p.11.

has the capacity to ignite his philosophizing through vivid images: 'Often I felt that I was engaged upon an extraordinary activity when I was composing; an activity other than writing or inventing; an activity that was closer to cleansing. I think I was like someone cleansing rust or dust off an image, looking for and renewing the basic pattern – looking for the patterns on the sea floor. If this cleansing, this scouring, is compared to a cough during a cold, then the basic pattern can be imagined as a lung. Or the activity can be thought of as a blind man reading Braille. We all know the pattern, this form which has been separated out from all other forms; we do not know how we know it; but we know it as being old, basic, authoritative, persistent, beautiful, and it is not possible to contact it without experiencing a thrust of joy'.[7]

That last phrase in Irish is superbly alive; 'ní féidir teangmháil leis gan geit áthais'. This searching of the sea floor of a thing or an experience (a horse, a love affair, despair) is the poetic activity. It is an objectless activity, in that it does not seek a particular transitive object; but it is a waiting for the 'geit', the thrust, of creation. No true poem, Ó Ríordáin says, is born without a 'beo-gheit' – a life-thrust.

Each being deals out of its own being, that which dwells indoors in 'each one'. But this 'being' is normally hidden, in the way that, according to the old philosophical maxim, truth takes care to keep itself hidden. The poetic activity, which is childish, ancient, and basic, looks to being in this sense. Ó Ríordáin, in a daring move of the argument, not entirely worked out logically, as far as I can see, then says that that being which poetry inclines to is analagous to the transformed body of Christ after the Resurrection, furiously citing St Augustine's *De Civitate Dei* in support of his leap. After the Resurrection, the body will be in continuous 'beo-gheit', life-thrust; it will be total prayer.

Poetry is the relation between essences discovered in an inclination of sympathetic loneliness from one to another. It is the Resurrection now, an earthly praying, for things,

---

7 *Ibid.*, p.12.

amidst things. This line of argument of Ó Ríordáin's is entirely
at one with the neo-Platonic line of poetic theory from the
Renaissance down: that poetry resurrects a golden world,
because it recovers man's creative ability from the fallen
state of time. In this aspect the poet becomes a Christ-
like person, figuring the potential redemption in things, in
time. His measuring, his metric, imitates the measuring,
the mathematics, of creation itself, the basic mathematics
ordained by the Creator. For the poet not to travel outwards
seeking those other 'dwellings' 'indoors' is damnation, *the* sin,
false creation. He moralizes this:

> And the damned person, what happened to him? I think he
> belied the truth: that he refused to humble himself to the forms
> of truth and that he continued to create his own pseudo-forms
> like an anti-Creator, so that he stayed inside himself always,
> like a badger.[8]

He quotes the poem of Séamus Dal MacCuarta on people
who stay underground in themselves, tunnelling away in
their egos:

> It's the badger's way to tunnel away
> In darkness day and night:
> He does not come out to all
> That was created in heaven and earth.

If the creative spirit is not to be turned in on itself it must seek
realization of otherness, and that involves the kind of intense
sympathy evident in the diary entry describing his feelings
after he took the dog to the dog's home, bathetic as this
instance might first seem. It also involves the self-scrutiny
that comes about when this action of sympathetic reaching
fails, or is aborted.

It is Ó Ríordáin's view that *everything* will have its own
prayerful instinct, deriving from its basic pattern. That
includes. a family, a village, a town, a city, a people, a
language. Language and the tradition of the people to whom
that language belonged mattered intensely to Ó Ríordáin. His

---

[8]   *Ibid.*, p.18.

poetic would lead him to think that way; or it may be that it was the importance of language and tradition to Ó Ríordáin, specifically the Irish language, Irish tradition, which led him to create a poetic which linked language, psychology, aesthetics and Christianity in the way that he did.

To be yourself you need to lose yourself into your tribe, your *dúchas* (tradition), your language, uncovering their basic patterns and in doing so discovering your own. Of Seán Ó Riada, the Irish musician who turned his back on the busy artistic life of Dublin to find his own place and his own quiet in the West Cork Gaeltacht, he wrote:

> He recognised his own ego in the accomplishment of the [Irish] language. He wanted to achieve his own completed self . . . The mind of the language, the mind of the music was older than the mind which was created with him . . . until he could come into full possession of this older mind his actions would be pastiche and futility, each one separated from the other.[9]

To achieve integrity involves integration, with the tradition, with the language, with the people. Not to do so is to lose the basic pattern, never to experience 'beo-gheit', to be lost in the sterile tunnelling of Séamus Dall MacCuarta's 'broc' (badger) in the labyrinth of the personal ego, one of the damned. Modern democratic notions of personal freedom are illusory. He excoriates freedom, in this sense, in the poem 'Saoirse' in *Eireaball Spideoige*:

> I'll go down amongst the people
> On foot,
> And I'll go down tonight.
>
> I'll seek release
> From the venomous freedom
> That's howling here.
>
> I'll chastise the pack of thoughts
> That snarl about me
> In the loneliness.

[9] Seán Ó Coileáin, *op.cit.*, p.189.

And I'll find the chapel
That's full of people
At fixed times.

I'll seek out people
Who've never hankered
To be free or lonely.

I'll listen to shilling-thoughts
Being exchanged
Like cash . . .

The mind that fell into the deep slough
Of freedom's exhausted.
The hill that God created's not there,
But there are abstract hills, fantasias,
Each one full of cravings
Scaling in futility.
There's no limit to freedom
Or to fantastic mountains;
And there's no limit to craving,
Or relief
To be had.[10]

This slough ('iomar' in Irish, linked to 'iomar na h-aimiléise'; the slough of despond) is not the sea floor of the preface to *Eireaballl Spideoige*, where the basic patterns can be come upon; this is mindlessness, self-betrayal and damnation. In 'Saoirse' he talks of going 'down amongst the people', but what people, where? His own people came from Baile Bhúirne in West Cork, but as a Gaeltacht that was an area where Irish as a spoken language had been steadily contracting since his youth. Dunquin in West Kerry, however, became for him a haven, a solace, God's country. It typified for him tradition, a place alive with significance.

His feelings about Dun Chaoin are revealed in a poem called 'An Feairín' in his second volume of verse, *Brosna* (*Kindlings*) (1964). A previously unpublished account of how the poem originated during a night in Dunquin has been given in O Coiléain's biography; 'An Feairín' ('The Little Man') is someone called Pound:

---

[10] *Eireaballl Spideoige*, pp.100-2.

One night we were night-visiting in John O'Connor's house. They were debating about the resettling of the people from [the Blaskets]. [The Blasket islanders were settled on the mainland in the 1950s.] The woman of the house, referring to Pound, said that the poor little man would want his own house and land like any other islander. I took particular notice of how she said the word 'feairín' ['little man'] and I composed this:[11]

 – 'He'd want a house and land
The little man,' she said, of Pound;
Pound sank into her word
And settled there.

I never saw him plain until she said it.
I studied him, fully,
In the light of what she called him,
And her meaning was correct.

She's nabbed Pound in her word
Because Pound's a little fellow;
All his living frame concurred with her
From tip of head to toe.

Pound's tenured in those words,
He's peaceful there;
And whoever' else's insecurity may occupy
Our minds, it won't be Pound's.[12]

The way the woman of the house spoke the ordinary word 'feairín' was poetic, because it touched the quintessence of Pound himself and in so doing it awoke; the word was, in her syntax, and with reference to the man, and the islands, the land round about, and the houses, a 'thrust of joy': 'geit áthais'. This attitude is, basically, a religious one. Ó Ríordáin holds it that such an awakening comes out of a live relation between essences; each essence is a basic pattern or form which has its own means of prayer, a potential activated when the relation is made between one pattern and another in the loneliness of time. The word, according to St John, was

[11] Seán Ó Coileáin, op.cit., p.190. The diary extract is from Ó Coileáin's biography; the poem is taken from Brosna. See note 12.
[12] Seán Ó Ríordáin, Brosna (Sáirséal agus Dill, Baile Atha Cliath, 1964), p.15.

God; the open mind of a child, the sympathy of a woman, the attentiveness of a poet can return the word, in the play of art, to Him, as a figuring of the Resurrection.

Dun Chaoin (Gentle Fortress), Dunquin, became a golden world for him, a figure of resurrected life. In an unpublished lecture describing the effect of the landscape around Slea Head, the view of the Blaskets and the Three Sisters, he writes 'You'll be startled [again he uses the Irish word 'geit'] with the life and vigour of the pattern . . . This country brings to mind miraculous days when God was with us.'[13]

The rational commonsensical mind knows that Dunquin is an underprivileged area, that the Irish language is dying out, that the glimmerings of insight may be only fancy or romantic self-indulgence. Ó Ríordáin fully admits all of this, indeed it torments him, and this torment is one of the factors that give his poetry edge and attentiveness, but nevertheless he asserts that there *is* something there, something basic, ancient, authoritative and *true*. This essential truth, which, if poetry can achieve it, puts the mind in touch with transfigured life, is seen as totally upsetting the normal commonsensical, matter-of-fact truth in 'Na Blascaodaí', a poem on the Blaskets and Dunquin, in which Peig Sayers, a famous Blasketwoman and a renowned storyteller, completely usurps everyday consciousness, replacing it with the basic, the prayerful, the ancient, the sea floor of the unconscious. The pattern stands out, revealed, in radical presence, in strangeness:

> A white subterranean house
> Dreams at the edge of Dunquin
> Where I listened to the ancient speech
> Of a bed-ridden woman, blinded with age;
> And the deep mind was up on the surface
> While reason was sent to the bottom.
>
> Peig Sayers' mind, a currach,
> Carried us over the waves;
> The froth of the intellect submerged
> While the undermind brightened like foam.
> Our voices were seized with a strangeness,
> Their sound acquired echo and substance.

13   Sean Ó Coileáin, *op.cit.*, p.192.

> We'd only heard this kind of echo
> From strange mountains out in the distance,
> But here is the broadcasting station
> Transmitting this resonant sound.
> Remoteness is near us,
> Order's transformed in the air.[14]

Ó Ríordáin here celebrates integration and unity. The isolated twentieth-century intellectual from Cork City, who works in the Motor Taxation Department of the City Hall, where what he described as the 'hollow men' (following Eliot and punning on *Halla* na Cathrach) walk about with papers in their hands, is integrated in the artistic statement with Dun Chaoin, Peig Sayers, the sea, the mountains, the Gaelic tradition itself: *dúchas*. Community becomes communion; things are themselves more completely in the golden world of the poem. The rhythmic drive of the poem (inadequately conveyed in the translation), conveys a sense of abundant life.

'Siollabadh' ('Syllables') is a poem with an entirely different setting – the ward of Sarsfield's Court Sanatorium outside Cork City – but the quality of prayerful realization of the presence of life is very like that in 'Na Blascaodaí'. A nurse comes into a ward to take the pulse of the patients. Her femininity, life and sexuality are conveyed in what is one of Ó Ríordáin's most perfect poems. The patients, their beds, the movements of the nurse, her expertise in taking the pulse, the pulse itself in each patient, the afternoon, the excitement and delight of life suddenly presenting itself, and the mysteriousness of the pulse of being; all these are gathered together and orchestrated in the rhythmic pulse of the saying of the different lives that the poem integrates in *its* own life. 'Ní insint dán ach bheith' – 'Poetry is being, not telling.'[15]

> A nurse in a hospital
> On a bright afternoon;
> Arteries in dormitories
> Effortlessly pulsing;

---

[14] *Eireaball Spideoige*, p.96.
[15] Compare the comments by Ó Coileáin in his biographical study, p.100; 'Beirthe air na rithimí seo go léir ag rithim bhreise, rithim an dáin ina dtéann siad chun suaímhnis. Comhrithim, comhbhualadh, cómheadaracht'.

And she stood at each bedside
Waiting and counting,
Writing down the metric
Of the syllables in her fingers;
And she syllabled rhythmically
Out of the room,
Leaving a symphony
Of arteries counting;
Syllables and murmurs,
And Amen all concluded
In a whisper in the sick room;
But the chanting continued
In the monastery of flesh,
Arteries like acolytes
Murmuring the nones.[16]

For sensual pleasure in the rhythmic possibility of words, for
the frank unintellectualized delight in the existential presence of the moment, for life re-presented as blessing, this
poem can stand alongside the miraculous moments of joy
and celebration to be found in Rilke's 'Ninth Duino Elegy',
Hopkins's 'That Nature is a Heraclitean Fire of the Comfort of the Resurrection', or Yeats's astonishing openness in
'Vacillation IV':

My fiftieth year had come and gone,
I sat, a solitary man
In a crowded London shop,
An open book and empty cup
On the marble table-top.
While on the shop and street I gazed
My body of a sudden blazed;
And twenty minutes more or less
It seemed, so great my happiness,
That I was blessed and could bless.[17]

Poems like 'Siollabadh', in which the isolated self moves out
of the labyrinths of the ego to confer with otherness, can be
found throughout Ó Ríordáin's work, from beginning to end.
In *Línte Liombó* (1971) there is a poem which translates the
aesthetic and theological principles underlying his theory

---

[16] *Eireaball Spideoige*, p.111.
[17] Yeats, *op.cit.*, pp.283-4.

into political terms. In Irish the poem is 'Ní Ceadmhach Neamhshuim' ('Indifference is not Acceptable'). The demand made by the poem is total: no indifference of any kind is acceptable; we must aspire to total commitment to Christ in others and in all else:

No fly, nor lion nor bee
Nor man nor woman
That God has made
Whose good is not our duty.
Indifference to their fear
Is not acceptable. No lunatic
In the madhouse whom
We shouldn't sit or walk with
While they carry in their hands
Our suffering for us.

No place, no stream or bush
Or flagstone, however lonely,
Whether north or south or east or west,
That we shouldn't think about
Wit love and tender feeling;

Though South Africa's a world away
And the moon's beyond our reach
They are part of us:
There's no where in all this life
Where we haven't been.[18]

The thinking here may owe something to Irish Christian tradition, but it is also a personal vision variously expressed throughout his writings. If the open mind of a child is basic to the discovery of what is essential in experience, then all experience should, ideally, be approached in openness. Only in this way can there be a prayerful interaction between the individual mind and the rest of being. Such interaction is a figuring of Christ's presence, and all of life should be approached as if it contained Him, potentially. False conscience, opinionatedness, the 'Galway Bray' of the bishops of Galway and elsewhere, all these blaspheme against the creative interaction there should be between people in a proper

---

[18]   *Línte Liombó*, p.40.

community. His outrage and disgust at the blasphemy of the blithely assured and corrupt is expressed in another powerful poem, 'To My Friends', in *Línte Liombó*, which follows immediately on from 'Ni Ceadmhach Neamhshuim':

> You make me sick, and not without reason,
> Your total statements,
> Your authoritative opinions,
> Your support for your own puny sort,
> Stand for the wrong done to the weak
> By the strong in this world, today,
> And for thousands of years;
> And done under cover of the lying treachery
> You still promulgate in the name of truth,
> In the name of the Christ you've lost.
>
> I will fight you to the death,
> Though you're my friends
> Because I can hear, through the corridors
> Of history the reverberations of your speechifying,
> Trampling and making carnage.[19]

Ó Ríordáin's aesthetic, moral and philosophical credo is absolutely simple and absolutely demanding: honour the thing as it is; do not intellectualize it; hear its essence speak to you through you; then you may share its being in communion. There is, perhaps, an Eastern element in this thinking, but it is also to be found in that European existentialist philosopher of the presence of being: Heidegger. He once said of himself: 'Bím i láthair' – 'I am *present*'.[20] Ó Ríordáin himself is conscious of an Eastern element in his Christian aesthetic which is playfully acknowledged in the first poem of his posthumous book *Tar Éis Mo Bháis* (*After My Death*) (1978), 'Piscín' ('Kitten'):

> In the West it's not enough
> For words to spring from things;
> Words deepening to themselves won't
> Do; we have to act.

---

[19] *Ibid.*, p.41.
[20] Seán Ó Caoileáin, *op.cit.*, p.72.

> I saw a kitten under the stool
> Tonight, perfectly framed.
> Terrified, he fled from
> The racket, the poor thing . . .
>
> In the East the limit's enough;
> That kitten there suffices,
> Not like here, because
> Paul expounded Christ.

To Westerners, he says:

> . . . a kitten under a stool, is not
> A fully legitimate kitten.[21]

It would not be right to give the impression that Ó Ríordáin's poetic is an effortless one. Life is there before him, he wishes to honour it and to gain access to its prayerfulness, but there is darkness as well, and terror. In a diary entry for 26 April 1940 he has the following account of an encounter in Cork city with a girl who was suffering from TB:

> I saw a girl on the South Mall. I took off my hat immediately, out of courtesy. We stopped. Maria O'Mahoney. A handsome young girl, with fine sturdy legs on her. But she has T.B. I saw her before in Heatherside [a sanatorium]. I hardly knew her . . . She was the most beautiful girl in the place without a sign of ill health . . . I think myself that one of the doctors used to be looking out for her. I used to be looking on, too, – the old story . . . But she frightened me. 'This Maria O'Mahoney was not the Maria O'Mahoney that was here before . . . ' She was much reduced. She was no longer a fine strapping girl. 'Consumption hath no pity for blue eyes or golden hair.' A slight redness was in her cheeks. That redness had a deadly meaning. Some of my fellow-patients are now in St. Patrick's Hospital. She had news about most of them. We parted. It is a terrible, sorrowful and bleak story. A beauty, in the vigour of her youth and goodness, rotting. The germs are powerful. You can't oppose them. Poverty caused a lot of this disease. And people are scared that Hitler will destroy this civilisation. If he does he didn't come soon enough. Well-fed Christianity, without a scruple![22]

---

[21] Seán Ó Ríordáin, *Tar Éis mo Bháis*, (Sáirséal agus Dill, Baile Atha Cliath, 1978), p.15.
[22] Seán Ó Coileáin, *op.cit.*, pp.124-5.

The writing here is halting because it is heartsmitten. The rage that mounts towards the end of this passage is the rage against confident complacent Christianity and its anodyne values that allow people to rot in poverty and disease through indifference. Charity and compassion have the same root, in Ó Ríordáin, as does the imagination, in real sympathy for the rest of life. But Maria O'Mahoney, the one he met on the street, was not the Maria O'Mahoney he knew in the sanatorium. Death had got a grip on her and transformed her. How can there be a basic pattern to anything or anyone if they can change so drastically? How can there be a prayerful exchange between essence, if those essences are unstable? How can there be the 'thrust of joy' in so much suffering? Might it not be better to have evil fully out, Hitler dominant, so-called civilization gone, than to continue in our overstuffed complacent lives?

In one of the most searching of all of his poems 'Oileán agus Oileán Eile' in *Eireaball Spideoige*, he meditates on the holy site of Gougane Bara, where St Finbarr settled, and built a tiny monastery, on an island in the lake. The informing idea of the poem is the old one that each person is an island, in the sense that each person has his own authentic territory, and that the attempt to uncover and reveal that is what inspired the saint and what should inspire us now. But is the whole activity just 'frantic illusion' in a time when words and life have gone 'vapid'?

> Words without verve,
> The imperiousness of years.
> Their grey film
> Fell on my thoughts . . .
>
> Finbarr and the saints
> Are years in the earth;
> Enthusiasm's no more
> Than frantic illusion.
>
> I'm sick to heart
> Of words gone vapid.
> Illusion or demon -
> Let them distract me.[23]

---

[23] *Eireaball Spideoige*, pp.789.

But bravely, the writing turns aside from this gloomy langour and moves into a section called 'An Bíogadh', 'The Stirring', in which the 'beo-gheit', the 'life-thrust', is attempted, and the saint's presence is attributed to the air, the wind and birdsong:

> Saintly intimations stir the air
> And the wind moves all through them.
> An ancient prayer's submerged in my mind
> Which thought now strives to breathe on.
>
> In this fold of saintly thought
> A sudden proposition took me,
> Enunciated in the bird's fierce song
> I heard a scorn towards the world.
>
> The birds' own island was in
> The music he flung at things;
> Without islands no-one lives
> Pity those men who've left them.[24]

Each person, then, must turn away from the clamour to his own special island, which was 'composed as a white prayer/On the lips of the Son of Man'. But that is easily enough said. How do you make poetry out of this? What Ó Ríordáin records is the struggle of the mind, in doubt, searching out the narrative of his experience at Gougane, trying to find a stillness and a central focus. The bleakness is there, the doubt, the search, and the looking for the basic pattern, whereby he and Finbarr can find at-one-ment:

> *St Finbarr's Island*
> At Gougane, on a bad afternoon,
> Fog whitened out the sheer
> Cliffs. I searched the island for
> A sign, found it in the trees.
>
> Around me, their contorted growth,
> The entangled order.
> They'd been driven into any shape
> Like a body burnt alive.

[24] *Ibid.*, p.80.

Or like writing on a page
With other writing over it.
I saw knee and nostril, back and foot,
And then I saw Mahatma Gandhi . . .

Freedom's zest, love for the turned
Eye, are in the treeshapes; love
For all that's crooked and bent,
And for the soft and straight, contempt . . .

Every man's island is
His narrative of Heaven,
The Christ that's leaping in his blood,
The implication in his words.[25]

This Gougane Bara poem is a poem of the ascetic will, intent on discovering a relation between the self, the past, and place; and also intent on conveying a sense of spiritual continuity. The sign is found; the stirring of the uncovering of its significance is recorded. But what of the two Maria O'Mahoneys? What if there is only the here and now and what if our insistence that there is a centre is pure invention? This doubt is the theme of a poem of intense metaphysical and spiritual anguish in *Brosna*, called 'Moths'.

The moths are creatures whom he wishes to realize, to present them in their pure aspect of integral form. Instead they remain moths, what they are, in exterior existential reality, and they threaten and terrify. So strong does their pressure become that they threaten to devour the identity of the speaker, whose job it is to control, order, possess and realize them. The trick is, of course, that the poem, while confessing failure to realize the essential 'mothness' of the moths, realizes, profoundly, the experience of the anguish of being excluded from any sense of integral identity. And yet what is being composed in this poem is the formation of identity in the experience of not being sure that there is such a thing. It is a poetry wrung from the beseeching heart, beset by all the circumstances of its doubt:

[25] *Ibid.*, pp.81-2.

Flutter of a delicate moth, turning of a page,
Crushing of the small wingspan,
In the bedroom of an autumn evening
Something fragile is being crazed.

Another night, in a dream, I saw
A pair of clothesmoth's wings,
They were extensive as an angel's
And fragile as a woman.

I had to hold them,
Not let them go astray,
And to possess without destroying them
And deliver them to complete delight.

But I spilled the holy dust
That powdered each wing,
And I knew then I hadn't the numbers
Of masculinity, and would never.

The ten digits marched out of the mess
Authority greater than ever before,
And generations were heard arguing arithmetic
And everyone heard but me.

Flutter of a delicate moth, turning of a page,
Destruction of a wing membrane;
This autumn evening I need the small
Agitation of the hovering moths.[26]

This is a poem of failure, of creative failure, and yet it is also a powerful piece of writing. He has 'spilled the holy dust' but the magic remains in the poem's attentiveness, patience and suffering.

Such a poem as 'Moths' achieves a convincing realization of metaphysical anguish because it is conveyed in an entirely direct manner. Even the obscurity of the 'numbers' does not really matter. They are a private symbol, and it is clear enough that they refer to male sexuality and creative power.

Ó Ríordáin began his career as a published writer with a statement, the preface to *Eireaball Spideoige*, in which he argued that sympathy was crucial to creativity, because

---

[26] *Brosna*, p.18.

it was the means by which the imagination could contact the pattern of something else, thereby moving towards the realization of itself. This poetic linked theology, instinct, ordinary human feeling and language. But it will be evident by now that Ó Ríordáin was not a programmatic writer; on the whole he did not write to justify an intellectual conception. As time went on his doubt about whether or not there really was a central meaning, a central pattern, increased; he did not repress that. As always is the case, the doubt increased the tension, so his belief in the basic pattern of each thing, each creature, was tested. In some poems, such as 'Moths', the doubt is very great, and the writing arises directly from uncertainty. I a late poem 'Oíche Gealaí' ('Moonlit Night') light and dark interplay. There is a mixture of serenity, terror, openness and resignation here that is like something in Hölderlin's later poems:

> Though the sky's cloudy
> The full moon's
> An eye of light
> Pouring down.
> Where it is in the sky
> Is war. Light's
> Declared war on dark.
> As much as it can
> This carnage of light
> Spreads and reveals itself.
> In that place, which is
> Neither light nor dark
> Huge mountains,
> Sea distances,
> And remote sunsets
> Are eaten by light out of dark.
> Terror resides
> In the unbearable beauty
> Of these reaches of light.
> This sudden loveliness
> Should be hidden.
> Nothing can stop it,
> All shapes obey it.
> Hide it in a cloud.
> Let us go in.[27]

27 *Línte Liombó*, p.32.

The mind opens to a not knowing, a terrible openness, in a language, Irish, which, commonsense tells us, is at the margin of European linguistic culture. But the margins are often where the activity is. In Rome who thought of Nazareth?

Celtic Art

Hilary Richardson

Religion and art were inseparably entwined in the culture of
the Celtic peoples. In both pagan and Christian times the
Celts expressed supernatural beliefs in their art.

It is their Christian art which concerns us here. There is
no doubt that it is of exceptional interest. Two reasons in
particular make it remarkable. In the first place it is an example without parallel of a native prehistoric style which was
adopted on a wide scale to proclaim the Christian message.
An abstract style of distinction had flourished for centuries
among the Celts under pagan patronage. This was reinter-
preted with verve and invention for the Church. The success
of the adaptation is astonishing. Although the material may
appear remote and unrelated, yet it is clear that the same
germ which had come to maturity in pagan Celtic art went
on to produce fresh growth in Christian surroundings.

In the second place the new use of Celtic art as a vehicle for
the Christian faith coincided with the most brilliant and creative period of all, certainly in Ireland. Thus it came about that
work produced by early Irish artists is not merely of academic
value, to be studied by historians, archaeologists or scholars
of church history, but has a vital presence. Art of this time

is still to some extent, even today, a living force.

In certain aspects Celtic art is more in tune with modern taste and the work of modern artists than art of the relatively recent past. I am reminded of a Glasgow art student twenty years ago, who referred to Michelangelo as 'old hat'; he found abstract Celtic work closer to his own ideal. In addition, as a medium for spiritual values, Celtic art still has meaning for Christians. There is an immediacy about it, and a completely original viewpoint not found elsewhere. For many centuries Celtic art was either unknown or ignored, appearing barbaric or incomprehensible. In recent years it has acquired a steadily growing relevance. As time goes on, we are slowly learning, little by little, to appreciate and understand it better.

Consequently, Christian Celtic art is alive at two levels. On the one hand it is a direct inspiration for artists and anyone interested in design, and on the other it is a revelation in visual terms of the Christian faith.

How is one to define the Celticness of Celtic art? John Scottus (Eriugena), the great Irish philosopher of the ninth century, says that 'a wise artist produces his art from himself in himself and foresees in it the things he is to make . . .'[1] The individual artist and individual work of art are of course unique. Yet at the same time, every human being is linked inescapably to his environment. The age in which he lives, and the country, determine the setting. Each artist's work is seen against the style of his own period. Certainly the art of the Celtic-speaking peoples has a special identity of its own.

There was a great sense of unity throughout the various branches of the Celtic world, with a common vision which can be traced back to the Iron Age. Accordingly, it is in the prehistoric Early Iron Age that one must start for an understanding of the later work. There is no other course. To appreciate Celtic art it is necessary to return to its very roots. Its subtle character is inextricably bound up with its past.

---

[1] *Periphyseon*, Book 2, ed. I.P. Sheldon-Williams, Dublin, 1972, p.117.

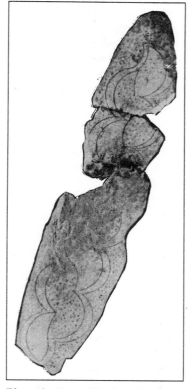

Plate 1a. Broighter Torc.
Photo: F. Henry

Plate 1b. Bone Slip from L. Crew
Photo: Nat. Mus. Dublin

The origins of prehistoric Celtic art are to be found in the Rhineland and eastern France in the fifth century BC with the emergence of the style associated with the name of La Tène, the famous site on Lake Neuchâtel in Switzerland. It was the La Tène conception of design which dominated later art in Britain and Ireland. This style had been devised to suit the taste of warrior chieftains and we know it mainly from its superb metalwork. At one time what one might call the 'empire' of the Celts was of vast extent, stretching right across Europe into Asia Minor. But with the ascendancy of Rome, and as Roman provincial civilization gained sway

Plate 2. Detail of letter Chi, *Book of Kells*, f-34r. *Photo: F. Henry*

over Europe, Celtic culture was pushed further and further towards the west. Eventually the art style, which had been developed in Central Europe to please native princes and warriors, continued to flourish only in the British Isles and Ireland.

Taking Ireland by itself, a radical difference was made by the complete absence of Roman rule there and the continuation of a Celtic way of life without interruption. Ireland was left as a place part. The sheer body of literature in Old Irish reflects a tradition stretching back into antiquity. It was into this milieu that Christianity took root in such a vital and original way. The free independent spirit of the Heroic Age of the Celts as depicted in their epic sagas, such as *Táin Bó Cúailgne*, survived. The very individual La Tène art style survived also. Irish artists retained a unique vision handed down to them uninterrupted from their prehistoric forbears. It is for this reason that Irish art gives the best insight into the distinctive structure of the Celtic eye.

Not only was Irish society never crushed under Roman provincial culture, but Ireland also escaped the barbarian invasions. Unlike her neighbours, Ireland remained relatively

undisturbed until the twelfth century. Therefore it is best
to concentrate on Ireland for a view of artistic work
encompassing the widest range both in time and development.

Here one may digress to consider the modern situation.
The visual arts do not normally spring to mind when thinking of the Celtic peoples in a general way. The Welsh, the
Bretons, the Irish and the Scots are renowned for other artistic gifts. David Bell, writing about art in Wales, admits 'that
the genius of the Welsh people has expressed itself primarily
in literature and in poetry and not in the visual arts.'[2] Wales,
in the national anthem, is a land of 'beirdd a chantorion'.
Music flourished along with the language, but perhaps the
nonconformist ethic finally extinguished any visual artistic
tradition. On the other hand, painters such as Gwen John or
David Jones still project a spiritual vitality which must surely

Illus. 1a & 1b. Details of design engraved on a bronze Scabbard from
Lisnacroghera, Co. Antrim

[2]   Bell, D., *The Artist in Wales*, London, 1957, p.16.

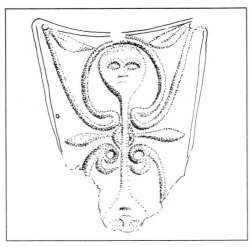

Illus. 2. Tal-y-llyn (Mer.), metal plaque c. 200
B.C.

be linked to their background. One could argue that history
(and the continuation of a native art style) would have been
very different if Latin had not been the official language of
the Church for so many centuries. If the native tongue had
been exploited by the Church from the earliest times, as in
Armenia for instance, a solidarity might have been maintained; but it was not to be. However, a gift for words and
the cultivation of an oral memory remained characteristic
of the Celts. Words and songs were free, whereas lack of
means of necessity put a brake on artistic output. Artists
in the nature of things require tangible materials, backed by
solid patronage, to produce worthwhile results. The prosperity of monasteries and the commissions of kings lay behind
the High Crosses. George Russell (AE) was astonished when
he received a copy of the *Crosses and Culture of Ireland* from
its author, Kingsley Porter, the American art historian, on
its publication in 1931. He wrote to Kingsley Porter to thank
him. 'I have been reading it with an interest I never imagined I
would have in Irish Crosses. I started my study of Christianity
in Ireland at the wrong end, that is, in my own time when it
produced neither art nor literature and was so sterile that I

could hardly imagine any period of fertility.'[3] Although AE
had been trained as a painter and was well informed on Irish
matters, he had never before encountered the rich heritage
of early medieval Christian sculpture in Ireland.

Almost sixty years later our knowledge has increased
considerably, not only through study but largely through
modern movements in art. Our viewpoint has been changed
by painters and sculptors in the twentieth century in their
search for new approaches. We no longer need to look for
naturalism and the accurate use of perspective. The general
acceptance of abstract art has made the popular vision more
objective, open and less prejudiced. Realistic representation,
as handed down from classical art to the Renaissance, is no
longer deemed to be essential; it is just one of many possible

Plate 3. Details of the Tara Brooch, much enlarged. *Photo: Nat. Mus.
Dublin*

---

[3] *AE's Letters to Mínanlábáin*, ed. Lucy Kingsley Porter, New York, 1937,
p.29.

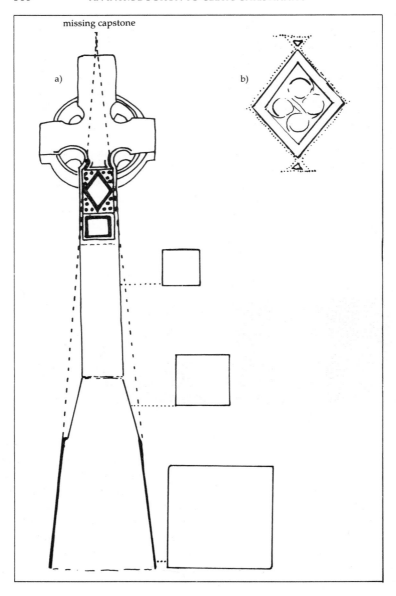

Illus. 3a. Plan of the Cross of Moone to show position of the lozer
Illus. 3b. Lozenge from *Book of Kells*, genealogy of Christ, f31r

South side   East side

Plate 4a & 4b. Cross of Moone, Co. Kildare. *Photo: Nat. Mon.*

solutions. There is no point in blaming Celtic artists for an apparent inability to draw realistic people or understand perspective. They had no interest in realism. Instead they had quite different aims in their work. Dom Louis Gougaud could write in 1932 of Celtic art that 'all sense of proportion, relief, perspective and expression is wanting.'[4] Opinion now is more sensitive to the intentions of these artists and is prepared

[4]   Gougaud, L., *Christianity in Celtic Lands*, London, 1932, p.374.

to recognize that their style, stemming back to prehistoric sources, has a validity of its own.

Returning again to the La Tène heritage, it is clear that it formed the core of Irish art up to medieval times. This long continuity of methods and ideas is a striking phenomenon. The Celtic chieftains on the Continent liked subtle abstract decoration to embellish weapons and jewellery. Their fashions gravitated with the Celtic tribes to Britain and Ireland. When the advancement of the Roman Empire undermined native Celtic life, the style prospered without restriction on the western seaboard of Europe, just as the Celtic languages had been pushed to the western extremities. Celtic artists had evolved their own methods of decoration and their own unique visual sense. Design was based on long-established semi-geometric principles. Grids and compasses were employed to build up running patterns of curves to give a feeling of life and movement (Pl. 1a). It was a linear art, largely covering surfaces, and the strict methods of construction achieved ungeometric flowing effects (Illus. 1a and 1b). It is characterized by a wonderfully free, uninhibited use of linear ornament. The style is ever changing, exploring new curvilinear ideas, and it is hard to pin down. The essence of La Tène art is the curve, with harmonious schemes worked out with care. Repetition and obvious groupings are avoided, to make sure that nothing bores the eye. La Tène art is non-representational, non-classical, applied in a subtle, restrained manner. Shapes are suggested rather than stated. Faces may lurk in a few floating indications. There is no attempt at realism in the treatment of figures. Cult heads and deities reflect the religious dimension, especially in stone carving (Illus. 2). In the formation of their style the Celts on the Continent had turned a blind eye to the lifelike figures of classical art. They treasured painted Attic ware among their possessions, yet chose to borrow only classical plant motifs, while ignoring realistic figured scenes. Even then the plant motifs became an excuse for pattern-making in running curves.

The unusual and successful abstract approach to decoration evolved by the Celts during the La Tène era went on thriving in Ireland with the same rigorous rules governing

North side   West side

Plate 5a & 5b. Cross of Moone, Co. Kildare. *Photo: Nat. Mon.*

the layout of designs. The grammar of the style stayed fundamentally unchanged up to medieval times. It suited the temperament and outlook of early Irish society and must have satisfied a wide general taste. Artists continued unreservedly to work within this tradition. As they came in contact with new influences and new neighbours they added an occasional borrowing into their repertoire. From the Saxons they copied chipcarving, a technique in cast metalwork to enhance the play of light and shade. Interlace with ribbons became a favourite motif and animal themes were introduced. Irish artists were adaptive. Their way of thinking remained constant, however.

When Christianity arrived in Ireland these sophisticated methods of seeing, symbolizing and constructing still held sway. The same mechanism for laying out designs can be seen in pagan and Christian work, in the surface ornament on metalwork or stone, and in the decoration of Gospel books. Using compass-drawn curves, flowing arrangements were produced. It required skill and practice to work out different combinations. The final effect could appear to be spontaneous, but in actual fact this was far from being the case.

A fascinating description which throws light on the methods of design is found in an early Irish saga. It recounts how a device had to be invented for Cú Chulainn's shield. A new law among the Ulstermen ruled that each warrior must have his own emblem blazoned on his shield. The armourer was unable to create an original composition for Cú Chulainn, and was threatened with death. Then, at the last moment, a

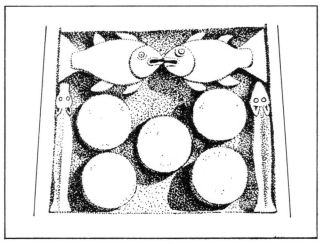

Illus. 4. The Multiplication of the Loaves
and Fishes, Cross of Moone

Plate 6a. Derrynavlan Paten. *Photo: Nat. Mus. Dublin*

supernatural being appeared through the skylight and drew a design of arcs on the workshop floor, which had been covered with ashes in order to make a good surface for sketching. A pronged instrument, like a pair of compasses, was used for drawing the curves of the new device. The day was saved, Cú Chulainn had his own individual emblem for his shield, and the armourer breathed a sigh of relief.

This story shows the premium that was set on originality and variety. It was plainly a difficult task to invent a new formula that was not derivative. Although mechanical means prepared the groundwork of compositions, it is rarely possible to analyze the structure at a brief glance. The forms are so carefully integrated that time is needed to unravel the way that they have been put together. Geometric art elsewhere can often be clear-cut, making a direct statement. The barbarians favoured open, symmetrical designs in their showy brooches, while the geometric constructions of Islamic art are a world apart from these elusive Celtic designs, where the eye is led on without rest. The quality

Plate 6b. View of Derrynavlan Chalice from radiograph
(*after Brit. Mus.*)

of elusion is a special feature of the Celts. They avoided the obvious at all costs. It is a balancing act between the abstract and the concrete. At the same time, ambiguity was grist to their mill. Shapes could imply several meanings, changing and disappearing, adding to the general richness. The word-juggling of James Joyce is another aspect of the same coin.

In Ireland some sketches are found on odd pieces of thin bone, antler or slate, which were used for blocking out designs and exploring the various combinations of arcs (Pl. 1b). In beautifully finished objects the same ideas prevail. Splendidly decorated Gospel books have elaborate multi-patterned carpet pages which are planned on a geometric framework, using compass-drawn curves in the ancient tradition. Perforations in the vellum reveal extremely intricate schemes, carried out to perfection.

Christianity was able to avail itself of the native artistic heritage. The long, unbroken tradition of visual skills, enriched by outside contacts, was now powered by a compelling new patron in the form of the Church. It was a recipe for extraordinary creative activity. A whole new field of enterprises opened for craftsmen. Churches and oratories had to be built and furnished, and gospels and psalters were in demand. Now metalworkers turned their long-cherished skills to the making of sacred vessels and shrines. Carving and stone-cutting came into their own, although much of the treatment of stone remained a surface ornament. Writing and the illumination of books, on the other hand, were radical innovations. Designs in metal, derived from the La Tène, were at hand as a source of inspiration when artists were first confronted with the task of decorating and copying texts on vellum for religious book. Brilliant enamelled discs, millefiori and glass studs were transposed into paintings (Pl. 2, 3).

It took a little time for Christian art to come to its full potential, but the expertise of artists was now matched only by their dedication. Just as the monastic life was dedicated to devotion, so much of the skilled craftsmanship was dedicated to the service of God. There had been no serious opposition to the new faith, and no martyrs. Instead, as far as the arts were concerned, there was a gentle adaptation of the age-old methods to an altogether grander sphere of operation, both on a material and spiritual level. Monastic centres had sprung up rapidly and they became the power-houses of early Irish culture. Monasticism was particularly congenial in Ireland since it fitted easily into the Celtic tribal pattern of society.

The early centuries of Christianity were imbued with a deep spirituality. Religion was central to all aspects of life at this time, in a way that we may find difficult to comprehend today. There was a direct and immediate response to the Gospels, with the Church as the mainspring of existence. Everything fell into place within a cosmic plan seen to be of God's creating. Life, including art, revolved around the Church. But it was not so much religious art as liturgical, expressing the Church's experience of God. It was an art constructed to aid contemplation and prayer.

Throughout Christendom a shared language of symbols was widely understood. Medieval thought was pervaded by mystical symbolism which was used to explain and expound the Scriptures. Philosophers following Pythagoras and the Neo-Platonists had established a system of celestial arithmetic allied to scriptural exegesis. A divine plan for the universe was expressed in numbers, measurements and geometry. No

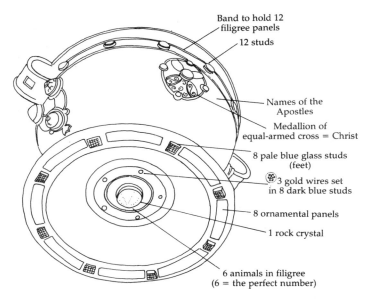

Illus. 5. Diagram to show some of the numbers used in the design
of the Ardagh Chalice

branch of medieval thought can have escaped the influence
of number symbolism. It was endemic to the age.

The writings of Pseudo Dionysius the Areopagite commanded an important role in the propagation of medieval
cosmology. It is significant that it was an Irishman, Eriugena,
who made these works available to the West. He was living
in France in the ninth century when he prepared his own
magnum opus, *On the Division of Nature*. Ideas of Christian
numerology had been circulating in Ireland long before this
time, however. They can be seen in an acrostic hymn composed by St Colmcille. The same influences appear in artistic
design also.

Craftsmen had reached an astonishing peak of excellence
by the eighth century, the Golden Age of Irish art. Their
style had developed in extraordinary profusion following
the merging of Christianity with the pagan heritage. Now
a wealth of mystical thinking associated with the Christian

theology of the period was included in designs. Of course it is dangerous to dogmatize on the exact intentions of an artist, especially in the remote past when documentation is in short supply. Yet there is no doubt that theories of the harmony of number and similar concepts were uppermost in contemporary thought and permeate art as well. A phrase often repeated by early Irish writers is 'to see with the eyes of the heart' or 'the eyes of the mind', and it is a good metaphor for understanding something of the aims of artists at this time. The beauty of an object may be enjoyed at a number of different levels. The physical eyes may appreciate certain attributes, such as colour, texture, materials or shape, for their own intrinsic loveliness. On the other hand the 'eyes of the heart' may perceive another dimension altogether, a dimension of spiritual values. Measurements, numbers, colours and motifs can be used with specific intentions, enclosing a wealth of meaning to the initiated. The ideas concealed in the composition of a carpet page or in the design of a chalice may have been forgotten over the years and go unrecognized. Enough beauty remains at more obvious, direct levels to be readily grasped by the beholder, who may be aware only of a entrancing arrangement of lines and colours.

Ireland could embrace the ideas of the Neo-Platonists without conflict. Neither were themes of Celtic mythology rejected, but were transformed by a Christian meaning. The pagan voyage tales reappear as the wandering of early saints, like St Brendan. On the one hand the old Celtic tradition could be adapted to Christianity, while on the other numerology and mystical philosophy had a strong appeal and could be applied with enthusiasm. The symbolic association of numbers and measurements for a theological purpose was attractive to the Celtic turn of mind. Nowhere can such a system have been more congenial than to the Irish, with their delight in names, numbers and derivations. Ambiguities and half-glimpsed perceptions continued their centuries-old native tradition. The richness of imagery gave multiple interpretations and layerings of meanings. An opportunity to build up allusions, display erudition and play with meanings was dear to the Celtic temperament. It is clear that the superlative decoration of the Book of Kells, unsurpassed in its complexity, is laden with Christian symbolism. Only a fraction of its meaning can be identified today with any confidence. Designs reach an incredible peak of intricacy here, yet Irish art of the whole period is shot through with similar qualities in less exaggerated form.

Turning to the Cross of Moone, Co. Kildare, one is faced with a monument which has been conceived in mathematical terms, with the proportions and measurements of each shape carefully worked out (Pl. 4, 5). It is the sole surviving work of a master sculptor. Carved in granite, this cross is an arrangement of geometric forms integrated into a harmonious whole, on a symbolic plan, just as the plans of early churches and basilicas have a mystical interpretation. Each unit of the design has its own value. Two truncated pyramids form the base, while the shaft rises in a square section. The lozenge, just below the cross head on the west side, is strategically placed, marking the convergence of the lines from the base (Illus. 3a, 3b). It is a Christian symbol and in all probability stands for Christ, the second person of the Trinity, the Logos. Significantly a lozenge is the central focus of the symbols page at the beginning of St John's Gospel in the Book of Kells. It is framed with a purple border, edged with gold, which is yellow paint in reality. These colours, purple and gold, were used for a special purpose to signify something precious. They were associated with imperial majesty in Byzantium. The monogram of Christ, the Chi-Rho page in the Book of Kells, is bordered with purple and gold to indicate the majesty of Christ (Pl. 2).

One could well imagine Eriugena's homily on the Loaves and Fishes from his *Commentary on the Gospel of St John* taking practical shape in front of the Multiplication scene carved on the Cross of Moone (Illus. 4). He tells us the five barley loaves are the five books of Mosaic Law to nourish man. On the other hand, five also is an image of the five senses of the body, implying that the faithful can abandon earthly for spiritual food. The two fish indicate the two Testaments, Old and New, though he says that others think they signify

Plate 7a. Underside of Ardagh Chalice. *Photo: Nat. Mus. Dublin*

the Prophets and the Psalms or the two faces of the Law, King and Priest.

The sculptor at Moone balances the five loaves and the two fish with an extraordinary simplicity and economy of line within the given space. By eliminating any pictorial reference to the scene of the miracle with the crowd or the Apostles, he concentrates on the numbers to great effect.

The twelve Apostles form a powerful composition on the west side of the base (Pl. 5b). They are divided into three rows of four figures, each row graded in size to fit the narrowing shape of the pyramid base and each figure reduced to an elementary unit. The carving of the Cross of Moone embraces at one and the same time a symbolism of the biblical scenes depicted, such as the sacrifice of Isaac, combined with a symbolism based on a mystical use of mathematics.

The programme of the applied decoration on the Ardagh Chalice and the Derrynavlan altar service of the eighth to ninth centuries is founded on Christian numerology and symbolism. These liturgical vessels are among the finest in the whole early Christian world. They have a robust design of a type only found in Ireland, yet the technical detail in the case of the Derrynavlan paten and the Ardagh Chalice is of extreme refinement and delicacy. The large size of the paten may be accounted for by the complex division of the bread, the *fractio panis*, described in the Stowe Missal (Pl. 6a). A short treatise on the Mass included in the Stowe Missal (c.800), the only early missal to come down to us intact, links numbers to mystical meanings in the Eucharist. It is of special interest because it throws light on the design of precious vessels for the altar.

The number symbolism is occasionally explicit. Twelve has obvious associations with the Apostles, whose names are engraved in stately insular script around the bowl of the Ardagh Chalice, immediately beneath the girdle running between the handles, which contains twelve spaces for gold filigree panels, punctuated by twelve blue and red studs. Eight symbolized the Resurrection. It is the number emphasized in the amazing ornamentation on the underside of the Ardagh Chalice and right through the decoration of the Derrynavlan Chalice (Pl. 6b). According to Eriugena, eight referred to Sunday and Easter, to regeneration, baptism and immortality, but above all to the Resurrection. 'Then the perfection of the number Eight, a supernatural cube, so to speak, will be established for ever, having been foreshadowed by the title of the sixth psalm: "Psalm of David, for the eighth day". For the resurrection of Our Lord also took place on the eighth day, in order to intimate mystically that blessed life which after the sevenfold rotation of the seven days of this life will follow upon the end of the world. Similarly, as we have said, human nature returns to its origin by an eightfold ascent: a fivefold one within the limits of its own nature, and a threefold one, transcending its nature and essence, within God Himself. When the Fiveness of created nature has been united to the Threeness of the creator, then there is nothing manifest at any step but God alone, similarly as in the purest

Plate 7b. The Ardagh Chalice. *Photo: F. Henry*

air only the light shines.'[5] Eight is called a supernatural cube here because it was considered perfect by virtue of its six surfaces, six being the perfect number.

This whole passage can be related to the crystal-centred underfoot of the Ardagh Chalice (Illus. 5). One splendid crystal is circled by five dark blue studs, each of which bears three C-shapes in gold filigree (Pl. 7a). The tiny gold coils were placed back to back inside the mould for the stud, and they slid naturally into position when the viscous glass was pressed on top. Following Eriugena, five stands for creation and three for the Creator. The band of gilt bronze decoration

---

[5] *Periphyseon*, Book 5, 39. Translation by L. Bieler.

6a. Cats and mice, *f-34r*

6b. Otter, *f-34r*

6c. Two moths and a lozenge, *f-34r*

6d. Goat, *f-41v*

6e. Cock and hens, *f-67r*

6g. Wolf, *f-76v*

6f. Fish and cat, *f-71r*

6h. Fish

Illus. 6a-6h. Details from *Book of Kells*

in which the studs are set contains five groups of three, compounded further by the three beaded wires adorning each of the studs. Certainly the design of the underside of the Ardagh Chalice emphasizes the numbers eight, five, three and one, a dramatic parallel to the passage from Eriugena quoted above (Pl.7b). In the foot girdle there are eight pale blue glass studs, backed by patterned silver foil, which act as feet on which the chalice stands, and eight decorated panels – two of copper, two of woven silver wire, and four of embossed silver in a design of three interlaced crosses. Five can also represent the five wounds of Christ and refer to the Passion. There is no difficulty because Eriugena piles on alternative interpretations to enrich the symbolism. To the medieval mind it was a merit to load allusion on allusion. The elucidation of these designs is as yet in its infancy, and demands a thorough study of the written sources. The careful arrangement of raised bosses in high relief on some of the High Crosses is likely to be based on this language of numbers also. But the Book of Kells is in a class apart in the profusion of its decoration, laden with meaning.

The illumination of manuscripts is the most renowned aspect of Irish art. The great insular Gospel-books were unrivalled in Europe and must still be regarded with awe and amazement. Extravagantly planned and magnificently ornamented in microscopic detail, these books were created for ceremonial use. It is only possible to understand such work in its religious context. Writing and manuscript art had come into being in Ireland for the sake of the Scriptures. Similarly, calligraphy has a spiritual purpose in Islamic art, where the text of the Koran itself is sacred. It is in this light that the illuminated Gospel-books must be viewed. The zeal and incredible expertise of the artist and scribes mirrors their faith. On his travels around Ireland in the twelfth century, Gerald the Welshman saw a wonderful early Gospels in Kildare; he believed it had been painted by angels. No other explanation could account for the miraculous handiwork. Already by his time the religious fervour was reduced to more mundane standards.

A single-mindedness of purpose is characteristic of the clerics and monks of the early Irish Church. It is reflected

Plate 8a. The Cross of the
Scriptures, Clonmacnois.
Photo: F. Henry

in whatever activity engaged their attention. Bede tells us that
St Aidan 'took care to neglect none of those things which he
found in the Gospels and the writings of the Apostles and
Prophets, but to the utmost of his power endeavoured to
fulfil them in all his deeds.'[6] The twenty-four hours of the day
were sanctified in the daily round of the life of the monk, with
its eight offices. In its wake came an extraordinary spiritual
refinement and sensitivity. The hermits and anchorites lived
in woodland retreats, by the sea coast and on islands. They
had a deep love for nature and a lively feeling for birds, animals and all creation. 'They brought into that environment

---

6   Bede, *A History of the English Church and People*, Book III, chap.17.

Plate 8b. Detail, Soldiers guarding the Tomb of Christ.
Photo: Nat. Mon.

an eye washed miraculously clear by a continual spiritual exercise,' so that 'they, first in Europe, had that strange vision of natural things in an almost unnatural purity.'[7] As a consequence, early Irish poetry has a freshness and a power of observation not found elsewhere until much later. Similarly, in between the lines of the Book of Kells, the artists loved to

[7] Flower, R., *The Irish Tradition*, Oxford, 1947, p.42.

depict tiny scenes of animal life, comments on nature, but illustrating the text or performing some practical function for the reader. No abstract monsters these, but thumbnail sketches of real creatures, catching their very essence. A greyhound stalks a hare; a cock parades with hens; a wolf, an otter, moths, eagles, salmon and cats of all shapes, fill the pages with unexpected entertainment (Illus. 6a-6h). There is the same affection for wildlife and domestic pets in early poems which scribes sometimes jotted down in the margins of manuscripts.

Birds are particular favourites. The tiny gold bird, decorated with delicate spirals of filigree, from Garryduff, Co. Cork, can be identified as a wren (Illus. 7). A little bird, representing the soul of Christ, is carved on some of the High Crosses in scenes showing the Soldiers Guarding the Tomb of Christ (Pl. 8a, b). It has all the appearance of a wren also, with its diminutive tail. This scene, with the Holy Women, takes the place of the Resurrection in later art. Christ's body lies beneath the horizontal stone of the tomb, while the soldiers have fallen asleep above it. The Irish version is unique in showing the bird or soul re-entering the mouth of Christ to bring back life.

Illus. 7. Gold bird ornament from ring-fort at Garryduff, Co. Cork
Max. dimension 14mm.

'He prayeth best who loved best, All things both great and small.' The truth of Coleridge's lines is borne out by these early Irish Christians who felt an intimate fellowship with nature, and at the same time a familiarity, almost, with the Almighty.

Reading List

This includes no articles from learned journals and is intended to be of use for the general reader.

Bieler, L. *Ireland, Harbinger of the Middle Ages*, Oxford, 1966.

Finlay, Ian, *Celtic Art: An Introduction*, London and New York, 1973.

Henry, Françoise, *Early Christian Irish Art* (Irish Life and Culture series), Dublin, 1979.

Henry, Françoise, *Irish Art*, 3 vols, London, 1965, 1967 and 1970.

Hickey, Helen, *Images of Stone*. Figure sculpture of the Lough Erne Basin. Fermanagh, 1985.

Laing, Lloyd, *Later Celtic Art in Britain and Ireland*, Aylesbury, 1987.

Nordenfalk, C., *Celtic and Anglo-Saxon Painting*, London, 1977.

Ross, Anne, *The Pagan Celts*, London, 1986.

Rowan, Eric, ed., *Art in Wales 2000 BC – AD 1850*, Cardiff, 1978.

Ryan, Michael, ed., *Treasures of Ireland, Irish Art 3000 BC – 1500 AD*, Dublin, 1983.

Acknowledgements

I am greatly obliged to the National Monuments Branch of the Office of Public Works, Ireland, to the National Museum, Dublin, to the Board of Trinity College, Dublin and to the Photographic Archives of the Dept. of Archaeology, U.C.D., for photographs or permission for photographs. The line drawings are by Hilary Richardson.

Celtic Theology: Pelagius

M. Forthomme Nicholson

Pelagius Britto (c.360 to c.430 AD) was a Celtic Briton by birth and a Roman citizen by right. He was too often called *Brito, Britto, ex Britanniis oriundus, Pelagius gente Britannus monachus, Pelagius Brito haeresiarches,* and derisively *Britannus* or *Britannicus noster* (in his own time) to leave any doubt about his Celtic British origin.[1]

His exact place of birth is unknown, but like Patrick (c.390 to c.460) or Gildas (over a century later, c.500 to c.570), Pelagius probably came into the world somewhere in the band of territory stretching from present-day Strathclyde through Cumbria to Wales. His name has been associated with the Greek *pelagios* (of the sea) and is rendered as Morgan or Morien in Welsh. It is possible he was born in the area of Roman Chester (perhaps at Bangor-is-y-coed) or of Caerlleon-ar-wsyg in South Wales near the Severn estuary.

Embroidering on the Welsh birth tradition, the writer of the Iolo manuscript speaks of 'Morien' (Pelagius) as the son of

---

[1] See among others Mercator, PL 48, 111-13, *Liber subnotationum in uerba Iuliani*, Praefatio, 2, ' . . . Pelagium gente Britannum monachum'. See also J.B. Bury, "The Origin of Pelagius", *Hermathena* XIII (Dublin, 1905): 26-35, esp. p. 28, para. 2 and p.33, para. 10.

Argad the Bard. Morien was the most learned person of any in the world and the writer notes that his superior knowledge gave rise to the expression 'Morien-ddysg' (one of 'Morienic learning'). Further, Morien was one of the three 'deceits' (or 'defects') manifested in the Ynys Prydain (the Isle of Britain).[2]

St Germanus had come with St Lupus to restore proper doctrine. Several places near the South Wales border appear to perpetuate the name of St Germanus, although the evidence is unclear and his anti-Pelagian campaign does not necessarily relate to the birthplace of Pelagius in any case.

Whatever his place of birth and upbringing, Pelagius came from a Christian romanized Celtic background with its emphasis on faith and good works, on the holiness of all life and the oneness-of-all. His father was probably a decurion (a local notable). He received an excellent Latin

---

[2] Hugh Williams, *Christianity in Early Britain*, Oxford, 1912, p.201 (notes 1, 2, 3 especially) discusses the Iolo manuscript tradition but expresses doubts about the 'Morgan' etymology. Hugh Williams might well have expressed doubt about much else in the Iolo manuscript (which was printed in Liverpool in 1888). The passage on Pelagius is from the chapter entitled 'A chronological account of times and remarkable occurrences . . . and of distinguished persons and circumstances.' Iolo footnoted this chapter as taken from Watkin Pywel O Ben Y Fai, itself a transcript from one of Caradoc's Chronicles, the *Lyfr Caradawc Llancarfan*. It is of particular note that the expression 'Morien-ddysg' is footnoted to the *Myvyrian Archaiology of Wales* (1801) volume I, p.410. The reference is to an old Welsh poem of the early fourteenth century from the *Red Book of Hergest*. The poet Gwilym Ddu O Arfon (who lived c.1280-1320) wrote three of the poems in this book. The poem in question mentions heroes of old like Morgan, Roland and Morien, while eulogizing Gwilym's patron Griffith. The fourth verse of the passage that concerns us reads 'Morien ddysg rodd ffysg reidd-ffyrf yngnhawd' (which translates as 'One of the learning of Morien of swift cause, one of strong compulsion, strong-willed in flesh').

Pelagius was known among his contemporaries for his great learning and knowledge. It is not unreasonable that his memory would be perpetuated several centuries later among the Brittones of Wales as 'Morien ddysg'. This point of view is that of the present writer, who is, however, greatly indebted to P.W. Davies of the Department of Manuscripts at the National Library of Wales in Aberystwyth, who welcomed questions and located the references; also to Dr R. Gruffydd and to Nerys A. Jones of the Centre for Advanced Celtic and Welsh Studies at the University College of Wales in Aberystwyth for their patience in translating the obscure four lines and discussing with me the plausibility of the present explanation, while not necessarily agreeing with me.

education and was taught Scripture well. He inherited the British Celtic tradition, which had links with the Church of Gaul and with the Eastern Church as well as with Milan, Aquileia and Imperial Rome in Italy. In the early 380s Pelagius went to Rome, initially to study law. He soon gave up his law career in favour of the Church. On this change of plans the hostile Jerome commented: 'The world is saved and inheritance and civil suits are plucked from the abyss, because this man, neglecting the law courts, has transferred to the Church.'[3] Nevertheless, Pelagius became the first-known major British writer and theologian. He was both a monk and a layman.

Even the physical portrait of Pelagius has to emerge from such hostile and unfavourable comments by Jerome and Orosius, for instance. Despite this, Pelagius comes through as a big, enthusiastic man. He was strong, tall, broad-shouldered and stout. Jerome often returns to the excessive physical size of Pelagius: 'You are inflated above the shoulders of Milo [the wrestler].' Even twenty years later, by 414 in Palestine, Jerome still describes Pelagius as most stupid and made heavy by Scottish (=Irish) porridge. An ageing and corpulent Pelagius walks slowly and ploddingly 'at the pace of a turtle'. For Jerome Pelagius is a dog from 'Albion' (some manuscripts have 'Alpine'). Later on, in a critical poem, Prosper of Aquitaine (c.390 to 463) wrote of 'sea-girt Britain's porridge' as having 'bred the twaddle' of the 'snakeling' Pelagius.[4]

In a similarly uncharitable vein Orosius (late fourth to early fifth centuries) describes Pelagius as a huge, proud Goliath, all blown up with his own physical strength, confident he can do anything by himself . . . with a ram-like jutting forehead and a preference for going bareheaded with a shaven pate. To cap the negative physical portrait Orosius addresses Pelagius directly: 'but for you it seems especially easy to carry the heavy weight [of Divine law] because being used to baths and banquets you owe it to your broad shoulders

[3]   This and the following quotations from Jerome are from his *Commentarius in Ieremiam*, Praefatio in I, 4; in III, 1; in IV, 1; and *Dialogus adversus Pelagianos*, I, 28, 29; II, 10; and III, 16, PL 34; *Ep.* 50, CSEL 54.
[4]   Bede's *Ecclesiastical History of the English People*, ed. by B. Colgrave and R.A.B. Mynors, Oxford, 1969, p.38 [N24]. This citation is from I, 10 of Bede.

and robust neck, showing your fat even on your forehead
. . .'5

For Jerome the physical outlandishness of Pelagius is matched by a mind which makes him presume to be the equal of his betters. Pelagius is portrayed as an argumentative and wrangling debater who strolls from crossroads and street corners to public squares talking to people and endeavouring to convince them to follow better ways. In argument he is not only crafty and tenacious; he also disputes with his head poised obliquely and tilted sharply forward, as if he were a ram butting with his horns. His brow is serious and stern. He discusses the doctrines of Scripture, in which he claims to be knowledgeable, with everyone, says Jerome, with young women among their spindles and their wickerwork wool baskets just as much as with educated men. Jerome refers mockingly to the wide circle of women around Pelagius and calls the aristocratic women who listen to him Pelagius's 'Amazons'. Jerome is sarcastic about Pelagius's opinion that women should be taught to read and interpret Scripture.

Behind the rhetorical caricature of those hostile to him, it is clear that Pelagius was the spiritual adviser to many Christians in Rome, and in fact moved about successfully in the Roman Christian circles of Jerome. In Rome Pelagius emerged as a theologian to be reckoned with and as a man who had great personal sanctity, moral fervour and charisma. Further, while in Italy, Pelagius often met the Celt Celestius, the Gaul Paulinus, the Easterner Rufinus and the very like-minded Bishop Chromatius of Aquileia.

Pelagius was evidently a major religious and intellectual force of his time. He always made a point of showing that his ideas had a solid basis in the writings of the Church Fathers. Otherwise, two other major figures of the stature of Augustine and Jerome would not have devoted substantial portions of their intellects and time to discussing and attempting to refute his religious message.

---

5 Orosius. *Liber apologeticus*, CSEL, 5, p.606 et seq. Orosius styles himself a David to the Pelagian Goliath, but a vivid picture emerges nevertheless, even if a contradictory one (porridge or banquets, hardly both).

At least until 415 Pelagius was widely accepted as an orthodox Christian theologian. In Augustine's words Pelagius was a man of high renown, a close friend of Paulinus of Nola, a great orator (*bonum ac praedicandum virum*) and a most excellent Christian (*vir ille tam egregie Christianus*).[6]

After the Fall of Rome to Alaric in 410 Pelagius and Celestius were among the numerous Roman refugees landing in Carthage, where they parted company. Pelagius moved on immediately to Palestine, but Celestius stayed in Carthage. There in 411-412 the African Church condemned Celestius as a heretic. A refugee from Milan, Paulinus by name, was the accuser for the bishops. The reasons for the condemnation related to baptism and the nature of infants. For Celestius original sin was a matter of inquiry, not a fixed dogma, denial of which would be heresy. The debate also included the idea that before the coming of Christ there existed some just men who were without sin (*inpeccabiles*).[7]

Augustine believed he discerned the root cause of Celestius's views in Pelagius's ideal of *inpeccantia*, the possibility of living a life without sin as a Christian requirement albeit a rare achievement. Consequently Augustine delivered two sermons against Pelagius as early as 413. In 415 he sent Orosius to Jerome in Palestine with the mission of convicting Pelagius of heresy. In that year Pelagius was twice acquitted of heresy: at the Synod of Jerusalem in June, Orosius being the accuser, and at the Council of Diospolis (Lydda) in December 415 where the accusers were two bishops deposed by the Gallic Church – Heros and Lazarus.

In reaction the African bishops convened two of their own Councils in 416 -at Carthage and at Milevum – where they condemned Pelagius and Celestius. They successfully persuaded Pope Innocent I to act against the Pelagians (as he already had against the Donatists at the Africans' request). Innocent issued a conditional condemnation on January 27, 417, effective only if Pelagius and Celestius did not return to orthodoxy. However, Innocent died on 12 March 417. Almost

---

[6] Augustine, *De gestis Pelagii*, BA 21, XXIII, 46; *Retractationes*, PL 32, II, 31; *Ep.* 186, 1.
[7] Augustine, . . . *de peccato originali*, IV, 4, PL 44, 359-410, CSEL 42, 123.

immediately, on 18 March 417, Zosimus was elected Pope. He was an Eastern Christian with a favourable judgment of Pelagius. Zosimus decided to re-examine the case and called a Synod, held in the Basilica of St Clement in Rome. Zosimus was not only impressed by the defence offered by Celestius, who was there in person; but he also had received the *Confession of Faith* that Pelagius, unaware of the previous Pope's death, had sent to Innocent. Pope Zosimus declared that Pelagius's *Confession* was totally orthodox and Catholic and that he was a man of unconditional faith – *absolutae fidei*. Pelagius had for many years been outstanding in good works and the service of God; he was theologically sound and had never left the Catholic faith. Zosimus condemned and excommunicated the accusers Heros and Lazarus and sent several letters to Africa, including one summoning Paulinus of Milan to Rome to account for his charges in Carthage in 411. Paulinus rudely refused in a letter that is extant. Writing on 21 September 417 Pope Zosimus advised the African bishops: 'Amate pacem, diligite caritatem, studete concordiam. Nam scriptum est: diliges proximum tuum tamquam te ipsum.'[8]

Since the African condemnation was going unheeded in Rome, the authority of the State was invoked. Consequently, Pelagius and Celestius were first condemned in an Imperial Rescript dated 30 April 418 – a civil document[9] – and in the further condemnation by 214 African bishops meeting in Carthage on 1 May 418.

The ecclesiastical document condemning Pelagius of heresy, the *Epistola Tractoria*, was written by Pope Zosimus only

---

[8] Zosimus Papa. *Epistola ad Aurelium II*, PL 45, 1752 ('Love peace, prize love, strive after harmony. For it is written: "Love thy neighbour as thyself".')

[9] Imperial Rescript on the Condemnation of Pelagius and Celestius. PL 45, 1726-7; PL 48, 379-86; PL 56, 490-2. Emperor Honorius orders immediate action against Pelagius and Celestius because public meetings and credulous adolescents affect the peace of Rome. It is intriguing to note that the terms of this condemnation are similar to imperial condemnations of the Druids of former times. For instance, in Gaul an Antonine Decree had ordered Pacatus to act in similar ways against the seers (the Druids) who provoked manifestations against the public peace and against the authority of the people of Rome (*contra publicam quietem imperiumque populi Romani*). See Camille Jullian, *Histoire de la Gaule*, Vol. 6, Paris 1909, p. 6, footnote, and *Collatio* XV, 1-4.

in the midsummer of 418. Except for unclear and perhaps contradictory minor fragments, it has unfortunately been lost. While the Canons of Carthage are known and may possibly have served as a blueprint for the *Tractoria*, the exact formal grounds on which Pelagius was condemned by the Church must thus remain a matter of speculation. Presumably they included the references to original sin, *inpeccantia*, the fate of unbaptized babies and the Augustinian approach to grace (which approach, however, the Church itself revised considerably twenty years later). Heresies indicate important local differences and are far from being temporary aberrations. The religious map of Europe was quite fragmented at the end of the Western Roman Empire and in early medieval times. Pelagius survived in Celtic Britain and in Ireland because his ideas were part of the local idiomatic expressions of the Christian faith.[10]

After Pelagius was condemned as a heretic and banned from Rome by the Emperor in April 418, he may perhaps have found his way back to his homeland. He was last seen in 420, some say in Egypt, some in Palestine, but no firm evidence is available. A stay in Lérins, where Julian of Aeclanum found asylum for a time, would seem more probable than Egypt. The great popularity of Pelagius's works in Ireland, and Meirion's manuscript from Wales, make a return to Western Britain by Pelagius plausible. Refuge in a friendly monastery in Wales is one possibility.

Such a return – to the vicinity of Bangor-is-y-coed, for instance – would explain: (a) the Welsh tradition's association of Pelagius with Bangor; (b) the meaning of Prosper of Aquitaine's words in *De gratia Dei et libero arbitrio contra collatorem* (a polemical work directed against John Cassián): [Pope Celestine expelled Celestius from Italy and showed no lesser concern] 'when he freed the Britannias from the same sickness (*ab hoc eodem morbo*) and expelled even from their distant retreat across the sea those persons, enemies of grace, who had taken possession of the land of their birth (*quosdam inimicos gratiae solum suae originis occupantes*), and,

---

[10]   Also Karl F. Morrison. *Europe's Middle Ages 565/1500*. Glenview, Illinois, 1970, p.16.

having ordained a bishop for the Scotti (i.e. Palladius), just as he strove to keep the Roman island [Britain] Catholic, he also made the barbarian one [Ireland] Christian.'[11] Here Prosper may be corroborating the Welsh tradition that Pelagius was at Bangor-is-y-coed; (c) the insistence of the Celtic British historian Gildas, in his work *About the Ruin and Conquest of Britain* (c.540), on references to Pelagius as *quidam*, but without ever mentioning him directly by name. Gildas refers to Pelagius in phrases such as: 'ut bene quidam noster ait' [as a certain person of ours says'], 'sicut bene quidam nostrorum ait' [thus does a certain one of our people say so well], and, more specifically, 'ut quidam ante nos ait' [as a certain person before our time says]. Gildas links the *quidam* with Pelagius in clear quotations such as 'non agitur de qualitate peccati, sed de transgressione mandati' [It is not a question of the quality of the sin, but of the transgression of a commandment].[12]

A return of Pelagius to Britain would also help explain why Germanus of Auxerre had to be sent on one anti-Pelagian crusade in 429 and possibly another a few years later. However, with or without the presence of the by then aged Pelagius himself, his spirit still pervaded the British Celtic Church. It does not seem credible that three authoritative bishops of the Gallic Church – Germanus of Auxerre, Lupus of Troyes and Severus of Trier – would have been sent by Rome to combat Pelagianism on its own 'ground of origin' in Britain if Pelagianism was then a recent, short-lived movement supported only *ab paucis auctoribus* [by a few partisans], a movement, moreover, traceable to a single individual – Agricola Pelagianus.[13] If Pelagianism was such a recent and sporadic novelty, why did it so alarm Pope Celestinus and Prosper, and the Gallican bishops, all of whom had much more pressing conversion work among the barbarian

---

[11]   Prosper. *Liber contra Collatorem*, c. 21, PL 51.

[12]   The original words of Pelagius are in *Virginitatis laus*, PL 30, 172. See also J. Morris, 'Pelagian Literature', *Journal of Theological Studies* 16 (1965); 26-60, and D. Dumville, 'Late-Seventh- or Eighth-Century Evidence for the British Transmission of Pelagius', *Cambridge Mediaeval Celtic Studies* 10 (Winter 1985); 39-52, note p.52.

[13]   Prosper. 1301 (*Chronica Minora*, ed. Mommsen, I, 472); see also Constance de Lyon, *Vie de Saint Germain d'Auxerre*, edited by René Borius, Paris, 1965. Sources Chrétiennes, N. 112.

waves of heathens on their own doorsteps? Yet the relevant passages in Constantius and Prosper (both Gallican clerics) show in their phrasing an unexplained urgency in 420-430. Evidently words such as 'new', 'recent' and 'few', common in later Roman polemics, are used to minimize the admitted strength of Pelagianism. It remains certain that in about 420-430 there were 'Pelagian' Christians in Britain and that they were making converts. The excessive emphasis in the *Vita Germani* (The Life of Germanus) on the British Pelagian episode may raise more questions than it answers about the nature of Christian orthodoxy in Britain as well as in Gaul itself around 429 AD. In any case, E.A. Thompson points out that the 'salient fact about the area which Germanus had visited was', later in that century, 'not the failure of Pelagianism to come to life again but the near destruction of Christianity itself there.'[14] While Pelagianism was strong in the Celtic Church in Britain, it may have appeared to vanish in the eyes of writers like Constantius, when the Church, the land and its institutions were taken over by the migrating German tribes. The Angles and the Saxons in Britain (like the Franks in France) were latecomers both to their new homelands and to Christianity. Their late conversions did not come about through the Celtic Church, so that their church customs and worship were of a different and later type. The earlier Celtic Christian inhabitants had to retreat west and northwards in what had been Roman Britannia, and some to Northern Gaul [Bretagne]. It is reasonable to assume they retained their 'Pelagian' tendencies which were deep-rooted among the Celts of Britain.

Pelagius as a Celtic Thinker

Mommsen considered that the Celtic world had a much greater affinity to the modern mind than to Graeco-Roman thought. This applies especially to the theology of Pelagius Britto. British Celtic Christianity must be distinguished from

---

[14]   E.A. Thompson, *Saint Germanus of Auxerre and the End of Roman Rule in Britain. Studies in Celtic History, 6,* Bury St Edmunds, 1984, p.85.

the much later English Anglo-Saxon Christianity. The British Church was certainly in existence by the final part of the third century. This church preceded and instructed Irish Christianity of the fourth century. Among Pelagius's own priorities was a defence of contemporary orthodox and Trinitarian theology in opposition to Arianism and Manichaeism. For the Manichaean man cannot avoid sin: . . . *hominem peccatum vitare non posse*. Pelagius believed the opposite. He opposed to such determinist theories the natural potentialities of man's God-given nature, emphasizing the freedom of the human will as a God-given human right and an individual responsibility. His concept of *inpeccantia* (sinlessness – the potential to avoid sin completely and the duty to strive toward it) can only be understood in this context and through the perfect example of Christ, God and man. Christians must not misuse the liberty given them at birth; they are to be judged, since they are able to come to the faith and merit the grace of God and keep his commandments.

Similarly, Pelagius insists that a baby is new-born innocence. A just and good God creates man both without virtue and without vice (*ut sine virtute, ita et sine vitio*): 'All the good and the bad, by which we are praiseworthy or reprehensible, is not born with us but is set in motion by our acts; because we are capable of either, we are not born full but we are procreated both without any virtue and similarly without any vice. Before the action of one's own will there exists in a human being only what God has established.'[15]

Man was created as an individual, with an individual soul, freewill and conscience to monitor his choices. There is no original sin in the individual soul at conception, and no double predestination. The ultimately valid criterion for Pelagius by which a Christian could be judged good or evil, was the Christian's own success or failure in following God's law in conscience. This view was shared by Faustus Britto (c.408 to 490), who became the much-loved Bishop of Riez, by Alcuin four centuries after Pelagius, by Abélard (1079-1142), and in the fifteenth to sixteenth centuries by Erasmus. It is striking that Abélard, a theologian from Brittany, held similar views to

---

[15] Augustine, *De gratia Christi* . . . II, c. XIII, p.180.

Pelagius on sin, was interested in the same kind of theological problems and employed teaching methods very close to those of Pelagius.

Concerning the links between Faustus and Pelagius, as late as 1528 (on the day after the Feast of St John the Baptist), in a letter sent from Basel Erasmus writes with enthusiasm about Faustus of Riez's defence of freedom of the will. Erasmus expresses his agreement that Pelagius was a Briton, although for Erasmus the *heresy* of Pelagianism probably originated in Gaul. On the title page of an old Cambridge manuscript (*Fausti Episcopi de gratia Dei, et humanae mentis libero arbitrio, opus insigne*), from Richard Holdworth's collection, someone has written in an old hand 'Faustus hic non Catholicus sed pelagianus erat . . .' [This Faustus was not a Catholic but a Pelagian].

There has always been much of the irrational and unfair in criticism of Pelagius, as if he touched some raw nerve. The important point is that, whatever Pelagius's qualities and defects may have been, he was not an innovator. He belonged to a Christian tradition that remained the norm in the Celtic Churches. In his extant works one detects a dedicated teacher, a terse Christian moralist, a competent scriptural commentator, a logical and pedagogical mind. At no time does he intend to startle rhetorically or show any penchant for extremism or new doctrine.

On the other hand, the known reactions in Italy, France, Dalmatia and elsewhere (but not in Eastern Christianity where the novelty was ignored) indicate that Augustine did innovate – on freewill, predestination and the corruption of human nature. As far as the Celtic British Church of the time is concerned, it is pertinent that neither Pelagius nor Patrick was taught the concept of birth-transmitted original sin, nor did they have a name for it.

Pelagius saw a harmonious division between what he called the *posse, velle* and *esse* of our human life. He referred to them as gifts from God.[16] Pelagius's tripartite division was subtly interacting and God-oriented. He certainly never negated the

---

[16] Augustine, *De gratia Christi et de peccato originali*, I, 5, citing Pelagius's *De libero arbitrio*, Book 3.

importance of God's grace in any human activity, or in any part thereof.

For Pelagius, before one is capable of acting of one's own will, there is in man only what God created. Thus, the ability (*posse*) to live a life of sinlessness (*inpeccantia*) comes only from God, it is God's free gift to man; the will (*velle*) to do this, and the being, the becoming or the action (*esse*) toward this aim, depend on the free decision of man. Since both the will and the action take their origin in man's decisions they are both to be referred to man and he is responsible for both will and action. Ability, will and action are all three necessary to living a life of *inpeccantia*. Striving for *inpeccantia* is obligatory. Inasmuch as men sin like Adam they die, and Adam's sin is strictly an example, not a debilitating substance that man inherits at conception (or birth), not an inborn sickness of the soul or a propensity to sin. Here, two anthropologies meet head-on – the Augustinian one of 'damned humanity' (*massa damnata*) and the Celtic concept that finds its justification in the Age of Saints.

It is important to realize, however, that Pelagius clearly thought God to be effective in all three parts of the harmonious tripartite division: *posse, velle, esse*. All three parts – ability, willing, action – interlock to the greater glory of God. Not only does the action (*esse*) appear to be the result of co-operation between God and man, but the will (*velle*) and action (*esse*), when turned towards good, belong to God. 'Therefore, praise of man is in good will and in good action: but moreover, there is praise of man and especially of God who afforded us the very possibility of will and action. God also furthers this possibility with his grace. Indeed, whatever good man may will and in fact does accomplish comes totally from God alone.' Pelagius enlarges on this interlocking division (*De gratia Christi*, I, 5, 8-11) and praises God for willing and acting the good and the saintly within us.

For Pelagius grace takes the form of the rule of *dilectio vel caritas* [great esteem, even love], on which he often comments. This was the law of nature for the just before the time of Moses. It was also the law of Moses, explained in Leviticus 6:13. Charles Wesley restates it poetically as: 'Still let me guard the holy fire / And still stir up the gift in me. /

Still let me prove thy perfect will / My acts of faith and love repeat . . .'

On the duty of love Pelagius wrote, using his favourite question and answer technique: 'In which ways is charity manifest? Charity is manifest in four ways. It is in the love of God, which is the first way. The second way is if we love ourselves next to God. The third way is that we love our neighbours (*proximos*). The fourth way is that we love our enemies. Accordingly we must love God more than we love ourselves, and we must love our neighbour as ourselves, and our enemy as our neighbour.'[17] This image of the rule of divine love probably holds the key to that compatibility of divine grace and human freedom which puzzled later theology.

Several authors have pointed out the intense preoccupation of Pelagius and the Pelagians with public morality and social justice. Also, for Pelagius, as for 'most Latin Christians outside Africa, *gratia* (Grace) was synonymous with bribery and to suggest that this quality was necessary to salvation was blasphemy.'[18] It is possible that the Pelagian phrases condemning rich and evil people also greatly contributed to the imperial condemnation of Pelagius and the Pelagians.

For Pelagius the law of love (*dilectio vel caritas*) was so important that he offered an unusually lengthy comment of twenty-four lines on Paul's Galatians 5:14. His comments on 1 Corinthians, 13 rise to a crescendo when he notes, on 'You follow charity' (*Sectamini caritatem*): 'with every effort, strive after it, because it is within your power.'[19]

Pelagius's essential concept of the law recurs insistently: 'Nothing else is sought in the old law than that you are to love God and your neighbour. And he who sins neither against God nor against neighbour is truly the fulfiller and

[17] Pelagius, PLS, *Fragmentum* 39, p.1570 which reads: PELAG 'Quibus modis karitas consistat? Karitas quatuor modis constitit. Hoc est in Dei dilectione quae prima est. Secunda si nosmetipsos secundum Deum amamus. Tercia proximos. Quarta etiam inimicos. Deus ergo plus quam nos diligere debemus. Proximos sicut nos. Inimicum ut proximum.'
[18] W.H.C. Frend, *The Early Church*, London, 1968, p.218.
[19] See A. Souter, *Pelagius' Expositions of Thirteen Epistles of St. Paul*. Texts and Studies IX, 2, Cambridge, 1922-6; reprint Kraus, Liechtenstein, 1967.

doer of the law' (*et vere ille Legis consummator et factor est*). In commenting on Paul's 'For the law of the spirit of life in Christ Jesu hath made me free from the law of sin and death' (*lex enim spiritus vitae in Christo Iesu . . .*) Pelagius writes: *Notandum quia gratiam legem appellat,*[20] thus emphasizing that in this passage grace is called the law. This is the clearest example of a major Pelagian tenet, namely that the *lex Christi* [the law of Christ] is equated with *gratia Dei* [the grace of God] during the era which for Pelagius was the final epoch of history (the era *sub gratia* [under grace] in his *Condiciones temporum*, or The Ages of Time). Pelagius's pithy comment (that grace is called the law) may be contrasted with the lengthy treatises on grace by Augustine during the grace controversy. The polemics did not originate with Pelagius, who had always emphasized grace as a free gift from God manifestly present in man's nature after conception. Nevertheless, Pelagius was described as the prime enemy of grace (*inimicus gratiae*). The complexities of the controversy make it inappropriate for detailed discussion here. However, two studies by scholars, different in scope but complementary, are the most useful contributions. These are:

1. Torgny Bohlin, *Die Theologie des Pelagius und ihre Genesis.* Uppsala/Wiesbaden, 1957; and
2. Gisbert Greshake, *Gnade als konkrete Freiheit. Eine Untersuchung zur Gnadenlehre des Pelagius.* Mainz, 1972.

These works make it clear that Pelagius's doctrine of grace was at once more orthodox and more complex than that with which he has generally been credited, and that British theology need feel no shame for any lack of sophistication in Pelagius. Also, any theological rehabilitation of Pelagius should be based on a careful study of his own writings (which are still being identified) and within the framework of the beliefs and concerns of the Celtic Churches (such as were found, for instance, at Columba's Iona).

The *De induratione cordis Pharaonis* of Pelagius, with his other works, shows that the criticism levelled at him that he was

---

[20] See A. Souter, *op.cit.*, in Ep. ad Romanos, viii, 2; PLS 1, 1145.

a Stoic cannot be sustained. In fact, he reacted impatiently to necessity (*saeva necessitas*) as embedded in original sin and double predestination. Pelagius criticized the assertion that God had made two masses of human beings, one saved and one damned, and that no man could reform himself from within.[21]

God was fair and just and would not tolerate such predestination with its fateful division into good and bad. Grace must mean equality of chances and is equal for all. Here of course, Pelagius ran up against the very much grace-and-favour definition of the Later Roman Empire. For him, God could not be a dispenser of favours (*gratiosus*); He is not a respecter of persons (*acceptor personarum*), and He would not choose some people arbitrarily. Christian morality must be based on justice towards all. The greatest freedom was to be free from sin.

'Christ, the Son of God, is my Druid.'
Columba of Iona

Druidism existed only in Gaul, Britain and Ireland. The druidic philosophy could therefore have had a possible impact only on the Celtic Churches. Despite the persecution of druidism it is more likely that there was an evolution of thought rather than a complete break. Local history in combination with insular geography gave the Celtic Churches a distinct tradition of thought in the British Isles. There, as in Gaul, the new country priests, seers and miracle-makers became the heirs of the ancient druids. They inherited the religious and moral power of the druids as well as their prophetic and poetic vision which were now enlisted to work for Christianity.

---

[21] PLS I, 1507 and 1537. In *De induratione* . . . Pelagius becomes aware of an opposite Christian anthropology. This could be Pelagius's most significant work from this point of view. Several manuscripts of the *De induratione* . . . circulated in the early Middle Ages, all British in origin and all as if written by Jerome. See also G. Martinetto, 'Les premières réactions antiaugustiniennes de Pélage', *Revue des études augustiniennes* 17 (1971); 83-117.

In the case of Pelagius much of his thinking appears to relate to the ancient wisdom of Britain, refined to fit in with the faith of the early Christian Celts.

For the Druids everything in nature was good, but it depended on the will of man for it to remain good. That man could attain to and keep in a state of perfection seems to relate to Pelagius's view of the potential of *inpeccantia*. The Druids' triple maxim was: 'Honour the Gods, do no evil, be brave', as Diogenes Laertius confirms (proem. 5 to his *Philosophoi bioi*). Pelagius's optimistic, almost pedagogical anthropology may have been inherited from the druidic system of thought. The Druids laid great emphasis on justice and morality. They sought an intense spirituality. Further, Trinitarian Christianity also related well to the older Celtic triads. On Pelagianism, Georges de Plinval cited a triad: 'Good or bad, all things being in equipoise between these two, and man having the power to join himself to one or the other according to his will.'[22] Other triads apply, such as the 'three candles that illume every darkness; truth, nature, knowledge.'[23]

Further, the Druids had formed an intellectual élite. One of their functions, for instance, was to act as the supreme court of justice at a set time every year at a sacred place on the territory of the Carnutes. It was for intellectual élitism that Pelagius and his followers were first condemned by Imperial Rescript on 30 April 418 (and since we have no religious Roman condemnation dating from 418, this imperial decree must remain the only official contemporary reason for the condemnation).

Earlier imperial decrees, at Lyons in Gaul, for instance, had appeared against druids and seers for provoking manifestations. Now, admittedly in Christian times but with the Empire recently divided into two rival parts and in the middle of a

[22] *Triades des Bardes de l'île de Bretagne*, ed. Le Fustec et Berthou, tr. du gallois, Paris, 1906, triade 24, p.21; as quoted by Georges de Plinval in his *Pélage, ses écrits, sa vie et sa réforme. Étude d'histoire littéraire et religieuse.* Lausanne, 1943, p.59.
[23] *1000 Years of Irish Poetry. The Gaelic and Anglo-Irish Poets from Pagan Times to the Present.* K. Hoagland, ed., Old Greenwich, Connecticut, 4th ed. 1947, p.23.

crisis of civilization and a contraction of territory, Emperor Honorius may have perceived more than a religious threat in the charismatic missionary appeal of Pelagius Britto.

Furthermore, when one examines Pelagius's Christian beliefs for possible links with Druidic spirituality, Pelagius's stubborn and absolute conviction that a human soul cannot be born with any original stain on it seems to interweave the two. For the Druids, the soul was divine, indeed part of the Deity, and it must try to return if necessary through several stages to its original state of divine perfection.[24] Pelagius comments several times on Christ living and triumphing in us and his *Commentary* written on 1 Corinthians, 12-14 is quite telling of what happens 'when one's conscience beats in unison with proper doctrine' (*quando eius pulsatur conscientia per doctrinam –* 14:25). A further illustration is his comment on 1 Corinthians, 14:33: 'For He is not a God of dissension, but of peace' (*Non enim est dissentionis Deus, sed pacis*): 'In other words, the mind agrees to the other prophet, so that they give way to each other in him. In other words: prophets must have a mind of humility and charity, because within them God is neither of dissension or pride.' 1 Corinthians is obviously the Pauline Epistle closest to Pelagius's heart.

With Pelagius as with the Druids religion is totally free from crude original sin and its traducianist explanation. In Christianity, the Celts found a reawakening of ancient deities that made heaven and earth, sun, stars, days and light, and ruled harmoniously over their energies. It was easy for them to relate to a good God that created everyone in his image and to whose Divinity all returned if they followed Christ's precept: 'be perfect' (*Estote perfecti*).

Pelagius and Patrick

In the Celtic Church the love of wisdom and of learning related closely to the study of Scripture and to scriptural

---

[24] J.W. Willis Bund, *The Celtic Church in Wales*, London, 1897, pp.103-8; see also Camille Jullian, *Histoire de la Gaule*, I-VIII, Paris, 1909, on druids.

commentary. Pelagius was the first major British commentator on biblical texts.

Pelagius and Patrick were both Britons. The *Confession of Faith of Patrick*, which was not in use in Rome, is in the same British tradition as Pelagius's *Confession of Faith*. In his 1919 work on Patrick, S. Czarnowski had already noted striking correspondences between Patrick's *Confession of Faith* and Pelagian or neo-Pelagian symbols of faith.[25]

The Confessions of both Pelagius and Patrick relate to the Gallican Symbols of Faith (cf. Bishop Phoebadius of Agen, who died in 392) and to those of several Eastern Churches. They originate in the Latin equivalent of a Greek version from before the third century, similar to the one from Victorinus of Pettavium, a martyr of 303. This Confession took its official form at the Synod of Philippopolis in 343 (repeating the fourth Antiochene formula from 341). It was translated into Latin by Hilary of Poitiers, using the same words as Pelagius (for instance: 'Quod Graeci dicunt homoousion' [which the Greeks call 'homoousion']. Pelagius's *Confession of Faith* even became the major source work in the instruction of Charlemagne, four centuries after Pelagius, by Alcuin (an Anglo-Saxon Briton), who believed the Confession had been written by Augustine or by Jerome, and was almost certainly unaware of its totally Pelagian origin.

In the writings of both Pelagius and Patrick there is an abundance of celestial and sun images of God, with his angels and archangels, together with the proud concept of Christians as sons of God, joint heirs with Christ (Pelagius's 'It is an imposing thing to be a son of God . . . ').[26] Illustrations are found in the ending of Pelagius's judgment day letter, 'Quantam de purissimae . . .', a masterpiece of Latin

---

[25] S. Czarnowski, *Saint Patrick et le culte des héros*, Paris, 1919, pp.40-42 and footnotes on the same pages. See also L. Bieler, 'The Creeds of St Victorinus and St. Patrick', pp.121-4 in *Theological Studies* 9 (1949); and R.P.C. Hanson, *St. Patrick. A British Missionary Bishop*, Nottingham, 1965; and *Dictionnaire de spiritualité* XII, 1, Paris, 1985, cols 477-483. For the Confessions of Faith see A. Hahn, C. Ludwig Hahn, A. Harnack, *Bibliothek der Symbole und Glaubensregeln der alten Kirche*, Hildesheim, 1962, esp. pp.162, 190, 259, 271 ff., 288-95 and 331.

[26] Pelagius, *De malis doctoribus et operibus fidei et de iudicio futuro* ('Quantam de purissimae . . . '), PLS I, 1418-57.

literature of the Later Roman Empire, and in chapters 59-60 of Patrick's *Confession*[27].

Pelagius and Patrick share a similar concept of grace. Neither believes in a confrontation between God's grace and human freedom. In the Celtic tradition, all was God's gift. For Patrick as for Pelagius there is no special gift that can be called "grace" in the Augustinian sense.'[28] At the same time, of course, while they each had clear philosophical views, neither of them was a philosopher 'in the manner of St. Augustine or St. Thomas Aquinas.'[29]

In both Pelagius and Patrick a just God rules as the supreme conscience of his own creation. At base 'a very straight affirmation of merit and reward . . . [seems to have] remained a constant within the Celtic Church . . . Yet . . . the Judge has . . . a human face,'[30] as N.D. O'Donoghue writes on Patrick.

Faustus Britto

Pelagianism in the sense that man has the God-given freedom to choose good and thus to strive for *inpeccantia* may well have been, even before the time of Pelagius himself, consistently the temper of the Celtic lands. Pelagius was in the synergist tradition. He believed human will should co-operate with divine grace. His optimism and ethics must have represented a cross-section of the views of the early Christians. That would explain why he, a Celtic Briton, was at home in Rome, in Antioch, in Jerusalem, and had friends in Aquileia, Nola, in Egypt and Constantinople.

Attempts were made to distinguish shades of Pelagianism (defined as Pelagianism, semi-Pelagianism or neo-Pelagianism) after the controversy arose with Augustine. Efforts were

[27] See p.117 in N.D. O'Donoghue, *Aristocracy of Soul. Patrick of Ireland*, London, 1987, who notes, on his p.97, the literary quality of C.H.H. Wright's translation which is used (from the latter's *The Writings of St. Patrick*, London, 1889).
[28] O'Donoghue, *op.cit.*, p.54.
[29] *Op.cit.*, p.55.
[30] *Op.cit.*, p.36.

made to compromise or mediate between the traditional christian views of Pelagius and the radical new opinions of Augustine on grace, original sin and predestination. It is noteworthy that Augustine himself (and Prosper) would have none of these distinctions. They saw no differences of substance in them and wanted what is now called 'semi-Pelagianism' outlawed too, since it had the same root principles as Pelagianism.

The 'semi-Pelagian' current is often identified with John Cassian, Vincent of Lérins and with Faustus Britto, Abbot of Lérins. Faustus Britto was himself a Celtic Briton living in Gaul, and had learned his Pelagianism in Britannia, well before Agricola (the target of Germanus's crusade) returned. The French scholar J. Turmel pointed out that 'the Pelagian spirit reigned in the monasteries of Britannia [la Grande Bretagne] before Agricola began his campaign.'[31] Turmel discusses the Pelagian doctrines which Faustus (Abbot of Lérins from about 433 until about 462) was disseminating in Southern Gaul and which Faustus himself had learned in Britannia circa 420. Since Pelagius had left Britannia at an early age and the Celtic Churches could not have learned anything from Pelagius directly, Turmel is 'brought to the conclusion' that these churches 'had long since professed these doctrines'[32] – that is, the ones proscribed by the Imperial Rescript of Honorius and presumably by the Tractoria of Zosimus in 418.

Faustus became Bishop of Riez in about 462. He appears to have been exiled from 477 until 484, and he died in 490. Like many saintly Celts he achieved only localized sainthood which was never sanctioned by Rome.

The life and thought of the later Faustus Britto may thus throw light on those of Pelagius. Similarly, in a later British Celtic generation yet, Gildas still insisted on morality and justice in Pelagian terms and made oblique references to Pelagius at a time when even mention of the name of

[31] Jean Turmel, 'Pélage et le Pélagianisme dans les églises celtiques', *Annales de Bretagne* XVII, 1901-1902, Rennes et Paris, p.318, footnote 1.
[32] Turmel, *op.cit.*, pp.317-18. The French reads: 'On est amené à conclure qu'elles [the Celtic Churches] professaient depuis longtemps ces doctrines.'

Pelagius had been proscribed. The Abbey at Lérins was more than a meeting-place between the Gallican Church and the Eastern monastic tradition. It also appears that the ecclesiastical thought currents of the Gallican and Celtic British Churches met there, coalesced and flourished under Faustus. As in many intellectual debates in the West ever since, the deliberations centred on authority and freedom.

Columbanus (543-615)

A noteworthy Celtic parallel to Pelagius the Irishman is Columbanus (543-615). Striking similarities exist between these two *peregrini*. Both were tall and solid in physical build. Each led a distinguished Christian circle, yet found the time to write biblical commentaries. They both tended to be perfectionists and wrote about self-discipline in lawyers' terms. Each found himself embroiled in theological controversies. In 602 Columbanus was accused by his enemies before a Synod in Gallia for his keeping the old British/Celtic Easter. Columbanus was sympathetic to the views of the earlier Theodore of Mopsuestia (350-428), who was condemned at the Councils of Ephesus (431) and Constantinople (553). Columbanus was banished. He fled first to Switzerland, and then had to move a second time, to Bobbio in Northern Italy where he died in the monastery he founded. Both Pelagius and Columbanus had a keen sense of justice, shared a common idealism, a belief in *inpeccantia* and a love of freedom. They both exhibited a missionary zeal directed against the Arians. They both were convicted by civil authority.

It is noteworthy that the earlier Columba (Columkille, 521-597), also Irish-born, was condemned by a synod in his day, but went on to found Iona and a monastic order which became the great defender of the independence of the Celtic Church. In fact, the missionary role of the Irish Church in the 7th century was in great part attributable to its Pelagian zeal, as de Plinval notes.[33]

---

[33] Georges de Plinval, *op.cit.*, p.406.

In addition to the major traditional beliefs of the early Celtic Christian Church which are in harmony with the beliefs of Pelagius, there are also secondary differences distinguishing the Celtic Church, such as setting the date of Easter, and choosing the proper mode of tonsure ('from ear to ear' – *ab aure usque ad aurem* for the Celts). There are also some points of difference less easy to define. The Druids tended to allot to women the same rights and hopes as to men. It is known from the criticisms of Jerome that Pelagius related well to the pastoral and intellectual needs of Christian women. There were certainly Celtic women leaders in the community (as there were among some of the Germanic tribes). The tradition of the Roman Empire did not allow this.

Pelagius and the Irish Celtic Church

Far more than just two different concepts of grace were opposed in what has been called the Pelagian controversy of the first half of the fifth century. Much more than the quality of heavenly mercy was involved since the controversy opposed two different anthropologies and two differing concepts of spirituality.

For Pelagius (as also for the Druids before him) a human soul created out of divine goodness could not, of necessity, be born with an original stain. Furthermore, there were political, social and especially geographic dimensions to what used to appear in the documents as a purely 'religious' conflict of the fifth century.

The British Celtic Church (after 406-410 especially) did not have the cohesion, the numbers, the well-defined orientation and political influence of the North African Church. Nonetheless, there was a Christian Church of the Brittones, with its own monastic and missionary traditions, which had been part of the Christian oekumene of the Roman Empire throughout the fourth century. The British Church gave birth to Pelagius and to Patrick. It is highly improbable that Hibernia was at that time barbaric and uncivilized, and that Patrick was the first apostle of Ireland. It is, however, probable that geography alone would have favoured numerous links between the Celtic Christian Churches of Ireland and Britain, especially through Wales.

Although the burden of proof still lies on the proponents, it is not unreasonable to believe that a Celtic Church may have been established in Ireland before Patrick and may have been visited by St Ninian. This Celtic Church, if set up and aided by the larger neighbouring Celtic island, would have had important components favourable to the development of Pelagianism later, such as the asceticism, the striving for perfection and the urge for peregrination that would characterize the Irish Church of the sixth and seventh centuries. This Irish Celtic Church would be expected to grow along its own lines, as West Britain (Cumbria, Wales and Cornwall) was cut off from the Roman Empire, and refugees from East Britain increasingly turned towards Ireland, as well as Armorica. The vitality of Pelagianism in the British Church may not unreasonably be linked to the love and use of Pelagius in the Irish Church.[34]

Thus, de Plinval considers the blossoming of the Irish Church to be a manifestation of the influence of Pelagius. The French scholar explains that the life and thought of that Church were Pelagian, and that it shared the Pelagian ambition of achieving *inpeccantia*. The Irish monks had access to the *De vita Christiana* and to the *Commentary* of Pelagius; they wanted to lead a perfect life and to turn a whole nation into a people of saints.[35]

Far from being a consequence of the isolation of the Irish Church, the strength of Pelagianism in Ireland would in fact be a consequence of the influence of British (Celtic) refugees fleeing from the Germanic barbarians.

One useful source for the early fifth century is Prosper of Aquitaine (390 to c.463), a follower of Augustine. Prosper

[34] There were early medieval links between Ireland and South Wales. For evidence of manuscripts of Pelagius in Welsh scriptoria see A. Souter, and more recently David Dumville, 'Late Seventh- or Eighth-Century Evidence for the British Transmission of Pelagius', *Cambridge Mediaeval Celtic Studies* (Leamington Spa: Vol. 10, Winter 1985), pp.39-52.

[35] Georges de Plinval, as above in the text and footnotes.

considered that Celestius, Pelagius's disciple, was of Irish origin. If this was so, then Celestius the Irishman would have been the first person condemned for holding Pelagian views. Prosper also cites the date of 429 AD for St Germanus's mission to Britain and 431 for the mission of Palladius to Ireland. Pope Celestine ordered both missions at the same time in 429. The Palladius in question may have been the same person as the *Palladius diaconus* who advised Pope Celestine to send Germanus of Auxerre to combat the British heretics in his place (*vice sua*), as Prosper records. Even if a different Palladius is involved, Celestine still thought it of the greatest importance to send a mission to Ireland very soon after he dispatched bishops from Gaul to repress Pelagianism in Britain. This too implies there were Pelagian links between the Celtic Churches of Britain and Ireland.

Concerning the general links between the two countries, as early as in Tacitus's time it could be written that 'the soil, climate, manners and habits of the people [of Hibernia] are similar to those of Britain. Its ports are well known to merchants.'[36]

Further, since it had remained unconquered by Rome, Ireland in the early fifth century would naturally have been described as *barbara insula* [a barbarous island]. St Jerome's statements that the Irish were cannibals and had communal wives indicate only that the Romans had not been there. At least the south-east of Ireland had some acquaintance with pre-Patrician Christianity.

Since Ireland was never a part of the Roman Empire the transmission of Latin grammatical and exegetic texts through Ireland to other parts of Europe is a significant fact. The multiple transmission of the *Expositiones* . . . of Pelagius (often under his own name, or in such forms as Pellagii, Pelg., Pel, Pil, Pela, Pelag, Pilag and the authoritative *Pl. ait* [Pl. states] or *Pl. dicit* [Pl. says]) is especially remarkable. Irish enthusiasm for acquiring and disseminating the knowledge of the time made the Irish the ideal transmitters of later Latin works. It also meant that Pelagius's *Expositiones*

---

[36] Tacitus, *Agricola*, Chapter 24.

. . . could not have been in the hands of better scribes and scholars. In fact, the fondness of the Irish for Pelagius has attracted frequent scholarly comment since the important early studies by Ludwig Traube and Heinrich Zimmer. The Irish persistently, indeed stubbornly, disseminated Pelagian texts with copious glosses in Old Irish and Latin. They not only helped save the Pelagian corpus, they at the same time demonstrated an almost natural Pelagian bent in the Irish Church.

Pelagius's *Expositiones* . . . were clear, concise and to the point. They contained a minimum of allegorical explanation and a maximum of commonsense dispensed in the most succinct yet passionate style. Pelagius's writings and style as well as his insistence that a human being could and indeed should strive toward *inpeccantia* were highly attractive to the Irish and compatible with their own convictions which were to guide them in their successful missions in Europe throughout the Early Middle Ages. Christianity in word and deed, missionary zeal for Christ, an originally untainted soul given individual freedom by its Creator, *inpeccantia* leading to celestial reward: this core of Pelagian thought was faithfully transmitted by early medieval Celtic Ireland.

The Pelagian aspects in the written record of the Irish Church are further corroborated by critical letters sent to that Church by the Popes and others. A common rhetorical device in such letters is the ironical emphasis that the British and Irish alone held the truth and that every other Church was mistaken. The Celts are then exhorted to abandon their individuality and rally to the superior wisdom of greater numbers elsewhere in the Church. One clear example occurs in the letter sent in 640 by Pope-elect John IV to the Irish. This letter not only attacks the separate Celtic date for Easter, it reiterates the standard Augustinian definition of Pelagius's *inpeccantia* in its condemnation of Pelagianism (see Bede, *op.cit.*., II, 19).

Three examples will suffice to demonstrate the continuity and influence of Pelagius in Ireland:

1. In the last quarter of the eighth century a manuscript of St. Paul's Epistles (The Würzburg MS), written in Irish miniscule,

probably in Ireland, refers at least 1000 times to Pelagius's *Expositiones*.

2. The *Liber Ardmachanus* or Book of Armagh – listed by Zimmer as MS LA – reflects the high esteem Irish scholars had for Pelagius and illustrates the written Irish transmission. It was written in Armagh circa 807 mostly by the scribe Fer-Domnach who transcribed Pelagius's Prologues to Paul's Epistles, and acknowledged Pelagius as the author.

3. The medieval Irish scholar Sedulius Scottus, in his *Collectaneum in Epistolas Pauli*, knew that he was transmitting Pelagius's thought when he wrote at the very beginning of the text: 'Aliter secundum Pil.' [Otherwise according to Pil.][37] Sedulius also annotated Pelagius extensively and with great care as his leading authority. Sedulius used a series of abbreviations, such as Pelag, Pilag, Pil, Pela and Pilg, as demonstrated by both Zimmer and Souter.[38]

Thus the Irish Church read and used texts written by Pelagius, and ones acknowledged to be by him, as well as the texts under the names of Jerome or Augustine which were in fact from the pen of Pelagius.

Pelagius was the prototype of the Celtic missionary travelling the roads to distant cities, preaching Christian baptism, redemption and the *testimonium adoptionis*. Pelagianism was essentially a love of Providence, a denial of transmitted sin, an emphasis on the law of nature, on Christian ethics and asceticism, an enthusiastic striving for *inpeccantia* and a peregrination for Christ.

Ultimately also, Pelagianism may have been or become a synonym for the Celtic Church's cherished individuality, which appears to have evoked continuing censure and reproof from Canterbury and Rome.

However, the central influence of Pelagius was exercised through his writings, and has been much more subtly pervasive than has hitherto been conceded. In many cases, his

---

[37] A. Souter, *loc.cit.*, p.337.
[38] For example 1 see J.F. Kenney, *The Sources for the early History of Ireland*, Vol. 1, New York, NY, 1929, p. 636 and H. Zimmer, *Pelagius in Ireland*, Berlin, 1901, pp. 112ff.; for example 2 see John Gwynn, ed., *Liber Ardmachanus*, Dublin, 1913, esp. pp. 476-478; and for No.3 see A. Souter, *Pelagius' Expositions of the Thirteen Epistles of St. Paul*, p. 333.

authorship has been identified only in the past century, although his works were read and had their influence under the names of other church writers. The thought of Pelagius, as transmitted by the Irish missionaries and their heirs, helped to inspire optimism and the belief that human nature had, by God's grace, the capacity for improvement. These ideas were to play an important role in the early Carolingian Renaissance to follow.[39]

Select Bibliography

A definitive classification of the extant works of Pelagius does not yet exist. There have, however, been several upward revisions of the corpus of his writings since the important research by Heinrich Zimmer at the end of the nineteenth century. Thus A. Souter in Britain, following Zimmer, devoted special attention to the text of the *Expositiones XIII epistularum Pauli*. The strong interest in theology in Germany has led to important studies of Pelagius. The most notable recent German scholars are Gilbert Greshake and Otto Wermelinger.

Church historians such as W.H.C. Frend and R.A. Markus, G.I. Bonner and J. Ferguson, historians such as the late J.R. Morris, and J.N.L. Myres, R.P.C. Hanson and D. Dumville, *solum originis occupantes*, have been particularly active in the Pelagian field.

In Europe, the late Georges de Plinval, and in the United States, the late R.F. Evans, by their scholarly work, heightened the consciousness of Pelagius among researchers. Unfortunately Volume IV (1986) of Quasten's *Patrology* (Vittorino Grossi, ed.) does not break any new ground on Pelagius.

Two recent works are very useful. The second part of Volume 12 of the *Dictionnaire de spiritualité* (Paris, 1986), with articles on Pelagius by Aimé Solignac and Flavio G. Nuvolone, is significant of the new Catholic scholarship on

---

[39] M. Forthomme Nicholson, 'Pélage et Alcuin', *Les Études Classiques* (forthcoming).

Pelagius. It also lists one of the better bibliographies on the subject which the present writer has seen.

For the convenience and clarity of its presentation and classification *A Bibliography of Celtic Latin Literature* 400-1200 by M. Lapidge and R. Sharpe (Dublin, 1985) must be recommended. One caveat must, however, be expressed. Their listings (while better than Solignac's and Nuvolone's) are too conservative on the corpus of Pelagius. Thus their items Nos 10, 11, 18, 19 and 20 are definitely included in the works of Pelagius by R.F. Evans (*Four Letters of Pelagius*, London, 1968), for instance. G. de Plinval's listing remains the best.

Celtic Scriptures:
Text and Commentaries

Martin McNamara

Introduction

The presence of the term 'Celtic' in the title both of this book
and this chapter calls for a few words of explanation. If the
word is to retain some of the force of an adjective (unlike for
instance the name of a football team) it must denote some
connection with one of the Celtic races: Breton, Welsh,
Cornish, Irish, (Scotch) Gaelic, Manx. This would clearly
be the case with regard to language, and to a certain extent
also to customs or peculiarities known to belong to the Celtic
races in general. Beyond such linguistic and racial connections, various Celtic groups may also be related in certain
other ways, as for instance in literary texts and monastic or
ecclesiastical customs. Affiliations of this sort may well be
due to cultural rather than to racial factors, and it can be
doubted whether they should be described by an adjective
primarily intended to denote racial affiliations. Thus, for
instance, if Christianity and monasticism came to Ireland
from Celtic Wales, or Celtic Britain, there would have come
with it certain Welsh or British influences. Whether it makes
for clarity to describe these as 'Celtic' could be open to

question. Likewise, if Breton Christianity came from Britain (Cornwall) with the Bretons, there would be a natural British (Cornish) influence, which need not be described by the more general designation 'Celtic'. If we are to pass beyond the more limited use to the more general 'Celtic', we must go on the evidence available to us from the documents at hand from Celtic-speaking countries rather than on any a priori assumption. Having said this much, it must be admitted on the one hand that the term 'Celtic' in recent years is becoming more widely used, as for instance to designate the Latin language and literature of Celtic-speaking countries; and on the other that certain common traits in this literature have been detected, as we shall see in the course of the present chapter. The use of the term is, thus, not altogether without foundation. Usages of the extended meaning is evidenced by the title of the dictionary in the process of preparation by the Royal Irish Academy and of its accompanying *Bibliography of Celtic-Latin Literature 400-1200* (1985; M. Lapidge and R. Sharpe, eds). The adjective with its broader reference is becoming ever more widely used in North American university and cultural circles to cater for 'Celts' of different ethnic backgrounds. The broader meaning might claim a precedent in such a designation as 'Celtic' cross. On the other hand, K. Hughes in 1981 brought forward strong arguments against the very concept of a 'Celtic Church', re-echoed by A. Firey in 1983.

Despite the title, the present chapter will deal principally with the text of the Bible in the early Irish Church (prior to AD 1200) and with the Irish commentary material on the Bible from this same period. The nature of the question and of the evidence will take us beyond Ireland itself, often to Europe although not specifically to the Celtic countries.

Brief History of Research

In recent decades there has been a remarkable reawakening of interest in the life and learning of the early Irish Church and this has become particularly keen over the past few years. Only two aspects of this interest will occupy us here, although summary reference will be made to a third one, namely the Apocrypha, and in particular the Apocrypha of the New Testament.

The great codices, such as the Book of Kells and the Book of Durrow, have through the centuries been witness to the honour in which the biblical text, or at least the Gospels, were held in Ireland. Only in the last century, however, did the Irish and related Gospel texts, come to be studied for the nature of their biblical texts rather than for their illumination. Beginning with B.F. Westcott in 1863, this study of 'Celtic' texts of the Gospels was carried through particularly by J. Wordsworth and H.J. White and was finally formulated in its classical position in their critical edition of the Vulgate Gospels (see Wordsworth and White, 1898, 707-708; 713-716; 717-719). Among Vulgate texts there was isolated a Celtic or Irish family, represented by the manuscripts, DELQR, the sigla respectively for the Book of Armagh, British Museum (now British Library), Egerton 609, the Lichfield Gospels, the Book of Kells and the Rushworth or Mac Regol Gospels. These texts represented Ireland (DR, possibly Q)), Wales or the English-Welsh border (L), probably Brittany (E) and possibly Scotland (Iona) or Northumbria (Lindisfarne) (Q). Samuel Berger (Berger 1893) popularized the idea of a strong influence of the mixed Irish text on the Continent through the work of Irish missionaries. In 1929 James Kenney gave a detailed account of the accepted views of his time on the text of the Latin Bible in Ireland. Little original work had been done on the matter since the beginning of the century. In 1950 A. Cordoliani took up the question without going noticeably beyond earlier positions, but stressing the need for a thorough study of the manuscripts. The most thoroughgoing examination of the Irish or Celtic texts has been made by Bonifatius Fischer as part of his study of the Latin Gospel texts. He called into question Roger's view on the influence of the Irish texts on the Continent and stressed the preponderant influence exercised by Italian texts. He emphasized the need for further study of Irish Gospel manuscripts before any worthwhile progress can be made in this field, and is himself currently engaged in such an examination. The present writer gave an overview of what is known concerning the Latin texts of both the Old and New Testaments in a study published in 1987, and in 1986 had occasion to make a preliminary study of some of the lesser-known Irish Gospel manuscripts during a research fellowship at the Ancient Biblical Manuscript Center, Claremont, California.

Passing from biblical text to exegetical and homiletic commentaries, it is agreed by all as flowing from the evidence that the early Irish monastic schools were renowned for their love of the Scriptures and for the Scripture training imparted in them. The Venerable Bede tells us of the English scholars who crossed over to Ireland to study the scriptures. It is the period known in Irish history as the Golden Age. One would dearly like to know the exact nature and quality of the instruction imparted in these schools, of the text- books used and the exegetical traditions on which they depended. Until a little over three decades ago the extant documentation at our disposal for this purpose was lamentably meagre (see McNamara, 1972, 337f.). In his extensive survey of the state of research in 1929 J. Kenney noted that scholars were hampered, in spite of the vast amount of study that had been expended on biblical texts, by the fact that accurate information was not at their disposal regarding much of this Irish, or semi-Irish, material; only a small number of the manuscripts had been described by persons having modern expert knowledge either of Irish palaeography or of Irish biblical texts (Kenney, 625). While these words refer primarily to the biblical texts, they hold good also for commentary material.

A significant contribution in this field was made in 1954 by Professor Bernhard Bischoff of Munich, the leading authority on Medieval Latin palaeography and Early Medieval Latin manuscripts. In his essay 'Wendepunkte in der Geschichte der lateinischen Exegese in Frühmittelalter' (see Bischoff, 1954, 1966, 1974; summary in McNamara 1972, 339-46) he brought to the attention of students a total of thirty-eight items of commentary material, most of them hitherto unpublished and unknown or neglected. Through a variety of specific symptoms within this body of material, he identified most of it as Irish or as having Irish connections, that is, as having been composed by Irish scholars whether in Ireland or on the Continent or at least as having been used by the Irish.

Since information on this matter is rather widely available elsewhere it need not detain us here.

The groundwork had been done by Professor Bischoff. It remained for others to take up the evidence, sift and evaluate it, and if needs be agree or disagree with Bischoff's views. Fr Robert McNally, a student of Bischoff, was one of the earliest scholars to promote the study of early Irish biblical learning (McNally, 1959, 1973). Not all agreed with Bischoff's assessment of the Irish origins or connections, or the importance of the material presented by him in the essay 'Wendepunkte . . .'. E. Coccia expresses such dissent in a lengthy study on the matter (Coccia, 1967). However, the greater the examination of the new evidence, all the more cogent did Bischoff's initial assessment become.

In 1974 the Irish Biblical Association devoted its Annual General Meeting to a consideration of the biblical text, and the exegetical and homiletic commentaries of the early and medieval Irish Church. The papers read at this meeting were published in 1976, together with an English translation of Bischoff's 1954 essay (McNamara 1976). However, between 1954 and 1984 very little of the material brought to scholars' attention by Bischoff had been published. It was becoming ever more obvious that a concerted effort should be made to have as much as possible of this material critically edited, and with it the other unpublished texts from the period prior to 1200. The question was again raised at the Annual General Meeting of the Irish Biblical Association in 1984 and a resolution passed to establish a Special Publications Trust having as its aim to edit and publish, and assist in editing and publishing, material of historical interest relating to the Bible in Ireland, with special reference to commentary material, the Apocrypha, and the text of the Latin Bible in Ireland. The Publications Committee of the IBA launched an appeal, principally among the hierarchy and clergy, which had remarkable success. Another body with a keen interest in the publication of this unedited biblical material was the Editorial Board of the Royal Irish Academy's 'Dictionary of Medieval Latin from Celtic Sources'. In 1986 an agreement was entered into between the Academy and the IBA for the production and publication of critical editions of

Hiberno-Latin texts containing material of a biblical interest: commentaries, homilies and works of a biblical-theological nature. An editorial board was established and the new series planned in detail. Shortly afterwards (1987) both organizations concerned concluded a most satisfactory agreement to enter into partnership with the Belgian publishing house Brepols to publish these works in the *Corpus Christianorum* series. Progress in future development of such studies and publications was also greatly helped by the foundation in 1986 of the *Hiberno-Latin Newsletter*, due principally to the initiative of Professor Denis Brearley of the Classical Studies Department, the University of Ottawa. Publication of this, from issue 2 (1987) onwards, was generously taken on by Brepols publishing house. These negotiations were successfully concluded through the interested involvement of Mr Roel Vander Plaetse on behalf of *Corpus Christianorum*.

Thanks to these latest developments a sure basis appears to have been laid for the thorough examination of the text of the Bible and the exegetical and homiletic commentaries on it in Ireland, in Celtic lands in general and for the investigation of the relationships of Ireland to the Continent of Europe. The entire question is now being examined in the context and against the background that best assure success and objectivity, namely Continental Europe from which the Latin tradition initially derived and to which both Irish and British missionaries and scholars later were to make their contribution.

Texts of the Latin and Greek Bible in Ireland

The quest for evidence on the Latin and Greek Bible texts in Ireland must be focused on direct transmission, as known to us through available manuscripts, and on indirect transmission through citations in ecclesiastical and other writings. Only on the evidence collected from these sources can sure conclusions be reached.

The Old Testament outside the Psalter

The ninth-century catalogue of writings in Irish script (*Libri scottice scripti*) in the library of the monastery of Sankt Gallen lists one book containing Genesis and another the prophet Ezekiel, each in a single volume. Both works were presumably written in Ireland. No trace of the book of Genesis in question now remains, but at Zürich (Staatsarchiv, A.G. 19, no. XII) there is preserved a small fragment of the text of Ezekiel, with glosses, in Irish script which presumably is what now remains of the volume found in the library of the abbey of Sankt Gallen. Manuscripts in Irish script in the course of time proved difficult to read for Continental monks. Because of this they tended to be set apart in a special section of a library, or worse still to be used as backing in bookbinding, or simply destroyed. In the Badische Landesbibliothek at Karlsruhe, in the palimpsested text MS Aug CXXXII we have fragments of the Old Latin version of Daniel (Dan 3:1 4, 5, 56). In this case the text was saved by being palimpsested and reused. In the Bibliothèque de l'Université, Ghent, MS 254 fol. 172, we have a fragment of the Book of Job in eighth-century Irish script (with Job 33:24-34:22).

Apart from these meagre remains nothing is known to have survived of the Old Testament text outside of the Psalter. This does not in any way mean that the Old Testament text was unknown in Ireland. There is overwhelming evidence that it was both known and used, but that the ravages of time have taken their toll. This is not the place to present this indirect evidence for the Old Testament text in the early Irish Church (see McNamara, 1987, 33-39).

Latin Psalter Texts

At least sixteen Latin Psalter texts of Irish origin are known to us (see Appendix II). None of these contains a copy of the Old Latin Psalter, in any of its forms. While this must have been the text known to St Patrick and brought to Ireland by the first missionaries in the fifth century, it must have soon afterwards been replaced by the Vulgate or *Gallicanum* text. The majority of the Irish Psalter texts contain the *Gallicanum*; a number of them, however, carry Jerome's direct rendering from the Hebrew, known as the *Hebraicum* or *Psalterium iuxta Hebraeos.*

Both these versions were very early known in Ireland (at least in the sixth century) and both have specifically Irish families of text. The Psalter, we may recall, lay at the very heart of Irish (as indeed of all) monasticism, and was learned by heart by every school-child at the age of seven. The *Gallicanum* was most probably the text for the Divine Office while the *Hebraicum* would be more at home in the classroom and the scholar's study.

Greek Psalter Texts with Irish Connections

In Paris, in the Bibliothèque de l'Arsenal MS 8407 (no. 2 of Greek series) we have an entire Psalter entirely in Greek and in the Greek alphabet from the ninth century, with a colophon saying that it was written by Sedulius Scotus (*sedylios skottos ego egrapsa*). The scribe is presumably the well-known Irish scholar of the ninth century. In MS Basel, Universitätsbibliothek A.vii.3 we have a further Greek Psalter from an Irish hand, this time accompanied by an interlinear Latin translation. The manuscript is from the second half of the ninth century. There are strong indications that this is but part of a triple bilingual, the other parts being the Gospels (now in Sankt Gallen, Stiftsbibl. Cod. 48) and the Pauline Epistles (now in Dresden, Sächische Landesbibliothek A. 145b).

This evidence indicates that at least certain Irish scholars had a special interest in the Greek text of the Bible during the ninth century. How typical this interest was and how widespread the knowledge of Greek, and whether the evidence holds good for the Irish on the European mainland only, are questions still exercising the minds of scholars and need not detain us here.

Latin Gospel Texts

Of all the Irish biblical texts those of the Gospels have been the most studied. However, the principal examination, as noted earlier, concerned a 'Celtic' rather than a specific Irish family, namely that of the manuscripts DELQR. Before we proceed further on this subject it needs to be recalled that in the earlier centuries of Latin Christianity there existed a large variety of Latin renderings (known as the Old Latin – *Vetus Latina* – versions). Many of them appear to have been made independent of one another from the Greek originals, although they fall into two major families in keeping with the major areas of use, i.e. African (*Afra*) and European or Italian (*Itala*). In the late fourth century Pope Damasus commissioned the great biblical scholar Jerome to make a revision of the New Testament Latin text. This Jerome did for the Gospels, and the work was later completed for the other New Testament books. This revision, which came to be accepted as the official text in the West, is known as the Vulgate NT. However, its text soon became contaminated by influences from the earlier *Vetus Latina*, with the result that down through the centuries we often find mixed texts rather than pure Vulgate or pure Old Latin. The 'Celtic' family DELQR has a mixed text, and is recognized as having five characteristics: (1) a good ancient text underlies it; (2) DLR especially, but also EQ, have been believed by some scholars to appear to have been occasionally corrected from Greek texts; (3) the manuscripts have many old readings, especially in Matthew (4, 5) and they contain many errors in redundancies and the inversion of word order. This is the more or less classic description of the DELQR family as found especially in Wordsworth's and White's *Epiloġus* to the critical edition of the NT (see J. Wordsworth and H.J. White, 1898, 713-716; Kenney 1929, 626).

It is presently being ever more clearly recognized that the study of the Irish (and 'Celtic') Gospel texts needs to be taken up anew and that serious conclusions can be arrived at only after a thorough analysis of all the known surviving texts. In all twenty-nine Gospel texts of Irish origin (i.e. written by Irish scribes whether at home or abroad) are known to exist and most of those still await critical textual examination. (See list in Appendix IIIA.) The present writer has made preliminary probes in some of these hitherto unexamined texts and found that a number of them appear to belong to the Irish or Celtic mixed family. Another curious fact that emerged from this examination is that the Mac Durnan Gospels (MS Lambeth Palace Library 1370 (Appendix IIIA no. 13), of Armagh origin, has an entire set of peculiar readings in common with the Echternach Gospels (MS Paris Bibl. Nat. lat. 89; Appendix IIIA no. 9), many of these readings being also found in the other Armagh manuscripts (Brit. Lib. Harley 1023 and

1802, this latter being the Gospels of Mael-Brigte. See further McNamara, 1986B, 1987, essays in press). The study of the Latin Gospel text in Ireland is really only in its infancy.

With regard to the form of Latin Gospel text used in Ireland, it has thus far been ascertained that we have one full Old Latin text, namely that known as Codex Usserianus Primus (with siglum r_1) of Trinity College, Dublin (MS no. 55; earlier A.IV.15). This is an early (seventh-century) text. We also have fragments of the Old Latin rendering of John 11 in a liturgical text with Mass for the Dead in MS Sankt Gallen Stiftsbibliothek MSS 47 and 1395 (see Appendix IIIA, no. 2). Old Latin readings of the kind found in these manuscripts tend to appear in later Irish Mixed or Vulgate texts. Another Trinity College, Dublin, (MS 56, earlier A.IV.6; Appendix IIIA no. 5) text, namely Codex Usserianus Secundus (r_2), known as 'The Garland of Howth', is so mixed that it is hard to classify either as Old Latin or Vulgate. In the renowned Book of Durrow (Trinity College, Dublin (MS 57, earlier A.IV.5)) we have a true Vulgate text. The Book of Armagh and the Book of Kells, and the Gospels of Mac Regol, as already noted, belong to the Irish or Celtic mixed type. It remains for future analysis to ascertain which other of the Irish manuscripts belong to this family, how much they really agree and differ among themselves, and to provide as far as possible an explanation of the emergence and development of this family of texts.

Greek Gospel Texts

We have already noted the existence of the bilingual Greco-Latin text of the Gospels, found in MS Sankt Gallen, Stiftsbibliothek 48 (Appendix IIIA no. 29). This ninth-century text contains the Gospels complete with the exception of Jn 19:17-35. The Greek text represents two quite distinct traditions: that of Mark belongs to the Alexandrian text and is very similar to that of the eighth- century Codex Regius (siglum L), while that of the other Gospels belongs to the ordinary Koine or Byzantine type. The Latin interlinear text is classed among the Old Latin but of the mixed type. Its affiliations, however, do not appear to have been fully investigated.

The evidence would seem to indicate that this bilingual Gospel text was copied on the Continent rather than in

Ireland. It represents the well-attested interest of Irish scholars on the Continent in Greek and Greek biblical texts. How much this interest existed also in Ireland remains unclear.

Other New Testament Texts

The ninth-century catalogue of the library of the monastery of Sankt Gallen notes the presence in the library of the following books in Irish script: the Epistles of St Paul, in one volume; the Acts of the Apostles, in one volume; the Seven Catholic Epistles, in one volume; the Apocalypse in one volume (two copies of this work); the Acts of the Apostles and the Apocalypse in one old volume. A further work included is the Gospel according to John, in one volume. This is probably still extant in manuscript no. 60 (Appendix III A, 19) in the same library. All the other volumes seem to have been lost. The only Irish manuscript with the entire New Testament we now possess is the Book of Armagh (Dublin, Trinity College, MS 52; Appendix IIIA no. 11). Together with this for the Pauline Epistles we have a complete manuscript in Würzburg (heavily glossed in Old Irish) and fragments in Sankt Gallen (see Appendix IV). We also have the Codex Boernerianus, the Greco-Latin bilingual now in Dresden (Appendix IV) written by an Irish scribe, most probably on the Continent, and originally, it appears, forming part of a single volume also containing the Psalms and the Four Gospels. In a Turin manuscript we have a palimpsested fragment of an eighth-century Irish manuscript of 2 Peter (and probably of all the seven Catholic Epistles) and in Durham we have small fragments of a 'Celtic-type' text of the Latin Apocalypse. (See further on all this McNamara, 1987, 48-53).

Indirect Transmission

I have presented above the textual evidence on the Old and New Testaments in the early Irish Church as known to me. The information for books other than the Psalter and the Four Gospels is rather meagre. It must be supplemented by the evidence for indirect transmission through citations in the various witnesses known to us, be these Latin, vernacular Irish or others. This, too, is a task that has scarcely begun. It is nonetheless highly important that this be carried out. Usage through citations brings the biblical text in Ireland to life. Such quotations show whether there was a diversity of text in use and much else besides.

All I can do here is to offer some examples of what appear to be such indirect citations. In the collection of ninth- or tenth-century homilies, known as the *Catechesis Celtica*, some of the Psalms citations belong to the Irish family of the *Gallicanum* and several of the Gospel citations to the Irish or 'Celtic' family. The same is not the case for citations from other biblical books. The Hiberno-Latin commentary material now being prepared for publication should have very interesting light to shed on the entire question of the biblical texts being used in early Ireland. From the little information so far available it appears that more than one text was known and used and that serious commentators knew but did not follow the mixed Irish or Celtic text. Thus, for instance, the Vulgate text of Mat 1:19 has: *Ioseph . . . cum esset iustus*, 'Joseph . . ., because he was just'. An early Hiberno-Latin commentary cites this text and comments on it, but adds: 'Many texts add the word "man"' (i.e. 'Joseph . . ., because he was a just man', *cum esset homo iustus*). The only texts now known to have this addition are from the Celtic family: DELR and Epternach of the critical edition, the Würzburg MS (see Appendix IIIA, no. 20) and MS Sankt Gallen, Stiftsbibliothek 51 (Appendix IIIA, no. 17). Likewise, at Mat 6:28 instead of the regular *neque nent* ('Neither do they spin'), the Irish or Celtic family DE Ept.mag.,LQR (found also in MSS J and T) has created a new Latin word *neunt*. So, too, has the Würzburg codex, yet the gloss on it notes that the better reading is *nent* (*melius nent*). It appears that a very interesting and informative new stage of textual research is being opened up for us by this commentary material, one which will probably show that a diversity of text forms was the order of the day in Ireland.

Commentary Material from the Early Irish Church

Extent of the Material
Only in our own day is it becoming possible to write the history of exegesis and of theological writing in the early Irish Church, and this in good part thanks to the newly

identified material that is being critically edited and analyzed. Exegetical and theological writings would have first
come to Ireland from abroad with Christianity itself in the
fifth century. A century later saw the beginnings of the
monastic schools and learning. The earliest writer of note
is Columbanus (530 or 545 to 615), who was keenly interested
in biblical matters. According to his biographer Jonas of
Bobbio, while still a young man he wrote a commentary on
the Psalms in elegant Latin (*elimato sermone*). It is not known
whether this work survives. The classical period of the early
Irish Church is regarded as having been 650 to 800. Written
compositions developed rather extensively after the impetus
given by the Paschal controversy. Analysis of the extant
material may make it possible to reconstruct the exegetical
and theological activity and writing of the earlier period. In
a recent essay Aidan Breen has made a contribution in this
direction. Until the publication of Dr Bischoff's essay in 1954
the extant recognizably Irish exegetical material from 650-800
was meagre indeed. The bulk of this was in vernacular Irish
in the form of glosses on the Pauline Epistles (the Würzburg
Codex) and on a Latin Commentary on the Psalms (the Milan
Codex), dating respectively from about 700-750 and 800.
Bischoff's catalogue of writings from this same period contains thirty-nine items. This is quite an impressive amount,
and an indication that the original output for the period
must have been quite extensive. Bischoff expresses himself
as follows on the matter (Bischoff, 1976, 89f.):

These commentaries, among which there are nine commentaries on or introductions to Matthew alone, are still only a
fraction of the total amount. The fact, however, that so many
writings are concentrated within a period of some hundred
and fifty years provides an insight into a literary activity
which differs essentially from that of the patristic age and
from that of the early continental Middle Ages. The purpose
behind their composition was not the production of scholarly
works, beautifully transcribed. To such a task but few are
called. There was no aversion to repetition and many of the
works apparently owed their origin to the mere transcription
of earlier works or to a new formulation of teaching widely
accepted in the schools. In fact, a great part of this literature is made up of scholastic teaching and contains different

presentations of similar material. What is remarkable is that so much of it has been written down.

Bischoff's list opens with a one-volume commentary on the entire Bible, from Genesis to the Apocalypse. This work he named 'Das Bibelwerk', generally rendered into English as 'The Reference Bible'. Dating from about this year 800, in a certain measure it brings the older Irish commentary to an end. Together with this, there are three commentaries on sections of Genesis, one on Job, two on the Psalter, one on Isaiah, and fragments of commentaries on Canticles and Amos. Two works have to deal with Mark, two with Luke, two with John, two with the Pauline Epistles, two with the Catholic Epistles, one with the Apocalypse and two on questions relating to the Bible.

From the ninth century we have commentary material by John Scottus Eriugena on John's Gospel and an extensive exegetical corpus by Sedulius Scottus, including full-length commentaries on Matthew's Gospel and on the Pauline Epistles (*Collectaneum in Matthaeum; Collectaneum in Apostolum*). From the tenth century we have in the Double Psalter of Rouen extensive glossing on the Psalter, and from about 1100 similar glossing on portions of Psalm 118 (119) in the so-called Psalter of Caimin. There are also extant glosses on the Pauline Epistles from the pen of Marianus Scottus (Muiredach Mac Robartaig), written in 1079. The same author also wrote a commentary on the Psalter which appears to have perished. The final commentary from this period is the glossed Gospel book, written in Armagh in 1138 and known from its scribe as the Gospels of Mael-Brigte.

Quality of the Material

Given the current state of research into early Irish exegesis only tentative conclusions can be reached regarding the quality of the exposition. It is undeniable that among early Irish scholars there existed a certain predilection for the marginal and the trivial, for finding equivalents for key words in the 'Three Sacred Language' (Hebrew, Greek and Latin) leading to many fictitious etymologies, an interest for the first occurrence of an event in the Bible or in sacred history. To regard their exegetical activity as flippant or inconsequential would, however, be to seriously miscontrue it. Their exegesis had both an expository and theological component. It was interested both in the historical, the theological and spiritual message of the sacred text and seems to have a special awareness of textual matters. Only a full analysis of the material, which fortunately is now in progress, will permit the writing of a history of early Irish exegesis.

Psalter Study and Antiochene Exegesis

An abiding problem in the Christian Church is how to meaningfully use the Psalter, Israel's prayer book, as the prayer book of believers in Christ. It is probably in this that there was most keenly felt the problem of the Christian use and interpretation of the Old Testament. By far the dominant approach to the question in both east and west was that of the Alexandrian School of exegesis. This, while not denying in theory that the Hebrew Scriptures had a literal sense, in practice tended to interpret them as if they were direct prophecies or foreshadowings of Christ. By skilfully passing from one form of exposition to another many of the Scripture passages more offensive to Christians could be explained or at least glossed over. In contrast, indeed in opposition, to this, the Antiochene School insisted that honesty required that the Scriptures be approached and interpreted as literary works, as units with a prior history in the people of Israel. This exegetical approach was applied to the Psalms by Diodorus of Tarsus and in particular by his student Theodore, later bishop of Mopsuestia. For Theodore only four of the entire 150 psalms were direct prophecies of Christ, i.e. Pss 2, 8, 44 (45) and 109 (110). Theodore's approach had no lasting success, except in the extreme East in the Syrian Church and in Ireland in the West. His lengthy commentary on the Psalms was translated into elegant Latin by Julian, Pelagian bishop of Eclanum, and was abbreviated by some later scholar. The extant sections of the full Latin commentary and the Epitome have been preserved for us almost solely in Irish sources. Both commentary and Epitome enjoyed a central place in Irish Psalms exegesis from the beginning right down to the twelfth century, and through it Irish Psalms

exegesis is strongly Antiochene. In fact, there is strong
evidence that already in the seventh century there was an
active and creative exegetical school in Ireland, one which
doubted the existence of any directly messianic psalm, even
Theodore's four messianic psalms being interpreted of events
and personages in Israel (2, 44, 109) or as speaking of divine
providence and of human dignity (8). See further, McNamara,
1973B, 1984A, 1986A. The spiritual interpretation of the Psalms
was not ignored because of this. Both historical and spiritual
exposition were attended to and various ways were devised
for combining them, such as Psalm Headings and the theory
of the fourfold sense of Scripture, particularly of the Psalms.
In fact it appears that the early Irish scholars worked out their
own peculiar theory of a twofold historical sense.

Exegesis of the Pauline Epistles and Pelagian Influence

Pelagius's commentaries on the Pauline Epistles are as central
to the early Irish exposition of Paul as Theodore's commentary in its translation by the Pelagian Julian is to the exegesis
of the Psalter. In these commentaries, from the very beginning right down to the latest by Marianus Scottus (1079)
Pelagius is unashamedly cited under his own name (*pil.*,
etc.). Irish sources, in fact, are among the principal ones for
a knowledge of Pelagius's text. This does not mean that the
early or medieval Irish Church was Pelagian. For one thing,
only Pelagius's exegetical commentaries were used, and in
these there is very little that is doctrinally reprehensible.
Together with this, Pelagius was not the only exegete drawn
on. Others, including his adversaries (e.g. Augustine), were
used, and ample place given in the exposition of Paul's letters to anti-Pelagian teaching, such as the doctrine on divine
grace.

Homiletic Commentaries and Homilies

Together with the more or less exegetical commentaries we
have the related genre of Homilies or Sermons and Homiletic
Commentaries on the Scriptures or biblical texts. A vernacular Irish eleventh-century homiliarium has been preserved
in the *Leabhar Breac* and in some other Irish manuscripts.

See Mac Donncha, 1976. It is now becoming clear that this later compilation had forerunners in Latin collections. Three major catechetical collections of this sort are now known to us. The best-known is that entitled 'Catéchèses Celtiques' by A. Wilmart, who published selections from the manuscript (Vat. Reg. Lat. 49) containing them (Wilmart, 29-112), but now generally known under the Latin designation 'Catechesis Celtica'. Wilmart favoured a Breton origin for the homilies, but strong arguments in favour of an Irish origin have since been advanced. A further collection of homilies, believed to be of Irish origin, has been identified in the Cracow MS, Cathedral Library 43, material found also in the Paris MS, Bibliothèque Nationale latin 13408. The third collection of such homilies is found in the Verona MS, Biblioteca Capitolare LXVII(64). Other collections of Hiberno-Latin (or Celto-Latin?) homilies probably still remain to be identified. As in other related fields, much pioneering work remains to be done before definite conclusions can be reached concerning these homilies.

Irish Apocrypha
Neither space nor the title of this chapter permits any more than mere mention of the rich corpus of Irish Apocrypha, preserved mainly in Irish, although occasional items are in Latin. It is an area closely related to that of Bible text and commentary and one to which scholarly attention is now being directed. It is hoped that in the not-too-distant future we will see this entire body of literature critically edited and analyzed in a *Corpus Apocryphorum Hiberniae*. See *Hiberno-Latin Newsletter*, no. 3, 1988.

Bibliography

Berger, Samuel, 1893: *Histoire de la Vulgate pendant les premiers siècles du Moyen Age*, Paris; reprinted New York 1961.

Bischoff, Bernhard, 1954, 1966: 'Wendepunkte in der Geschichte der lateinischen Exegese im Frühmittelalter',

Sacris Erudiri 6 (1954), 189-279; revised in same author's *Mittelalterliche Studien. Aufsätze zur Schriftkunde und Literaturgeschichte*, Stuttgart: Hiersemann, 1966, 205-273; 1976: 'Turning-Points in the History of Latin Exegesis in the Early Middle Ages', in *Medieval Studies. The Medieval Irish Contribution*, M. McNamara (ed.), Dublin, 1976, 73-160 (English translation of 'Wendepunkte . . . ').

Breen, Aidan, 1987: 'The Evidence of Antique Irish Exegesis in Pseudo-Cyprian, *De duodecim abusivis saeculi*', *Proceedings of the Royal Irish Academy* 87C (1987), 71-101.

Coccia, E., 1967: 'La cultura irlandese precarolina: miracolo o mito?', *Studi medievali*, 3rd ser. 8 (1967), 257-420.

Cordoliani, A., 1950: 'Le texte de la Bible en Irlande du Ve au IXe siècle. Étude sur les manuscrits', *Revue Biblique*, 57 (1950), 5-39.

Doyle, Peter, 1967: 'A Study of the Text of St Matthew's Gospel in the Book of Mulling and of the Palaeography of the Whole Manuscript', Ph.D. Dissertation, National University of Ireland (through University College, Dublin); 1973: 'The Text of St. Luke's Gospel in the Book of Mulling', *Proceedings of the Royal Irish Academy* 73C (1973), 177-200; 1976: 'The Latin Bible in Ireland: Its Origins and Growth', in *Biblical Studies. The Medieval Irish Contribution*, M. McNamara (ed.), 1976, Dublin, 30-45.

Firey, A., 'Cross-Examining the Witness: Recent Research in Celtic Monastic History', *Monastic Studies* 14 (1983), 31-49, esp. 31-3.

Fischer, Bonifatius, 1963: 'Bibelausgaben des frühen Mittelalters', in *La Biblia nell'alto medievo*, Settimane . . . Spoleto 10, 519-600; 685-704.
1965: 'Bibeltext und Bibelreform unter Karl dem Grossen', in B. Bischoff (ed.), *Karl der Grosse, Lebenswerk und Nachleben*, vol. 2, *Das geistige Leben*, Düsseldorf, 156-216.

Gougaud, Louis, 1932: *Christianity in Celtic Lands*, London.

Hughes, Kathleen, 'The Celtic Church: Is this a Valid Concept?', *Cambridge Medieval Celtic Studies* 1 (1981), 1-20.

Hiberno-Latin Newsletter, 1986; 1987-, Turnhout: Brepols).

Kelly, Joseph F., 1976: 'Bibliography on Hiberno-Latin Biblical Texts', in *Biblical Studies. The Medieval Irish Contribution*, M. McNamara (ed.), Dublin, 1976, 161-4;

1987: '*Das Bibelwerk*: Organization and *Quellenanalyse* of the New Testament Section', *Ireland and Christendom. The Bible and the Missions*, P. Ní Chatháin and M. Richter (eds), Stuttgart: Klett-Cotta, 1987, 113-23.

Scriptores Hiberniae Minores (Corpus Christianorum, Series Latina vol. 108C), Turnhout: Brepols, 1974.

Kenney, James, *The Sources for the Early History of Ireland: Ecclesiastical. An Introduction and Guide*, Columbia University Press: reprinted New York: Octagon Books, 1966, and later by other publishers.

Lapidge, Michael, and Sharpe, Richard, 1985: *A Bibliography of Celtic-Latin Literature 400-1200* (Royal Irish Academy Dictionary of Medieval Latin from Celtic Sources Ancillary Publications 1), Dublin: Royal Irish Academy.

Mac Donncha, Frederick, 1976: 'Medieval Irish Homilies', in *Biblical Studies. The Medieval Irish Contribution*, M. McNamara (ed.), Dublin, pp. 59-71.

McNally, Robert E., 1959: *The Bible in the Early Middle Ages* (Woodstock Papers, no. 4);
1973: *Scriptores Hiberniae Minores, (Corpus Christianorum* vol. 108B), Turnhout: Brepols.

McNamara, Martin, 1972: 'A Plea for Hiberno-Latin Studies', *ITQ* 39 (1972), 337-353;
1973A: 'Hiberno-Latin Studies', *ITQ* 40 (1973), 364-370;
1973B: 'Psalter Text and Psalter Study in the Early Irish Church (AD 600- 1200)', *Proceedings of the Royal Irish Academy* 73C (1973), 201-98;
1975: *The Apocrypha in the Irish Church*, Dublin Institute for Advanced Studies (second corrected printing 1984).
1976 (ed.) *Biblical Studies. The Medieval Irish Contribution* (Proceedings of the Irish Biblical Association no. 1), Dublin: Dominican Publications;
1979: 'Ireland and Northumbria as Illustrated by a Vatican Manuscript', *Thought* (Robert E. McNally Memorial Issue; Fordham University), 54 (1979), 274-90;
1981: 'The Bible in Irish Spirituality', in *Irish Spirituality*, Michael Maher (ed.), Dublin: Veritas Publications, pp.33-46, 146f.;
1982: 'Antiochene Commentary on the Psalms: by Diodorus of Tarsus', *Milltown Studies*, no. 10, 66-75;

1983: 'The Psalter in Early Irish Monastic Spirituality', *Monastic Studies*, no. 1, 173-206;

1984A: 'Tradition and Creativity in Early Irish Psalter Study', in *Ireland and Europe. The Early Church*, P. Ní Chatháin and M. Richter (eds), Stuttgart: Klett-Cotta, 338-9;

1984B: 'Early Irish Exegesis. Some Facts and Tendencies', *Proceedings of the Irish Biblical Association* 8 (1984), 57-96;

1986A: *Glossa in Psalmos. The Hiberno-Latin Gloss on the Psalms of Codex Palatinus Latinus 68 (Psalms 39: 11-151:7)*. Critical Edition of the Text together with Introduction and Source Analysis (Studi e Testi 310), Città del Vaticano: Biblioteca Apostolica Vaticana;

1986B: 'The Text of the Irish Latin Gospels', *The Folio. The Newsletter of the Ancient Manuscript Center for Preservation and Research* (Claremont, Ca), vol. 6. no. 2;

1987A: 'The Text of the Latin Bible in the Early Irish Church. Some Data and Desiderata', in *Ireland and Christendom. The Bible and the Missions*, P. Ní Chatháin and M. Richter (eds), Stuttgart: Klett-Cotta, pp. 7-55;

1987B: 'Plan and Source Analysis of *Das Bibelwerk*, Old Testament', *Ireland and Christendom. The Bible and the Missions*, P. Ní Chatháin and M. Richter (eds), Stuttgart: Klett-Cotta, 1987, 84-112;

in press: 'The Text of the Latin Bible in Ireland', *Peritia*;

in press: 'The Echternach Gospels and Mac Durnan Gospels. Some Common Readings and their Significance', *Peritia*.

Westcott, B.F., 1863: 'Vulgate, The (Latin Versions of the Bible)', in W. Smith, *A Dictionary of the Bible*, vol. 3, London, 1688-1718.

White, H.J., 1894; 'The Latin Versions', in F.H.A. Scrivener, *A Plain Introduction to the Criticism of the New Testament for the use of Biblical Students*, 4th ed., London, 1894, 41-90;

1902: 'Vulgata', in J. Hastings (ed.), *A Dictionary of the Bible*, vol. 4, Edinburgh, 873-90.

Wilmart, André 1933: *Analecta Reginensia. Extraits des manuscrits latins de la Reine Christine conservés au Vatican* (Studi e Testi 59), Città del Vaticano: Biblioteca Apostolica Vaticana).

Wordsworth, J. and White, H.J., 1889-1895: *Nouum Testamentum Domini Nostri Iesu Christi secundum editionem sancti Hieronymi*, vols 1-4;
1898: section 5: *Epilogus*.

Appendix I

Irish Biblical Texts –
The Old Testament outside of the Psalter

1. Zürich, Staatsarchiv, A.G.19, No. XII (fol. 24-25 = pp.61-4). Ezechiel (frag.): Ezech 2:6-3:5; 3:7-15; 16:4-21; 16:26-42. With interlinear glosses from Homilies of Gregory on Ezech. CLA VII.1008. Probably from St Gall, and MS of Libri scottice scripti: *Ezechiel propheta, in volumine I*, saec. VIII-IX.
2. Karlsruhe, Badische Landesbibliothek Aug. CXXXII (fol. 86, 91, 92, 97-99, 101-104, 106, 107). Palimpsested MS. Below Priscian stands Dan. 3:1, 4, 5, 56. Probably s.VII. Ed. B. Bischoff, *Miscellanea Mercati* I, 1946, p.420, cf. CLA VIII, 1084.
3. Ghent. Bibl. de l'Univ. 254 (Catal. 445) (fol. 172). Job (frag.), with Job 33:24-34:22. CLA X, 1557. Saec. VIII.
4. St Omer, Bibliothèque Municipale 342b (fol. B). Amos (1:6-3:12; 4:1-6:8). Biblical text according to B. Fischer, 'Bibelausgaben des frühen Mittelalters', in *La Biblia nell'Alto Medievo* (Spoleto, 1963), pp.544f., note 65. Or commentary? cf. B. Bischoff, 'Wendepunkte . . . ', no. 10 and Lowe, CLA VI, 826. Saec. VII-VIII.

Old Testament Books (outside of Psalter) Among *Libri scottice scripti*.

Catalogue of St Gall Library:
Liber I genesis i quaternionibus.
Ezechiel propheta, in volumine I.

New Testament Books Among *Libri scottice scripti* of European 9th-cent. catalogues

Catalogue of St Gall Library:
Epistolae Pauli, in volumine I.
Actus apostolorum, in volumine I.
Epistolae canonicae VII, in volumine I.
Evangelium secundum Iohannem, in volumine I.
Apocalypsis, in volumine I.
Item apocalypsis, in volumine I.
Actus apostolorum et apocalypsis, in volumine I vetere.

Appendix II

Early Irish Psalter Texts (AD 600-1200): Gallicanum, Hebraicum/Iuxta Hebraeos.

1. Dublin, National Museum S.A. 1914:2. Early Irish Minuscule, CLA Supplement 1684. Psalmi XXX-XXXII. 'Springmount Box Wax Tablets'. VII (ca. 600).
2. Dublin, Royal Irish Academy S.N. – Psalterium. 'Cathach of St Columba'. VII (ca. 630). Gallican. Irish family.
3. Florence, Bibl. Medico-Laurenz. Amiatino I. Biblia. CLA III, 299. VIII but before 716. Psalter belongs to Hebraicum, Irish family (A).
4. Karlsruhe, Landesbibliothek Aug. CXCV (fol. 3, 5, 8). Irish majuscule, saec. VIII. Psalterium Gallicanum (frag.) probably written in Ireland. CLA VIII. 1088.
5. Paris, Bibl. Nationale fr. 2452 fol. 75-84. Psalterium Hebraicum (frag.). CLA. Sec. IX in.
6. Basel, Universitätsbibliothek A.vii.3. Psalterium Graeco-Latinum. Sec. IX[2].
7. Paris, Bibliothèque de l'Arsenal 8470 (no. 2 of Greek series). Psalterium Graecum of Sedulios Skottos. Saec. IX.
8. Rouen, Bibliothèque Publique 24 (A.41). Double Psalter with Gallicanum (Irish family) and Hebraicum (Irish family) (I). Saec. X.

9. Dublin, Trinity College 1137 (H.3.18), fols 2*-3*. Fragments (Ps 70:9-20a; 70:20b-71:9a (Fragments 2*r, 2*v, with Hebraicum and Gallicanum respectively), 72:3-17a, 72:17b. 73:2a (3*r, 3*v, as above). From sister codex of Rouen Psalter. Saec. X.

10. Edinburgh, University Library 56. Psalterium Hebraicum. Ca. AD 1025.

11. London, British Library, Codex Vitellius F. XII. Psalterium Gallicanum, Irish family. Ca. AD 920.

12. Vatican Library, Vatican Latin. 12910. Gallican Psalter, later Irish family. Saec. XI.

13. Dublin, Trinity College 50 (A.4.20). Psalterium Hebraicum. 'The Psalter of Ricemarch', ca. AD 1080.

14. Cambridge, St John's College, C. 9. Psalterium Gallicanum. Irish family, saec. XI. 'The Southampton Psalter'.

15. Killiney, Co. Dublin, Ireland. Franciscan Fathers Library A; 6 fols. Psalterium Gallicanum, frag. (Ps 118:1-16, 33-116). Ca. AD 1100.

16. London, British Library Codex Galba A.V. Psalterium Gallicanum. Saec. XII.

17. Vatican Library, Codex Palatinus Latinus 65. Psalterium Gallicanum. Text later Parisian recension. 'The Coupar Angus Psalter'. Ca. AD 1170.

18. British Library, Additional 36929. Psalterium Gallicanum. Text later Parisian recension. 'The Psalter of Cormac'. AD 1150-1200.

Appendix III

A. Irish Gospel Books and Related Texts, ca. 600 to 1200.

CLA = E.A Lowe, *Codices Latini Antiquiores*; L.G.B. = Patrick McGurk, *Latin Gospel Books from AD 400 to AD 800*.

1. Dublin, Trinity College 55 (A.IV.15). Evangelia. Codex Usserianus Primus (r.). CLA II, 267; LGB 83. --- VII

2. Sankt Gallen, Stiftsbibliothek 47 and 1395 (pp.430-433). Fragments of a liturgical text, with *Missa pro defunctis*, and Gospel reading from John 11:14-44 (MS 47 with John

11:19, 20, 29, 30, 37-8). CLA VII.989 B. Bischoff, in *Miscellanea Mercati* I, (Studi e Testi 121, Vatican, 1946) pp.425-6. --- VII

3. Dublin, Trinity College 60 (A.I.5). Evangelia. 'The Book of Mulling'. CLA II.276; LGB 89. --- VII

4. Dublin, Trinity College 60 (A.IV.5), fol. 95-98. Mulling Fragments (with Mt 26:42-27:35; Mk 1:1-4:8:5:18-6:350. CLA II.273:LGB 90. --- VIII-IX

5. Dublin, Trinity College 56 (A.IV.6). Evangelia. Codex Usserianus Secundus ('The Garland of Howth' (r_1). CLA II,272; LGB 85. --- VIII-IX

6. Cambridge (Mass.), Harvard University, Houghton Library MS Typ 620 (purchased from Bernard Rosenthal, San Francisco). Luke 16:27-17:26. Described by B. Bischoff and V. Brown in: 'Addenda to Codices Latini Antiquiores', in *Medieval Studies* 47 (1985), 323-4, and pl. 3b; Evangelia Antihieronymiana, Irish minuscule, s. VIII[2].

7. Paris, Bibl. nat., nouv.acq.lat. 1587. Evangelia. Gospels of St Gatien. From monastery of St Gatien, Tours. Written in Brittany? From Insular or Irish original? CLA V.684; LGB. --- VIII-IX

8. Dublin, Trinity College 57 (A.IV.5). Evangelia. The Book of Durrow. CLA II.273; LGB 86. --- ca. AD 700

9. Paris, Bibl. Nat., Lat. 9389. Evangelia. The Echternach Gospels. Written at Echternach? Lindisfarne? Ireland (Rathmelsigi)? CLA V.587; LGB. --- ca. AD 700.

10. Dublin, Trinity College 58 (A.I.6). Evangelia. 'The Book of Kells'. (Q). CLA II.274; LGB 87. --- ca. AD 700.

11. Dublin, Trinity College 52. Novum testamentum. Patriciana. Martiniana. 'The Book of Armagh'. CLA II.270. --- ca. AD 800

12. Oxford, Bodleian Library Auct. D.2.19 (3946). Evangelia. 'Mac Regol Gospels'. Codex Rushworthianus). (R). CLA II,231; LGB 33. --- ante 822.

13. London, Lambeth Palace Library 1370. Evangelia. 'Mac Durnan Gospels'. Kenney, *Sources*, pp.644f. (No. 475). --- IX ex.

14. Dublin, Trinity College 59 (A.IV.23). Evangelia. 'Book of Dimma'. CLA II.275; LGB 88. --- VIII[2]

15. London, British Library Additional 40618. Evangelia. Imperfect. Beg. Mt 21:32; ends Jn 21:16. CLA II.179; LGB 20. --- VIII-IX

16. Fulda, Landesbibliothek Bonifatius 3. Evangelia. 'Cadmug Gospels'. CLA VIII.1198; LGB 68. --- VIII (ante 750)

17. Sankt Gallen, Stiftsbibliothek 51. Evangelia. CLA VII. 901; LGB 117. --- VIII²

18. Milan, Bibl. Ambrosiana I.61 sup. Evangelia. CLA III.350; LGB 96. --- VIII.

19. Sankt Gallen, Stiftsbibliothek 60. St John's Gospel. CLA VII.902; LGB 118. --- VIII-IX

20. Würzburg, Universitätsbibliothek M.p.th.f.61. St Matthew's Gospel. CLA IX.1415; LGB 79. – VIII-IX

21. Sankt Gallen, Stiftsbibliothek 1394 (pp.1014). Evangelia (frag.): Lk 112-32; 2:43-3:9). Two folios forming a bifolium. CLA VII.980; LGB 121. --- VIII

22. Turin, Biblioteca Nazionale O.IV.20. Evangelia (frag.). Partly palimpsest. CLA IV.466; LGB lo7. --- VIII

23. Dublin, Royal Irish Academy D.II.3, fol 1-11. Excerpts from John's Gospel. CLA II.267; LGB 82. --- VIII-IX.

24. Dublin, Royal Irish Academy 24.Q.23. Evangelia. The manuscript of the 'Domnach Airgid'. CLA II.269; LGB 83. --- VIII-IX.

25. Oxford, Bodleian Rawlinson G. 167 (14890). Evangelia. Imperfect. (Luke 1:1-24:47; John 1:14-6:53; 7:1-21:16). CLA II.256; LGB 35. --- VIII or VIII-IX

26. Oxford, Corpus Christi College 122. Evangelia. Imperfect (John 1:1-33; 7:33-18:20 missing). Kenney, *Sources*, pp.647-48 (no. 481). --- XII; after 1140

27. London, British Library Harley 1023. Evangelia. Imperfect. Kenney, *Sources*, p.648 (no. 482). --- XII

28. London, British Library Harley 1802. Evangelia. 'Gospels of Mael-Brigte'. Kenney, *Sources*, p.648 (no.483). --- AD 1138

29. Sankt Gallen, Stiftsbibliothek 48. Evangelia. Greek, with Latin interlinear translation. Kenney, *Sources.*, p.558 (no. 364v). --- IX

B. Texts Connected with Irish Tradition Written Outside of Ireland

Biblical Text

1. Lichfield, Cathedral, s.n. Evangelia. 'Gospels of St Chad'. Symbol: L. Written in England, in centre near Welsh border following Irish calligraphic traditions. Imperfect (ends Luke 3:9). CLA II,159; LGB 16. --- ca. VIII[2]

2. Hereford, Cathedral Library, P.I.2. Evangelia. Text related to Lichfield MS as original to copy, or as sister MS. Written in England near Welsh border? CLA II.157; LGB 15. --- VIII

3. London, British Library, Egerton 609. Symbol: E. From Tours monastery. Written apparently in Brittany. --- IX.

C. Introductory Material (Monarchian Prologues; Nomina Hebraica) etc.

1. Trier, Bistumsarchiv MS 420 (Domschatzkammer MS 61; olim 13). LGB 76. --- VIII

2. Freiburg im Breisgau, Universitätsbibliothek 702. CLA VIII.1195; LGB 67. -- - VIII

3. Augsburg, Universitätsbibliothek (formerly Schloss Harburg, Fürst. Oettingen-Wallterstein Bibl.) I.2.4.°2. CLA VIII.1216. Evangelia. The Maihingen Gospels. --- VIII

4. Würzburg, Universitätsbibliothek, M.p/th.f.67. Evangelia. CLA IX.1411. --- VIII-IX

5. Berne, Bürgerbibliothek 85.

6. Berne, Stadtbibliothek 671. Evangelia. In format, an Irish pocket Gospel Book.

7. Stoneyhurst (England), College Library. St John's Gospel. In format, an Irish pocket Gospel Book. CLA II.260. LGB. --- VII-VIII

8. Durham, Cathedral Library A.ii. 17. Evangelia. 'Durham Gospels'. CLA II.150. --- ca. AD 700.

9. New York, Public Library. Evangelia. 'Landevennec Gospels'. --- VIII ex.

Appendix IV

Irish Biblical Texts – *New Testament other than Gospels*

For all books:
Dublin, Trinity College 52, Novum testamentum . . . , 'Book of Armagh', ca. AD 807.

Pauline Epistles
Würzburg Universitätsbibliothek P.p.th.f. 12. CLA IX.1403. VIII ex. All Pauline Epistles, except latter portion of Hebrews, Kenney, no. 461 (pp.635f.).
St Gall, Stiftsbibliothek 1395 (pp.440-1) – fragmentary single page, with Coloss. 3:5-25 (ca. 235 x 190 mm) with marginal glosses, on intentionally broad margin. The remnants of a collection of Pauline letters. Perhaps from *Epistolae Pauli* of the *Libri scottice scripti* of St Gall Library, 9th- cent. catalogue. saec. IX
Dresden, Sächische Landesbibliothek. Msc. A 145b, fol. 1-99v. Pauline Epistles, except Hebrews. Greek with interlinear Latin translation. Kenney, no. 364 (vi) (p.559), IX. Hermann Josef Frede, *Altlateinische Paulus-Handschriften*, 1954, pp.50-79.

Catholic Epistles
Turin, Bibl. Naz. F.IV.24, last page (fol. 93). 2 Peter (frag.): 2 Pet 2:9, 11, 13, 15; 2:1, 3, 4, 6-9, 9-12 (only portions of palimp-sested text legible). CLA IV, 457. Saec. VIII